# *Linguistics for Non-Linguists*

*Second Edition*

# *Linguistics for Non-Linguists*

## *A Primer with Exercises*

**Frank Parker**
*Louisiana State University*

**Kathryn Riley**
*University of Minnesota, Duluth*

**Allyn and Bacon**
*Boston • London • Toronto • Sydney • Tokyo • Singapore*

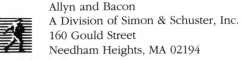

Allyn and Bacon
A Division of Simon & Schuster, Inc.
160 Gould Street
Needham Heights, MA 02194

**Library of Congress Cataloging-in-Publication Data**

Parker, Frank,
   Linguistics for non-linguists: a primer with exercises / Frank
Parker, Kathryn Riley. — 2nd ed.
     p.  cm.
   Includes bibliographical references and index.
   ISBN 0-205-15083-7
   1. Linguistics.  I. Riley, Kathryn Louise       II. Title.
P121.P334  1994
410—dc20                        93–17981
                                    CIP

Printed in the United States of America

10  9  8  7  6  5  4  3  2      97  96  95  94

# Contents

# *Acknowledgments*

We are indebted to John Algeo, Jody Bailey-Teulon, Lionel Bender, Kim Campbell, Jonathan Conant, C. B. Dodson, Alan Manning, Chuck Meyer, Anna Schmidt, and Tom Walsh for reading and commenting on various parts of this book. Special thanks to Dick Veit for his many valuable suggestions. Thanks also to Lance Fox and JoAnne Johnson for their help with manuscript preparation.

# Chapter 1

# Introduction

The title of this book, *Linguistics for Non-Linguists*, delimits both its scope and audience. Let us say something about each one. The primary audience for which this book is intended are people who are not linguists, but who feel they need some familiarity with the fundamentals of linguistic theory in order to help them practice their profession. This includes specialists in such fields as speech-language pathology, experimental phonetics, communication, education, English as a second language (ESL), composition, reading, anthropology, folklore, foreign languages, and literature. The common thread among these disciplines is that, in one form or another and at one time or another, they all deal with language. For example, a researcher in business communication might try to characterize how different managerial styles are reflected in the way that managers give directions to their employees, noting that some managers give instructions like *Type this memo* while others say *Could you type this memo?* A kindergarten teacher might observe that students give more correct responses to questions like *Which of these girls is taller?* than to questions like *Which of these girls is shorter?* A composition instructor might encounter a student who writes *I wanted to know what could I do* rather than *I wanted to know what I could do.* An ESL teacher might have a student who writes *I will taking physics next semester*, rather than *I will take* or *I will be taking physics next semester.* A speech-language pathologist might attempt to evaluate a child who says *tay* for *stay*, but never *say* for *stay.* In each case, these specialists have encountered phenomena that cannot be thoroughly understood without some familiarity with concepts from linguistic theory.

Realistically speaking, however, there are several practical reasons that may have prevented these specialists from acquiring a background in basic linguistic theory. First, courses in linguistics are relatively rare in colleges and universities, and are virtually nonexistent in high schools. Even universities that have such courses generally do not require them of all students. Second, each university curriculum (especially a professional curriculum) quite naturally tends to focus its students' attention on the central concerns of its discipline. Of course, the more courses required of students within their discipline, the fewer they can take from fields outside of their major. Such factors often prevent students in allied areas from being exposed to linguistics. Third, once people complete their formal education, it is often difficult, if not impossible, for them to supplement their knowledge with formal coursework, especially in an unfamiliar area. Finally, linguistics, at least at first glance, appears to be incredibly complicated. Articles and books on the subject are often filled with charts, tables, diagrams, and notation that seem to be uninterpretable, and many people simply give up in frustration. In short, there are a number of practical reasons for this gap in the flow of information between linguistics and other fields that deal with language. This book is an attempt to solve this problem, at least in part. It is specifically designed to convey a basic understanding of linguistic theory to specialists in neighboring fields, whether students or practicing professionals.

As for its scope, this book is essentially a primer in linguistics: a short work covering the basic elements of the subject. As such, it is not meant to substitute for an exhaustive linguistics text or for an introductory course in linguistics. Rather, this book is best viewed as a sort of "pre-text"—a work that might be read before taking up a more comprehensive text or before taking a basic course in linguistics. Alternatively, it might be used as supplementary reading in an introductory course.

The book is organized as follows. Chapters 2 through 6 cover the theoretical areas of pragmatics, semantics, syntax, morphology, and phonology, respectively. Chapters 7 through 11 cover the applied areas of language variation, first-language acquisition, second-language acquisition, written language, and the neurology of language. Each chapter is divided into four parts: text, supplementary readings, 10 practice problems with answers, and 50 additional unanswered exercises. The text of each chapter focuses on a handful of the basic ideas in that area of linguistics; we have not tried to cover each subject in breadth or in detail. Also, we have made an effort to make explicit the reasoning that lies behind each area discussed. Each chapter begins with a set of observations that can be made about that subject, and the rest of the chapter constructs a partial theory to account for the original observations. Throughout the text, we have tried to emphasize the fact that linguistic theory is a set of categories and principles devised by linguists in order to explain observations about language. (More on this subject later.)

The supplementary readings at the end of each chapter consist of an annotated list of several articles and books that we have found useful in introducing others to the field. We have made no attempt to cover each field exhaustively or to restrict the readings to the latest findings, since each of the ten areas covered here has numerous textbooks and primary works devoted to it. However, anyone interested in pursuing one of these areas can at least begin by consulting the supplementary readings. The practice problems and exercises at the end of each chapter are included as a means for you to check your understanding of the text and internalize the basic concepts. The questions are in most cases discrete rather than open-ended. That is, each question has a specific answer or range of answers within the framework of the chapter (for example, "Would a child exposed to English be more likely to acquire the meaning of *long* or *short* first?" "What principle accounts for this?") We believe that the process of reading the text, working the practice problems and checking your answers, and then working the 50 exercises will enable you to teach yourself the basics of linguistics.

Obviously, an introductory book such as this has several potential limitations. First, there are entire subdomains of linguistics that are not included—language change, animal communication, and psycholinguistics, to name just a few. Our reason for omitting these areas is that our primary purpose is to focus on the central concepts of linguistic theory in the simplest and most straightforward way possible. The experience of having taught linguistics for 15 years convinces us that students and professionals from neighboring fields are most often in need of a solid grounding in the core areas of pragmatics, semantics, syntax, morphology, and phonology. Once they have a basic understanding of these areas, they have little trouble in mastering the applied areas that overlap with their own field of specialization. We have included chapters on language variation, first- and second-language acquisition, written language, and the neurology of language—five applied areas which seem to us to be of the most importance to the greatest number of neighboring fields.

Second, this book is limited by our own understanding and interpretation of the field of linguistics. This is a factor that should not be underestimated. No one can study an academic field without incorporating some of his or her own prejudices into a view of that field, and certainly we are no exceptions. For example, our own views of the field of linguistics are biased toward the work of Noam Chomsky, who is undoubtedly the most influential linguist alive today. Consequently, most of this book is written from the perspective of **generative grammar**, a view of language which Chomsky began developing 35 years ago. (Some of the properties of this theory are discussed in detail in Chapter 12.) In short, it is wise to keep these limitations in mind as you read this book. It represents neither all there is to know about linguistics nor the only way of looking at the field.

Having discussed the audience and scope of this book, let's now turn to its primary subject matter—linguistic theory. There are two questions central to an understanding of this field. First, what do linguists study? And second, how do they go about studying it? Let's take these questions one at a time. First, one common understanding of linguistic theory is that it is the study of the psychological system of unconscious knowledge that underlies our ability to produce and interpret utterances in our native language. It is not the study of how human beings actually produce speech with their vocal mechanism, nor is it the study of speech itself. Thus, we need to distinguish three different domains: (1) the psychological system of language; (2) the means of implementing this system (the vocal tract); and (3) the product (speech).

An analogy may help clarify the distinction among these three areas. In talking about computers, specialists differentiate at least three domains: software, hardware, and output. The software (or program) is essentially the mind of the machine; it is the set of instructions that tells the machine what to do. The hardware is the machine itself; it is the physical mechanism that carries out the instructions contained in the software. The output is the final product that comes out of the hardware; it is the tangible result of the software having told the hardware what to do. Thus, in a very loose sense the psychological system of language is like the software; it is essentially the mind of the system; it provides the instructions. The vocal mechanism is like the hardware; it is the physical system that implements the language. Speech is like the output; it is the final product of the vocal tract, the tangible result of the language faculty having told the vocal tract what to do. This analogy is illustrated in Figure 1–1. Thus, linguistic theory is the study of the psychological system of language. Consequently, the vocal tract and speech are of interest to linguists to the extent that they shed light on this psychological system: the internalized, unconscious knowledge that enables a speaker to produce and understand utterances in his or her native language.

Now that we have some idea of what theoretical linguists study, let's consider how they study it. At this point, our computer analogy breaks down. If a computer specialist wants to study the software of a particular computer system, he or she can access it and examine it directly (by requesting the hardware to produce the software as output) or question the person who designed it. In other words, an understanding of how the software works is part of the conscious knowledge of the person who designed it, and consequently it is directly accessible to anyone who wants to examine it. Language, on the other hand, it not so easily accessible. First, knowledge of language is unconscious in the sense that speakers of a language cannot articulate the rules of that language. Moreover, although linguists can examine the vocal tract and the sounds it produces, they cannot examine language directly. Rather, they must approach the properties of this psychological system *indirectly.*

There are a number of methods that linguists use to infer properties of the system. Some linguists look at language change: they compare different historical stages in the development of a language and try to infer what properties of the system would account for changes. Other linguists look at language pathology: they compare normal language output to that of aphasic patients (people with brain damage that has disrupted normal linguistic functioning) and try to infer what properties of the system would account for such abnormalities. Still others look at language universals—features that all human languages seem to have in common—and try to infer what properties of the system would account for these similarities. The list of approaches goes on and on.

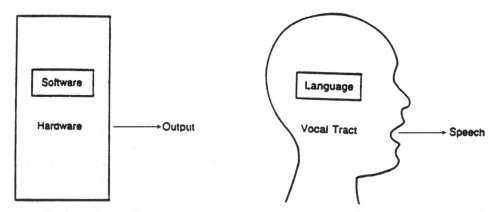

**FIGURE  1–1.  Analogy between computer system and linguistic system.**

Here, however, we will discuss in some detail another common method that theoretical linguists use to infer properties of language: investigating speakers' judgments about sentences. Under this method, the linguist asks informants (native speakers of the language under investigation) questions such as the following: Is utterance X an acceptable sentence in your language? Does utterance X have the same meaning as utterance Y? In utterance X, can word A refer to word B? And so on and so forth. Consider, for example, the following sentences.

(1)   John thinks that Bill hates him.
(2)   John thinks that Bill hates himself.

The linguist might present (1) and (2) to some informants and ask them to judge the two sentences for acceptability. In response, the informants would undoubtedly say that both (1) and (2) are perfectly acceptable. That is, both are completely unremarkable; people say such things day in and day out, and they go completely unnoticed. (In contrast, note that sentences such as *Him thinks that Bill hates John* and *John thinks that himself hates Bill* are remarkable; that is, speakers of English do not typically produce such sentences.) After having determined that both (1) and (2) are acceptable, the linguist might ask the informants the following questions. (The expected answers appear in parentheses.) In (1), can *him* refer to *John*? (Yes.) Can *him* refer to *Bill*? (No.) In (2), can *himself* refer to *John*? (No.) Can *himself* refer to *Bill*? (Yes.) Do sentences (1) and (2) have the same meaning? (No.)

Having gathered these data, the linguist would then try to infer the properties of the internal linguistic system of the informants that would account for these judgments. For example, the linguist might hypothesize that English contains at least two kinds of pronouns: **personal pronouns** (e.g., *him*) and **reflexive pronouns** (e.g., *himself*). Moreover, the linguist might hypothesize that a pronoun may have an **antecedent** (i.e., a preceding word or phrase to which the pronoun refers). Finally, the linguist might infer that the antecedents of these two types of pronouns have different distributional properties; that is, the antecedent for a personal pronoun and the antecedent for a reflexive pronoun cannot occupy the same position within a sentence. In order to determine exactly what the distributional limitations are on these antecedents, the linguist might construct some related sentences (e.g., *John hates him, John hates himself,* and so on) and present them to informants for different types of judgments. This process would continue until the linguist had formed a picture of what the psychological system of the informants looks like, at least with respect to the distribution of antecedents for personal and reflexive pronouns.

There are several points to note about this method of inquiry. First, if the linguist is a native speaker of the language being studied, the linguist himself can, and often does, serve as both informant and analyst. In the previous example, any native speaker of English would be able to determine that (1) and (2) are both acceptable, but that they have entirely different meanings. Moreover, any native speaker of English would be able to trace these differences in meaning to the fact that in (1) *him* can refer to *John* but not to *Bill,* and in (2) *himself* can refer to *Bill* but not to *John.* In a clear-cut example like this, there is no need to present these sentences to thousands, hundreds, dozens, or even two speakers of English. The linguist can be reasonably certain in advance that they would all judge the sentences in the same way. Second, the linguist, in forming a picture of the internal linguistic system of the informant, is in essence constructing a **theory** of that system. That is, concepts such as personal pronoun, reflexive pronoun, antecedent, and distribution are not directly observable in the utterances themselves. Rather, the linguist *hypothesizes* such concepts to account for the observable fact that speakers of English can make such clear-cut judgments about sentences like (1) and (2). In short, the linguist uses the directly observable judgments of the informant (i.e., the data) to draw inferences about the unobservable internal system that governs such judgments (i.e., to construct a theory). This procedure can be schematized as follows.

| *Observable Data* → | *Linguist* → | *Theory* |
|---|---|---|
| Speaker's judgments of acceptability, sameness of meaning, reference, and so forth. | Makes hypotheses about internal structure of speaker's psychological linguistic system. | English has two kinds of pronouns, whose antecedents have different distributions. |

This, of course, is not a complete theory of English; it is not even a complete theory of the distribution of antecedents for personal and reflexive pronouns in English. After all, the linguist in this hypothetical example has not determined where the antecedent for each type of pronoun can occur, but simply that they cannot occur in exactly the same positions within a sentence. The point of this example has been to illustrate one central goal of linguistics: constructing a theory about the unobservable, based upon observable data. And one type of data that linguists commonly use is the judgments of informants.

Having drawn a distinction between data and theory, let's pursue our example further and try to construct a more precise theory of the distribution of antecedents for personal and reflexive pronouns. The sentences in (1) and (2) are repeated in (1a-b) and (2a-b), but here we have incorporated the judgments of our hypothetical informants. (An arrow indicates the antecedent of a pronoun, and an asterisk indicates an unacceptable sentence.)

(1a)   *John* thinks that Bill hates *him.*

(1b)   *John thinks that *Bill* hates *him.*

(2a)   **John* thinks that Bill hates *himself.*

(2b)  John thinks that *Bill* hates *himself.*

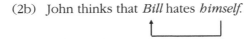

Each of these structures is to be interpreted as follows.

(1a) is acceptable, if *John* is the antecedent of *him.*
(1b) is unacceptable, if *Bill* is the antecedent of *him.*
(2a) is unacceptable, if *John* is the antecedent of *himself.*
(2b) is acceptable, if *Bill* is the antecedent of *himself.*

How can we explain these observations? That is, what principle accounts for the distribution of antecedents for personal and reflexive pronouns? There is no fool-proof method for knowing where to begin. We simply have to start with an educated guess and see how accurately it accounts for our observations. We can begin by noting that each of our sample sentences is complex; that is, it contains more than one clause. In fact, each of our sample sentences has exactly two clauses. Moreover, within each sentence, the dividing line between the two clauses comes precisely between *thinks* and *that.* The sentences in (1) and (2) are repeated once more, with a vertical line separating the clauses in each sentence.

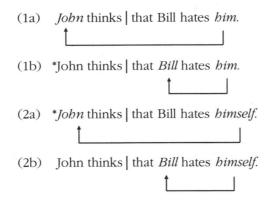

(1a)  *John* thinks | that Bill hates *him.*

(1b)  *John thinks | that *Bill* hates *him.*

(2a)  *John* thinks | that Bill hates *himself.*

(2b)  John thinks | that *Bill* hates *himself.*

Now, if we consider just the examples in (1), it is clear that the personal pronoun *him* requires an antecedent *outside* of its clause. Note that in (1a), which is acceptable, the antecedent for *him* is in a different clause; but in (1b), which is unacceptable, the antecedent for *him* is in the same clause. Likewise, if we consider just the examples in (2), it is clear that the reflexive pronoun *himself* requires an antecedent *inside* of its clause. Note that in (2b), which is acceptable, the antecedent for *himself* is in the same clause; but in (2a), which is unacceptable, the antecedent for *himself* is in a different clause.

At this point, we might abstract away from the particular data in (1) and (2) and propose the following general theory governing the antecedents of personal and reflexive pronouns:

- The antecedent for a personal pronoun *cannot* be within the clause containing the pronoun.
- The antecedent for a reflexive pronoun *must* be within the clause containing the pronoun.

The next step would be to test our theory on additional examples containing personal and reflexive pronouns. If our theory predicts speakers' judgments about these other sentences, then it gains strength. If, on the other hand, it makes incorrect predictions, then we need to go back and revise the theory.

Let's consider a few other examples. The sentence *Mary lies to herself* is acceptable if *herself* refers to *Mary*; likewise, this sentence is unacceptable if *herself* refers to someone other than *Mary*. Both of these judgments are predicted by our theory: *herself* is a reflexive pronoun and thus must have an antecedent within the same clause, in this case *Mary*. Consider another example. The sentence *Mary lies to her* is acceptable only if *her* is someone other than *Mary*. Once again our theory predicts this judgment; *her* is a personal pronoun and thus cannot have an antecedent within the same clause; since *Mary* is in the same clause as *her*, it can't serve as the antecedent.

Both of these examples fit within the theory we have constructed, but what about a sentence like *\*John thinks that Mary hates himself*? This sentence is unacceptable regardless of whether *himself* refers to *John* or *Mary*. Our theory correctly predicts that *himself* cannot refer to *John*, since *himself* is reflexive and *John* appears in a different clause. However, our theory incorrectly predicts that *himself* should be able to refer to *Mary*, since *Mary* is in the same clause. The problem, of course, is that *himself* can refer only to words designating a male, and the word *Mary* normally designates a female. Thus, we would have to revise our rule to stipulate that pronouns and their antecedents must match in gender. This process of testing and revising the theory goes on until the theory predicts the data (in this case, speakers' judgments) exactly.

There are several points worth making about this process of theory construction. First, we have been able to account for some fairly puzzling phenomena (e.g., why can't *him* refer to *Bill* in *John thinks that Bill hates him?*) with two simple and apparently exceptionless statements concerning the distribution of antecedents for personal and reflexive pronouns. Second, in the process of devising these statements (or rules), we had to try several guesses (or hypotheses) before we hit upon one that seems to provide a reasonable explanation (or theory) of the data in (1) and (2). (In fact, the theory we ended up with is still not precise enough to predict every judgment a speaker can make about the distribution of antecedents for pronouns in English. For example, our revised theory, as it stands, cannot explain why *he* can refer to *John* in a sentence like *After he came home, John ate lunch*. Here the "antecedent" follows the pronoun, thus violating our theory.) Third, and most importantly, our theory is made up of categories (e.g., pronoun, antecedent, clause, gender) and rules (e.g., a reflexive pronoun must have an antecedent within the same clause) which are not part of the data themselves. Rather, these categories and rules are products of our own creation that enable us to account for the fact that speakers of English interpret sentences such as (1) and (2) in a specific, limited, and uniform manner. In short, this is what linguistic theory is all about: we try to form a theory of a psychological system that we cannot observe directly, by examining the superficial manifestations of this system (i.e., speakers' judgments about utterances).

This idea of trying to model what we cannot directly observe by drawing inferences from what we can observe is not restricted to linguistic theory. In 1938, the physicists Albert Einstein and Leopold Infeld wrote a book entitled *The Evolution of Physics*. In it they had this to say:

> In our endeavor to understand reality we are somewhat like a man trying to understand the mechanism of a closed watch. He sees the face and the moving hands, even hears its ticking, but he has no way of opening the case. If he is ingenious he may form some picture of a mechanism which could be responsible for all the things he observes, but he may never be quite sure his picture is the only one which could explain his observations. He will never be able to compare his picture with the real mechanism and he cannot even imagine the possibility of the meaning of such a comparison. (1938:31)

These physicists are essentially describing the same position that theoretical linguists are in: they are trying to formulate hypotheses about the structure of what they cannot observe, based upon what they can observe. In studying language, linguists cannot observe a speaker's mind. They can, however, observe the speaker's judgments about sentences. On the basis of these observable judgments, linguists can construct a theory of the unobservable psychological system that underlies these judgments. Moreover, they will never know for sure if their theory is correct; all they can do is continue to test it against an ever-expanding range of data and revise it as necessary.

To summarize, this book is intended to provide specialists in fields neighboring linguistics with a basic introduction to the principles and methods of linguistic theory. Under one common definition, linguistic theory is the study of the psychological system of language; that is, of the unconscious knowledge that lies behind our ability to produce and interpret utterances in a language. However, since this system cannot be observed directly, it must be studied indirectly. One common method is to infer properties of the system by analyzing speakers' judgments about utterances. The goal of this enterprise is to construct a theory of the psychological system of language. This theory is composed of categories, relationships, and rules, which are not part of the directly observable physical world. We will take up the topic of theories again in the final chapter.

*C h a p t e r* **2**

# *Pragmatics*

**Pragmatics** is the study of how language is used to communicate within its situational context. Pragmatics is distinct from grammar, which is the study of the internal structure of language. (Grammar is generally divided into a number of particular areas of study: semantics, syntax, morphology, and phonology. These areas are covered in Chapters 3–6.) Keeping in mind this distinction between pragmatics (language use) and grammar (language structure), let's consider some observations that we can make about how language is used.

(1)  If Jack says *Kathy's cooking dinner tonight*, and Jill replies with *Better stock up on Alka-Seltzer*, an observer might conclude that Kathy is not a good cook.

(2)  The utterance *I apologize for stepping on your toe* can constitute an act of apology. The utterance *John apologized to Mary for stepping on her toe* cannot.

(3)  The utterance *I now pronounce you man and wife* can constitute an act of marriage if spoken by an appropriate authority, such as an ordained Catholic priest. If uttered by an 8-year-old child, however, it cannot.

(4)  An appropriate answer to the question *Do you have the time?* might be *7:15*; an inappropriate answer would be *Yes*.

(5)  When a friend says something that you agree with, you might respond by saying *You can say that again*. But it would be inappropriate for your friend to then repeat what he or she originally said.

Observation (1) illustrates the fact that sentences can imply information that is not actually stated. Observation (2) illustrates the fact that we can do things by uttering sentences, as well as say things. Observation (3) illustrates the fact that the nature of the participants in a verbal exchange can determine the effect of what is actually said. Observation (4) illustrates the fact that a correct answer to a question is not necessarily appropriate. Observation (5) illustrates the fact that speakers don't always mean exactly what they say.

All of these phenomena are pragmatic in nature. That is, they have to do with the way we use language to communicate in a particular context rather than the way language is structured internally. Moreover, we will assume that the phenomena in (1–5) are systematic; that is, they are governed by a system of principles. What we will now try to do is construct the system of principles that will account for these phenomena. Keep in mind that what follows is a theory (a set of unobservable hypotheses) designed to account for the data in (1–5) (a set of observable phenomena).

# Implicature

In a 1975 article entitled "Logic and Conversation," the philosopher Paul Grice pointed out that an utterance can *imply* a proposition (i.e., a statement) that is not part of the utterance and that does not follow as a necessary consequence of the utterance. Grice called such an implied statement an **implicature**. Consider the following example. John says to his wife Mary *Uncle Chester is coming over for dinner tonight*, and Mary responds with *I guess I'd better lock up the liquor*. An observer of this interchange might draw the inference that Uncle Chester has a drinking problem. Thus, in Grice's terms, we might say that Mary's utterance *raises the implicature* that Uncle Chester has a drinking problem.

It is important to make three points about this example of implicature. First, the implicature (Uncle Chester has a drinking problem) is not part of Mary's utterance (*I guess I'd better lock up the liquor*). Second, the implicature does not follow as a necessary consequence of Mary's utterance. A necessary consequence of an utterance is called an **entailment** and will be covered in the chapter on semantics. Consider an example of entailment: the sentence *John fried some fish* entails that John cooked some fish, since it is impossible to fry fish without cooking them. If a sentence is true then its entailment must be true, but not vice versa. (Note that it is possible to cook fish without frying them—they could be broiled, for instance.) However, an implicature, as opposed to an entailment, does not follow as a necessary consequence from the utterance which implies it. Third, it is possible for an utterance to raise more than one implicature, or to raise different implicatures if uttered in different contexts. For instance, in the previous example, Mary's response (*I guess I'd better lock up the liquor*) might raise the implicature that Uncle Chester is a teetotaler and a prohibitionist. That is, the mere sight of alcohol and its consumption offends Uncle Chester, so Mary is locking it up to keep it out of sight. Thus, implicatures are heavily dependent upon the context of an utterance, including the participants. However, we have not yet constructed any hypotheses about how these implicatures arise. We will now consider what such a theory might look like.

## Conversational Maxims

Grice proposes that conversations are governed by what he calls the Cooperative Principle, namely that participants in a conversation cooperate with each other. This Cooperative Principle, in turn, consists of four **conversational maxims**: **Quan-**

**tity**—a participant's contribution should be informative; **Quality**—a participant's contribution should be true; **Relation**—a participant's contribution should be relevant; and **Manner**—a participant's contribution should be clear. Grice's claim, however, is not that we strictly adhere to these maxims when we converse; rather, he claims that we interpret what we hear *as if* it conforms to these maxims. That is, when a maxim is violated, we draw an inference (i.e., an implicature) which makes the utterance conform to these maxims. Grice used the term **flouting** to describe the *intentional* violation of a maxim for the purpose of conveying an unstated proposition. This, then, would constitute a theory of how implicatures arise. Let's now consider how this theory of conversational implicature applies in some hypothetical cases.

**Maxim of Quantity.** This maxim states that each participant's contribution to a conversation should be just as informative as is required; it should not be less informative or more informative. Suppose Kenny and Tom are college roommates. Kenny walks into the living room of their apartment, where Tom is reading a book. Kenny asks Tom *What are you reading?* Tom responds with *A book.* Kenny reasons (unconsciously) as follows: I asked Tom what he was reading and the context of my question required him to tell me either the title of the book or at least its subject matter. Instead, he told me what I could already see for myself. He appears to be flouting the Maxim of Quantity; there must be a reason for him giving me less information than the situation requires. The inference (i.e., the implicature) that I draw is that he does not want to be disturbed (and thus is trying to terminate the conversation).

**Maxim of Quality.** This maxim states that each participant's contribution should be truthful and based on sufficient evidence. Suppose an undergraduate in a geography class says, in response to a question from the instructor, *Reno's the capital of Nevada.* The instructor, Mr. Barbados, then says *Yeah, and London's the capital of New Jersey.* The instructor's utterance raises an implicature. The student reasons (unconsciously) as follows: Mr. Barbados said that London is the capital of New Jersey; he knows that is not true. He appears to be flouting the Maxim of Quality; there must be a reason for him saying something patently false. The inference (i.e., the implicature) I draw is that my answer is false (i.e., Reno is not the capital of Nevada).

**Maxim of Relation.** This maxim states that each participant's contribution should be relevant to the subject of the conversation. Suppose a man wakes up in the morning and asks his wife *What time is it?* She responds with *Well, the paper's already come.* Her statement raises an implicature. The husband reasons (unconsciously) as follows: I asked about the time and she told me about something seemingly unrelated—the arrival of the newspaper. She appears to be flouting the Maxim of Relation; there must be some reason for her seemingly irrelevant comment. The inference (i.e., the implicature) I draw is that she doesn't know the exact time but the arrival of the newspaper has something to do with the time, namely that it is now past the time of day that the newspaper usually comes (i.e., 7:00 a.m.). (This example is adapted from Levinson [1983].)

**Maxim of Manner.** This maxim states that each participant's contribution should be expressed in a reasonably clear fashion; that is, it should not be vague, ambiguous, or excessively wordy. Suppose Mr. and Mrs. Jones are out for a Sunday drive with their two preschool children. Mr. Jones says to Mrs. Jones *Let's stop and get something to eat.* Mrs. Jones responds with *Okay, but not M-c-D-o-n-a-l-d-s.* Mrs. Jones' statement raises an implicature. Mr. Jones reasons (unconsciously) as follows: she spelled out the word *McDonald's*, which is certainly not the clearest way of saying it. She appears to be flouting the Maxim of Manner; there must be reason for her lack of clarity. Since the kids cannot spell, the inference (i.e., the implicature) I draw is that she does not want the children to understand that part of her statement.

In summary, an implicature is a proposition implied by an utterance but neither part of nor a logical consequence of that utterance. An implicature arises in the mind of a hearer when the speaker flouts (i.e., intentionally violates) one of the maxims of Quantity, Quality, Relation, or Manner.

## Speech Acts

In 1955, the British philosopher John Austin delivered the William James lectures at Harvard. (These lectures were published in 1962 as *How to Do Things with Words.*) Austin's fundamental insight was that an utterance can be used to perform an act. That is, he was the first to point out that in uttering a sentence, we can *do* things as well as *say* things. (Before Austin, philosophers held that sentences were used simply to say things.) For example, if you say to someone who is leaving your office *Please close the door*, you are not just saying something but also making a request. Likewise, if you say to a friend after a fight *I'm sorry for the way I acted*, you are not just saying something but also apologizing. Finally, if you say to your boss *I'll come in on Saturday to finish the Katznelson Project*, you're not just saying something but you're also making a commitment.

Thus, each speech event (or **speech act**) has at least two facets to it: a **locutionary act** (i.e., the act of saying something) and an **illocutionary act** (i.e., the act of doing something). These concepts are defined in more detail as follows.

**Locutionary Act.** This is the act of simply uttering a sentence from a language; it is a description of what the speaker *says*. Typically, it is the act of using a referring expression (e.g., a noun phrase) and a predicating expression (e.g., a verb phrase) to express a proposition. For instance, in the utterance *You should stop smoking*, the referring expression is *you* and the predicating expression is *stop smoking*.

**Illocutionary Act.** This is what the speaker *does* in uttering a sentence. Illocutionary acts include such acts as stating, requesting, questioning, promising, apologizing, and appointing. For example, if a mother says to her child *Take your feet off the table*, the illocutionary act is one of ordering. The illocutionary act is sometimes called the **illocutionary force** of the utterance. Thus, in the previous example, we might say that the illocutionary force of the mother's utterance is an order.

In the rest of this section we will examine speech acts first from the perspective of the illocutionary act involved and then from the perspective of the locutionary act.

## *Classification of Illocutionary Acts*

In a 1976 article entitled "The Classification of Illocutionary Acts," the philosopher John Searle, one of Austin's former students, pointed out that there is a seemingly endless number of illocutionary acts. There are statements, assertions, denials, requests, commands, warnings, promises, vows, offers, apologies, thanks, condolences, appointments, namings, resignations, and so forth. At the same time, he observed that some illocutionary acts are more closely related than others. For example, promises and vows seem to be more alike than, say, promises and requests. Thus Searle attempted to classify illocutionary acts into the following types.

**Representative.** A representative is an utterance used to describe some state of affairs—for example, *I have five toes on my right foot*. This class includes acts of stating, asserting, denying, confessing, admitting, notifying, concluding, predicting, and so on.

**Directive.** A directive is an utterance used to try to get the hearer to do something—for example, *Shut the door*. This class includes acts of requesting, ordering, forbidding, warning, advising, suggesting, insisting, recommending, and so on.

**Question.** A question is an utterance used to get the hearer to provide information—for example, *Who won the 1968 presidential election?* This class includes acts of asking, inquiring, and so on. (Note: Searle treated questions as a subcategory of directives; for our purposes, however, it is more useful to treat them as a separate category.)

**Commissive.** A commissive is an utterance used to commit the speaker to do something—for example, *I'll meet you at the library at 10:00 p.m.* This class includes acts of promising, vowing, volunteering, offering, guaranteeing, pledging, betting, and so on.

**Expressive.** An expressive is an utterance used to express the emotional state of the speaker—for example, *I'm sorry for calling you a dweeb*. This class includes acts of apologizing, thanking, congratulating, condoling, welcoming, deploring, objecting, and so on.

**Declaration.** A declaration is an utterance used to change the status of some entity—for example, *You're out* uttered by an umpire at a baseball game. This class includes acts of appointing, naming, resigning, baptizing, surrendering, excommunicating, arresting, and so on.

### *Felicity Conditions*

Early on, Austin realized that context was an important factor in the *valid* performance of an illocutionary act. He noted, for example, that the participants and the circumstances must be appropriate: an umpire at a baseball game can cause a player to be out by uttering *You're out!*, but an excited fan in the bleachers cannot. Likewise, the act must be executed completely and correctly by all participants; if during a game of hide-and-go-seek, Suzy says to Billy *You're it*, and Billy responds with *I don't want to play*, then the act of naming is not valid. Finally, the participants must have the appropriate intentions: if a friend says to you *I promise I'll meet you in your office at 10:00 a.m.*, but actually plans to be on his way to Mexico at the time, the act of promising is not valid. Austin called these conditions **felicity conditions**. Searle expanded on this basic idea by trying to categorize felicity conditions into four types.

**Preparatory Conditions.**  Preparatory conditions are those existing *antecedent* to the utterance, including the speaker's beliefs about the hearer's capabilities and state of mind. For example, an apology requires that the speaker believe that some act has occurred that is harmful to the hearer.

**Sincerity Conditions.**  Sincerity conditions relate to the speaker's state of mind. For example, a valid apology requires that the speaker feel remorse for his act.

**Essential Condition.**  The essential condition requires that the utterance be recognizable as an instance of the illocutionary act in question. For example, a valid apology requires that the utterance be recognizable as an apology: if a speaker attempts to apologize for something he's said by saying *I have a big mouth*, it would violate the essential condition if the hearer fails to recognize the utterance as an apology. Such a failure would be indicated by the response *Are you trying to apologize?*

**Propositional Content Conditions.**  Propositional content conditions relate to the state of affairs predicated in the utterance. For example, a valid apology must predicate a past act of the speaker: *I'm sorry I screamed*.

Figure 2–1 gives the four types of felicity conditions for a representative example of each of the six different types of illocutionary acts.

This theory of felicity conditions helps to account for the relationship between specific illocutionary acts within the same category. Consider the difference between two different types of representatives: assertions and lies. Note that the preparatory, essential, and propositional content conditions are identical for both types of representatives. However, the sincerity condition for a lie is the exact opposite of that for an assertion. In an assertion, *S believes p* and in a lie, *S doesn't believe p*. This is illustrated in the diagram following Figure 2–1.

| | PREPARATORY | SINCERITY | ESSENTIAL | PROPOSITIONAL CONTENT |
|---|---|---|---|---|
| Representative: ASSERTION | 1. S believes H doesn't know p. | 1. S believes p. | 1. Counts as an assertion of p. | 1. Any p. |
| Directive: REQUEST | 1. S believes H able to do A. 2. A is something H would not normally do. | 1. S wants H to do A. | 1. Counts as attempt to get H to do A. | 1. Future A of H. |
| Question: QUESTION | 1. S doesn't know p. 2. P is something H would not normally provide. | 1. S wants to know p. | 1. Counts as attempt to elicit p from H. | 1. Any p. |
| Commissive: PROMISE | 1. S believes H wants A done. 2. A is something S would not normally do. | 1. S intends to do A. | 1. Counts as obligation to do A. | 1. Future A of S. |
| Expressive: THANKING | 1. S believes A benefits S. | 1. S feels appreciation for A. | 1. Counts as expression of appreciation for A. | 1. Past A of H. |
| Declaration: NAMING | 1. S has authority to name X. | 1. S intends to name X. | 1. Counts as naming of X. | 1. Name for X. |

(KEY: S = speaker, H = hearer, A = Act, p = proposition.)

**FIGURE 2–1. Felicity conditions on different types of speech acts.**

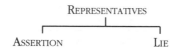

SINCERITY CONDITION:     1. S. believes p.     1. S doesn't believe p.

Now consider the difference between two different types of directives: requests and orders. The felicity conditions for orders are exactly the same as those for requests except that orders have the additional preparatory condition that *the speaker has authority over the hearer.* This is illustrated in the following diagram:

PREPARATORY CONDITIONS:     1. S believes H able to do A.     1. Same
2. A is something H would not normally do.     2. Same
3. S has authority over H

Consider, finally, the difference between two types of commissives: promises and threats. Note that the sincerity, essential, and propositional content conditions are identical for both types of commissives. However, the first preparatory condition for a threat is opposite that for a promise. In a promise, *S believes H wants A done* and in a threat, *S believes H doesn't want A done*. This is illustrated in the following diagram.

|  | PROMISE | THREAT |
|---|---|---|
| PREPARATORY CONDITION: | 1. S believes H wants A done. | 1. S believes H doesn't want A done. |

## Explicit vs. Nonexplicit Illocutionary Acts

One of Austin's most fundamental insights was the realization that English contains a set of verbs, each of which actually *names* the illocutionary force of that verb. Consider the following sentences.

(a)  I *confess* that I stole the family jewels.
(b)  I *warn* you to stop teasing your sister.
(c)  May I *inquire* where you got that gun?
(d)  I *promise* I'll come to your birthday party.
(e)  I *apologize* for calling you "a special assistant to James Brown."
(f)  I *name* this "The Good Ship Lollipop."

Note that, if said under the right circumstances, each of the sentences (a-f) constitutes the performance of the act named by the verb: (a) constitutes a confession (a type of representative); (b) constitutes a warning (a type of directive); (c) constitutes an inquiry (a type of question); (d) constitutes a promise (a type of commissive); (e) constitutes an apology (a type of expressive); and (f) constitutes an act of naming (a type of declaration). Consequently, the verbs in each sentence are known as **performative verbs**.

In order for a performative verb to have its **performative sense** (i.e., to actually perform the illocutionary act it names), it must (i) be positive, (ii) be present tense, (iii) have a first-person agent (i.e., performer of the action of the verb), and (iv) refer to a specific event. Consider, for example, the following sentences.

(a)  I *promise* I'll bring the beans.
(b)  I *can't promise* to bring the beans. (not positive)
(c)  I *promised* I would bring the beans. (not present)
(d)  *Big Bob promises* that he'll bring the beans. (not first person)
(e)  I *promise* people things from time to time. (not specific)

Sentence (a) contains a performative verb (*promise*) used in its performative sense (positive, present tense, first-person agent). Thus, uttering (a) can constitute a promise. On the other hand, (b-e) contain the same verb (*promise*), but in these cases it does not have its performative sense. Thus, uttering (b-e) do not constitute promises; they merely describe some state of affairs (i.e., they are all representatives).

On the other hand, not all verbs are performative verbs. Consider, for example, the verb *know*, as in the utterance *I know that the cube root of 27 is 3. Know* is not a performative verb because performative verbs must meet the following criteria: (1) a performative verb describes a *voluntary* act (you can't choose to know or not know something); (2) a performative verb describes an act that can only be performed *with words* (i.e., you can know something without saying you know it); and (3) a performative verb can be used with the performative indicator *hereby* (you can't say *\*I hereby know such and such* [an asterisk before an expression means it is unacceptable]). These three tests for distinguishing performative verbs from nonperformative verbs are summarized in the following chart.

| *Performative Verbs* | *Nonperformative Verbs* |
|---|---|
| *(e.g., deny)* | *(e.g., know)* |
| (a) *voluntary* act (e.g., 'denying X' is voluntary) | (a) *involuntary* act (e.g., 'knowing X' is involuntary) |
| (b) act can be performed *only with words* (e.g., 'denying X' requires words) | (b) act can be performed *without words* (e.g., 'knowing X' doesn't require words) |
| (c) can be used with *hereby* (e.g, *I hereby deny X*) | (c) can't be used with *hereby* (e.g., *\*I hereby know X*) |

An utterance which contains a performative verb (used in its performative sense), Austin called an **explicit performative**; any utterance *not* containing a performative verb (used in its performative sense), we will call a **nonexplicit performative**. The following chart illustrates that virtually any type of illocutionary act can be achieved through either an explicit or a nonexplicit performative utterance.

| | *Explicit Performative* | *Nonexplicit Performative* |
|---|---|---|
| REPRESENTATIVE | I *deny* that I killed Cock Robin. | I did not kill Cock Robin. |
| DIRECTIVE | I *forbid* you to leave your room. | Don't leave your room. |
| QUESTION | I *ask* you where you were on the night of May 21st. | Where were you on the night of May 21st? |
| COMMISSIVE | I *vow* that I'll be faithful to you. | I'll be faithful to you. |

| | | |
|---|---|---|
| EXPRESSIVE | I *thank* you for your help. | I appreciate your help. |
| DECLARATION | I *resign*. | I don't work here anymore. |

It should be noted, however, that occasionally performative verbs can be used to carry out more than one illocutionary act. For example, consider the verb *ask*, which can be used to issue an explicit question or an explicit directive, as in (a-b).

(a)    I'm asking you *if Jack drinks*.
(b)    I'm asking you *to drink this*.

Utterance (a) has the illocutionary force of a *yes-no* question (an appropriate response would be for the hearer to answer *Yes* or *No*), whereas (b) has the illocutionary force of a directive (an appropriate response would be for the hearer to drink whatever *this* refers to). In such cases, the use of the performative verb *ask* can be determined by reference to the propositional content condition on questions and directives. The propositional content condition on directives is very specific: the utterance must predicate a future act of the hearer. Utterance (b) meets this condition, but (a) does not. Thus, (b) is a directive but (a) is not. On the other hand, since any proposition can serve as the propositional content of a question, (a) must be a question. The point is that an utterance containing an explicit performative verb should be double checked to determine the illocutionary act it performs.

Moreover, it may be necessary to expand the concept of explicit performative to include such stock utterances as *Thanks* and *Congratulations*, which serve as conventional ways of expressing *I thank you* and *I congratulate you*, respectively. Along the same lines, we might treat nouns derived from performative verbs (e.g., *advice* from *advise*) as capable of functioning as explicit performatives. Note that an utterance such as *My advice is for you to X* corresponds directly to the explicit performative *I advise you to X*.

## Direct vs. Indirect Illocutionary Acts

In "Indirect Speech Acts," published in 1975, Searle pointed out that a nonexplicit performative can be carried out *indirectly* by appearing to carry out another illocutionary act. For example, if you say to someone *Bring me my coat*, you are issuing a directive *directly*. Thus, uttering this sentence under these circumstances would constitute, among other things, a **direct illocutionary act**. However, if you issue the same directive by saying *Could you bring me my coat?*, you are doing something quite different. Here, you appear to be asking a question, but actually you are issuing a directive *indirectly*. Thus, this utterance would constitute an **indirect illocutionary act**. It turns out that there is a relatively simple way of differentiating direct and indirect illocutionary acts.

**Direct Illocutionary Acts.** In general, an illocutionary act is issued directly when the syntactic form of the utterance matches the illocutionary force of the utterance. Consider the following examples.

| *Utterance* | *Syntactic Form* | *Illocutionary Force* |
|---|---|---|
| (a) It's raining. | Declarative | Representative |
| (b) Keep quiet. | Imperative | Directive |
| (c) Do you know Mary? | *Yes-No* Interrogative | *Yes-No* Question |
| (d) What time is it? | *Wh*-Interrogative | *Wh*-Question |
| (e) I'll help you with the dishes. | Declarative | Commissive |
| (f) How nice you are! | Exclamatory | Expressive |
| (g) You're fired. | Declarative | Declaration |

In each of these examples, the syntactic form of the utterance matches the direct illocutionary act. In (a) a declarative form is used to issue a representative; in (b) an imperative form is used to issue a directive; in (c) a *yes-no* interrogative form is used to ask a *yes-no* question (one to which you can respond *Yes* or *No*); in (d) a *wh*-interrogative is used to ask a *wh*-question (one to which you *cannot* respond *Yes* or *No*; they also contain a *wh*-word: *who, what, when, where, how*, etc.); in (e) a declarative form is used to issue a commissive; in (f) an exclamatory form is used to issue an expressive; and in (g) a declarative form is used to issue a declaration.

The ideal situation from our point of view would be one in which there is a one-to-one correspondence between each of the categories of illocutionary act and a particular syntactic form. Unfortunately, however, this is not the case. Instead, we have only a partial correspondence between syntactic form and illocutionary act, as illustrated in the following table.

| *Syntactic Form* | *Illocutionary Act* |
|---|---|
| Declarative | Representative |
| Declarative | Commissive |
| Declarative | Declaration |
| Imperative | Directive |
| *Yes-No* Interrogative | *Yes-No* Question |
| *Wh*-Interrogative | *Wh*-Question |
| Exclamatory | Expressive |

Note that a declarative form is used to issue commissives and declarations, as well as representatives. On the other hand, even though the correspondence between syntactic form and illocutionary force is not one-to-one, it is nonetheless possible to identify four situations where it is clear that the illocutionary act is being performed directly (see boxed material): (a) an imperative used to issue a directive; (b) a *yes-no* interrogative used to issue a *yes-no* question; (c) a *wh*-interrogative used to issue a *wh*-question; and (d) an exclamatory used to issue an expressive.

**Indirect Illocutionary Acts.**   In general, an illocutionary act is issued indirectly when the syntactic form of the utterance does *not* match the illocutionary force of the utterance. Consider the following examples. (For purposes of comparison, the direct phrasing is given in parentheses below each utterance.)

| *Utterance* | *Syntactic Form* | *Illocutionary Force* |
|---|---|---|
| (a) You might give me a hand with this. (Give me a hand with this.) | Declarative | Directive |
| (b) And you are . . . (Who are you?) | Declarative | Declarative |
| (c) Could yŏu keep quiet? (Keep quiet.) | *Yes-No* Interrogative | Directive |
| (d) Do you have the time? (What time is it?) | *Yes-No* Interrogative | *Wh*-Question |
| (e) Can I give you a hand with that? (I can give you a hand with that.) | *Yes-No* Interrogative | Commissive |
| (f) I'm sorry to hear about your loss. (How sorry I am to hear about your loss!) | Declarative | Expressive |
| (g) Why don't you be quiet? (Be quiet.) | *Wh*-Interrogative | Directive |

Let's summarize this section on illocutionary acts. The illocutionary part of a speech act is what the utterance does (rather than what it says). Illocutionary acts can be grouped into six types: representatives, directives, questions, commissives, expressives, and declarations. Illocutionary acts are valid only if their felicity conditions are met. These conditions can be grouped into four categories: preparatory, sincerity, essential, and propositional content. Illocutionary acts can be achieved through either an explicit or a nonexplicit performative. A nonexplicit performative is, in turn, either direct or indirect. The various means of performing illocutionary acts are illustrated in the following diagram.

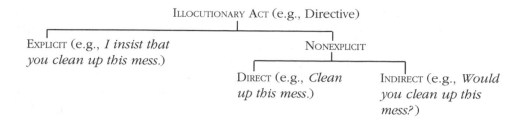

ILLOCUTIONARY ACT (e.g., Directive)

EXPLICIT (e.g., *I insist that you clean up this mess.*)

NONEXPLICIT

DIRECT (e.g., *Clean up this mess.*)

INDIRECT (e.g., *Would you clean up this mess?*)

## Expressed vs. Implied Locutionary Acts

As we said earlier, a speech act consists of an illocutionary act (what is done) and a locutionary act (what is said). At this point we want to turn our attention from illocutionary acts to locutionary acts. The locutionary act is concerned with the propositional content of the utterance, which is what follows the performative verb in an explicit performative and the entire utterance in a nonexplicit performative. In the following examples, the propositional content is in italics.

(a) EXPLICIT:      I promise *I'll come to your birthday party.*
(b) NONEXPLICIT:      *I'll come to your birthday party.*

The propositional content of a locutionary act can be either expressed directly or implied via implicature. The propositional content is **expressed** if the utterance actually contains an expression of the propositional content condition for the illocutionary act involved. For example, consider a warning, which is a type of directive. The propositional content condition on all directives is to predicate a future act of the hearer. Thus a warning such as *I warn you to stop smoking* constitutes an *expressed* locutionary act because its propositional content predicates a future act (to stop smoking) of the hearer (you).

On the other hand, the propositional content is **implied** if the utterance does *not* contain an expression of the propositional content condition for the illocutionary act involved. For example, consider the warning *I warn you that cigarette smoking is dangerous.* This utterance constitutes an *implied* locutionary act because its propositional content does not predicate a future act of the hearer; instead, it predicates a property of cigarettes. The hearer must infer the relevant propositional content, which he or she does via implicature. The hearer reasons (unconsciously) something like this. The speaker issued an explicit warning, which is a type of directive, but he failed to fulfill the propositional content condition on directives (i.e., predicate a future act of me, the hearer). Thus, since the utterance is not overtly relevant, he appears to be flouting Grice's Maxim of Relation. However, he knows I smoke cigarettes, and since there must be some reason for his seemingly irrelevant comment, the inference (i.e., implicature) I draw is that he is trying to get me to stop smoking.

Some types of illocutionary acts, however, don't have any specific propositional content conditions. Questions, for example, can have virtually any proposition as their propositional content. Thus, a common method for implying a locution is for the speaker to express a *pre-condition* for the proposition of interest. For example,

*Do you have a watch?* (as opposed to *Do you have the time?*) expresses a precondition for having the time. Likewise, representatives can have virtually any proposition as their propositional content. Thus, a speaker can imply the proposition of interest by expressing a pre-condition on that proposition. For example, *The battery's dead* (as opposed to *The car won't start*) expresses a pre-condition for the car starting.

Make no mistake: it's not always obvious if you're dealing with an expressed or an implied locutionary act. The same utterance may contain an implied locution on one occasion but an expressed locution on another. For example, if an uncle asks his niece *Do you have a watch?* in order to help him decide what to get her for her birthday, then the proposition of interest is *expressed* by the utterance. However, as we saw in the preceding paragraph, if the same utterance is used to ask the time, then the proposition of interest is only *implied* by the utterance.

The following table displays a representative example of each of the six types of illocutionary act, the propositional content condition (if any), and examples of locutions that express and imply the proposition of interest.

| Type of Illocution (and Example) | Propositional Content Condition | Utterance with Expressed Locutionary Act | Utterance with Implied Locutionary Act |
|---|---|---|---|
| Representative (assertion) | any p | The car won't start. | The battery's dead. |
| Directive (request) | future A of H | Please do the dishes. | The dishes are piling up. |
| Question (*Yes-no* question) | any p | Do you have the time? | Do you have a watch? |
| Commissive (volunteering) | future A of S | I'll help with the dishes. | You look like you could use some help with the dishes. |
| Expressive (condolence) | past event related to H | I am sorry to hear your mother died. | I am sorry to hear of your loss. |
| Declaration (firing) | H fired | You're fired. | You'll need to start looking for a new job. |

Directives in particular are prime candidates for implied locutionary acts. This is because, as we noted earlier with regard to indirect illocutionary acts, directives constitute an imposition on the hearer. Thus, in such cases it is quite often more polite to *implicate* the propositional content rather than express it directly. For example, consider an employee asking his boss for a raise with the following utterances.

| Utterance | Illocutionary Act | Locutionary Act |
|---|---|---|
| (a) Give me a raise. | Direct | Expressed |
| (b) Could you give me a raise? | Indirect | Expressed |
| (c) I could sure use a raise. | Indirect | Implied |

As we move from (a) to (c), the utterances become increasingly oblique but also increasingly polite. In fact, (c), since it does not express the propositional content of a directive, could be (intentionally) misconstrued by the boss as simply a comment on the general state of the economy. The point is that implied locutionary acts serve the same function as indirect illocutionary acts. They both serve to distance the speaker from the speech act.

Consider the distancing effect of the implied locutionary act in another example. The following sign appears in the botanical gardens at Oxford: *Please make a donation to help us maintain this Historic Garden and unique collection of plants. Visiting similar gardens often costs at least two pounds.* The implied proposition in the second sentence is 'a donation is two pounds.' Moreover, this proposition is implied by an implicature which flouts Grice's Maxim of Relation. The reader of the sign reasons (unconsciously) as follows: the sign requests a donation but refers to something seemingly unrelated—the admission cost to other gardens; there must be some reason for the seemingly irrelevant comment. The inference (i.e., implicature) the reader draws is that the garden owners don't want to specify the amount of the donation directly, since a donation is voluntary and without limit. Instead, they state what other gardens charge for admission and hope the reader makes the connection.

## Literal vs. Nonliteral Locutionary Acts

A locutionary act can be either literal or nonliteral, depending upon whether the speaker actually means what is said or not. Consider, for example, the warning on a pack of cigarettes, which reads *Cigarette smoking is dangerous to your health*. The warning means exactly what it says; thus, it constitutes a **literal locutionary act**. On the other hand, consider an anti-smoking poster which depicts a bleary-eyed, disheveled man with a cigarette hanging out of his mouth; the caption reads *Smoking is glamorous*. The caption does not mean what it says (in fact, it means quite the opposite); thus, the caption constitutes a **nonliteral locutionary act**.

Nonliteral locutionary acts are those for which a literal interpretation is either impossible or absurd within the context of the utterance. For example, the famished husband who walks through the door and says to his wife, *I could eat a horse* (instead of, say, *I am very hungry*) is performing a nonliteral locutionary act. The locution is nonliteral because most human beings could not (and certainly *would* not) eat an entire horse. Likewise, the college student who says to her roommate *I guess it would kill you to turn down that radio* (instead of, say, *Please turn down the radio*) is performing a nonliteral locutionary act. The locution is nonliteral because there is no known causal connection between turning down radios and death. Another example is the teacher who says to the schoolyard bully, who is picking on Little Timmy, *Pick on someone your own size* (instead of *Don't pick on Little Timmy*). The teacher is performing a nonliteral locutionary act because the teacher (presumably) does not really want the bully to pick on someone larger, but rather to stop tormenting his current victim. Consider, finally, the following comedy routine. Laurel and Hardy are sitting in a jail cell commiserating about being captured in the act of robbing a bank. Laurel says to Hardy *Ollie, when you said "Why don't you scream so everyone can hear?" . . . Well, I thought you really meant it. . . .* The locution *Why don't you scream so everyone can hear?* is clearly nonliteral. In fact, the "humor" of the routine depends upon the audience knowing this.

Note that all of these examples have something in common. They all can be analyzed as flouting Grice's Maxim of Quality. That is, they all involve someone saying something that is blatantly false under the circumstances. Moreover, note that all cases of sarcasm essentially involve nonliteral locutionary acts (e.g., *Smoking is glamorous, I guess it would kill you to turn down the radio, Why don't you shout so everyone can hear*), but not all nonliteral acts are sarcastic (e.g., *I could eat a horse*).

Nonliteral locutionary acts, however, can be quite complex. For example, a shop owner in England erected the following sign in front of his store: *If you want your wheel clamped, by all means park here.* (A wheel clamp is a device that, once attached to a car, keeps the car from being moved.) Note that the literal way to word the sign would be something like *Don't park here* or *Parked cars will be clamped*. The sign as worded, however, is nonliteral because a literal interpretation would be absurd within the context of the utterance. That is, to interpret the sign literally would require the reader to assume that there are drivers who would actually like to have their wheels clamped.

## Overview of Speech Act Theory

Speech acts, as we have seen, each have two facets: an illocutionary act (i.e., what is *done*) and a locutionary act (i.e., what is *said*). The illocutionary act can be achieved either with an *explicit* performative (i.e., a performative verb used in its performative sense) or a *nonexplicit* performative. Moreover, a nonexplicit illocutionary act can be performed either *directly* (i.e., syntactic form matches illocutionary force) or *indirectly*. On the other hand, the locutionary act can be either *expressed* (i.e., articulates propositional content condition) or *implied*. Likewise, the locutionary act can be expressed either *literally* (i.e., does not require a nonliteral interpretation) or *nonliterally*.

These four variables define 16 theoretically possible types of speech acts. However, since any nonexplicit illocutionary act can, at least in theory, be made explicit by prefixing a performative verb to it (e.g., *Shut up* → *I hereby order you to shut up*), we will ignore explicit performatives for present purposes. The remaining 8 types of nonexplicit illocutionary acts are illustrated in the following table. (Each utterance could be used in a particular context to get someone to refrain from smoking.)

| Utterance | Direct | Expressed | Literal |
|---|---|---|---|
| (a) Please don't smoke. | + | + | + |
| (b) By all means, go right ahead and smoke. (sarcastic) | + | + | − |
| (c) Think about what you're doing to your lungs. | + | − | + |
| (d) Would you please not smoke? | − | + | + |
| (e) Go ahead and kill yourself, see if I care. | + | − | − |
| (f) I guess it would kill you to stop smoking. | − | + | − |
| (g) Cigarette smoking is dangerous to your health. | − | − | + |
| (h) Smoking is glamorous. (under picture of derelict smoking) | − | − | − |

## Summary

Let's review what we have done. We started with five observations about the way language is used to communicate. However, we had no ready explanation for these phenomena. We constructed a (partial) theory of pragmatics to account for our original observations. This theory makes use of such concepts as implicature and conversational maxims (i.e., quantity, quality, relation, and manner), speech act (i.e., illocutionary and locutionary acts), a classification of illocutionary acts, felicity conditions on illocutionary acts, explicit/nonexplicit and direct/indirect illocutionary acts, expressed/implied and literal/nonliteral locutionary acts. These theoretical constructs were developed by such people as Grice, Austin, and Searle in order to help explain the observations noted in (1–5). This theory will no doubt require revision, but it is the best we have at the present time.

Moreover, it is important to realize that there is much more to the study of pragmatics than what has been presented in this one short chapter. However, you have now been exposed to some of the basic ideas in the field; if you want to learn more about the subject, see the readings at the end of the chapter. Following the readings is a short set of practice problems with the answers, which you can use to check your understanding of the material in this chapter. After that is a set of 50 exercises for you to work on your own.

## Supplementary Readings

### Primary

Austin, J. L. (1962). *How to do things with words.* Oxford: Clarendon Press.

Grice, H. P. (1975). Logic and conversation. In P. Cole and J. L. Morgan (Eds.), *Syntax and semantics 3: Speech acts*, pp. 41–58. New York: Academic Press.

Searle, J. R. (1969). *Speech acts.* Cambridge, England: Cambridge University Press.

Searle, J. R. (1975). Indirect speech acts. In P. Cole and J. L. Morgan (Eds.), *Syntax and semantics 3: Speech acts*, pp. 59–82. New York: Academic Press.

Searle, J. R. (1976). The classification of illocutionary acts. *Language in Society, 5*, 1–24.

### Secondary

Bach, K., and Harnish, R. M. (1979). *Linguistic communication and speech acts.* Cambridge, MA: MIT Press.

Coulthard, M. (1977). *Discourse analysis.* London: Longman.

Sperber, D., and Wilson, D. (1986). *Relevance.* Cambridge, MA: Harvard University Press.

Levinson, S. (1983). *Pragmatics.* Cambridge, England: Cambridge University Press.

Coulthard provides a clear introduction to pragmatics. The other works are more advanced and would be more accessible after you've had an introductory course in linguistics. Levinson is a comprehensive textbook on pragmatics; since it has a detailed index and bibliography, you can also use it as a reference tool.

## Practice

**1.** In the movie *The Doctor*, an orderly is wheeling patient Jack McKee (William Hurt) down a hospital corridor on a gurney. McKee is nearly naked except for a single sheet draped over him. McKee looks up at the orderly and says *Do you think you could get me a thinner sheet? I'm not sure everybody can see through this one.* McKee's utterance raises an implicature, namely that he wants more covering. Which of Grice's maxims does McKee flout?

**2.** Assume that you are teaching a course. A fellow instructor approaches you after you have graded a test and asks *How did Mr. Jones do?* You respond with *Well, he wrote something down for every question.*

   a.  Which of Grice's maxims does your response appear to flout?

   b.  What is the implicature raised by your response?

**3.** You ask a friend *Do you know where Billy Bob is?* The friend responds with *Well, he didn't meet me for lunch like he was supposed to.*

   a.  Which of Grice's maxims does your friend's statement appear to flout?

   b.  What is the implicature raised by your friend's statement?

**4.** Identify the class of illocutionary act (i.e., representative, directive, etc.) performed by each of the following utterances.

    a.  A child says to her playmate, *Happy birthday.*

    b.  A doctor says to a patient, *I advise you to stop smoking.*

    c.  One secretary says to another, *My daughter's getting married in August.*

    d.  A priest says over an infant, *I baptize you in the name of . . .*

    e.  A mother says to her daughter, *Who washed the dishes?*

    f.  A passerby says to a motorist with a flat tire, *Let me help you with that.*

**5.** Assume that each of the following utterances constitutes a nonfelicitous (i.e., invalid) act of apologizing. Which type of felicity condition (i.e., preparatory, sincerity, etc.) is violated by each one?

    a.  I apologize for what I'm about to do.

    b.  I apologize for not running over you with my car.

    c.  I apologize for Little Freddie's having dumped potato soup in your lap.

**6.** Explain why each of the performative verbs in the following utterances is *not* being used in its performative sense.

    a.  I *warned* you not to go to that movie.

    b.  *Promise* me anything, but give me Arpege.

    c.  I *won't insist* that you leave.

**7.** For each of the following utterances, state (i) the syntactic form, (ii) the illocutionary act it performs, and (iii) whether the illocutionary act is performed directly or indirectly.

    a.  A clerk says to a customer, *And your account number is . . . ?*

    b.  A mother says to a neighbor's child, *Have some candy.*

    c.  An impatient husband grouses to his wife, *Shouldn't we be leaving soon?*

**8.** For each of the following utterances, state whether the relevant proposition is expressed or implied.

    a.  A sign on a fence reads *Parking here prohibits rubbish collection.*

    b.  A warning on a can reads *Do not incinerate.*

    c.  A train conductor points to a NO SMOKING sign and says to a passenger who is smoking, *Look at that sign.*

**9.** For each of the following utterances, state whether the locutionary act is literal or nonliteral.

    a.  You go to a movie and the Warthog family comes in and sits down behind you. They crumple candy wrappers and talk for the first 20 minutes of the movie. Finally you have had enough, and you turn to them and say *I don't want to have to call the manager.*

    b.  Assume the context is the same as in (a), except you say *I can still hear the movie; would you mind speaking up?*

**10.** For each of the following speech acts, state if it is (i) explicit or nonexplicit; (ii) direct or indirect (applies to nonexplicit only); (iii) expressed or implied; (iv) literal or nonliteral.

    a.  To express agreement, a friend says *How right you are!*

    b.  A teacher says to his student, *I suggest you spend more time on your homework.*

    c.  A sign on the side of the road reads *Construction Ahead.*

## Answers

The following answers are not always the only ones possible; they are meant solely to be suggestive. Discussion of other possible answers is part of the practice.

**1.** quality

**2.** a. quantity; b. Jones did not do well on the test.

**3.** a. relation; b. Your friend doesn't know where Billy Bob is.

**4.** a. expressive; b. directive; c. representative; d. declaration; e. question; f. commissive

**5.** a. propositional content (speaker must predicate *past* act)
b. preparatory (speaker must believe hearer is *displeased* by the act)
c. propositional content (speaker must predicate an act of *him/herself* )

**6.** a. *warned* is not present tense
b. *promise* does not have a first-person agent
c. *won't insist* is not positive

**7.** a. i. declarative; ii. *wh*-question; iii. indirect
b. i. imperative; ii. directive; iii. direct
c. i. *yes-no* interrogative; ii. directive; iii. indirect

**8.** a. implied ('Don't park here')
b. expressed
c. implied ('Don't smoke')

**9.** a. literal; b. nonliteral

**10.** a. i. nonexplicit; ii. direct; iii. expressed; iv. literal
b. i. explicit; ii. not applicable to explicit performatives; iii. expressed; iv. literal
c. i. nonexplicit; ii. indirect; iii. implied; iv. literal

## Exercises

**1.** The italicized phrase indicates that the speaker is trying to avoid violating a conversational maxim (i.e., Quantity, Quality, Relation, or Manner). Name the maxim.

WAITER: What can I get you, sir?
CUSTOMER: I'll have the roast beef. Oh, *incidentally*, where's the phone?

**2.** The italicized phrase indicates that the speaker is trying to avoid violating a conversational maxim (i.e., Quantity, Quality, Relation, or Manner). Name the maxim.

JOHN: What happened during your interview today?
MARY: Well, *to make a long story short*, they didn't hire me.

**3.** John and Mary are leaving a movie.

JOHN: That was a great movie.
MARY: It sure was. Oh, *by the way*, do you have the car keys?

The italicized expression in Mary's response indicates that she is trying to avoid violating the maxim of _____.

a. manner    c. quality    e. memory
b. relation    d. quantity

**4.** Gretchen is married and has two children, ages 7 and 4. In a conversation concerning her father-in-law, held in the presence of her children, she referred to her father-in-law as *the first generation* and to her children as *the third generation.*

     a. Which of Grice's maxims did Gretchen flout?
     b. What is the implicature raised by Gretchen's utterance?

**5.** For the following exchange, determine (a) which of Grice's maxims Ray is flouting, and (b) the implicature raised by her reply.

BOB:      Do you want some dessert?
RAY:      Do birds have wings?

     a. _____

     b. _____

**6.** For the following exchange, determine (a) which of Grice's maxims Susan is flouting, and (b) the implicature raised by her reply.

DIANE:      Don't you think John is a wonderful guy?
SUSAN:      Yeah, he's about as sensitive as Rambo.

     a. _____

     b. _____

**7.** For the following exchange, determine (a) which of Grice's maxims Mary is flouting, and (b) the implicature raised by her reply.

JOHN:      Who was that man I saw you with yesterday?
MARY:      That was just someone.

     a. _____

     b. _____

**8.** For the following exchange, determine (a) which of Grice's maxims the customer is flouting, and (b) the implicature raised by her reply.

SALES CLERK:      Could I have your name?
CUSTOMER:      It's K-A-T-H-R-Y-N   R-I-L-E-Y.

     a. _____

     b. _____

**9.** Grice (1975: 55) cites the following example. Determine (a) which maxim the critic is flouting, and (b) the implicature raised by the critic's reply.

PATRON:      How was Miss X's performance?
CRITIC:      Miss X produced a series of sounds that corresponded closely with the score of *Home Sweet Home.*

     a. _____

     b. _____

**10.** Traugott and Pratt (1980: 237) cite the following joke. Determine (a) which of Grice's maxims Sam flouts in his first utterance, and (b) the implicature it raises.

FARMER BROWN: Hey, Sam, my mule's got distemper. What'd you give yours when he had it?
SAM:            Turpentine.
(a week later)
FARMER BROWN: Sam, I gave my mule turpentine like you said and it killed him.
SAM:            Did mine, too.

a. _____

b. _____

**11.** A sign on the door of a Shoney's restaurant in Gatlinburg, Tennessee, says *Shoney's is a family restaurant. No one allowed without shoes or shirts.* Determine (a) which of Grice's maxims is flouted by the sign, and (b) the implicature it raises.

a. _____

b. _____

**12.** Classify the following as a directive, commissive, representative, expressive, question, or declaration. One friend says to another, *I swear I won't see Martha again.*

**13.** Classify the following as a directive, commissive, representative, expressive, question, or declaration. A parent says to her child, *I forbid you to leave your room.*

**14.** Classify the following as a directive, commissive, representative, expressive, question, or declaration. A man says to a stranger, *Do you know what time it is?*

**15.** Classify the following as a directive, commissive, representative, expressive, question, or declaration. A buyer says to a seller, *I agree to your terms.*

**16.** In the movie *The Lonely Passion of Judith Hearne*, James Madden is telling Judith how he has been wronged by his daughter. The following interchange ensues.

JUDITH:    Oh, I'm sorry.
JAMES:    You don't have to be sorry; you didn't do anything.

James misinterprets Judith's remark, because it is ambiguous as to what illocutionary act it performs. Explain this ambiguity.

**17.** On the TV show *Little House on the Prairie*, the preacher says to Mrs. Ingalls, *Family discipline is based on promises kept—whether punishment or reward.* The preacher is treating two different types of illocutionary acts as promises.

a. What are the two illocutionary acts the preacher is referring to?
b. What general category of illocutionary acts do they both belong to?
c. How do the two illocutionary acts differ in terms of their felicity conditions?

**18.** Pat and Chris are having an argument, and Pat punches Chris in the nose. Chris responds with *Thanks a lot.* What preparatory condition on thanking does Chris's utterance violate?

a. The act for which one is thanked must be in the hearer's best interest.
b. The act for which one is thanked must be a past act.
c. The act for which one is thanked must be witnessed by the speaker.
d. The act for which one is thanked must be in the speaker's best interest.
e. both (b) and (d)

19. What type of felicity condition on apologies (Preparatory, Sincerity, Essential, Propositional Content) is violated by the following utterance: *I apologize for what I'm about to do.*

20. At noon a woman goes to a pharmacy to check on a prescription that is being filled. The woman is told that the prescription has to be brought from another location but that it will arrive no later than 6:00 p.m. The woman fumes for a minute and then says, *I'm sorry but I can't come back later this evening.* The woman's utterance appears to be an apology (i.e., *I'm sorry . . .* ). However, it is not. (a) What felicity condition on apologizing does it violate? (b) If the utterance is not an apology, what is it?

    a. _____

    b. _____

21. Searle distinguishes ordinary questions from what he calls "exam questions"—the type of question a teacher asks a student (for example, *What is the cube root of 27?*). Ordinary and exam questions differ in their felicity conditions, in particular their preparatory and sincerity conditions. How do the preparatory and sincerity conditions for ordinary questions and exam questions differ?

22. You walk into a shop in a mall. There is a sign on the wall that reads *Thank you for not smoking.* You correctly take the sign as a directive rather than an expressive, because it violates a propositional content condition on thanking. What is that condition?

23. On the TV show *Hawaii 5–0*, Steve McGarrett has the following conversation with an old girlfriend named Kathy.

    KATHY:     I made a promise to someone; I promised to marry him.
    STEVE:     Okay, a promise, but not a vow. You have a right to change your mind.

    Explain McGarrett's distinction between a promise and a vow in terms of their respective felicity conditions.

24. A self-proclaimed "preacher" was recently observed at LSU's Free Speech Alley, an area of campus where speakers may publicly address passersby. In the heat of his fervor, the preacher addressed a nearby squirrel as follows: *Repent, you squirrel; repent, you evil fornicating squirrel.* Explain why this utterance is an infelicitous directive.

25. Explain why the following utterance is not an explicit performative: *The boss insists that you work late tonight.*

26. Explain why the following utterance is not an explicit performative: *Apologize to your Aunt Martha immediately.*

27. A sign over a bar door says *Minors are forbidden to enter.*
    a. What is the illocutionary force of this utterance?
    b. Is the illocutionary act explicit? Explain. (Hint: change passive voice [e.g., *Mr. X was sentenced to death*] to active [e.g., *The judge sentenced Mr. X to death*].)

28. The following announcement is made over a public address system at an airport: *Passengers are requested to proceed to gate 10.*
    a. What is the illocutinary force of this utterance?
    b. Is the illocutionary act explicit? Explain. (Hint: see question [27].)

29. The envelope supplied for paying your credit card bill carries the following notice: *Did you remember to sign your check?* Identify (a) the syntactic form, (b) the illocutionary act it performs, and (c) whether the illocutionary act is performed directly or indirectly.

    a. _____

    b. _____

    c. _____

30. A student, wheedling a teacher for an A, says *If I don't get an A in this course, I'll lose my scholarship.* Identify (a) the syntactic form, (b) the illocutionary act it performs, and (c) whether the illocutionary act is performed directly or indirectly.

    a. _____

    b. _____

    c. _____

31. Smith is fixing a flat tire as Jones looks on. Smith says *You can give me a hand with this* in order to get Jones to help him. The syntactic form of the utterance is _____. The illocutionary act is _____. The illocutionary act is performed (directly, indirectly).

32. Smith is fixing a flat tire as Jones looks on. Smith says *Why don't you give me a hand with this?* in order to get Jones to help him. The syntactic form of the utterance is _____. The illocutionary act is _____. The illocutionary act is performed (directly, indirectly).

33. A friend comes to visit you for the first time and, being positively impressed by where you live, says, *What a nice house you have!* The syntactic form of your friend's utterance is _____. The illocutionary act is _____. The illocutionary act is performed (directly, indirectly).

34. A sign in front of a garage states *Don't even think of parking here.*
    a. Is the locution expressed or implied?
    b. Is the locution literal or nonliteral?

35. A highway sign says *Do not exceed 55.*
    a. Is the locution expressed or implied?
    b. Is the locution literal or nonliteral?

36. A highway sign says *Speed Limit 55.*
    a. Is the locution expressed or implied?
    b. Is the locution literal or nonliteral?

37. One night you go to visit a friend in her apartment. When you walk in, your friend is sitting there with all the lights off. In an attempt to get her to turn on a light, you say *What is this, a mausoleum?*
    a. Is the locution expressed or implied?
    b. Is the locution literal or nonliteral?

38. One night you go to visit a friend in her apartment. When you walk in, your friend is

sitting there with all the lights off. In an attempt to get her to turn on a light, you say *It's kinda dark in here.*

   a.  Is the locution expressed or implied?
   b.  Is the locution literal or nonliteral?

**39.**  One night you go to visit a friend in her apartment. When you walk in, your friend is sitting there with all the lights off. In an attempt to get her to turn on a light, you say *It's kinda dark in here.* She says *What are you talking about?* and you say *I'm asking you to turn on a light.* Answer the following regarding your *second* utterance.

   a.  Is the illocution explicit or nonexplicit?
   b.  If nonexplicit, is the illocution direct or indirect?
   c.  Is the locution expressed or implied?
   d.  Is the locution literal or nonliteral?

**40.**  The following sign was observed on a British Rail train car: *Passengers are reminded that a valid ticket is required for each journey made.* This seems to be a roundabout way of saying *Buy a ticket.*

   a.  Is the illocutionary act performed by the sign explicit or nonexplicit?
   b.  Is the locutionary act performed by the sign expressed or implied?

**41.**  We recently came across a congratulations card which depicted a baby and had the words *Your baby boy has arrived.*

   a.  What type of illocutionary act is performed by the card?
   b.  Is the illocutionary act explicit or nonexplicit?
   c.  Is the illocutionary act performed directly or indirectly?
   d.  Is the locutionary act expressed or implied?
   e.  Is the locutionary act literal or nonliteral?

**42.**  In the movie *Honky Tonk Man*, Marlene Mooney tries to get Red Stovall to give her his sandwich by saying, *If you're not gonna eat this [sandwich], I can finish it for you.*

   a.  What type of illocutionary act is performed by this utterance?
   b.  Is the illocutionary act explicit or nonexplicit?
   c.  Is the illocutionary act performed directly or indirectly?
   d.  Is the locutionary act expressed or implied?
   e.  Is the locutionary act literal or nonliteral?

**43.**  In the corner of an envelope, there's a printed message stating, *Post Office will not deliver mail without proper postage.* Identify the type of speech act conveyed by this utterance, given the context.

   a.  explicit, expressed, nonliteral
   b.  nonexplicit, direct, implied, literal
   c.  nonexplicit, indirect, implied, literal
   d.  explicit, implied, literal
   e.  nonexplicit, indirect, implied, nonliteral

**44.**  John shows up for class after missing the previous session. He turns to his friend Mary and says, *Did you take notes during the last class?* If this is intended as a request to borrow Mary's notes, then it is being used as which type of speech act:

   a.  explicit, expressed, literal
   b.  nonexplicit, direct, expressed, literal

    c. nonexplicit, indirect, implied, literal
    d. explicit, implied, nonliteral
    e. nonexplicit, indirect, implied, nonliteral

**45.** A parent, attempting to get his child to close her mouth, says, *You're so attractive when you talk with your mouth full.* Identify the type of speech act conveyed by this utterance, given the context.

    a. explicit, expressed, literal
    b. nonexplicit, direct, implied, literal
    c. nonexplicit, indirect, implied, literal
    d. explicit, implied, nonliteral
    e. nonexplicit, indirect, implied, nonliteral

**46.** A sign on the interstate reads *Speed limit enforced by radar.* Identify the type of speech act conveyed by this utterance, given the context.

    a. nonexplicit, indirect, implied, literal
    b. nonexplicit, direct, implied, nonliteral
    c. explicit, expressed, literal
    d. explicit, implied, literal
    e. nonexplicit, indirect, implied, nonliteral

**47.** Dirty Harry, in trying to get a criminal to give up his gun, says *Go ahead—make my day.* Identify the type of speech act conveyed by this utterance, given the context.

    a. explicit, expressed, literal
    b. nonexplicit, direct, implied, nonliteral
    c. nonexplicit, indirect, implied, literal
    d. explicit, implied, literal
    e. nonexplicit, indirect, implied, nonliteral

**48.** For the following utterance, state whether it is explicit or nonexplicit, direct or indirect, expressed or implied, literal or nonliteral: A highway sign reads *YIELD.*

**49.** For the following utterance, state whether it is explicit or nonexplicit, direct or indirect, expressed or implied, literal or nonliteral.

Count Monte Crisco has been insulted by Count Marmaduke; Monte Crisco says to Marmaduke, *I challenge you to a duel.*

**50.** Francine wants to find out from Jolene the name of Jolene's date. For each of the following utterances, state whether it is explicit or nonexplicit, direct or indirect, expressed or implied, literal or nonliteral.

    a. You haven't told me your date's name, Jolene.
    b. What's your date's name, Jolene?
    c. For the last time, Jolene, I'm asking you to tell me the name of your date.
    d. Please don't bore me with the name of your date, Jolene.

# Chapter 3

# Semantics

**Semantics** is the study of linguistic meaning; that is, the meaning of words, phrases, and sentences. Unlike pragmatics, semantics is part of grammar proper, the study of the internal structure of language. (Other areas of grammar are syntax, morphology, and phonology; these are covered in Chapters 4–6.) Unfortunately, because semantics is the most poorly understood component of grammar, it can be one of the most difficult areas of linguistics to study. The fact is that no one has yet developed a comprehensive, authoritative theory of linguistic meaning. Nonetheless, we can discuss some of the phenomena that have been studied within the domain of semantics and some of the theories that have been developed to explain them. It is important to keep in mind, however, that much of what follows is tentative and subject to debate.

Let's first consider some observations we can make about the meaning of words and sentences.

(1)  The word *fly* has more than one meaning in English. The word *moth* does not.

(2)  The word *hide* can mean the same thing as *conceal*.

(3)  The meaning of the word *fear* includes the meaning of the word *emotion*, but not vice versa.

(4)  The words *sister* and *niece* seem to be closer in meaning than are the words *sister* and *girl*.

(5)  In the sentence *Jimmy Carter was the 39th president of the United States*, the phrases *Jimmy Carter* and *the 39th president of the United States* refer to the same person. The phrases, however, don't "mean" the same thing.

(6)  In the sentence *Monica believes that she is a genius*, *she* can refer either to *Monica* or to someone else. However, in the sentence *Monica believes herself to be a genius*, *herself* can refer only to *Monica*.

(7)  If someone were to ask you to name a bird, you would probably think of a robin before you would think of an ostrich.

(8)    The sentences *A colorless gas is blue* and *Oxygen is blue* are both false, but for different reasons.

(9)    The sentence *John's wife is six feet tall* is neither true nor false, if John does not have a wife.

The observations in (1–9) are all essentially semantic in nature. That is, they have to do with the meaning of words and sentences. As is standard procedure in linguistics, we will assume that these phenomena are systematic; that is, they are rule-governed. What we will try to do now is construct a set of categories and principles that will at least partially explain these phenomena. Keep in mind that what follows is a (partial) theory designed to account for the observations in (1–9). It may eventually be replaced by other theories, but it is the best we have, given the present state of the art.

## Background

Contributions to semantics have come essentially from two sources—linguistics and philosophy. Linguists have contributed primarily to the study of the core meaning or **sense** of individual words. One method that they have used to characterize the sense of words is called **lexical decomposition**. This method represents the sense of a word in terms of the **semantic features** that comprise it. For example, consider the words *man, woman, boy,* and *girl*. The sense of each of these words can be partly characterized by specifying a value (+ or −) for the features [±adult] and [±male], as follows.

|          | *man* | *woman* | *boy* | *girl* |
|----------|-------|---------|-------|--------|
| [adult]  | +     | +       | −     | −      |
| [male]   | +     | −       | +     | −      |

Lexical decomposition, as a method for characterizing the sense of words, has several advantages. First, it explains our intuitions as speakers of English that the meanings of *man* and *boy* are more closely related than are the meanings of *man* and *girl*. *Man* and *boy* have the same value for one of these features [±male], whereas *man* and *girl* do not have the same value for either of these features. Second, it is easy to characterize the senses of additional words by adding features. For example, we can account for part of the meanings of *stallion, mare, colt,* and *filly* simply by adding the feature [±human], as follows.

|          | *man* | *woman* | *boy* | *girl* | *stallion* | *mare* | *colt* | *filly* |
|----------|-------|---------|-------|--------|------------|--------|--------|---------|
| [adult]  | +     | +       | −     | −      | +          | +      | −      | −       |
| [male]   | +     | −       | +     | −      | +          | −      | +      | −       |
| [human]  | +     | +       | +     | +      | −          | −      | −      | −       |

Finally, this method allows us, at least in principle, to characterize the senses of a potentially infinite set of words with a finite number of semantic features. (Note that in the previous example, we were able to differentiate the senses of eight words with only three features.) In general, the fewer the number of statements required by a theory to account for a given set of observations, the more highly valued the theory.

On the other hand, lexical decomposition has several practical limitations. First, linguists have been unable to agree on exactly how many and which features constitute the universal set of semantic properties, especially once we go beyond the handful of features already mentioned. Moreover, nouns, especially concrete nouns, seem to lend themselves to lexical decomposition more readily than do other parts of speech. For example, what features could be used to characterize the sense of *carefully, belligerent*, and *assassinate*, not to mention *the, of*, and *however*? In sum, then, lexical decomposition in terms of semantic features provides a useful, if somewhat limited, account of the meaning of words.

Philosophers, on the other hand, have contributed primarily to the study of the meaning of sentences. However, rather than trying to characterize the core meaning or sense of sentences directly—which, as we have just seen, is a difficult undertaking—they have approached the semantics of sentences from two other directions: the study of **reference** and the study of **truth conditions**. Reference is the study of what objects linguistic expressions (i.e., words, phrases, sentences, and so on) refer to. For example, in the sentence *Mulroney is the Prime Minister of Canada*, the expression *Mulroney* and the expression *the Prime Minister of Canada* refer to the same entity, namely Brian Mulroney. Truth-conditional semantics, on the other hand, is the study of the conditions under which a statement can be judged true or false. In actuality, much of what goes under the name of truth conditions involves truth relations that hold between sentences. For example, if the sentence *Fred is 80 years old* is true, then the sentence *Fred is over 50 years old* is necessarily true.

Like lexical decomposition, both the study of reference and the study of truth conditions have advantages as well as limitations. The major advantage of both avenues of inquiry is that they have very restricted domains, which can be probed in a reasonable amount of detail. The drawback, of course, is that both of them overlook a great deal of what might fall within the domain of "meaning." For example, in the sentence *Mulroney is the Prime Minister of Canada*, determining the referents of *Mulroney* and *the Prime Minister of Canada* skirts the question of what these expressions "mean."

So far, we have considered semantics from the point of view of the contributors to the theory: linguists, who have studied meaning through lexical decomposition, and philosophers, who have tried to characterize meaning through the study of reference and truth conditions. (We should add that there has been a great deal of cross-fertilization between linguistics and philosophy, especially in the last 15 years or so.) Nonetheless, a certain amount of disagreement exists among researchers in the field and, consequently, a great deal of confusion can exist in the mind of anyone trying to learn the field. All we can do is try to impose some order on the diverse array of approaches to the subject. If we abstract away from the material we've been discussing, we can divide the study of semantics into three areas: **sense**, **reference**, and **truth**. Let's now consider each one in turn.

# Sense

The study of sense (or meaning) can be divided into two areas: speaker-sense and linguistic-sense. **Speaker-sense** is the speaker's intention in producing some linguistic expression. For example, if someone utters the sentence *Fred is a real genius* sarcastically, then the speaker-sense of the sentence might be 'Fred is below average in intelligence.' Speaker-sense, because it has to do with nonliteral meaning, is outside the domain of semantics; rather, it is part of pragmatics (discussed in Chapter 2). Consequently, no further mention of speaker-sense will be made in this chapter. **Linguistic-sense**, on the other hand, is the meaning of a linguistic expression as part of a language. For example, if the sentence *Fred is a real genius* means literally something like 'Fred has a truly superior intellect,' then the linguistic-sense is within the domain of semantics, since it deals solely with literal meaning and is independent of speaker, hearer, and situational context. Note, however, that in this example we presently have no better way of indicating the linguistic-sense of a sentence than by simply paraphrasing it. All we have done so far is differentiate situationally dependent meaning (speaker-sense, part of pragmatics) from situationally independent meaning (linguistic-sense, part of semantics).

Now let's consider some sense properties and relations that any descriptively adequate theory of semantics should account for.

**Lexical Ambiguity.**    A word is lexically ambiguous if it has more than one sense. For example, the English noun *fly* is ambiguous because it has more than one sense: an insect, a zipper on a pair of pants, or a baseball hit into the air with a bat. Thus, the sentence *Waldo saw a fly* is three-ways ambiguous. One way a semantic theory might account for this fact is to list the word *fly* in the **lexicon** of English (i.e., a dictionary listing of all English words) three times, once with each sense of the word. It is not clear, however, exactly what form each of these **lexical entries** should take. For the time being, we will assume that each one takes the form of a paraphrase, e.g., *fly*: (i) an insect having the following characteristics . . .; (ii) a zipper . . .; (iii) a ball . . . .

Note, by the way, that not all cases of ambiguity are lexical. Consider the phrase *American history teacher*, which can mean either 'a teacher of American history' or 'a history teacher who is American.' The ambiguity here does not derive from the ambiguity of a particular word, as in the case of *fly*. Neither *American*, nor *history*, nor *teacher* has more than one sense. Instead, the ambiguity of *American history teacher* is syntactic, in that we can assign two different structures or bracketings to the phrase: for example [[American history] teacher] = 'a teacher of American history,' and [American [history teacher]] = 'a history teacher who is American.' Syntactic ambiguity will be discussed in Chapter 4.

**Synonymy.**    Two words are synonymous if they have the same sense; that is, if they have the same values for all of their semantic features. For example, the pairs *conceal* and *hide, stubborn* and *obstinate*, and *big* and *large* seem to be synonymous in English. Presumably, the meaning of each pair consists of the same set of features marked for the same values. As mentioned earlier, however, note that it is not clear what the relevant features are for each of these pairs. Moreover, in all likelihood there are no absolute synonyms in any language—that is, words that mean exactly the same thing in all contexts. For example, even though *big* and *large* are (near) synonyms, the phrases *my big sister* and *my large sister* certainly do not have the same meaning.

**Hyponymy.** A **hyponym** is a word that contains the meaning of another word; the contained word is known as the **superordinate**. For example, *oak* contains the meaning of *tree*; therefore, *oak* is a hyponym of the superordinate *tree*. In other words, a hyponym is a word whose meaning contains all the same feature values of another word, plus some additional feature values. For instance, the meaning of the word *sow* has exactly the same feature values as the word *pig* (e.g., [−human]) plus some additional ones (e.g., [+adult], [−male]). This relationship is represented in Figure 3–1.

In general, there are a number of hyponyms for each superordinate. For example, *boar* and *piglet* are also hyponyms of the superordinate *pig*, since the meaning of each of the three words *sow, boar,* and *piglet* "contains" the meaning of the word *pig*. (Note that in defining a word like *sow, boar,* or *piglet,* the superordinate word *pig* is often used as part of the definition: "A *sow* is an adult female *pig*.") Thus, it is not surprising that hyponymy is sometimes referred to as **inclusion.** The superordinate is the included word and the hyponym is the including one.

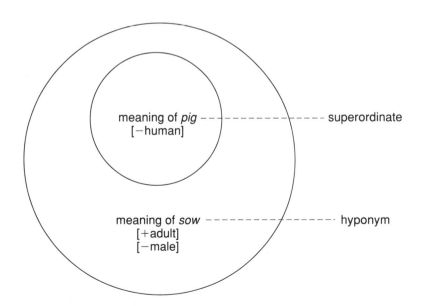

**FIGURE  3–1.  Representation of hyponymy.**

**Overlap.** Two words overlap in meaning if they have the same value for some (but not all) of the semantic features that constitute their meaning. For example, the words *sister, niece, aunt,* and *mother* overlap in meaning. This relationship can be captured by stating that part of the meaning of each of these words is [+human/–male/+kin]. If we were to add the words *nun* and *mistress* to the list above, then this set of words would overlap because they are all marked [+human/–male]. If we were to further add *mare* and *sow* to this list, then the meanings of this set would overlap by being marked [–male]. And so on. This relationship is displayed in the following diagram.

|  | *sister* | *niece* | *aunt* | *mother* | *nun* | *mistress* | *mare* | *sow* |
|---|---|---|---|---|---|---|---|---|
| [human] | + | + | + | + | + | + | – | – |
| [male] | – | – | – | – | – | – | – | – |
| [kin] | + | + | + | + | – | – | – | – |

It is important to distinguish overlap from hyponymy. With hyponymy, the meaning of one word is entirely included in the meaning of another. (The meaning of *pig* is entirely included in the meaning of *sow*; i.e., all sows are pigs, but not all pigs are sows.) With overlap, on the other hand, the meanings of two words intersect, but neither one includes the other. The meanings of *sister* and *niece* intersect, but neither includes the other: not all sisters are nieces, and not all nieces are sisters. Overlap is represented in Figure 3–2.

**Antonymy.** Two words are antonyms if their meanings differ only in the value for a single semantic feature. The following pairs are all antonyms: *dead* and *alive, hot* and *cold,* and *above* and *below.* The meanings of the members of each pair are presumably identical, except for opposite values of some semantic feature. The meanings of *dead* and *alive,* for instance, are identical except that *dead* is marked [–living] and *alive* is marked [+living]. Once again, however, note the difficulty in determining the relevant semantic feature that distinguishes the members of each pair. Antonyms, moreover, fall into at least three groups. **Binary antonyms** are pairs that exhaust all possibilities along some dimension. *Dead* and *alive* are exam-

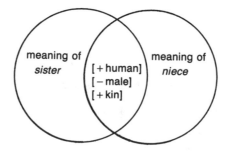

**FIGURE 3–2. Illustration of overlap.**

ples of binary antonyms. Everything that can be dead or alive is, in fact, either dead or alive: there is no middle ground between the two. All people, for example, are either dead or alive. **Gradable antonyms**, on the other hand, are pairs that describe opposite ends of a continuous dimension. *Hot* and *cold* are examples of gradable antonyms. Not everything that can be hot or cold is, in fact, either hot or cold. A liquid, for example, may be neither hot nor cold; it can be in between, say, warm or cool. **Converse antonyms** are pairs that describe a single relationship between two items from opposite perspectives. *Above* and *below* are examples of converse antonyms. If a picture, for example, is above a sofa, then the sofa is necessarily below the picture. The difference among binary, gradable, and converse antonyms is represented in Figure 3–3.

It is not always easy to decide if a pair of antonyms is binary, gradable, or converse. There are, however, several useful tests. First, test the pair to see if they are converse antonyms. This can be done by putting them into the following form: *If X is _____ Y, then Y is _____ X.* For example, *if X is above Y, then Y is below X.* If the pair fits this form, they are converse antonyms. If they don't, then test them to see if they are binary. This can be done by putting the pair in the following form: *If X is not _____, then X must be _____.* For example, *If John is not dead, then he must be alive.* If the pair fits this form, they are binary antonyms. If they don't, then test them to see if they are gradable. This can be done by putting each member of the pair in the following form: *X is very _____.* For example, *This soup is very hot/cold.*

It is also worth pointing out that some pairs which have traditionally been treated as antonyms might be better handled as hyponyms of the same superordinate. For example, *liquid* and *solid* are not converse antonyms (*\*If X is liquid Y, then Y is solid X* ); they are not binary antonyms (*\*If X is not a liquid, then it must be a solid*—it could be neither; it could be a gas); and they are not gradable antonyms (*\*This is very liquid/solid*—neither is literally true). Instead, *liquid* and *solid* (along with *gas*) seem to be hyponyms of *matter.*

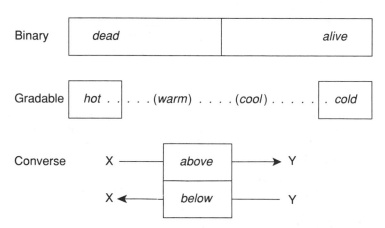

**FIGURE 3–3. Illustration of binary, gradable, and converse antonyms.**

# *Reference*

The study of reference, like the study of sense, can be divided into two areas: speaker-reference and linguistic-reference. **Speaker-reference** is what the speaker is referring to by using some linguistic expression. For example, if someone utters the sentence *Here comes Queen Elizabeth* facetiously, to refer to a snobbish acquaintance, then the speaker-reference of the expression *Queen Elizabeth* is the acquaintance. Speaker-reference, because it varies according to the speaker and context, is outside the domain of semantics; instead it is part of pragmatics. **Linguistic-reference**, on the other hand, is the systematic denotation of some linguistic expression as part of a language. For example, the linguistic expression *Queen Elizabeth* in the sentence *Here comes Queen Elizabeth* refers in fact to the public figure Queen Elizabeth. Linguistic-reference, in contrast to speaker-reference, is within the domain of semantics, since it deals with reference that is a systematic function of the language itself, rather than of the speaker and context.

Let's now consider some concepts that seem useful in thinking and talking about reference (**referent**, **extension**, **prototype**, and **stereotype**); then we will take a look at some different types of linguistic reference (**coreference**, **anaphora**, and **deixis**).

**Referent.**    The entity identified by the use of a referring expression such as a noun or noun phrase is the referent of that expression. If, for example, you are standing in your back yard and point to a particular yellow-bellied sapsucker and say *That bird looks sick*, then the referent for the referring expression *That bird* is the particular yellow-bellied sapsucker you are pointing at.

**Extension.**    Extension refers to the set of all potential referents for a referring expression. For example, the extension of *bird* is the set of all entities (past, present, and future) that could systematically be referred to by the expression *bird*. In other words, the extension of *bird* is the set of all birds.

**Prototype.**    A typical member of the extension of a referring expression is a prototype of that expression. For example, a robin or a bluebird might be a prototype of *bird*; a pelican or an ostrich, since each is somewhat atypical, would not be.

**Stereotype.**    A list of characteristics describing a prototype is said to be a stereotype. For example, the stereotype of *bird* might be something like the following: has two legs and two wings, has feathers, is about six to eight inches from head to tail, makes a chirping noise, lays eggs, builds nests, and so on.

**Coreference.**    Two linguistic expressions that have the same extralinguistic referent are said to be coreferential. Consider, for example, the sentence *The Earth is the third planet from the Sun*. The expressions *the Earth* and *the third planet from the Sun* are coreferential because they both refer to the same extralinguistic object, namely the heavenly body that we are spinning around on right now. Note, however, that the expressions *the Earth* and *the third planet from the Sun* do not "mean" the same thing. Suppose, for example, a new planet were discovered between Mercury (now the first planet from the Sun) and Venus (now the second planet from the Sun). If so, then the Earth would become the fourth planet from the Sun, and Venus would become the third. Thus, the linguistic expressions *the Earth* and *the fourth planet from the Sun* would become coreferential. Note, moreover, that if we were to claim that these two expressions "mean" the same thing, then we should be able to substitute *the third planet from the Sun* for *the Earth* in a sentence like *The Earth is the fourth planet from the Sun,* assuming, of course, our discovery of a new planet between Mercury and Venus. However, this substitution procedure would give us *\*The third planet from the Sun is the fourth planet from the Sun.* (Recall that an asterisk indicates an unacceptable form.) As this example illustrates, *the Earth* and *the third planet from the Sun* have separate meanings in English, even though they now happen to be coreferential.

      **Anaphora.**   A linguistic expression that refers to another linguistic expression is said to be anaphoric or an anaphor. Consider the sentence *Mary wants to play whoever thinks himself capable of beating her.* In this sentence the linguistic expression *himself* necessarily refers to *whoever*; thus *himself* is being used anaphorically in this case. Note, moreover, that it would be inaccurate to claim that *whoever* and *himself* are coreferential (i.e., that they have the same extralinguistic referent). This is because there may in fact not be anyone who thinks himself capable of beating Mary; that is, there may not be any extralinguistic referent for *whoever* and *himself*.

      It is common, however, for coreference and anaphora to coincide. Consider, for example, the sentence *The media reported that Congress voted themselves a raise.* The expressions *Congress* and *themselves* are coreferential since they refer to the same extralinguistic body, namely the legislative branch of the federal government. At the same time, *themselves* is an anaphor since it necessarily refers to the expression *Congress*. Note that there is no reading of this sentence such that *themselves* can be construed as referring to the expression *the media*. In sum, coreference deals with the relation of a linguistic expression to some entity in the real world, past, present, or future; anaphora deals with the relation between two linguistic expressions.

      **Deixis (pronounced DIKE-sis).**   An expression that has one meaning but can refer to different entities within the same context of utterance is said to be deictic. Deictic terms crucially depend on the speaker's point of reference. Obvious examples are expressions such as *you* and *I*, *here* and *there*, and *right* and *left*. Assume, for instance, that Jack and Jill are speaking to each other face-to-face. Note that *I* refers to Jack and *you* refers to Jill, when Jack is speaking. The referents for these expressions reverse when Jill speaks. Likewise, *here* refers to a position near Jack and *there* refers to a position near Jill, when Jack is speaking; the referents for these expressions reverse when Jill speaks. Similarly, *right* and *left* can refer to the same location, depending upon whether Jack or Jill is speaking; his left is her right and vice versa.

      Note, moreover, that deixis can intersect with anaphora. Consider, for example, the sentence *Members of Congress believe they deserve a raise.* The expression *they* can refer either to the expression *members of Congress* or to some other plural entity in the context of the utterance. When, as in the first case, a pronoun refers to another linguistic expression, it is used anaphorically; when, as in the second case, it refers to some entity in the extralinguistic context, it is used deictically.

## Truth

The study of truth or truth conditions in semantics falls into two basic categories: the study of different types of truth embodied in individual sentences (**analytic**, **contradictory**, and **synthetic**) and the study of different types of truth relations that hold between sentences (**entailment** and **presupposition**).

**Analytic Sentences.** An analytic sentence is one that is necessarily true as a result of the words in it. For example, the sentence *A bachelor is an unmarried man* is true not because the world is the way it is, but because the English language is the way it is. Part of our knowledge of ordinary English is that *bachelor* "means" *an unmarried man*, thus to say that one is the other must necessarily be true. We do not need to check on the outside world to verify the truth of this sentence. We might say that analytic sentences are "true by definition." Analytic sentences are sometimes referred to as **linguistic truths**, because they are true by virtue of the language itself.

**Contradictory Sentences.** Contradictory sentences are just the opposite of analytic sentences. While analytic sentences are necessarily true as a result of the words in them, contradictory sentences are necessarily false for the same reason. The following sentences are all contradictory: *A bachelor is a married man, A blue gas is colorless, A square has five equal sides*. In each case, we know the sentence is false because we know the meaning of the words in it: part of the meaning of *bachelor* is 'unmarried'; part of the meaning of *blue* is 'has color'; part of the meaning of *square* is 'four-sided.' It is not necessary to refer to the outside world in order to judge each of these sentences false. Consequently, contradictory sentences are sometimes referred to as **linguistic falsities**, because they are false by virtue of the language itself.

**Synthetic Sentences.** Sentences that may be true or false depending upon how the world is are called synthetic. In contrast to analytic and contradictory sentences, synthetic sentences are not true or false because of the words that comprise them, but rather because they do or do not accurately describe some state of affairs in the world. For example, the sentence *My next door neighbor, Bud Brown, is married* is a synthetic sentence. Note that you cannot judge its truth or falsity by inspecting the words in the sentence. Rather, you must verify the truth or falsity of this sentence empirically, for example by checking the marriage records at the courthouse. Other examples of synthetic sentences include *Nitrous oxide is blue, Nitrous oxide is not blue, Bud Brown's house has five sides*, and *Bud Brown's house does not have five sides*. In each case, the truth or falsity of the sentence can be verified only by consulting the state of affairs that holds in the world. Thus, synthetic sentences are sometimes referred to as **empirical truths** or **falsities**, because they are true or false by virtue of the state of the extralinguistic world.

The examples that we have considered so far seem fairly straightforward. Analytic and contradictory sentences are true and false, respectively, by definition. Synthetic sentences, however, are not—they must be verified or falsified empirically. Nevertheless, some sentences do not seem to fall neatly into one of these two groups. Consider, for example, the sentence *Oxygen is not blue*. It is true. But is it analytic—true by virtue of the words that make it up (i.e., part of the meaning of oxygen is 'without color')? Or is it synthetic—true because it coincides with the state of the world (i.e., because it just so happens that oxygen has no color)? This can get to be a thorny issue and the experts don't always have a uniform answer to such questions. However, it would probably be reasonable to treat such cases as synthetic truths rather than analytic truths. This is because it is easy to imagine conditions under which the sentence *Oxygen is not blue* would be false. For example, suppose scientists froze oxygen and found that solid oxygen is in fact blue. Such a finding would not cause a change in the meaning of the word *oxygen*, but rather a change in our understanding of the substance oxygen. In contrast, consider the sentence *A colorless gas is not blue*. It is impossible, at least for us, to imagine a situation in which this sentence would be false. If a gas is colorless, it cannot be blue; if it is blue, it cannot be colorless. Thus it seems reasonable, at least until more light can be shed on the subject, to consider sentences like *Oxygen is not blue* as synthetically true.

**Entailment.**    An entailment is a proposition (expressed in a sentence) that follows *necessarily* from another sentence. For example, *John fried fish* entails *John cooked fish*, because fish cannot be fried without being cooked. The test for entailment is as follows: sentence (a) entails sentence (b) if the truth of sentence (a) insures the truth of sentence (b) and if the falsity of sentence (b) insures the falsity of sentence (a). Consider the following sentences: (a) *The Duke of New York suffered a fatal heart attack* and (b) *The Duke of New York is dead*. In this case, sentence (a) entails sentence (b) because the truth of (a) insures the truth of (b) (if the Duke of New York suffered a fatal heart attack, he necessarily is dead), and the falsity of (b) insures the falsity of (a) (if the Duke of New York is not dead, he necessarily didn't suffer a fatal heart attack). The relationship of entailment is represented in Figure 3–4.

Note, however, that the relation of entailment is unidirectional. For instance, consider our example sentences again, but in the opposite order: (b) *The Duke of New York is dead* and (a) *The Duke of New York suffered a fatal heart attack*. In this case, sentence (b) does not entail (a) (if the Duke of New York is dead, he did not necessarily die of a heart attack—he may have died of kidney failure or he may have been hit by a bolt of lightning); and the falsity of (a) does not insure the falsity of (b) (if the Duke of New York did not suffer a fatal heart attack, it is not necessarily the case that he is not dead—he may, once again, have died of kidney failure or he may have been hit by a bolt of lightning). In short, then, it should be clear that the relation of entailment is unidirectional.

This is not to say, however, that there cannot be a pair of sentences such that

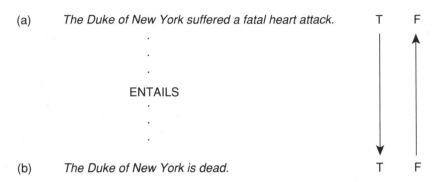

(a)        *The Duke of New York suffered a fatal heart attack.*        T    F

ENTAILS

(b)        *The Duke of New York is dead.*                              T    F

**FIGURE 3–4.  Representation of entailment.**

each entails the other. Rather, when such a relation holds, it is called **paraphrase**. For example, the sentences *Biff and Tammy are good scouts* and *Tammy and Biff are good scouts* are paraphrases of each other. Likewise, *Tammy was driven home by Biff* is a paraphrase of *Biff drove Tammy home.*

**Presupposition.**  A presupposition is a proposition (expressed in a sentence) that is *assumed* to be true in order to judge the truth or falsity of another sentence. For example, *John didn't pass chemistry* presupposes that *John took chemistry*, because not passing chemistry assumes the person in question actually took chemistry. The test for presupposition is as follows: sentence (a) presupposes sentence (b) if the falsity of (b) renders (a) without a truth value. A sentence without a truth value is one that cannot be judged true or false. Questions, for example, are typical of sentences without truth values. What sense would it make to say that a sentence like *Do you have blue eyes?* is true or false? Likewise, imperatives have no truth value. It wouldn't make any sense to say that a sentence like *Shut up!* is either true or false.

Now, let's consider an example of presupposition and examine how this concept relies on the notion of "sentence without a truth value." As stated before, one sentence presupposes another if the falsity of the second renders the first without a truth value. Consider the following sentences: (a) *The Duke of New York is dead* and (b) *There is a Duke of New York.* Sentence (a) presupposes (b) because if (b) is false, then (a) has no truth value. Note that if (b) is false—that is, if there is no Duke of New York—then it doesn't make sense to say that (a) *The Duke of New York is dead* is true or false. For (a) to be true, there would have to be such a thing as the Duke of New York and he would have to be dead. On the other hand, for (a) to be false, there would have to be such a thing as the Duke of New York and he would have to *not* be dead.

Another property of presupposition is that a sentence and its denial (i.e., the negative version of the sentence) have the same set of presuppositions. Thus if sentence (a) *The Duke of New York is dead* presupposes sentence (b) *There is a Duke of New York*, then the denial of sentence (a) *The Duke of New York is not dead*

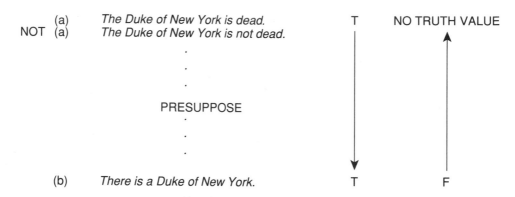

**FIGURE 3-5. Representation of presupposition.**

also presupposes sentence (b). If there is no Duke of New York, then *The Duke of New York is not dead* cannot be judged true or false. The relationship of presupposition is represented schematically in Figure 3–5.

It might be of some comfort to know that presupposition is a much more slippery concept than entailment. Consequently, more investigators agree on the semantic concept of entailment than on that of presupposition.

## *Summary*

Let's go back over what we have done. We started with a number of observations about the meaning of words and sentences that we had no ready explanation for. We then constructed a (partial) theory of semantics to account for our original observations. Contributions to this theory have come from two main sources: from linguists who have traditionally been interested in the core meaning or sense of linguistic expressions (especially words) and from philosophers who have traditionally been concerned with the reference of linguistic expressions and the truth of sentences. The study of sense makes use of such concepts as lexical decomposition, semantic features, lexical ambiguity, synonymy, hyponymy, overlap, and antonymy. The study of reference utilizes concepts such as referent, extension, prototype, stereotype, coreference, anaphora, and deixis. Finally, the study of truth conditions relies on the notions of analytic, contradictory, and synthetic sentences, as well as entailment and presupposition. These theoretical constructs were developed to help explain the observations in (1–9). This theory will undoubtedly turn out to need revision in some of its details; however, it is the best we have for the time being. Think of the discussion in this chapter as a (partial) working hypothesis concerning the nature of semantic structure.

In addition, keep in mind that there is much more to the study of semantics than has been presented so briefly here. Nonetheless, you have now had some exposure to most of the basic concepts in the field; if you want to investigate the subject further, consult the reading list at the end of the chapter. Following the readings are practice problems and answers to help you check your understanding of the material in this chapter. After that are 50 exercises for you to do on your own.

## Supplementary Readings

Allwood, J., Andersson, L.-G., and Dahl, Ö. (1977). *Logic in linguistics.* Cambridge, England: Cambridge University Press.

Chierchia, G., and McConnell-Ginet, S. (1991). *Meaning and grammar: An Introduction to semantics.* Cambridge, MA: MIT Press.

Cruse, D. A. (1986). *Lexical semantics.* Cambridge, England: Cambridge University Press.

Hurford, J. R., and Heasley, B. (1983). *Semantics: A coursebook.* New York: Cambridge University Press.

Kempson, R. (1977). *Semantic theory.* Cambridge, England: Cambridge University Press.

Lyons, J. (1977). *Semantics,* 2 vols. New York: Cambridge University Press.

Palmer, F. R. (1976). *Semantics: A new outline.* New York: Cambridge University Press.

Salmon, W. C. (1973). *Logic* (2nd ed.). Englewood Cliffs, NJ: Prentice-Hall.

All of these readings are, or can be used as, textbooks. However, they differ in the amount of preparation you will need in order to benefit from them. You are ready to read Hurford and Heasley, Palmer, and Salmon right now. Allwood et al., Chierchia and McConnell, Cruse, Kempson, and Lyons require a minimum background of an introductory course in linguistics. We suggest you begin with Hurford and Heasley, which is a combination text and workbook. Lyons, which is probably the most comprehensive treatment of semantics available, is invaluable as a reference tool.

## Practice

1. What semantic feature or property differentiates the following sets of nouns? (Hint: start by figuring out what the two subsets have in common.)

   a. *niece, daughter, sister* vs. *nun, woman, girl*
   b. *mailman, nephew, priest* vs. *gander, stag, bull*
   c. *hen, ewe, cow* vs. *rooster, ram, bull*
   d. *table, chair, pencil* vs. *love, thought, idea*
   e. *table, chair, pencil* vs. *water, dirt, cream*

2. *Riddle:* A father and son are riding in a car. The car hits a truck. The father dies and the son is rushed to the emergency room of a nearby hospital. The doctor comes in and says *I can't operate on this boy. He's my son.* What is the relationship between the doctor and the boy?
   *Answer:* The doctor is the boy's mother.
   A listener's inability to answer this riddle rests on his or her semantic representation of the word *doctor.* Explain.

3. What sense relation is illustrated by the following words: *chair, sofa,* and *desk?*

**4.** What reference relation holds between the italicized expressions in each of the following sentences?

    A. *George* won't give *himself* an injection.

    B. *Maxine* has been named *secretary of the Student Government Association*.

**5.** Consider the following interchange:

    FRED: It's the one on the right.
    ETHEL: My right or yours?

    The area of semantics that accounts for Ethel's confusion is _____.

    a. overlap              d. deixis
    b. entailment        e. none of the above
    c. synonymy

**6.** In the sentence *John gave me all his money, his* can be interpreted _____.

    a. anaphorically        d. all of the above
    b. deictically           e. (a) and (b) only
    c. coreferentially

**7.** What truth relation holds between the following sentences? How can it be demonstrated?

    A. Fred is mortal.

    B. Fred is a man.

**8.** What truth relation holds between the following sentences? How can it be demonstrated?

    A. Fred's wife is ten feet tall.

    B. Fred is married.

**9.** What kind of truth is illustrated by each of the following sentences?

    A. Waldo's living room has four right angles.

    B. A square has four right angles.

**10.** True/False.

    a. Philosophers' most important contributions to the study of semantics have been in the area of sense.

    b. *Fat* and *skinny* are binary antonyms.

    c. The meaning relation illustrated by *hen, cow, mare*, and *vixen* is overlap.

    d. The phrase *French literature teacher* constitutes a case of lexical ambiguity.

    e. The sentence *John killed Bill* presupposes the sentence *Bill died*.

    f. The following sentence is analytic: *If George killed the deer, then the deer died.*

    g. Two words overlap in meaning if they share the same specifications for at least one semantic feature.

    h. The pronoun in the following sentence is deictic: *Sam is extremely pleased with himself.*

    i. The sentence *Buckaroo Bonzai loves his wife* entails the sentence *Buckaroo Bonzai is married.*

    j. The pronouns in the following sentence are anaphoric: *I like you a lot.*

    k. *Smart* and *stupid* are gradable antonyms.

    l. The sense relation illustrated by *rooster, bull, stallion*, and *buck* is hyponymy.

# Answers

The following answers are by no means the only possible ones; they are meant solely to be suggestive. Discussion of other possible answers is part of the practice.

**1.** a.  [±kin]
   b.  [±human]
   c.  [±male]
   d.  [±abstract] (or [±concrete])
   e.  [±count] Note: *table*, *chair*, and *pencil* each have a plural form and thus are called **count** nouns. *Water*, *dirt*, and *cream* don't have a plural form and consequently are called **non-count nouns**. However, what's going on when someone goes into a restaurant, orders coffee, and asks for *two creams*?

**2.** The listener's semantic representation of *doctor* apparently includes the feature specification [+male]. This would then preclude the listener from associating *doctor* with a female referent, in this case the boy's mother.

**3.** overlap

**4.** A.  anaphora
   B.  coreference

**5.** d.  deixis

**6.** d.  all of the above

**7.** (B) entails (A). Note: if *Fred is a man* is true, then *Fred is mortal* must be true; likewise, if *Fred is mortal* is false, then *Fred is a man* must be false.

**8.** (A) presupposes (B). Note: if *Fred's wife is ten feet tall* is true, then *Fred is married* must be true; likewise, if *Fred is married* is false, then *Fred's wife is ten feet tall* has no truth value.

**9.** A.  empirical (synthetic sentence)
   B.  linguistic (analytic sentence)

**10.** a.  F (reference and truth)
    b.  F (gradable)
    c.  T
    d.  F (syntactic)
    e.  F (entailment)
    f.  T
    g.  T
    h.  F (anaphoric)
    i.  F (presupposes)
    j.  F (deictic)
    k.  T
    l.  F (overlap)

# Exercises

**1.** If a floozle is a type of schtek, then _____.
   a. *floozle* is a hyponym of *schtek*
   b. *floozle* is a superordinate of *schtek*
   c. *schtek* is a hyponym of *floozle*
   d. *schtek* is a superordinate of *floozle*
   e. both (a) and (d)

**2.** The sentence *We saw three stars tonight* is _____.
   a. lexically ambiguous      d. both (a) and (c)
   b. structurally ambiguous   e. both (b) and (c)
   c. a synthetic sentence

**3.** What sense relation holds among the following words: *book, magazine, pamphlet?*

**4.** What sense relation holds between the following words: *hate, despise?*

**5.** What sense property is illustrated by the word *bar* in *George passed the bar?*

**6.** Provide three hyponyms for the following term: *walk.*

**7.** Provide three hyponyms for the following term: *talk.*

**8.** Identify a superordinate (included term) for the following set: *aunt, grandmother, cousin, nephew.*

**9.** Rearrange the following set of terms from most general (the highest superordinate) to most specific (the lowest hyponym): *animal, feline, lynx, mammal, vertebrate.*

**10.** Rearrange the following set of terms from most general (the highest superordinate) to most specific (the lowest hyponym): *rectangle, quadrilateral, polygon, parallelogram, square.*

**11.** Classify the following terms as binary antonyms (B), gradable antonyms (G), or converse antonyms (C).
   a.  B  G  C  wide/narrow
   b.  B  G  C  smoking/nonsmoking
   c.  B  G  C  near/far
   d.  B  G  C  defeat/lose to
   e.  B  G  C  innocent/guilty
   f.  B  G  C  wife/husband
   g.  B  G  C  in front of/behind

**12.** Classify the following terms as binary antonyms (B), gradable antonyms (G), or converse antonyms (C).
   a.  B  G  C  true/false
   b.  B  G  C  open/closed
   c.  B  G  C  debtor/creditor
   d.  B  G  C  deciduous/evergreen
   e.  B  G  C  teacher/student
   f.  B  G  C  cheap/expensive
   g.  B  G  C  man/woman

**13.** Consider the following positions on the semantic relation between *house* and *building*.

    A. The semantic relation between *house* and *building* is hyponymy.

    B. The semantic relation between *house* and *building* is overlap.

How do the semantic systems of those holding the two positions differ?

**14.** Consider the following data.

    A. *Come* to me.        C. *Come* to him.

    B. *Go* to him.         D. *Go* to me.

    a. Which of these sentences is absolutely unacceptable?

    b. *Come* and *go* both have a deictic component to their meaning. That is, they both depend on the speaker's point of reference. What is the deictic component of each?

    c. Explain the deviance of the absolutely unacceptable sentence.

**15.** Consider the following data.

    A. Fred *went* to New York last night.

    B. Fred *came* to New York last night.

    C. Fred *arrived* in New York last night.

    a. Which of these verbs does not have a deictic component?

    b. Explain.

**16.** The following sign was hanging on the front of a pub in Birmingham, England: *Music of the 60's and 70's every other Tuesday night*. The reader is unsure when to show up to hear the music. The area of semantics that most likely accounts for the reader's confusion is _____.

    a. overlap          d. presupposition

    b. entailment      e. none of the above

    c. antonymy

**17.** You go to see one of your professors and find a note on the office door that says (in its entirety) *Back in 20 minutes*. You are not sure when the professor will return.

    a. What area of semantics accounts for the confusing nature of this note?

    b. Explain.

**18.** For the following term, identify (a) a prototype, (b) a nonprototypical member, and (c) a stereotype: *car*

    a. _____.

    b. _____.

    c. _____.

**19.** For the following term, identify (a) a prototype, (b) a nonprototypical member, and (c) a stereotype: *house*

    a. _____.

    b. _____.

    c. _____.

**20.** What reference relation holds between *who* and *anyone* in the following sentence: *Anyone who parks illegally will be towed*.

21. What principle from the study of reference is illustrated by the following three sentences? Your answer should explain why (A) and (B) are acceptable, while (C) is not.

   A.  Jack Parr used to be the host of the Tonight Show.
   B.  Johnny Carson used to be the host of the Tonight Show.
   C.  *Jack Parr used to be Johnny Carson.

22. Which of the following deals with a particular entity in the real world?

   a.  stereotype
   b.  prototype
   c.  sense
   d.  all of the above
   e.  none of the above

23. You look up the word *aardvark* in a dictionary and find a written definition accompanied by a picture of an aardvark. In this case it could be argued that the dictionary relies on _____.

   a.  sense
   b.  reference
   c.  both sense and reference
   d.  none of the above

24. **Ostention** deals with defining linguistic expressions by "pointing." For example, if a speaker says to someone who does not know English *That is a TV* while pointing at a TV, then this constitutes a definition by ostention. Ostention is most closely related to which of the following theoretical constructs?

   a.  sense
   b.  stereotype
   c.  presupposition
   d.  truth
   e.  prototype
   f.  none of the above

25. In the sentence *John gave me all his money, me* can be interpreted _____.

   a.  anaphorically only
   b.  deictically only
   c.  coreferentially only
   d.  both anaphorically and deictically
   e.  none of the above

26. The men John F. Kennedy and Ronald Reagan are related to the term *President of the U.S.* as follows:

   a.  Kennedy and Reagan are hyponyms of *President of the U.S.*
   b.  Kennedy and Reagan are part of the extension of *President of the U.S.*
   c.  Kennedy and Reagan are stereotypes of *President of the U.S.*
   d.  Kennedy and Reagan are superordinates of *President of the U.S.*
   e.  none of the above

27. The word *robin* and the word *bird* are related as follows:
   a.  *robin* is a prototype of *bird.*
   b.  *robin* is a stereotype of *bird.*
   c.  *robin* is a hyponym of *bird.*
   d.  *robin* and *bird* overlap.
   e.  none of the above

28. Consider the following description: chases cars, barks, is about two feet long, is covered with fur, wags its tail when happy. This is a _____.

   a.  prototype of *dog*
   b.  stereotype of *dog*
   c.  referent of *dog*
   d.  description of *Buick*

29. A man calls up an auto supply store on Florida Boulevard and asks if the store is located east or west of Airline Highway. The clerk who answers the phone says *It depends on*

*where you are.* Using the relevant concept from semantics, explain why the clerk's response is nonsense.

**30.** A vet tells a cat owner to put medicine into the left ear of the cat. The owner appears confused and asks the vet to show her which ear he means. What concept from semantics accounts for the owner's confusion? Explain.

**31.** In the sentence *Mary shot herself in the toe, herself* can be interpreted (either deictically or anaphorically, anaphorically only, deictically only).

**32.** Consider the following pair of sentences:
    A.  Ralph likes anchovy pizza.
    B.  Ralph has tasted anchovy pizza.
    Which of the following truth relations holds between (A) and (B)?
    a.  (A) entails (B).          d.  (B) presupposes (A).
    b.  (B) entails (A).          e.  none of the above
    c.  (A) presupposes (B).

**33.** Which of the following pairs illustrates entailment?
    a.  *George Washington chopped down a cherry tree* entails *George Washington chopped down a tree.*
    b.  *George Washington chopped down all the cherry trees* entails *George Washington chopped down all the trees.*
    c.  *George Washington did not chop down a tree* entails *George Washington did not chop down a cherry tree.*
    d.  both (a) and (b)
    e.  both (a) and (c)

**34.** The sentence *Siblings are not relatives* is _____.
    a.  analytic               d.  both (a) and (b)
    b.  contradictory          e.  none of the above
    c.  synthetic

**35.** The sentences *Wally gave Beaver a dog biscuit* and *Wally gave a dog biscuit to Beaver* _____.
    a.  are paraphrases of each other     d.  are analytic
    b.  are contradictory                 e.  both (a) and (c)
    c.  entail each other

**36.** For the following pair of sentences, state which truth relation holds between (A) and (B): presupposition or entailment.
    A.  I regret having my hair dyed green.
    B.  I had my hair dyed green.

**37.** *Boys will be boys* is an example of a(n) _____ sentence or linguistic truth.

**38.** *A widow is a man whose wife has died* is an example of a(n) _____ sentence or linguistic falsity.

**39.** *My mother is a widow* is an example of a(n) _____ sentence or empirical truth/falsity.

**40.** Consider the following sentences.

A. Fester has children.
B. Fester's middle son is a dentist.

Which of the following best describes the relation between (A) and (B)?

a. (A) presupposes (B).
b. (A) entails (B).
c. (B) presupposes (A).
d. (B) entails (A).
e. both (c) and (d)

**41.** For the following set of sentences, state what truth relation holds between (A) and (B): presupposition or entailment.

A. John knew that the window was open.
B. The window was open.

**42.** For the following pair of sentences, state what truth relation holds between (A) and (B): presupposition or entailment.

A. John passed the test.
B. John took the test.

**43.** For the following pair of sentences, state what truth relation holds between (A) and (B): presupposition or entailment.

A. Biff likes Muffy's new car.
B. Biff likes Muffy's new Mercedes-Benz.

**44.** Identify each sentence as analytic (A), synthetic (S), or contradictory (C).

a. A  S  C   This pentagon is six-sided.
b. A  S  C   A horse is a horse.
c. A  S  C   A triangle is a three-sided figure.
d. A  S  C   My cat is not a mammal.
e. A  S  C   Young Juan's pet is not a mammal.
f. A  S  C   Young Juan's snake is not a reptile.

**45.** The following sentence is from a letter received by a former student of ours: *It is amazing how easy it is to get by with no Japanese but it is really difficult.* What concept from truth-conditional semantics describes this sentence?

**46.** What truth relation holds between the following set of sentences?

A. Fred got wet.
B. Fred took a shower.

**47.** Consider the following interchange between a father and son.

SON:      Bob Feller pitched two no-hitters. True or false?
FATHER:   True.
SON:      False. He pitched three.

Actually, the son is wrong. If Bob Feller pitched three no-hitters, it is also true that he pitched two no-hitters. What concept from semantics explains why this is so?

**48.** O'Barr (1981) describes a study similar to the following: an experimenter shows a film of a car crash to two groups of students. The first group is asked *Did you see a broken headlight?* Thirty percent say *Yes*. The second group is asked *Did you see the broken headlight?* Seventy percent say *Yes*. What area of truth conditional semantics can be used to explain these different results? Explain.

**49.** Consider the following question: *Have you stopped beating your wife?* What truth relation can be used to explain why this is a "loaded" question? Explain. (Hint: consider the meaning of either a *yes* or *no* response.)

**50.** Consider the following joke: *One million people in this country aren't working. But thank God they've got jobs.* What concept from semantics can be used to explain the source of humor in this joke? Explain.

# Chapter *4*

# *Syntax*

**Syntax** is the study of the structure of phrases, clauses, and sentences. In contrast to semantics, syntax is one of the better understood areas within linguistics. In fact, during the past 35 years, more has probably been written about syntax than about any other area within linguistics. This interest in syntax has stemmed largely from the pioneering work of Noam Chomsky, who in 1957 first set out his ideas in a little book (117 pages) entitled *Syntactic Structures*. Since then, Chomsky's name has become almost synonymous with the study of generative grammar in general. However, the fact that syntactic theory has undergone such rapid and detailed development over the past several decades raises a problem for us here. What points can we discuss in just a few pages that will provide a basic grasp of the core elements of the theory of syntax? As usual, we will begin by considering some observations that we can make about the structure of phrases, clauses, and sentences.

(1) The phrase *the biggest house* is acceptable English; *theest big house* is not.
(2) The sentence *Sergeant Preston was shot in the arm by a terminator* is acceptable in English; *Sergeant Preston in the arm was shot by a terminator* is not.
(3) The interrogative *What will Tiny Abner put on his head?* is acceptable in English; *What will Tiny Abner put a hat on his head?* is not.
(4) The sentence *Katznelson is expected to run* is acceptable in English; *Katznelson is expected will run* is not.

Observation (1) illustrates the fact that the words in a language are organized into different **categories** or, in traditional terms, parts of speech. Observation (2) illustrates the fact that words in sentences are not just strings of elements arranged in left-to-right order, but are also arranged in hierarchical **constituent structures**. Observation (3) illustrates the fact that sentence structures are related by **transformations**: operations that move a category from one location to another within a structure. Observation (4) can be used to argue that transformations are subject to various **constraints** that limit their application.

All of these phenomena are essentially syntactic in nature. That is, they all have to do with the internal architecture of phrases, clauses, and sentences. Moreover, we will make the now familiar assumption that the phenomena in (1–4) are systematic; that is, they are governed by a system of principles stated in terms of theoretical constructs. What we will do now is investigate four of these constructs (categories, constituent structure, transformations, and constraints), without which we cannot even begin to account for the observations in (1–4). It is important to bear in mind that what follows is part of an (unobservable) theory designed to account for the (observable) data in (1–4).

## Categories

The classification of words into categories or parts of speech goes back at least as far as Plato, who first mentioned the categories **noun**, **verb**, and **sentence**. (He, of course, used the Greek terms *noma*, *rhema*, and *logos*, respectively.) Even today, school children learn that there are eight parts of speech in English. However, because categories have been with us so long, it is easy to be misled into thinking that they are part of the *observable* aspect of language. Nothing could be farther from the truth: categories are theoretical constructs, part of the *unobservable* theory of syntax. Linguists have historically classified words into categories solely because postulating such categories helps them explain phenomena that they otherwise could not explain.

For example, some words can be made plural (*table-tables, boy-boys, idea-ideas*), whereas others cannot (*quick-\*quicks, of-\*ofs, the-\*thes*). (An asterisk in front of a form means that it is not acceptable in the language in question; it is ungrammatical or ill-formed.) One way to account for this phenomenon is to categorize English words into two groups: nouns (which can be made plural) and others (which cannot). Now we can make a general statement about English: nouns can be made plural; other words can't. Note that if we did not postulate a category such as noun, we would have to state as an idiosyncratic fact about each word in English whether or not it can be made plural. Before leaving this example it is worth pointing out that there is nothing sacred about the term *noun* itself. If we wanted to, we could call this group of words that can be made plural *category one*, or make up some other term, such as *dook*. The point is that words in human languages can be categorized in terms of their behavior; what we choose to call these categories is immaterial.

Consider another example. Children are taught in school that articles are a type of adjective. Is this, however, a legitimate claim? The answer, unfortunately, is "no." The reason is that adjectives and articles behave differently; that is, they have different properties. First, adjectives can be made comparative and superlative (*tall-taller-tallest*), whereas articles can't (*the-\*theer-\*theest, a-\*aer-\*aest*). Second, if both an adjective and an article modify a noun, then the article must precede the adjective (*the tall man*, *\*tall the man*). Finally, a noun can be modified by more than one adjective, but not by more than one article (*a short, fat man*, *\*a the fat man*).

Let's go back and take a look at what we've done here. First, we have justified postulating a category **adjective** by virtue of the fact that some words can be made comparative and superlative (*short-shorter-shortest*) whereas others can't (*boy-\*boyer-\*boyest*). Second, we have provided three different pieces of evidence that articles are not a type of adjective simply because they do not behave like adjectives. There is in fact reason to believe that articles are members of another category **determiner**, which includes demonstratives (*this, that, these, those*) as well as perhaps possessive personal pronouns (*my, your, his, her, its, our, their*). Try the tests we've discussed on these words, and see what you think.

The point of this section on categories is straightforward. First, we cannot make even the most commonplace statement about the observations in (1) without reference to the concept **category**. Second, we can group words in a language into categories based on their behavior (e.g., the types of endings they allow and their position in phrases and sentences).

Before leaving this section, we should further note that linguists have grouped words into two corresponding types of categories: **lexical** (or word) **categories**, which include items such as nouns, verbs, adjectives, and adverbs; and **phrasal categories**, which include items such as noun phrases, verb phrases, adjective phrases, and adverb phrases. For example, the sentence *The fat man ate* contains a noun phrase (NP) *the fat man*, which in turn contains the noun (N) *man*. The theory is that every phrasal category contains at least one lexical category of the same basic type. For example, every NP contains at least an N, every VP contains at least a V, and so on. Conversely, every lexical category belongs to a phrasal category of the same basic type: every N belongs to an NP, and so on. As usual, however, even such straightforward claims such as these can be problematic. For example, in the sentence *To win is everything*, the words *to win* seem to be functioning as the subject NP of the sentence yet that NP does not contain an N (*to win* is a verb form). One way around this problem might be to claim that *to win* is not a member of the category NP at all, but rather a reduced S(entence). Note, incidentally, that *to win* can take a subject and an object just like an S can: *For the Cubs to win the pennant would be a miracle*. Regardless of how this particular problem is resolved, however, the point is that it is representative of the types of problems linguists run into in theorizing about categories.

## Constituent Structure

Phrases, clauses, and sentences are more than just a set of words or, as we have just discussed, categories arranged in left-to-right order. Rather, they are sets of categories organized into a *hierarchical* structure. As was the case with categories, linguists have postulated hierarchical structures for sentences solely in order to account for phenomena that they otherwise could not explain. For example, consider the phrase *American history teacher*, which was mentioned briefly in the chapter on semantics.

As any native speaker of English can verify, this phrase is ambiguous: it can mean either 'a teacher of American history' or 'a history teacher who is American.' However, we saw earlier that this ambiguity is not lexical; none of the words (*American, history*, or *teacher*) has more than one sense. If this is the case, how then are we to account for the ambiguity of *American history teacher*?

One way to explain this phenomenon is to assume that phrases are organized into hierarchical structures and that there are cases where more than one such structure can be assigned to a particular phrase. Such cases are said to exhibit **structural ambiguity**. Under this hypothesis, *American history teacher* can be assigned two different structures and, therefore, is structurally ambiguous. The two structures are given in Figure 4–1. An informal explanation of how these structures account for the ambiguity of *American history teacher* is as follows. In (i), *American* modifies *history*. In alternative terms, we might say that *American history* is a **constituent**. Two or more words form a constituent if there is a point (i.e., **node**) in their associated tree structure that dominates all and only these words. In structure (i), there is a node Y which dominates all and only the words *American history*. Note also that there is no such node in (i) which dominates all and only the words *history teacher*. Thus, in (i) *history* does not modify *teacher* or, in alternative terms, *history teacher* is not a constituent. Moreover, note that structure (i), in which *American history* is a constituent, corresponds exactly to the interpretation of (i), namely that *American* describes *history*.

Now consider structure (ii). Here *history teacher* is a constituent, whereas *American history* is not. There is a node X in (ii) which dominates all and only *history teacher*; there is not a node which dominates all and only *American history*. Structure (ii), in turn, corresponds exactly to the interpretation of (ii), namely that *history* describes *teacher*.

Before moving on, it is worth mentioning several points about these two structures. First, they are theoretical constructs (i.e., part of a theory) postulated by linguists in order to account for the fact that the phrase *American history teacher* has two different senses or interpretations. Second, without postulating these hierarchical structures, there is no transparent explanation for the ambiguity of *American history teacher*. (As we saw earlier, this is not a case of lexical ambiguity.) Third, the justification for these two hierarchical structures is independent of the justification for

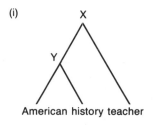

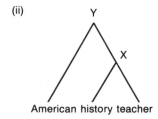

'a teacher of American history'    'a history teacher who is American'

**FIGURE  4–1.  Structural ambiguity.**

categories. Note that, in these two structures, the words *American, history,* and *teacher* are not labeled for categories. In fact, it is immaterial what category each of these words falls into. The point is that the structures are motivated independently of the need for categories. Note, incidentally, that the argument for categories discussed earlier in this chapter was completely independent of the argument for hierarchical structure.

However, the concepts of categories and constituent structure do interact in many syntactic phenomena. Consider the following sentences.

(A.1)   A terminator shot Sergeant Preston in the arm.
(A.2)   Sergeant Preston was shot in the arm by a terminator.
(A.3)   *Sergeant Preston in the arm was shot by a terminator.
(B.1)   The police examined a photograph of the accident.
(B.2)   *A photograph was examined of the accident by the police.
(B.3)   A photograph of the accident was examined by the police.

What observations can we make about these sentences? First, (A.1) and (B.1) are **active** sentences, whereas (A.2–3) and (B.2–3) are their respective **passive** counterparts. (Active and passive sentences are paraphrases of each other in which the object of the active verb corresponds to the subject of the passive verb. Thus, *X saw Y* is active and *Y was seen by X* is the corresponding passive.) Second, (A.1) and (B.1) seem to contain the same categories arranged in the same order, as illustrated here.

| | *NP* | *V* | *NP* | *PP*<br>*(Prepositional Phrase)* |
|---|---|---|---|---|
| (A.1) | A terminator | shot | Sergeant Preston | in the arm |
| (B.1) | The police | examined | a photograph | of the accident |

Third, in (A.2) the NP *Sergeant Preston* is the subject; in (A.3) the NP-PP sequence *Sergeant Preston in the arm* is the subject. In (B.2) the NP *a photograph* is the subject; in (B.3) the NP-PP sequence *a photograph of the accident* is the subject. Fourth, (A.2) is an acceptable passive version of (A.1), but (A.3) isn't. On the other hand, (B.3) is an acceptable passive version of (B.1), but (B.2) isn't. It is this last observation that seems to have no ready explanation. That is, why should the acceptable passive version of (A.1) have only an NP (*Sergeant Preston*) as its subject but the acceptable passive version of (B.1) have an NP-PP sequence (*a photograph of the accident*) as its subject?

This state of affairs can be explained if we make three assumptions. First, a passive sentence will have the direct object of its active version as subject. That is, the direct object of the active corresponds to the subject of the passive. Second, the direct object of an active sentence is the NP directly under VP (or, in more technical terms, the NP **directly dominated** by VP). Third, (A.1) and (B.1) have different constituent structures, as shown in Figure 4–2. These structures provide a simple

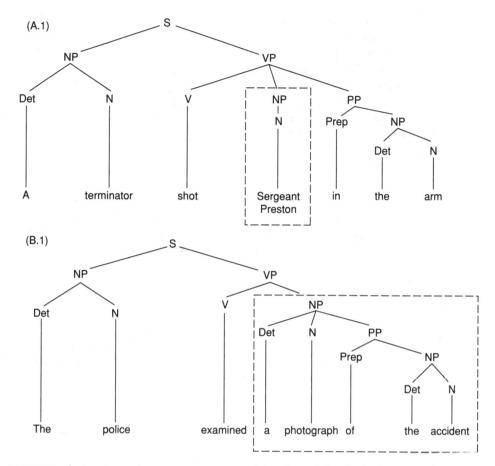

**FIGURE 4–2. Constituent structures of (A.1) and (B.1), indicating their direct objects.**

account of the problem we noted earlier, namely that in the acceptable passive of (A.1), the NP *Sergeant Preston* is the subject, but in the acceptable passive of (B.1), the NP-PP sequence *a photograph of the accident* is the subject. Note that in diagram (A.1), *Sergeant Preston* is the direct object (the NP directly under VP) and thus corresponds to the subject of the passive version (A.2). On the other hand, in diagram (B.1), *a photograph of the accident* is the direct object (i.e., *a photograph of the accident* is all part of the NP directly under VP) and thus corresponds to the subject of the passive version (B.3).

(As an informal exercise, try to explain how the diagram in (A.1) rules out the unacceptable passive in (A.3) and how the diagram in (B.1) rules out the unacceptable passive in (B.2).)

The main point of this example is that our explanation of the data in (A.1–3) and (B.1–3) depends crucially on the concepts of categories and constituent structure. Note our reference to categories (e.g., the object is the NP directly under VP) and to constituent structure (e.g., the PP in (B.1) is part of the direct object NP, whereas the PP in (A.1) is not). As this example shows, it is difficult, if not impossible, to make even the most commonplace observations about syntactic phenomena without using notions such as categories and constituent structure.

Constituent structure diagrams, in turn, allow us to define a number of useful structural relationships. Consider, for example, the following abstract structure:

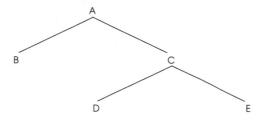

In this structure, node A **dominates** B, C, D, and E, and node C dominates D and E. Node A **directly dominates** B and C, and node C directly dominates D and E. Nodes B and C are **daughters** of A, and nodes D and E are daughters of C. Nodes B and C are **sisters**, as are nodes D and E.

These structural relationships are codified in terms of **phrase structure (PS) rules**. PS rules specify the left-to-right ordering of elements, whether the elements are optional or obligatory, and so on. Consider the following illustrations.

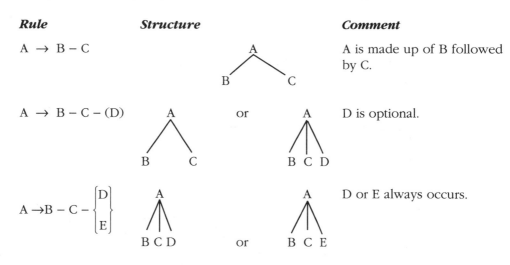

Using these formalisms, we can construct a specific set of PS rules, for example those that generate the structures in Figure 4–2.

$$S \rightarrow NP - VP$$
$$NP \rightarrow (Det) - N - (PP)$$
$$VP \rightarrow V - NP - (PP)$$
$$PP \rightarrow Prep - NP$$

Note, for example, that in Figure 4–2, S is always made up of NP followed by VP; NP can be made up of N only, or a Det followed by an N, or a Det followed by an N followed by a PP; and so on. In essence, PS rules such as these essentially *define* (a subset of) the structural relationships for a given language.

Before leaving the topic of constituent structure, we want to cover two concepts that deal with the relationships between constituents. **Subcategorization restrictions** are syntactic constraints on the kinds of complements (e.g., direct object, prepositional phrase) that lexical categories (e.g., verbs) can take. For example, *conceal* requires a direct object (*He concealed the bed*); *sleep* cannot have a direct object (*\*He slept the bed*). On the other hand, **selectional restrictions** are semantic constraints on the arguments (e.g., subject and object) that lexical categories (e.g., verbs) can take. For example, *admire* requires a human subject (*My neighbor/\*My dog admires my begonias*); *frighten* requires an animate object (*Franklin frightened his dog/\*his chainsaw*).

# Transformations

In addition to postulating categories and constituent structure, many linguists have proposed that a complete account of the syntactic structure of sentences must include the concept of **transformation**. A transformation is an operation that moves a phrasal category (e.g., NP, VP, PP) from one location to another within a structure. As with categories and constituent structure, linguists have postulated transformations in order to account for phenomena that they otherwise could not explain.

Let's consider a concrete example. In English, the verb *conceal* is subcategorized for one direct object NP. That is, *conceal* requires one and only one direct object NP. This property is illustrated in (C.1–.).

> (C.1)   Tiny Abner concealed the document.
> (C.2)   Tiny Abner concealed Mary.
> (C.3)   *Tiny Abner concealed.
> (C.4)   *Tiny Abner concealed the document Mary.

Sentences (C.1–2) are acceptable because *conceal* is followed in each case by one and only one direct object (*the document* in (C.1) and *Mary* in (C.2)). Sentence (C.3) is unacceptable because *conceal* has no direct object, and (C.4) is unacceptable because *conceal* has more than one direct object (*the document* and *Mary*). We can account for these facts very simply with the following generalization: any sentence containing the verb *conceal* will be acceptable if it contains one and only one direct object NP; conversely, any sentence containing the verb *conceal* will be unacceptable if it contains no direct object or more than one direct object.

In passing, it is worth mentioning that sentences such as *Tiny Abner concealed the document and the microfilm* appear to violate this generalization, since there seem to be two direct objects, *the document* and *the microfilm*. One method linguists have used to solve this apparent problem is to assume that sentences containing compound NP's (e.g., *the document and the microfilm*) behave as if they were compound sentences (e.g., *Tiny Abner concealed the document and Tiny Abner concealed the microfilm*). Note that in this example each half of the compound sentence has one occurrence of *conceal* and exactly one direct object, which conforms to our generalization.

Now let's look at some *wh*-interrogatives containing the verb *conceal*. (A *wh*-interrogative is one introduced by a *wh*-word: *who, what, when, where, why,* or *how*.) Examples are given in (D.1–4).

> (D.1)   What did Tiny Abner conceal?
> (D.2)   Who did Tiny Abner conceal?
> (D.3)  *What did Tiny Abner conceal Mary?
> (D.4)  *Who did Tiny Abner conceal the document?

These sentences seem to present a problem. Note that our generalization about the declarative sentences in (C.1–) makes exactly the *wrong* predictions about (D.1–). The generalization predicts that (D.1–2) should be unacceptable, since neither of these sentences apparently has a direct object, and that (D.3–) should be acceptable, since each of these sentences apparently has one and only one direct object. (Recall our definition of direct object as an NP directly under VP.) Actually, the facts are just the reverse: (D.1–2) are perfectly acceptable, and (D.3–) are absolutely unacceptable.

One way out of this predicament would be to say that sentences containing the verb *conceal* are subject to two different generalizations, depending upon whether they are declaratives or interrogatives. We can state these generalizations as follows:

> GENERALIZATION 1: A declarative sentence containing the verb *conceal* is acceptable if it contains one and only one direct object.
> GENERALIZATION 2: An interrogative sentence containing the verb *conceal* is acceptable if it contains no direct object.

Although this solution seems to work, it raises three additional problems. First, it requires us to double our number of generalizations concerning sentences containing *conceal*. This problem is not insurmountable, but it does make our analysis suspect, since it opens the door to proliferating the number of generalizations we need to cover various types of sentences. Second, there are acceptable interrogative sentences such as *Where did Tiny Abner conceal the document?* that contain the verb *conceal* and do have a direct object. Third, there are other interrogative sentences (non-*wh*-interrogatives) that conform to Generalization 1 (the one for declaratives) rather than to Generalization 2 (the one for interrogatives). Consider the non-*wh*-interrogatives in (E.1–).

> (E.1)   Did Tiny Abner conceal the document?
> (E.2)   Did Tiny Abner conceal Mary?
> (E.3)  *Did Tiny Abner conceal?
> (E.4)  *Did Tiny Abner conceal the document Mary?

Note that these interrogative sentences do not behave like the interrogatives in (D.1–4), but instead like the declaratives in (C.1–). That is, Generalization 2, the one concerning interrogatives, *incorrectly* predicts that (E.1–2) are unacceptable, since they contain a direct object; and that (E.3) is acceptable, because it contains no direct object. On the other hand, Generalization 1, the one concerning declaratives, *correctly* predicts that (E.1–2) are acceptable, since they contain one and only one direct object; that (E.3) is unacceptable, because it contains no direct object; and that (E.4) is unacceptable, because it contains more than one direct object. How can we avoid these problems?

We could, of course, state that (for some unknown reason) declaratives and non-*wh*-interrogatives behave one way with respect to *conceal* and that *wh*-interrogatives behave another way. This solution would describe some of the facts, but it doesn't really explain them. That is, it doesn't give us any insight into why the facts are the way they are.

Let's consider another, completely different way of analyzing the *wh*-interrogatives in (D.1–). Let's assume that our original generalization about *conceal* was correct, namely that *conceal* requires one and only one direct object. Let's further assume that *wh*-words do not originate in clause-initial position, but instead originate elsewhere in the structure and are moved into clause-initial position by a transformation that is stated something like this: move the *wh*-word into clause-initial position. We will call this transformation **wh-Movement**. We will further identify the structure that exists before the *wh*-word is moved as the **underlying structure** and that which exists after the *wh*-word is moved as the **surface structure**. Finally, we will stipulate that our original generalization—that the verb *conceal* requires one and only one direct object—applies only to underlying structures.

Now we are in a position to provide a straightforward account of *wh*-interrogatives containing the verb *conceal*. The underlying structure of (D.1) *What did Tiny Abner conceal?* is given in Figure 4–3. Note that this underlying structure is consistent with our original generalization, namely that *conceal* requires one and only one direct object NP (the direct object here is the NP *what*). The *wh*-Movement transfor-

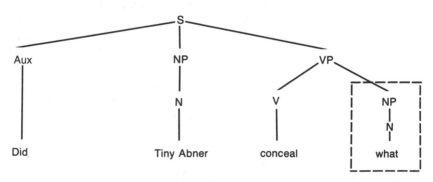

**FIGURE 4–3. Underlying structure of sentence (D.1).**

mation applies to the underlying structure in Figure 4–3, transforming it into the surface structure in Figure 4–4.

The *wh*-Movement transformation accounts for the fact that even though *what* originated as the direct object in the underlying structure, it ends up in clause-initial position in the surface structure. The main point is that this analysis provides a unified treatment of sentences (C.1), (D.1), and (E.1), repeated here.

(C.1)    Tiny Abner concealed the document.
(D.1)    What did Tiny Abner conceal?
(E.1)    Did Tiny Abner conceal the document?

The underlying structure of all three sentences contains one and only one direct object, and thus meets the criterion for acceptability set out in our original generalization, namely that *conceal* requires one and only one direct object. The direct object in (D.1) (*what*) is moved to clause-initial position by the *wh*-Movement transformation. The direct object in both (C.1) and (E.1) (*the document*) remains in its original position since it is not a *wh*-word and thus is not subject to *wh*-Movement.

Note, too, that our transformational analysis provides a straightforward account of the unaccceptability of (D.3) *\*What did Tiny Abner conceal Mary?* The underlying structure of this sentence is given in Figure 4–5. This structure violates our generalization that *conceal* requires one and only one direct object NP in the underlying structure. Even though *wh*-Movement would move *what* to clause-initial position, leaving only one direct object (i.e., *Mary*) in the surface structure, the "damage" is already done. Our generalization applies to underlying structures, not to surface structures.

Another transformation that plays a major role in Chomsky's theory is **NP-Movement**: move any NP to any empty NP position. This rule moves the object of a passive verb into subject position to create a passive sentence, as shown in the diagram immediately below Figure 4.5.

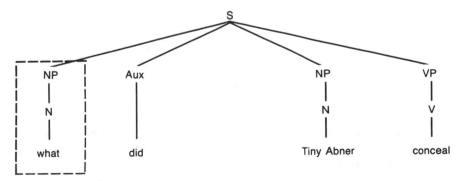

**FIGURE 4–4. Surface structure of sentence (D.1).**

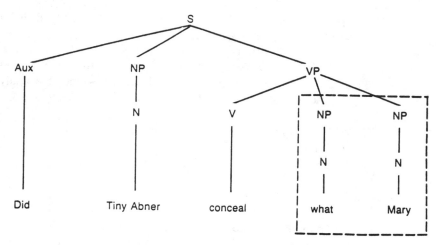

**FIGURE 4–5. Underlying structure of sentence (D.3).**

*Muffy* was being pursued _____ by the police.

NP-Movement

The arguments for NP-Movement here are exactly the same as those for *wh*-Movement in the case of *conceal. Pursue* is subcategorized for a direct object; therefore, *pursue* must have a direct object in the underlying structure of any sentence containing it. Thus, in the passive sentence *Muffy was being pursued by the police, Muffy* must originate as the direct object of *pursue.*

NP-Movement also moves the subject of a dependent infinitive clause to subject position of the adjacent main clause, as follows.

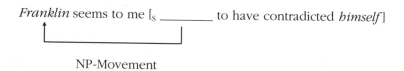

*Franklin* seems to me [s _____ to have contradicted *himself*]

NP-Movement

The arguments for NP-Movement in this situation are somewhat different. One argument rests on the fact that a reflexive pronoun (*himself*) requires an antecedent (*Franklin*) within the same clause. (This was discussed in the Introduction.) Thus, *Franklin* must originate in the dependent clause, so it can serve as antecedent to *himself.*

To conclude this section, we have looked at the motivation for positing transformations as part of a theory of syntax. Like the concepts of categories and constituent structure, the concept of transformations is postulated in order to account for phenomena that otherwise could not be explained, at least in any systematic, principled way. Before leaving the subject of transformations, let us again emphasize that transformations are part of an (unobservable) theory of syntax—that is, part of a method for describing and analyzing the structure of sentences. It would be a mistake to assume that transformations are involved in the actual production and perception of sentences by speakers and listeners. In other words, the fact that sentences can be described in terms of their underlying and surface structures should not be interpreted as meaning that a speaker "starts out" with an underlying structure and "transforms" it into a surface structure during the act of producing a sentence. A theory that includes the notions of transformations, underlying structures, and surface structures does not make any direct claims about how speakers go about producing sentences, but instead about how sentences themselves can be analyzed.

### Constraints on Movement

During the last 20 years, Chomsky has extended the theory of transformational grammar to include **constraints** on transformations. Each constraint is not part of a particular rule, but rather a restriction on what transformations can do in general. Consider the following constraints (adapted from Radford, 1981: 212–248) and an example of how each one serves to block transformational movement in a derivation. (Movement is indicated by an arrow.)

**Coordinate Structure Constraint.**   This constraint states that no element can be moved out of a coordinate structure.

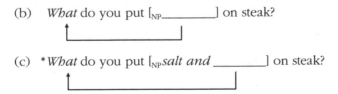

(a)   Do you put [NP*salt and pepper*] on steak?

(b)   *What* do you put [NP_____] on steak?

(c)   **What* do you put [NP*salt and* _____] on steak?

*Salt and pepper* is a coordinate structure, as illustrated in (a). The whole structure can be questioned and then moved to clause-initial position, as in (b). However, one member of the coordinate structure cannot be questioned and moved, as in (c).

**Unit Movement Constraint.**   This constraint states that no string of elements which do not form a constituent can be moved together in a single application of a movement rule.

(a)    Did he climb [PP*up the ladder*]?

(b)    *Where* did he climb [PP_____]?
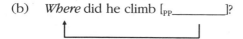

(c)    Did he [V fold *up*] [NP*the ladder*]?

(d)    *Where* did he [V fold _____] [NP_____]?
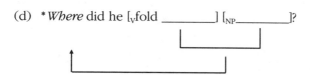

*Up the ladder* is a constituent (i.e., a PP) in (a), and thus can be questioned and subsequently moved, as illustrated in (b). However, *up the ladder* is not a constituent in (c), and thus cannot be questioned and moved, as in (d).

**Subjacency Constraint.** This constraint prohibits an element from being moved across more than one S or NP boundary in a single application of a movement rule. (The rule in this example is called **Extraposition**, which moves a relative clause or prepositional phrase away from the NP that contains it to clause-final position.)

(a)    The fact that [S[NPan article *about Trump*NP] was just published S] was unexpected.

(b)    The fact that [S[NPan article _____NP] was just published *about Trump* S] was unexpected.

(c)    *The fact that [S[NPan article _____NP] was just published S] was unexpected *about Trump.*

*About Trump* is a PP contained in the NP *an article about Trump*, as illustrated in (a). Thus, *about Trump* can be moved via Extraposition to the end of the interior clause as in (b), since it crosses only one NP boundary. However, it cannot be moved to the end of the exterior clause as in (c), since it would have to cross both an NP and an S boundary.

**Sentential Subject Constraint.**  This constraint states that no element can be moved out of a clause which is the subject of another clause.

(a)   Would Desi Arnaz hate [$_S$for me to play *Babaloo* ]?

(b)   *What* would Desi Arnaz hate [$_S$for me to play _____ ]?
         └─────────────────────────────────────────────┘

(c)   Would [$_S$for me to play *Babaloo* ] infuriate Desi Arnaz?

(d)   \**What* would [$_S$for me to play _____ ] infuriate Desi Arnaz?
         └─────────────────────────────────────┘

*For me to play Babaloo* is the object of the clause *Would Desi Arnaz hate* _____ in (a). Thus, part of that clause (e.g., *Babaloo*) can be questioned and then moved out of that clause, as in (b). However, *for me to play Babaloo* is the subject of the clause _____ *infuriate Desi Arnaz* in (c). Consequently, no part of it may be moved out of that clause, as in (d).

**Tensed S Constraint.**  This constraint prohibits an element from being moved outside of a tensed clause.

(a)   All hell is expected [$_S$_____ to break loose]
         └─────────────────────────┘

(b)   \**All hell* is expected [$_S$_____ might break loose]
         └─────────────────────────┘

*All hell* is the subject of an untensed verb (*to break*) in (a) and thus can be moved outside of that clause. However, *all hell* is the subject of a tensed verb (*might break*) in (b) and thus cannot be so moved.

These constraints on movement represent a major step in the evolution of Chomsky's thought on syntax and the nature of language in general. In the late 1950's and 1960's Chomsky viewed each language as a set of complicated idiosyncratic rules. Twenty years later, he had begun to see the syntax of all languages as a set of very simple rules (e.g., NP-Movement and *wh*-Movement) plus the interaction of a number of very simple constraints. It is the *interaction* of the constraints (rather than the rules or constraints themselves) that Chomsky began to see as accounting for the differences among languages.

## *Summary*

Let's review the main points of this chapter. We began with four observations concerning the structure of sentences. However, we had no transparent explanation for these phenomena. We therefore constructed a (partial) theory of syntax to account for our original observations. This theory makes use of four crucial concepts: category, constituent structure, transformation, and constraints on transformations. These theoretical constructs are postulated solely to help us account for phenomena that otherwise would go unexplained. Of course, some of the details surrounding these concepts may turn out to need revision; however, they enable us to account for syntactic phenomena better than any competing theory that has been proposed so far.

Since the study of syntax has received more attention than any other area of linguistics during the past 35 years, it is especially important to understand that there is much more to the study of syntax than we have been able to cover here. However, you have now been exposed to some of the seminal concepts that form the basis of syntactic investigation. If you want to learn more, take a look at some of the supplementary readings listed below. As usual, it would be wise to check your understanding of the material in this chapter by working through the practice problems and answers, then attempting the 50 exercises on your own.

## *Supplementary Readings*

Cowper, E. (1992). *A concise introduction to syntactic theory: The government-binding approach.* Chicago: University of Chicago Press.

Haegeman, L. (1991). *Introduction to government and binding theory.* Cambridge, MA: Blackwell.

Leiber, J. (1975). *Noam Chomsky: A philosophic overview.* New York: St. Martin's Press.

Lyons, J. (1977). *Noam Chomsky.* New York: Penguin.

Newmeyer, F. J. (1986). *Linguistic theory in America* (2nd ed.). Orlando: Academic Press.

Radford, A. (1981). *Transformational syntax: A student's guide to extended standard theory.* Cambridge, England: Cambridge University Press.

So much has been written about syntax that it is a difficult area to break into on your own. Our best advice is to take an elementary course in syntax, where you will read Cowper, Haegeman, Radford, or something like them. Then read Leiber, Lyons, and Newmeyer for background. If you are in a position where you cannot take a course, read these books in the following order. Lyons and Leiber provide an introduction to Chomsky's thought; Cowper is a short introduction (under 200 pages) to current syntactic theory; Haegeman and Radford are standard texts; and Newmeyer discusses the social and intellectual context surrounding the development of syntactic theory from the mid-1950's up to 1980.

## *Practice*

1. In the phrase *the brick house*, the word *brick* appears to be an adjective as is *old* in *the old house.* Cite one piece of evidence that *brick* is in fact not an adjective. (Hint: consider the suffixes that can be attached to adjectives.)

**2.** What generalization about English is violated by the following sentence: *Some those books were on the table.*

**3.** Each of the following phrases is structurally ambiguous—that is, it can be assigned two different constituent structures. For each phrase, use tree diagrams to show the two different structures. Also, provide a paraphrase which indicates the meaning associated with each tree structure.

   A. abnormal psychology professor
   B. red oak table
   C. foreign student organization
   D. second language teacher
   E. big truck driver

**4.** Identify the daughter node(s) of S in the following structure:

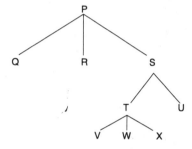

**5.** What is the difference between the structures defined by the following two rules?

A. $VP \rightarrow be \begin{Bmatrix} NP \\ PP \end{Bmatrix}$     B. $VP \rightarrow be \begin{Bmatrix} PP \\ NP \end{Bmatrix}$

**6.** Consider the following data and tree structure:

   A. *Muffy might rob the 7–11 and Biff might rob the, too.
   B. *Muffy might rob the 7–11 and Biff might rob, too.
   C.  Muffy might rob the 7–11 and Biff might, too.
   D. *Muffy might rob the 7–11 and Biff too the 7–11.
   E. *Muffy might rob the 7–11 and Biff too rob the 7–11.

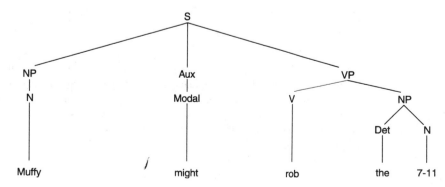

Based on these data, which of the following generalizations is true?

   a. *too* can substitute for any phrasal category.
   b. *too* can substitute for any lexical category.
   c. *too* can substitute only for NP.
   d. *too* can substitute only for VP.
   e. *too* can substitute only for V.
   f. *too* can substitute for either an auxiliary or a main verb.

7. Consider the following sentence: *Where has John put the car?* How can the following data be used to argue that *where* originated to the right of *the car* in the underlying structure (i.e., *John put the car where*) and was moved to clause-initial position in the surface structure?

   A.  John has put the car in the garage.
   B.  *John has put.
   C.  *John has put the car.

Hint: both *where* and *in the garage* indicate location.

8. Negative sentences in English follow a predictable pattern in terms of where *not* can occur within the sentence. Based on the following data, state a generalization about where *not* can occur.

   A.1.  John has put the car in the garage.
   A.2.  *John *not* has put the car in the garage.     *before aux.*
   A.3.  John has *not* put the car in the garage.
   A.4.  *John has put *not* the car in the garage.     *after past participle*

   B.1.  John must have put the car in the garage.
   B.2.  *John *not* must have put the car in the garage.
   B.3.  John must *not* have put the car in the garage.
   B.4.  *John must have *not* put the car in the garage.
   B.5.  *John must have put *not* the car in the garage.

   C.1.  John must have been putting the car in the garage.
   C.2.  *John *not* must have been putting the car in the garage.
   C.3.  John must *not* have been putting the car in the garage.
   C.4.  *John must have *not* been putting the car in the garage.
   C.5.  *John must have been *not* putting the car in the garage.
   C.6.  *John must have been putting *not* the car in the garage.

9. The following two sentences appear to have the same structure:

   A.  John threw away the magazine.
   B.  John walked down the street.

However, certain tests can be used as evidence that one of these sentences contains a one-word verb followed by a prepositional phrase, while the other sentence contains a two-word verb followed by an object noun phrase. Try each of the following tests on these two sentences. What conclusions can you draw about which sentence has which structure?

   I.  A prepositional phrase can appear in both sentence-final and sentence-initial position.
      i.  He went *up the chimney.*
      ii.  *Up the chimney* he went.

II. A two-word verb can be separated by a direct object:
i. John *picked up* the garbage.
ii. John *picked* the garbage *up.*

**10.** What constraint (if any) is violated by the following derivation:

*I remember the man *whom* you mentioned [<sub>NP</sub> _____ and the woman]

# Answers

The following answers are meant only to be suggestive; discussion of other possible answers is part of the practice.

**1.** *Brick* cannot be made comparative (*\*bricker*) or superlative (*\*brickest*), whereas adjectives, in general, can (e.g., *older, oldest*).

**2.** An NP can contain no more than one determiner; *some* and *those* must both be analyzed as determiners.

**3.** A.

abnormal psychology professor = 'professor of abnormal psychology'

abnormal psychology professor = 'psychology professor who is abnormal'

B.

red oak table = 'table made of red oak'

red oak table = 'oak table painted red'

C.

foreign student organization = 'organization of foreign students'

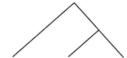

foreign student organization = 'student organization that is foreign'

D.

second language teacher = 'teacher of a second language'

second language teacher = 'additional teacher of language'

E.

big truck driver = 'one who drives big trucks'

big truck driver = 'truck driver who is big'

**4.** T and U

**5.** No difference.

**6.** d. *Too* can substitute only for VP.

**7.** Sentences (a–c) indicate that the verb *put* must be followed (although not immediately) by a phrase indicating location (e.g., *in the garage*). In the sentence *Where has John put the car?*, there is no phrase indicating location following *put*, yet the sentence is perfectly acceptable. One way to account for the acceptability of this sentence is to assume that *where* (a phrase indicating location) originated to the right of *put* in the underlying structure (i.e., . . . *put the car where*) and was later moved into clause-initial position by the rule of *wh*-Movement.

8. *Not* can occur after the first verb form in a sentence. (Actually, we might say after the first auxiliary verb, since forms of *must, have,* and *be* are auxiliary verbs and *put* is a main verb.)

Note that some of the starred sentences may be acceptable to you (e.g., (B.4), (C.4), (C.5)). If you assume that these sentences are acceptable, along with the unstarred ones, how would you have to state the generalization concerning the occurrence of *not*?

9. A.   John threw away the magazine. (= two-word verb + NP)
   B.   John walked down the street. (= one-word verb + PP)


   I.   *\*Away the magazine* John threw.
   I.   *Down the street* John walked.

   II.  John *threw* the magazine *away.*
   II.  *John *walked* the street *down.*

10. Coordinate Structure Constraint

# Exercises

1. Consider the following English words. Some can be made past tense; others can't. Some can be made superlative; others can't. Some can be made plural; others can't. What concept from syntactic theory will enable you to account for this? Explain.

   A. walk - walked
   B. wok - *woked
   C. weak - weakest
   D. week - *weekest
   E. beast - beasts
   F. best - *bests

2. Consider the claim that possessive pronouns (as in *my book, your book, their books*) constitute a type of adjective. Cite two pieces of evidence that possessive pronouns are in fact not adjectives at all.

   a. _____

   b. _____

3. In the movie *Funny Farm*, a couple moves from the city to a farm and they end up spending the first night on the floor. The next morning the wife says to the husband, *What they really mean when they say "hardwood floors" is "hard, wood floors."* What concept from syntax accounts for the "humor" of this line? Explain.

4. Consider the following data:

   A.   I wrote a letter and a postcard.        D.   I wrote to Fred and Ricky.
   B.   *I wrote a letter and to Fred.          E *   I wrote carefully and slowly.
   C.   I wrote to Fred and to Ricky.           F.   *I wrote carefully and a letter.

The analysis that best explains these data is that:

    a.  Only items belonging to identical categories can be conjoined by *and*.
    b.  Only items belonging to different categories can be conjoined by *and*.
    c.  Only NP's can be conjoined by *and*.
    d.  Only PP's can be conjoined by *and*.
    e.  none of the above.

**5.** Consider the following data and its associated structure.

    A.  Fred should get a haircut, and so should Ricky.
    B.  *Fred should get a haircut, and so Ricky.
    C.  *Fred should get a haircut, and so should Ricky a haircut.

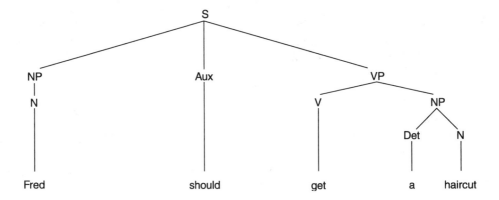

The analysis that best explains these data is that

    a.  *so* substitutes for the material dominated by AUX and VP.
    b.  *so* substitutes for the material dominated by VP.
    c.  *so* substitutes for the material dominated by NP.
    d.  *so* substitutes for the material dominated by AUX.

**6.** In traditional grammar, forms such as *he*, *she*, and *it* are called *pronouns* because they are said to substitute for nouns. Now consider the phrase *the man from the CIA*, its associated structure, and some relevant data.

    A.  *The man from the CIA* came in and then *he* left.
    B.  *The *man* from the CIA came in and then the *he* from the CIA left.
    C.  *_The man_ from the CIA came in and then *he* from the CIA left.
    D.  *The *man from the CIA* came in and then the *he* left.
    E.  *The man *from the CIA* came in and then the man *he* left.

Based on these data, what category do *pronouns* substitute for?

**7.** Consider the following sentences:

    A.  Meet me at the bank.
    B.  Dr. Smith is a European history professor.

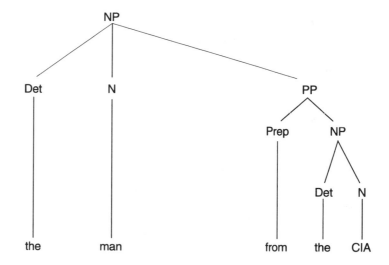

C. The men examined the plant.
D. Jane hid the letter from Dan.
E. Muffy saw some old men and women.

Which of these are structurally ambiguous?

a. (A) and (B) only
b. (A), (B), and (C) only
c. (D) only
d. (B), (D), and (E) only
e. (A), (B), (C), (D), and (E)

8. Identify the structurally ambiguous sentences in the group below.

   A. Professor Jones is an ancient history teacher.
   B. Visiting relatives are sometimes a nuisance.
   C. Visiting relatives can sometimes be a nuisance.

9. Consider the following sentences:

   A. Ralph put the note on the door.
   B. Ralph found the key to the door.

   Provide evidence that (A) and (B) have different structures with respect to their direct objects and their prepositional phrases. (Hint: your evidence should consist of one grammatical and one ungrammatical sentence.)

10. The following caption appears on a bumper sticker: *I need someone really bad. Are you really bad?*

    a. What concept from syntactic theory can be used to explain the source of humor in this caption?

    b. Explain.

**11.** Consider the following sentences (adapted from Akmajian and Heny [1975: 72–73]):

A. John ran up the hill.
B. John ran up the bill.

Which pair below does *not* provide evidence that these two sentences have different syntactic structures?

a.  *John ran the hill up.
    John ran the bill up.
b.  Up the hill John ran.
    *Up the bill John ran.
c.  John was running up the hill.
    John was running up the bill.

**12.** The insertion of parenthetical material (e.g., *in my opinion*) into a sentence is sensitive to syntactic structure. Given the following structure and data, construct a rule governing the insertion of parenthetical material into a sentence. (Hint: parenthetical material can be inserted into a structure only under the _____ node(s).)

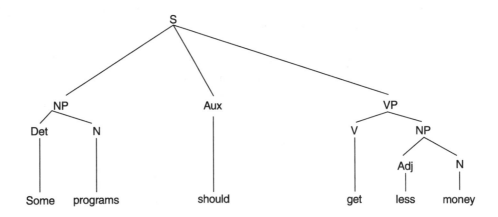

A.  *In my opinion*, some programs should get less money.
B.  *Some, *in my opinion*, programs should get less money.
C.  Some programs, *in my opinion*, should get less money.
D.  Some programs should, *in my opinion*, get less money.
E.  *Some programs should get, *in my opinion*, less money.
F.  *Some programs should get less, *in my opinion*, money.
G.  Some programs should get less money, *in my opinion*.

**13.** What tree structure is permitted by rule (A) that is not permitted by rule (B)?

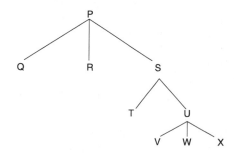

A.   $VP \rightarrow be - ( \left\{ \begin{matrix} NP \\ Adj \\ PP \end{matrix} \right\} )$     B.   $VP \rightarrow be - \left\{ \begin{matrix} NP \\ Adj \\ PP \end{matrix} \right\}$

**14.** Identify the node(s) directly dominated by S in the following structure:

**15.** Identify the sister node(s) of S in the structure in (14).

**16.** Label each of the following sentences as active or passive, positive or negative, and declarative or non-declarative.

    A. Ralph should have given Mary a birthday present.
    B. Should Ralph have given Mary a birthday present?
    C. Mary should have been given a birthday present by Ralph.
    D. Ralph is giving a birthday present to Mary.
    E. Mary wasn't given a birthday present by Ralph.
    F. Mary isn't being given a birthday present by Ralph.
    G. Isn't Mary being given a birthday present by Ralph?

**17.** Consider the following sentences:

    A.  John noticed a mistake.
    B.  What did John notice?
    C.  *John noticed.
    D.  *What did John notice a mistake?

These data can be explained by assuming that:

    a. *what* is moved to clause-initial position by means of the *wh*-Movement transformation.
    b. *notice* requires exactly one direct object NP in the underlying structure.
    c. *notice* requires exactly one direct object NP in the surface structure.
    d. both (a) and (b).
    e. both (b) and (c).

**18.** Based on the following data, state the selectional restrictions on the object of *kill*.

    A.  kill a man
    B.  kill a dog
    C.  kill a tree
    D.  *kill a rock

**19.** Based on the following data, state the selectional restrictions on the object of *murder.*

    A.   murder a man
    B.   *murder a dog
    C.   *murder a tree
    D.  *murder a rock

**20.** Consider the following sentences containing *frimble,* a hypothetical verb:

    A.   Martha is frimbling her parakeet with a garden hose.
    B.   Martha frimbled her husband in the dining room.
    C.   Little Freddy might frimble the parakeet.
    D.  *Little Freddy frimbled with a garden hose.
    E.   *Martha is frimbling the bed with a garden hose.
    F.   *Little Freddy shouldn't frimble.

Based on these data, what is the best statement of the subcategorization restrictions on *frimble?*

    a.   must be followed by both NP and PP
    b.   can be followed by NP, must be followed by PP
    c.   does not have to be followed by either NP or PP
    d.   must be followed by NP, can be followed by PP

**21.** Based on the data in question (20), what is the best statement of the selectional restrictions on *frimble?*

    a.   must be followed by a [−human] NP
    b.   must be followed by a [+human] NP
    c.   must be followed by a [+animate] NP
    d.   can be followed by any type of NP

**22.** Consider the following data:

    A.   I saw the man who lives down the street.
    B.   *I saw the man which lives down the street.
    C.   *I called the dog who was chasing the cat.
    D.   I called the dog which was chasing the cat.
    E.   *I found the hammer who I lost last week.
    F.   I found the hammer which I lost last week.

Based on these data, what are the selectional restrictions on the relative pronouns *who* and *which?*

**23.** Consider the following data (the italicized portion of each sentence is a relative clause):

    A.   I met the man *who told the story.*
    B.   *I met the man *told the story.*
    C.   I've read the story *which the man told.*
    D.   I've read the story *the man told.*
    E.   I met the man *whom you told me about.*
    F.   I met the man *you told me about.*
    G.   I wrote the story *which won first prize.*
    H.   *I wrote the story *won first prize.*

Under what circumstances can a relative pronoun (*who(m)* or *which*) be omitted from a relative clause and still yield a grammatical sentence? (Hint: consider the function of the relative pronoun within the relative clause.)

**24.–31.** English contains a structure called a *yes/no*-question which, as its name implies, asks for a *yes* or *no* response from the addressee. *Yes/no*-questions can be described as systematic deviations from their declarative counterparts. Consider the following data:

A.1.  Ed has gone home.
A.2.  Has Ed gone home?

B.1.  The incumbent will win the primary.
B.2.  Will the incumbent win the primary?

C.1.  Bubba can do better than this.
C.2.  Can Bubba do better than this?

As these data illustrate, forming a *yes/no*-question involves moving a verb. However, these data are insufficient for making a conclusive statement about exactly where the verb is moved.

**24.** Based on the data above, formulate two hypotheses about where the verb is moved during the formation of a *yes/no*-question.

(a) _____

(b) _____

**25.** Use the following data to decide between the two hypotheses stated in your answer to question (24). That is, complete the following statement: To form a *yes/no*-question from the corresponding declarative, move the verb to _____.

A.1.  In 1492, Columbus was sailing to America.
A.2.  In 1492, was Columbus sailing to America?
A.3.  *Was in 1492 Columbus sailing to America?

B.1.  After Joan is fired, I can have her office.
B.2.  After Joan is fired, can I have her office?
B.3.  *Can after Joan is fired I have her office?

**26.** As already illustrated, forming a *yes/no*-question from a declarative structure involves moving a verb to the left of the subject NP. Use the following data to specify more precisely which verb is moved. (Assume that each sentence has one or more auxiliary verbs and a main verb.)

A.1.  You should have taken the last left turn.
A.2.  Should you have taken the last left turn?
A.3.  *Should have you taken the last left turn?
A.4.  *Have you should taken the last left turn?

B.1.  Congress could be planning to vote for the bill.
B.2.  Could Congress be planning to vote for the bill?
B.3.  *Could be Congress planning to vote for the bill?
B.4.  *Be Congress could planning to vote for the bill?

C.1.  The cat has been eating this fish.
C.2.  Has the cat been eating this fish?
C.3.  *Has been the cat eating this fish?
C.4.  *Been the cat has eating this fish?

**27.** Formulate the *yes/no*-question that corresponds to each of the following declaratives. You will find that two general patterns emerge, one similar to the *yes/no*-questions examined so far and one different from them. What do the declarative structures associated with the new pattern have in common?

A. Ralph parked the car next to a fire hydrant.
B. I should have sent this letter by certified mail.
C. Toby would like to ride on the merry-go-round.
D. Wonder Bread builds strong bodies.
E. The dentist removed two of her wisdom teeth.
F. You can use your American Express card at this store.

**28.** As illustrated in (27), it appears that *yes/no*-questions exhibit one of two patterns, depending on what verbs are present in the corresponding declarative. If the declarative contains an auxiliary verb, then the first auxiliary verb is moved to the left of the subject NP. If the declarative contains only a main verb (i.e., no auxiliary verb), then a form of *do* is added to the *yes/no*-question where an auxiliary verb would be expected to occur. Now consider the following data in light of these generalizations.

A.1. Someone is in the yard.
A.2. Is someone in the yard?
A.3. *Does someone be in the yard?

B.1. Someone is knocking at the door.
B.2. Is someone knocking at the door?
B.3. *Does someone be knocking at the door?

C.1. John has the keys.
C.2. *Has John the keys?
C.3. Does John have the keys?

D.1. Mino has eaten my blueberry muffin.
D.2. Has Mino eaten my blueberry muffin?
D.3. *Does Mino have eaten my blueberry muffin?

a. Which set of sentences contains auxiliary *be*? main verb *be*? auxiliary *have*? main verb *have*?
b. Which set of sentences illustrates an exception to the following generalization: If the declarative contains only a main verb, then a form of *do* is added in forming a *yes/no*-question.
c. Based on these data, do sentences containing main verb *be* pattern more like sentences containing auxiliary verbs or like those containing only main verbs?
d. Based on these data, do sentences containing main verb *have* pattern more like sentences containing auxiliary verbs or like those containing only main verbs?

**29.** *Yes/no*-questions provide an **operational definition** of "subject"; that is, the subject of a sentence can be defined operationally as the NP that the first auxiliary verb moves to the left of in the formation of a *yes/no*-question. Based on this definition, underline the subject of each of the following sentences.

A. The resident manager has been given a raise.
B. Wally and Beaver could have gone to the movies.
C. Kim and Kevin sent us a postcard from the French Quarter.
D. Some of the people at the garage sale paid by check.
E. There should have been someone at that counter.
F. It will be necessary for the applicants to submit three letters of recommendation.
G. It will be necessary to submit three letters of recommendation.

**30.** What generalization about *yes/no*-questions in English is violated by the following structure: *\*Does John can take the babysitter home?*

**31.** What generalization about *yes/no*-questions in English is violated by the following structure: *\*Had he some cake?*

**32.–41.** English contains a type of structure called a tag question, which consists of a declarative sentence with a *yes/no*-question "tagged" onto the end of it. Tag questions are illustrated by the following:

    A. Fred hasn't been drinking, has he?
    B. Ralph should do his homework, shouldn't he?
    C. Mary is driving to Utah, isn't she?
    D. Betsy won't miss the meeting, will she?

**32.** Consider the following data:

    A.  Fred hasn't been drinking, has he?
    B. *Fred hasn't been drinking, is he?
    C.  Ralph should do his homework, shouldn't he?
    D. *Ralph should do his homework, hasn't he?

Use these data to construct a generalization about the verb form that appears in the tag. That is, given a declarative structure, what predictions can be made about the verb that will appear in the tag?

**33.** Consider the following data:

    A.  Ralph should do his homework, shouldn't he?
    B. *Ralph should do his homework, shouldn't she?
    C. *Ralph should do his homework, shouldn't I?
    D. *Ralph should do his homework, shouldn't they?
    E. *Ralph should do his homework, shouldn't him?

Use these data to construct a generalization about the pronoun that appears in the tag. That is, given a declarative structure, what predictions can be made about the pronoun that will appear in the tag? (Make sure that your generalization accounts for the unacceptability of (B–E).)

**34.** Form tag questions based on each of the following sentences:

    A. The phone is ringing.
    B. The phone rang.
    C. Ralph took a shower.
    D. Dinner will be ready in a minute.
    E. Helen walked three miles this morning.
    F. The boys have been playing in the mud again.
    G. Martha and George couldn't make it to dinner.
    H. Ralph and Ed bought Trixie some flowers.

    a. What auxiliary appears in the tag, which never appears in the main clause in these examples?
    b. In what other structure in English does this auxiliary occur?
    c. State a generalization concerning the appearance of this auxiliary that covers both tag questions and the structure you named in (b).

**35.** Examine the following data:

A.1.   Alan is a Republican, isn't he?
A.2.   *Alan is a Republican, doesn't he?

B.1.   Those books are going back to the library, aren't they?
B.2.   *Those books are going back to the library, don't they?

C.1.   Mino has been eating steadily, hasn't he?
C.2.   *Mino has been eating steadily, doesn't he?

D.1.   *This TV has remote control, hasn't it?
D.2.   This TV has remote control, doesn't it?

a.   Which set of tag questions contains main verb *be*? auxiliary *be*? main verb *have*? auxiliary *have*?
b.   Does main verb *be* pattern like other main verbs in a tag question?
c.   Does auxiliary *be* pattern like other auxiliary verbs in a tag question?
d.   Does main verb *have* pattern like other main verbs in a tag question?
e.   Does auxiliary *have* pattern like other auxiliary verbs in a tag question?

**36.** Tag questions, like *yes/no*-questions, provide an **operational definition** of "subject"; that is, the subject of a sentence can be defined as the NP with which the pronoun in the tag must agree. Use this operational definition to identify the subject of each of the following sentences.

A.   Barney and Andy captured a thief.
B.   It looks like rain.
C.   There won't be enough food for another guest.
D.   "The Facts of Life" is Tammy's favorite show.
E.   A woman with 10 children just walked by.

**37.** What generalization about tag questions in English is violated by the following structure:
*The mail hasn't come yet, had it?*

**38.** What generalization about tag questions in English is violated by the following structure:
*"Cosmos" was written by Carl Sagan, didn't he?*

**39.** What generalization about tag questions in English is violated by the following structure:
*The mail hasn't come yet, hasn't it?*

**40.** What generalization about tag questions in English is violated by the following structure:
*We have enough gas, don't they?*

**41.** What constraint (if any) is violated by the following derivation:
*Big Ed* seems [$_S$ _____ will be incompetent]

**42.** What constraint (if any) is violated by the following derivation:
*What* might [$_S$ for him to do _____ ] irritate you?

**43.** What constraint (if any) is violated by the following derivation:

*The car into the garage* was put _____ by Muffy.

**44.** What constraint (if any) is violated by the following derivation:

*What* are you dating [$_{NP}$ a man [$_S$ that believes in _____ ]

**45.** What constraint (if any) is violated by the following derivation:

*John* appears [$_S$ _____ and Karen to be looking for Mr. Goodbar]

**46.** What constraint (if any) is violated by the following derivation:

*The commissioner* is expected [$_S$ the police to want [$_S$ _____ to die] ]

**47.** What constraint (if any) is violated by the following derivation:

*What* do you regret [$_{NP}$ the fact [$_S$ that you said _____ ]]

**48.** Consider the following derivation:

*Who* did he say [$_S$ _____ might fail]

This sentence is perfectly acceptable even though it appears to violate one of Chomsky's constraints on transformations.

a. What constraint does it violate?

b. The fact that this sentence is acceptable can be used to argue that the transformational rule of _____ is not subject to this constraint.

**49.** Chomsky's constraints were originally formulated as restrictions on movement. Some of these constraints, however, had to be re-formulated to block not only movement but also anaphoric relations between two NP's (i.e., where one NP refers to another NP). Consider the following derivation involving anaphora (indicated by an arrow).

*Pasquale Bubba* considers [$_S$ *himself* is a sensitive humanitarian]

Which of Chomsky's constraints on movement is similar to the violation in this derivation?

**50.** The following derivation violates the Sentential Subject Constraint.

*What* [$_{NP}$ [$_S$for me to do _____ ] ] might get on your nerves

a.   What other constraint does it violate?

b.   Which of these constraints subsumes the other?

c.   Which of these constraints is redundant?

# Chapter 5

# *Morphology*

**Morphology** is the study of word formation. (The word *morphology* itself comes from the Greek work *morphē*, which means 'form.') Morphology is to words what syntax is to sentences. That is, morphology is concerned with the structure of words, just as syntax is concerned with the structure of sentences. Let's begin by considering some of the observations we can make about the structure of words in English.

(1)   *Boldest* can be divided into two parts (i.e., *bold* + *est*), each of which has a meaning; *bold* cannot.

(2)   The word *boy* has a meaning in and of itself; the word *at* does not. Rather, *at* indicates a relationship between two meaningful expressions (e.g., *The boy at the door*).

(3)   The form *serve* can stand alone as a word; the form *pre-* (as in *preserve*) cannot.

(4)   *Friendliest* is a word; *friendestly* is not.

(5)   *TV* and *telly* are both formed from *television*.

Observation (1) illustrates the fact that words are made up of meaningful units (**morphemes**). Observation (2) illustrates the fact that some morphemes, called **lexical morphemes**, have meaning in and of themselves; others, called **grammatical morphemes**, specify the relationship between one lexical morpheme and another. Observation (3) illustrates the fact that some morphemes, called **free morphemes**, can stand alone as words; others, called **bound morphemes**, cannot. Observation (4) can be used to argue that bound morphemes can be divided into two types, **inflectional** and **derivational**. Observation (5) illustrates the fact that languages create new words systematically.

All of these phenomena are essentially morphological in nature. That is, they have to do with the internal structure of words. Moreover, we will make our standard assumption that the phenomena in (1–5) are governed by a system of rules. What we will do now is attempt to construct a set of concepts and principles that will help us account for the phenomena in (1–5). As usual, keep in mind that what follows is a theory designed to account for the data in (1–5).

## *Morphemes*

A **morpheme** can be loosely defined as a minimal unit having more or less *constant meaning* associated with more or less *constant form*. Consider a simple example: the word *buyers* is made up of three morphemes {buy} + {er} + {s}. (Braces are sometimes used to indicate morphemes.) Each of these morphemes has a unique meaning: {buy} = verb 'buy' (however it might be represented semantically); {er} = 'one who performs an action'; {s} = 'more than one.' Together they mean something like 'more than one person who buys things.' The strongest evidence that each of these word parts is a morpheme is the fact that each one can occur with other morphemes without changing its core meaning. For example, {buy} occurs in *buy, buying,* and *buys,* as well as in *buyers.* {er} occurs in *farmer, driver,* and *mover,* as well as in *buyers.* {s} occurs in *boys, girls,* and *dogs,* as well as in *buyers.* The more combinations a morpheme can occur in, the more **productive** it is said to be; the more productive a morpheme is, the stronger the evidence that it is a separate morpheme.

There are five points to note about morphemes. First, they are distinct from syllables. The word *alligator,* for example, consists of one morpheme but has four syllables; *cats,* on the other hand, consists of two morphemes but has only one syllable. Second, morphemes are distinct from semantic features, in that morphemes have a more or less constant form, which is usually reflected by their spelling. (After covering the chapter on phonology [Chapter 6], we will be able to define morphemes a little more precisely in terms of pronunciation rather than spelling.) For example, the senses of *man, boy, stallion,* and *colt* all might be specified with the semantic feature [+male], yet all four words constitute different morphemes. One way of looking at the difference between semantic features and morphemes would be to say that features combine vertically to form morphemes, and morphemes combine horizontally to form words. The semantic and morphological structure of the word *girls* is illustrated in the following diagram. (The dotted line represents other semantic features, whatever they may be, that are necessary for specifying the meaning of {girl}.)

[–adult]
[–malc]
[+human]

.

.

.

.

---

{girl} + {s} = *girls*

Moreover, note that words such as *conceal* and *hide* constitute different morphemes (because they have different forms or spellings), even though their senses might be represented by identical sets of semantic features.

Third, identical spellings do not necessarily indicate identical morphemes. For example, consider *buyer* and *shorter*, each of which ends in *-er*. Note that the *-er* in *buyer* means something like 'one who,' while the *-er* in *shorter* means something like 'to a greater degree than.' Note, moreover, that the *-er* which means 'one who' always attaches to a verb (e.g., *buy*) and the *-er* which means 'to a greater degree than' always attaches to an adjective (e.g., *short*). Thus, even though the two *-er*'s have the same form or spelling, they have different meanings, and we therefore have to treat them as different morphemes. The former is sometimes called the agentive morpheme (abbreviated {AG}), since it indicates one who performs an action, and the latter is termed the comparative morpheme ({COMP}), since it indicates the comparative degree of an adjective.

Fourth, the definition of a morpheme as a minimal unit with *more or less* constant meaning associated with *more or less* constant form should be taken as a general rule of thumb rather than a hard and fast criterion. The words *boys* and *girls* conform to this definition rather closely. That is, *boys* can be divided into {boy} + {s} and *girls* can be divided into {girl} + {s}, where the *-s* in each word represents the same plural morpheme. (The plural morpheme is often symbolized {PLU} rather than {s} to distinguish it from other morphemes spelled with *-s*, such as the possessive morpheme in *boy's*.) The word *men*, however, does not seem to be as easily divisible into morphemes, since plurality is marked not by the addition of an *-s* but rather by a change in vowel (from *man*). Do we want to say, then, that *men* has nothing in common with *boys* and *girls*, simply because there is no consistency in form (i.e., spelling)? Probably not. This solution would overlook the obvious generalization that the meaning relationship between *man* and *men* is identical to that between *boy* and *boys*, *girl* and *girls*, and so on, even though the form (or spelling) relationship between such pairs is not identical. In order to capture such obvious meaning relationships, some linguists have opted to represent the morphology of *men* as {man} + {PLU}. Note, moreover, that we will have ample opportunity to make further use of this type of abstraction. For example, *went* is to *go* as *walked* is to *walk*. Thus, *went* might be represented morphologically as {go} + {PAST}, just as *walked* would be characterized as {walk} + {PAST}. In short, all exceptional cases (e.g., *men* and *went*) can be treated on analogy with regular cases (e.g., *boys* and *walked*).

Fifth, the goal of morphological analysis is to determine the rules that speakers actually follow for forming words in a particular language. However, it is often difficult for the linguist to distinguish between the etymology (i.e., history) of a word and its structure in the minds of present-day speakers. Consider, for example, the word *hamburger*. Historically, the word is derived from {Hamburg} = 'a city in Germany' + {er} = 'originating from' (as in *Southerner* or *New Englander*). Nowadays, speakers analyze *hamburger* (unconsciously, of course) as something like {ham} = 'ham' + {burger} = 'hot patty served on a round bun.' This is evidenced by the fact that {burger} can combine with virtually any substance that could conceivably be eaten (e.g., *cheeseburger, shrimpburger, veggieburger,* etc.) and can even occur alone, as in *a burger and fries*. Thus, over time, not only has the morpheme boundary shifted in this word, but the meanings of the morphemes themselves have changed. The fact is that the {ham} + {burger} analysis is undoubtedly "psychologically real" for most present-day speakers of American English. Nonetheless, the {Hamburg} + {er} analysis is just as real for a small subset of these same speakers. In short, it is a recurring source of frustration in morphology to decide just how much of the history of a word modern-day speakers are able to infer from the samples of the language available to them.

Let's summarize the main point of this section. A morpheme is a linguistic unit that is defined by a (more or less) constant core meaning associated with a (more or less) constant form.

## Lexical and Grammatical Morphemes

The distinction between lexical and grammatical morphemes is not well defined, although many linguists seem to agree that it is a useful division to make. **Lexical morphemes** have a sense (i.e., meaning) in and of themselves. Nouns, verbs, and adjectives (e.g., {boy}, {buy}, and {big}) are typical of lexical morphemes. **Grammatical morphemes**, on the other hand, don't really have a sense in and of themselves; instead, they express some sort of relationship *between* lexical morphemes. Prepositions, articles, and conjunctions (e.g., {of}, {the}, and {but}) are typical of grammatical morphemes.

## Free and Bound Morphemes

In contrast to the division between lexical and grammatical morphemes, the distinction between free and bound morphemes is straightforward. **Free morphemes** are those that can stand alone as words. They may be lexical (e.g., {serve}, {press}) or they may be grammatical (e.g., {at}, {and}). **Bound morphemes**, on the other hand, cannot stand alone as words. Likewise, they may be lexical (e.g., {clude} as in *exclude, include,* and *preclude*) or they may be grammatical (e.g., {PLU} = plural as in *boys, girls,* and *cats*).

## Inflectional and Derivational Morphemes

This distinction applies only to the class of bound, grammatical morphemes. (See the right-hand branch of Figure 5-1.) The more familiar term for the class of bound grammatical morphemes is **affix**. Affixes, in turn, can be subdivided into **prefixes** and **suffixes**, depending upon whether they are attached to the beginning of a lexical morpheme, as in *depress* (where {de} is a prefix), or to the end of the lexical morpheme, as in *helpful* (where {ful} is a suffix). Note that this division of affixes into prefixes and suffixes appears to present a bit of a problem in cases such as *men* = {man} + {PLU}, which technically has neither a prefix nor a suffix. What we are forced to say here is that the plural morpheme in English *generally* appears as a suffix, never as a prefix. A summary of these divisions is presented schematically in Figure 5–1.

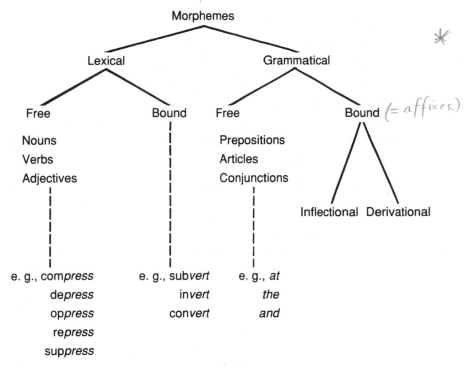

**FIGURE 5–1. Division of morphemes into various types.**

## Inflectional Affixes

Let's now return to the distinction between inflectional and derivational affixes (i.e., bound, grammatical morphemes). English has eight inflectional affixes; all other affixes are derivational. The eight inflectional affixes are listed in the following table, along with the type of root (i.e., lexical morpheme) that each one attaches to, and a representative example.

| Inflectional Affix | Root | Example |
|---|---|---|
| {PLU} = plural | Noun | boy*s* |
| {POSS} = possessive | Noun | boy*'s* |
| {COMP} = comparative | Adjective | old*er* |
| {SUP} = superlative | Adjective | old*est* |
| {PRES} = present | Verb | walk*s* |
| {PAST} = past | Verb | walk*ed* |
| {PAST PART} = past participle | Verb | dri*ven* |
| {PRES PART} = present participle | Verb | driv*ing* |

Each one of these requires some comment.

    {*PLU*}. All plural nouns in English can be represented morphologically as a root

+ {PLU}, regardless of how the plural morpheme is actually spelled or pronounced. For example, *boys* = {boy} + {PLU}, *men* = {man} + {PLU}, and even the plural of *sheep* (as in *Those sheep have big noses*) = {sheep} + {PLU}.

{*POSS*}. All possessive nouns in English can be represented morphologically as a root + {POSS}. For example, *boy's* = {boy} + {POSS}, and *man's* = {man} + {POSS}. (The reason that {PLU} and {POSS} are both generally spelled with -*s* in Modern English is the result of historical accident. The plural -*s* comes from the Old English masculine nominative-objective plural suffix -*as*, while the possessive -*s* comes from the Old English masculine possessive singular suffix -*es*.)

{*COMP*} *and* {*SUP*}. All comparative and superlative adjectives in English can be represented morphologically as a root + {COMP} or {SUP}. For example, *happier* = {happy} + {COMP}, and *happiest* = {happy} + {SUP}. Note, even *good, better*, and *best* can be represented in this fashion: *good* = {good}, *better* = {good} + {COMP}, and *best* = {good} + {SUP}. On the other hand, it isn't clear how best to handle forms like *most beautiful*. Under some circumstances it might be reasonable to treat them as a root plus an affix (e.g., *most beautiful* = {beautiful} + {SUP}), on analogy with regular cases such as *prettiest* = {pretty} + {SUP}. However, *most* in *most beautiful* is clearly not an affix, as is -*est* in *prettiest*; rather, it's a free grammatical morpheme. Since linguists do not always agree on how to handle forms such as *most beautiful*, we will simply leave this as an open question.

{*PRES*}. All present tense verbs in English can be represented morphologically as a root + {PRES}. For example, *loves* (as in *John loves Mary*) = {love} + {PRES}. Note, however, that the only time this affix is spelled out is when there is a third person singular subject (i.e., *he, she, it*, or an NP for which one of these can substitute—for example, *John, Mary, the dog*). With all other subjects (e.g., *I, you, we, they, John and Mary*, and so on), the present tense verb has no surface affix. Nonetheless, the verb *love* as in *John and Mary love each other*) can be represented as {love} + {PRES}.

{*PAST*}. All past tense verbs in English can be represented morphologically as a root + {PAST}. For example, *walked* (as in *John walked on hot coals*) = {walk} + {PAST}. Thus, any past tense verb, regardless of its spelling, can be represented in this fashion. For example, *drove* = {drive} + {PAST}. Note, moreover, that in English (as in all Germanic languages), the first and only the first verb form in a simple sentence is inflected for tense (i.e., {PRES} or {PAST}); no verb following the first is ever inflected for tense. Thus, for example, in the sentence *I think, think* is inflected for tense ({think} + {PRES}); in *I have thought, have* is inflected for tense ({have} + {PRES}); in *I am thinking, am* is inflected for tense ({be} + {PRES}); and so on.

{*PAST PART*}. All past participles in English can be represented morphologically as a root + {PAST PART}. For example, *driven* (as in *John has driven his mother crazy*) = {drive} + {PAST PART}. One potential problem in identifying past participles results from the fact that there is so much variation in their spelling. For example, *gone* = {go} + {PAST PART}, *come* (as in *They've come home*) = {come} + {PAST PART}, *hit* (as in *He's hit three home runs*) = {hit} + {PAST PART}, and *walked* (as in *He's walked three miles*) = {walk} + {PAST PART}. Nonetheless, there is a very simple method for identifying a past participle in a simple active sentence: a past participle always follows a form of the auxiliary verb *have*. Thus, in the sentence *they have walked home*, *walked* is a past participle since it immediately follows a form of *have*. However, in the sentence *They walked home*, *walked* is not a past participle since it does not follow a form of *have*. In fact, it is a tensed form (here past), since it is the first verb form in the sentence.

{PRES PART}. All present participles in English can be represented morphologically as a root + {PRES PART}. For example, *drinking* = {drink} + {PRES PART}. Unlike other verb forms in English, present participles always appear in a constant form (i.e., with an *-ing* suffix). In addition, the present participle in a simple active sentence can be identified as the verb form following a form of the auxiliary verb *to be*, as in *They were laughing*.

We should add a footnote at this point concerning verb forms in English. In simple, active sentences there are five different types of verbs that can occur: main verbs and four different auxiliary verbs (modal verbs, forms of *have*, forms of *be*, and forms of *do*). We will take these up one at a time.

The **main verb** is always the right-most verb in a simple sentence. Thus, in the sentence *John should have gone*, *gone* is the main verb; in *John might have a cold*, *have* is the main verb; and so on. Note that forms of *have*, *be*, and *do* in English can function as both main verbs and auxiliaries. If they are farthest to the right, they are main verbs; if not, they are auxiliaries.

The primary **modal verbs** are *can/could, shall/should, will/would, may/might,* and *must*. Modals are characterized by the absence of the third person singular *-s* that occurs on all other types of verbs in the present tense. For example, in the sentence *John has seen Mary*, note the *-s* on *has*. However, in the sentence *John may see Mary*, note that there is no *-s* on *may* (cf. *\*John mays see Mary*). Furthermore, when a modal occurs in a sentence, it is always the first verb form and it is always followed by an uninflected verb form; for example, in *John will be going*, the modal *will* is first in the series, and the following verb *be* is uninflected (cf. *\*John is will go* and *\*John will been going*).

If the auxiliary *have* occurs in a simple active sentence, it is always followed by a past participle. For example, in the sentence *John has eaten*, *eaten* follows *have* and thus is a past participle; in the sentence *John has been eating*, *been* follows *have* and thus is a past participle; and so on. Moreover, if both a modal and the auxiliary *have* occur in the same sentence, *have* follows the modal; for example, in *We may have gone*, *have* follows the modal *may* (cf. *\*We have may gone*).

If the auxiliary *be* occurs in a simple active sentence, it is always followed by a present participle. For example, in the sentence *John is eating*, *eating* follows a form of *be* (i.e., *is*) and thus is a present participle; in the sentence *John will be eating*, *eating* follows *be* and thus is a present participle; and so on. Furthermore, if both the auxiliary *have* and the auxiliary *be* occur in the same sentence, the form of *be* always follows the form of *have*; for example, in *We have been eating*, the form of *be* (i.e., *been*) follows the form of *have* (cf. *\*We are have eating*).

The auxiliary *do* never occurs with any of the other auxiliary verbs in a simple active sentence. When two items (e.g., *do* and other auxiliaries) never occur in the same environment (e.g., in a simple active sentence), the two items are said to be in **complementary distribution**. In other words, auxiliary *do* occurs only with a main verb, never with another auxiliary verb. For example, in the sentence *I do eat corn*, *do* is an auxiliary and *eat* is a main verb (cf. *\*I do may eat corn*, *\*I do have eaten corn*, *\*I do am eating corn*). Moreover, the main verb that appears with *do* is always uninflected. For example, in the sentence *We did see that movie*, *see* is the main verb and thus is uninflected (cf. *\*We did saw that movie*, *\*We did seen that movie*, *\*We did seeing that movie*).

In short, then, verbs in English are perfectly systematic. For example, using the sentence *Someone may have been knocking at the door*, we can make several observations based on this system. First, *knocking* is the main verb, because it is the right-most verb. Moreover, it is a present participle, because it immediately follows a form of *be*. Second, *been* is an auxiliary verb, because it is not the right-most verb. Furthermore, it is a past participle, because it immediately follows a form of *have*. Third, *have* is an auxiliary verb, because it is not the right-most verb. Also, it is uninflected, because it immediately follows a modal (*may*). Fourth, *may* is a modal, because it lacks the third person singular *-s*. Moreover, it is inflected for present tense (*might* would be past), since the first and only the first verb in a simple sentence in English is inflected for tense.

Before ending this section on inflectional affixes, we should say something about **tense**. As we have been using the term, it refers to a particular *form* of a verb. All Germanic languages (including English) have two inflected tenses: present and past. Furthermore, a past tense verb in English is generally characterized by a *-t* or *-d* suffix. Thus, *may* is present and *might* is past; *can* is present and *could* is past; and so on. The main point to note, however, is that inflected tense does not correlate perfectly with time reference. For example, the sentence *I might go with you tonight* contains a past tense verb form (*might*) but the sentence refers to future time. Likewise, the sentence *Yesterday this guy comes up to me on the street* contains a present tense verb form (*comes*) but the sentence refers to past time.

## Derivational Affixes

After this rather long detour into inflectional affixes, let's return to their counterparts, the derivational affixes. Unlike the inflectional affixes, which number only eight in English, the set of derivational affixes is open-ended; that is, there are a potentially infinite number of them (although the number is finite at any one time for a particular speaker). Since it would be impossible to enumerate them exhaustively, let us look at a few representative examples. The suffix {ize} attaches to a noun and turns it into the corresponding verb, as in *criticize, rubberize, vulcanize, pasteurize, mesmerize*, and so on. (This suffix can also be added to adjectives, as in *normalize, realize, finalize, vitalize, equalize*, and so on.) The suffix {ful} attaches to a noun and changes it into the corresponding adjective, as in *helpful, playful, thoughtful, careful*, and so on. The suffix {ly} attaches to an adjective and turns it into the corresponding adverb, as in *quickly, carefully, swiftly, mightily*, and so on. Note that there is another separate derivational affix, also spelled *-ly*, which attaches to a noun and changes it into the corresponding adjective, as in *friendly, manly, neighborly*, and so on. Obviously, we would need to come up with two different morphological symbols for these two derivational affixes spelled *-ly*, just as we came up with {AG} and {COMP} for the two affixes generally spelled *-er*.

In addition to these derivational affixes, English also has derivational prefixes. The following all exhibit some variation on the meaning 'not.' The prefix {un} appears in forms like *unhappy, unwary, unassuming,* and *unforgettable.* The prefix {dis} occurs in words such as *displeasure, disproportionate, dislike,* and *distrust.* The prefix {a} appears in forms such as *asymmetrical, asexual, atheist,* and *atypical.* And the prefix {anti} occurs in words like *anti-American, anti-Castro,* and *anti-aircraft.*

## Differences Between Types of Affixes

So far, we have simply assumed that there are two classes of bound grammatical morphemes: inflectional and derivational. Let's now consider some evidence for this division. Remember that one of our fundamental assumptions is that if two items exhibit different behavior under the same conditions, they must belong to different categories.

**Historical Development.** All inflectional affixes are native to English (i.e., they have been part of English since Old English was spoken—around 500–1000 AD). On the other hand, many (but not all) derivational affixes are borrowings from other languages, in particular Latin and Greek. For example, {ize} is borrowed from Greek; {dis}, {de}, and {re} are borrowed from Latin; and {a} and {anti} are borrowed from Greek through Latin. Moreover, while derivational prefixes tend to show a high percentage of borrowings, there are still a number of derivational affixes (especially suffixes) that are native to English. For example, {ful}, {ly} (both varieties), {like}, and {AG} all derive ultimately from Old English. Thus we can make the generalization that if an affix is borrowed, it is derivational (i.e., all borrowed affixes are derivational).

**Distribution.** All inflectional affixes are suffixes; derivational affixes may be either suffixes or prefixes. That is, {PLU}, {POSS}, {COMP}, {SUP}, and the four verbal inflectional affixes all appear as suffixes, at least in the unexceptional cases. (Recall that the exceptional cases are analyzed on analogy with the regular cases; for example, *sang* = {sing} + {PAST}, since *walked* = {walk} + {PAST}.) On the other hand, it should be clear by now that derivational affixes may be either prefixes or suffixes. For example, *unfriendly* consists of the free lexical morpheme {friend} plus the derivational prefix {un} and the derivational suffix {ly}. In sum, we can say that if an affix is a prefix, then it is derivational (i.e., all prefixes are derivational).

**Range of Application.** Inflectional affixes have a relatively wide range of application, while derivational affixes have a wide to narrow range of application. Wide application means that an affix joins with (almost) all members of a particular category. For example, the inflectional affix {PLU} adjoins to (almost) all members of the category noun. Note that it is difficult to find a noun in English that cannot be made plural. Even proper names can be made plural (for example, *There are two Marthas in my syntax class*). Derivational affixes, on the other hand, have a varying range of applications. Many of them (especially prefixes) have a fairly narrow range of application. For example, the derivational prefix {a} can be prefixed to a very limited number of lexical morphemes: *asexual, atypical, asymmetrical, atheist,* *agnostic, amoral, apolitical, aseptic, aphasia.* The derivational prefix {un} seems to have a somewhat wider range of application. It is prefixed to adjectives (among other things) to form the negative: *unhappy, unreliable, unpatriotic, unpopular, unbearable, unimportant, unremarkable,* and so on. Note, however, that not all adjectives will take this prefix: *\*unshort, \*unsad, \*untall, \*ungullible,* and so forth. Other derivational affixes, especially the suffixes, tend to have a wider range of application. For example, the {AG} affix can be suffixed to a wide range of verbs: *doer, achiever, thinker, builder, baker, pusher,* and so on. On the other hand, some derivational suffixes have a very limited range of application. For example, {hood} appears in the kinship terms *motherhood, fatherhood, sisterhood,* and *brotherhood,* but not *\*aunthood, \*unclehood, \*niecehood,* or *\*nephewhood.* In short, we can make the following generalization: if an affix has a narrow range of application, it is derivational.

**Order of Appearance.** Inflectional suffixes follow derivational suffixes. That is, if a word contains both a derivational and an inflectional suffix, then the inflectional suffix comes last. For example, the word *friendliest* can be broken down as follows (R = root, D = derivational, and I = inflectional).

$$\{friend\} \quad + \quad \{ly\} \quad + \quad \{SUP\}$$
$$R \qquad\qquad D \qquad\qquad I$$

Note that reversing the suffixes results in the unacceptable form *\*friendestly.* Consider another example. The word *lovers* consists of the following morphemes.

$$\{love\} \quad + \quad \{AG\} \quad + \quad \{PLU\}$$
$$R \qquad\qquad D \qquad\qquad I$$

As in the previous case, reversing the suffixes results in the unacceptable form *\*loveser.*

This principle of inflectional suffixes following derivational suffixes, in turn, accounts for some apparently problematic cases. Consider, for example, the forms *spoonsful* and *spoonfuls.* Proponents of prescriptive or "school" grammar would claim that *spoonsful* is "correct" and *spoonfuls* is "incorrect." On the other hand, many (if not most) speakers of English would unselfconsciously say *spoonfuls* rather than *spoonsful.* Our principle governing the order of derivational and inflectional affixes helps explain what is going on here. Historically, *spoon* and *ful* (from *full*) were two separate lexical morphemes, as in *a spoon full of castor oil.* Thus, since *spoon* was a noun and nouns take the {PLU} affix, an *-s* was added to *spoon* to make the phrase plural, as in *two spoons full of castor oil.* However, over time *spoon full* (two lexical morphemes) was reanalyzed as *spoonful* (a lexical morpheme plus a derivational suffix). Note that if you were to hear *spoon full* or *spoonful* spoken, you wouldn't be able to tell if it were one word or two. Once *full* was reanalyzed as a derivational suffix attached to the noun *spoon,* then our principle would predict that the plural morpheme would be attached to the right of the derivational affix *ful,* yielding *spoonfuls* as follows.

$$\underset{\text{R}}{\{spoon\}} \quad + \quad \underset{\text{D}}{\{ful\}} \quad + \quad \underset{\text{I}}{\{PLU\}}$$

Note that *spoonsful* is a violation of the principle governing the order of suffixes.

$$\underset{\text{R}}{*\{spoon\}} \quad + \quad \underset{\text{I}}{\{PLU\}} \quad + \quad \underset{\text{D}}{\{ful\}}$$

In short, the morphological rules of English dictate that *spoonfuls* will eventually supplant *spoonsful.* An identical argument could be used to explain the preference for *cupfuls* over *cupsful* and *mother-in-laws* over *mothers-in-law.*

Consider a related example. What is the plural of *attorney general: attorneys general* or *attorney generals*? Again the purists would probably claim that *attorneys general* is "correct," since *attorney* is a noun and thus takes the plural suffix, while *general* is an adjective and thus should not be inflected for {PLU}. On the other hand, most speakers of English would unselfconsciously say *attorney generals* for the plural form. As in our earlier example, this can be explained as a by-product of reanalysis. English borrowed the term *attorney general* from French, in which an adjective generally follows the noun it modifies. Thus, this phrase in French would have the structure shown in Figure 5–2. As a result, since the plural inflection is affixed to nouns, the plural form in French would be *attorneys general.* In English, on the other hand, an adjective generally *precedes* the noun it modifies. Thus, *attorney general,* once borrowed, has been reanalyzed to conform to English structure as shown in Figure 5–3. Given this structure, it is perfectly predictable that

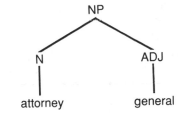

**FIGURE 5–2. Structure of *attorney general* in French.**

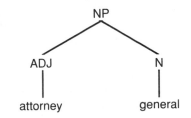

**FIGURE 5–3. Structure of *attorney general* in English.**

English speakers will pluralize *attorney general* as *attorney generals*. In short, then, inflectional and derivational affixes are governed by a system of principles that predict both their order and the categories to which they can be attached.

**Effect on Syntactic Category.**     Inflectional affixes do not change the syntactic category (i.e., part of speech) of the root they are attached to; derivational affixes, however, may. First, let's consider some inflectional suffixes. *Boy* is a noun and *boys* ({boy} + {PLU}) is also a noun. *Short* is an adjective and *shorter* ({short} + {COMP}) is likewise an adjective. *Drive* is a verb and *driven* ({drive} + {PAST PART}) is also a verb. Now consider some derivational suffixes. *Critic* is a noun, but *criticize* ({critic} + {ize}) is a verb. *Quick* is an adjective, but *quickly* ({quick} + {ly}) is an adverb. *Read* is a verb, but *readable* ({read} + {able}) is an adjective. It is important to realize, however, that some derivational suffixes do not change the category of the root. For example, *brother* is a noun and so is *brotherhood* ({brother} + {hood}). Now consider derivational prefixes. Some change the category of the root: *freeze* is a verb, but *antifreeze* ({anti} + {freeze}) is a noun. Others don't: *do* is a verb and so are *undo* ({un} + {do}) and *redo* ({re} + {do}). Therefore, we can make the following generalization: if an affix changes the syntactic category of the lexical morpheme to which it is attached, it is derivational.

**Number of Allowable Affixes.**     No more than one inflectional morpheme can be affixed to a particular syntactic category; however, there is no limit to the number of derivational morphemes that can be affixed to one category. Let's first consider the inflectional affixes. In nontechnical terms, this principle essentially says that no noun, adjective, or verb can have more than one inflectional affix at any one time. Thus, for example, *\*happierest* ({happy} + {COMP} + {SUP}) is correctly predicted by this principle to be unacceptable, since the adjective {happy} has been inflected with two inflectional affixes: {COMP} and {SUP}. Likewise, the verb form *\*droven* ({drive} + {PAST} + {PAST PART}) is ungrammatical for the same reason.

However, what about a form like *men's*, which appears to violate this principle? That is, it looks like the form *men's* is constructed from a noun plus *two* inflectional affixes: {man} + {PLU} + {POSS}. Actually, neither this example nor plural possessives in general violate our principle. It turns out that {PLU} and {POSS} do not affix to the same category at all. In fact, {PLU} affixes to N's (nouns), while {POSS} affixes to NP's (noun phrases). To see this, consider the NP *the man on the moon*, which contains the head N *man*. If we want to make this phrase plural, we inflect the N *man* for plurality: *the men on the moon*; we do not add a plural suffix to the end of the NP: *\*the man on the moons*. The significant point is that {PLU} attaches to the N *man*, not to the whole NP *the man on the moon*. On the other hand, if we want to make the phrase possessive, we inflect the entire NP: *the man on the moon's wife*; we do not inflect the N *man* for {POSS}: *\*the man's on the moon wife*. In short, then, *men's* does not violate our principle that there can be no more than one inflectional affix per syntactic category. Rather, the morphological structure of *men's* is represented as follows.

$$[_{NP} [_N \{man\}] + \{PLU\}] + \{POSS\}$$

Thus, the N *man* is inflected for {PLU} and the NP *man* is inflected for {POSS}.

Derivational affixes, on the other hand, are subject to no such constraint; a given syntactic category can take an infinite number of derivational affixes, at least in theory. For example, {cover} is a verb and from it we can build, by way of derivational affixes, the following forms: *coverable, recover, recoverable, uncover, unrecoverable, recoverability, unrecoverability,* and so on. Thus, we can make the following generalization: a syntactic category can take a (theoretically) infinite number of derivational affixes, but no more than one inflectional affix.

## Word-Formation Processes

Another area of interest to linguists is the formation of new words in a language. The following are common word-formation processes.

**Derivation.** This involves the addition of a derivational affix, changing the syntactic category of the item to which it is attached (e.g., *orient* (V) → *orientation* (N)).

**Category Extension.** This involves the extension of a morpheme from one syntactic category to another (e.g., *chair* (N) → *chair* (V)).

**Compounding.** This involves creating a new word by combining two free morphemes (e.g., *put-down*).

**Root Creation.** A root creation is a brand new word based on no pre-existing morphemes (e.g., *Kodak*).

**Clipped Form.** A clipped form is a shortened form of a pre-existing morpheme (e.g., *bra* < *brassiere*).

**Blend.** A blend is a combination of parts of two pre-existing forms (e.g., *smog* < *smoke* + *fog*).

**Acronym.** An acronym is a word formed from the first letter(s) of each word in a phrase (e.g., *NASA* < *National Aeronautics and Space Administration*).

**Abbreviation.** An abbreviation is a word formed from the *names* of the first letters of the prominent syllables of a word (e.g., *TV* < *television*) or of words in a phrase (e.g., *FBI* < *Federal Bureau of Investigation*).

**Proper Name.** This process forms a word from a proper name (e.g., *hamburger* < *Hamburg*).

**Folk Etymology.** This process forms a word by substituting a common native form for an exotic (often foreign) form (e.g., *cockroach* < Spanish *cucuracha* 'wood louse').

**Back Formation.** A back formation is a word formed by removing what is mistaken for an affix (e.g., *burgle* < *burglar*).

## Summary

Let's review what we've done in this chapter. We started with five observations about the internal structure of words. At first, however, we had no obvious explanation for these phenomena. We then constructed a (partial) theory of morphology to account for our original observations. Central to this theory is the concept of morpheme, as well as the distinctions between lexical and grammatical morphemes, bound and free morphemes, inflectional and derivational morphemes, and word-formation processes. These theoretical constructs have been developed by linguists in order to help explain the observations in (1–5).

This, of course, is only part of the theory of morphology; there is much more to this subject than what has been discussed in this one short chapter. However, you have now been exposed to some of the basic ideas in the field. If you want to investigate the subject further, take a look at the reading list below. Following the readings are some practice problems and answers to test your understanding of the chapter. After that are 50 exercises for you to do on your own.

## Supplementary Readings

### Primary

Aronoff, M. (1976). *Word formation in generative grammar.* Cambridge, MA: MIT Press.

Marchand, H. (1969). *The categories and types of present-day English word-formation* (2nd ed.). Munich: Beck.

Selkirk, E. O. (1982). *The syntax of words.* Cambridge, MA: MIT Press.

### Secondary

Adams, V. (1973). *An introduction to modern English word formation.* London: Longman.

Bauer, L. (1983). *English word-formation.* Cambridge, England: Cambridge University Press.

Matthews, P. H. (1974). *Morphology: An introduction to the theory of word-structure.* Cambridge, England: Cambridge University Press.

You are now prepared to tackle all of the secondary readings: Adams, Bauer, and Matthews are general introductions to the field of morphology; however, the first two are restricted to English. The primary readings are more advanced and require at least an introductory course in linguistics. (A course each in phonology and syntax would enable you to get more out of these works.) Aronoff is a revised and expanded version of his MIT doctoral dissertation and deals primarily with derivational morphology. Selkirk is a monograph based on developments in morphology and syntax since 1977. Marchand is probably the most comprehensive work written on the subject of English morphology.

# *Practice*

1. True - False. Every English word ending in -*ly* is an adverb.

2. Divide the following words into morphemes. For each morpheme, identify the type (lexical or grammatical, free or bound, prefix or suffix, inflectional or derivational), where applicable.

   a. restate
   b. strongest
   c. actively
   d. precede

3. Consider the following data from Logarpilk, a language spoken only at the Student Union:

   | faldep | 'pink flamingo' | meldep | 'big flamingo' |
   |--------|-----------------|--------|----------------|
   | falmok | 'pink flower'   | faldepu | 'pink flamingos' |

   a. List the five morphemes in these words and assign a meaning to each one.
   b. Based on these data, how would you say 'big flowers' in Logarpilk?

4. List the morphemes that make up the following Spanish words, and assign a meaning to each one. (For example, the meaning of {re} in *rewrite* and *reenter* might be 'perform an action again.')

   | tío | 'uncle' | hermano | 'brother' |
   |-----|---------|---------|-----------|
   | muchacha | 'girl' | abuelo | 'grandfather' |
   | abuela | 'grandmother' | nieta | 'granddaughter' |
   | nieto | 'grandson' | tía | 'aunt' |
   | hermana | 'sister' | muchacho | 'boy' |

5. Give an example (other than the one in this chapter) which illustrates the principle that in English the plural inflection attaches to nouns and the possessive inflection attaches to noun phrases. (Hint: you will need an NP containing a head N such that the boundaries of the NP and the N are not the same.)

6. State the morphological principle that each of the following forms violates.

   a. *cupsful* for *cupfuls*
   b. *\*loveding* for *loved* or *loving*
   c. *\*photographser* for *photographers*
   d. *\*two coffee blacks* for *two coffees black*

7. What kind of evidence could be used to argue that *action* and *package* each contain two

morphemes: {act} + {ion} and {pack} + {age}? (Hint: A morpheme can appear independently in other words.)

**8.** What kind of evidence could be used to argue that {age} in *package* is a derivational morpheme?

**9.** State the general principle that accounts for the deviance of the following sentence: *She is make a lot of money at her new job.*

**10.** State the word-formation process involved in the creation of the following word: *fan < fanatic.*

# Answers

The following answers are by no means the only possible ones; they are meant solely to be suggestive. Discussion of other possible answers is part of the practice.

**1.** False (e.g., *fly*)

**2.** a.  restate = {re} + {state}
   {re} = grammatical, bound, prefix, derivational
   {state} = lexical, free
   b.  strongest = {strong} + {SUP}
   {strong} = lexical, free
   {SUP} = grammatical, bound, suffix, inflectional
   c.  actively = {act} + {ive} + {ly}
   {act} = lexical, free
   {ive} = grammatical, bound, suffix, derivational
   {ly} = grammatical, bound, suffix, derivational
   d.  precede = {pre} + {cede}
   {pre} = grammatical, bound, prefix, derivational
   {cede} = lexical, bound (Note: {cede} is a separate morpheme because it appears in other words: *secede, intercede,* and so forth.)

**3.** a.

| {fal} | 'pink' | {mok} | 'flower' |
|-------|--------|-------|----------|
| {dep} | 'flamingo' | {u} | plural |
| {mel} | 'big' | | |

   b.  melmoku

**4.**

| {a} | 'female' |
|-----|----------|
| {o} | 'male' |
| {muchach} | 'child' |
| {abuel} | 'grandparent' |
| {niet} | 'grandchild' |
| {herman} | 'sibling' |
| {tí} | 'parent's sibling' |

**5.** The kids next door's pool = $_{NP}$[the $_N$[kid] + {PLU} next door] + {POSS}

**6.** a.  Inflectional suffixes must follow any derivational suffixes.

b.  No more than one inflectional affix per syntactic category.

c.  Same as (a).

d.  {PLU} attaches to nouns, not to noun phrases.

7.  {act} occurs in *act, actor, active, react*.
    {ion} occurs in *construction, projection, inflection, rejection*.
    {pack} occurs in *pack, packs, packed, packing, packer*.
    {age} occurs in *wreckage, baggage, breakage*.

8.  *packages, packaged, packaging*. An inflectional morpheme can be added after {age}. Since a lexical morpheme can take only one inflectional affix, {age} must be derivational. (Note that this bound grammatical morpheme is completely distinct from the free lexical morpheme of the same spelling, meaning 'number of years alive.')

9.  The verb following a form of *be* should be the {PRES PART} form.

10. Clipping.

# Exercises

1.  True - False. Any one-syllable English word will also be a one-morpheme word.

2.  True - False. Any English word with more than one syllable will contain more than one morpheme.

3.  True - False. Every English word ending in the suffix *ly* is an adverb.

4.  Divide the word *disentangled* into morphemes. Identify each morpheme as lexical or grammatical; free or bound; prefix, suffix, or root; inflectional or derivational (as applicable).

5.  The morpheme {er}, as in *teachers*, is _____.
    a.  bound, grammatical, inflectional
    b.  bound, lexical, derivational
    c.  bound, grammatical, derivational
    d.  lexical, grammatical, inflectional

6.  The morpheme {cur}, as in *recur, incur*, and *occur*, is _____.
    a.  bound, lexical
    b.  bound, inflectional
    c.  free, derivational
    d.  free, lexical
    e.  bound, grammatical

7.  The morpheme represented by *ing* in *Bed coverings on sale* is _____.
    a.  bound, grammatical, inflectional
    b.  bound, grammatical, derivational
    c.  free, grammatical
    d.  free, lexical
    e.  none of the above

8.  {at}, {to}, and other prepositions are _____.
    a.  free, lexical
    b.  free, grammatical
    c.  bound, lexical
    d.  bound, grammatical, derivational
    e.  bound, grammatical, inflectional

**9.** List at least five different verbs that contain the bound, lexical morpheme {mit} 'send, go.'

    a. _____        d. _____

    b. _____        e. _____

    c. _____

**10.** List the terms needed to describe the morpheme {pel}, as in *repel, compel, impel.* (Choose from the following: free, bound, lexical, grammatical, inflectional, derivational.)

**11.** What morpheme (if any) is represented by *-er* in each of the following words: *heater, hotter, heather*?

**12.** Consider the following words from Drulingua, a hypothetical language.

| | | | |
|---|---|---|---|
| sutel | 'old dog' | wotel | 'small dog' |
| bantel | 'big dog' | wolantel | 'smaller dog' |

Based on these data, which morpheme in English corresponds to the Drulingua morpheme {lan}:

    a. {dog}                 d. {old}

    b. {COMPARATIVE}    e. {big}

    c. {SUPERLATIVE}

**13.** Consider the following data from Glorificandum, a language spoken only during the World Series.

| | | | |
|---|---|---|---|
| tapto | 'chemistry student' | tapda | 'history student' |
| kelto | 'chemistry professor' | itapto | 'chemistry students' |

    a. List the five morphemes in these words and assign a meaning to each one.

    b. Based on these data, how would you say 'history professors' in Glorificandum?

**14.** Below are some words from Holtiana, a hypothetical language. Identify the five morphemes that appear in these words and assign a meaning to each morpheme.

| | | | |
|---|---|---|---|
| bekumtan | 'chemistry students' | bekfam | 'chemistry professor' |
| shartan | 'history student' | sharumfam | 'history professors' |

**15.** What is the meaning of the morpheme {Mc} as in *McMuffin, McNuggets,* and *McDLT*?

**16.** What is the meaning of the morpheme {oholic} as in *workoholic, chocoholic,* and *foodoholic?*

**17.** English contains a group of words called **reflexive pronouns**. These pronouns are formed by adding the suffix *-self* or *-selves* to a form of the personal pronoun (e.g., *I* = nominative, *me* = objective, *my* = possessive).

    a. Based on the following data, which form of the personal pronoun is *-self* or *-selves* added to in order to form a reflexive pronoun?

       *myself*         *ourselves*
       *yourself*       *yourselves*

    b. Based on your answer to question (a), try to explain why some nonstandard dialects of English use the following reflexive pronouns:

       *hisself* (instead of *himself*)
       *theirselves* (instead of *themselves*)

**18.** Consider the claim that *may* in the sentence *John may have been lying* is a modal. Which of the following facts supports this view?

    a.  Main verbs are obligatory in English.

    b.  The right-most verb in a simple sentence is the main verb.

    c.  Auxiliary verbs are optional in English.

    d.  Modal verbs lack the third person, singular *-s*.

    e.  none of the above

**19.** For the following sentence, choose the generalization that explains why the sentence is ungrammatical: *\*King Tusk has ate Perry the Squirrel.*

    a.  The verb following a form of auxiliary *have* should be inflected for {PRES PART}.

    b.  The verb following a form of auxiliary *have* should be inflected for {PAST PART}.

    c.  The verb following a form of auxiliary *have* should be inflected for {PRES}.

    d.  The verb following a form of auxiliary *have* should be uninflected.

    e.  The verb following a form of auxiliary *have* should be inflected for {PAST}.

**20.** Consider the sentence: *\*Have you came here before?* Assume *came* is a past tense form. Explain the deviance of this sentence using principles of English verb morphology.

**21.** Consider this overheard sentence: *He give $500 for that old car.* What is one piece of evidence that *give* in this sentence is past tense rather than present tense? (Hint: what property would the verb exhibit if it were present tense?)

**22.** Consider the following data:

    A.  Ralph drives. / Ralph drove.  
    B.  Ralph has driven. / Ralph had driven.  
    C.  Ralph is driving. / Ralph was driving.  
    D.  Ralph will drive. / Ralph would drive.  
    E.  Ralph has been driving. / Ralph had been driving.  
    F.  Ralph will have driven. / Ralph would have driven.  
    G.  Ralph will be driving. / Ralph would be driving.  
    H.  Ralph will have been driving. / Ralph would have been driving.

    a.  Which verb form is inflected for tense?

    b.  Where does the main verb occur with respect to the other verbs?

    c.  Where do auxiliaries occur with respect to the main verb?

    d.  If there is a modal, where does it occur?

    e.  If there is a form of auxiliary *be*, where does it occur?

    f.  If there is a form of auxiliary *have*, where does it occur?

    g.  What form of the verb follows a modal? auxiliary *be*? auxiliary *have*?

**23.** For each of the italicized verbs, state the form (e.g., uninflected, past participle, etc.) and explain your answer (e.g., right-most verb is main verb): He *might have gone* home early.

**24.** For each of the italicized verbs, state the form (e.g., uninflected, past participle, etc.) and explain your answer (e.g., right-most verb is main verb): He *has done* his work.

**25.** For each of the italicized verbs, state the form (e.g., uninflected, past participle, etc.) and explain your answer (e.g., right-most verb is main verb): They *have been* in the kitchen.

**26.** For each of the italicized verbs, state the form (e.g., uninflected, past participle, etc.) and explain your answer (e.g., right-most verb is main verb): *Did* he *walk* home?

**27.** For the following sentence, state the tense of the verb and the time reference of the sentence: *John leaves for Chicago tomorrow.*

**28.** For the following sentence, state the tense of the verb and the time reference of the sentence: *He might go with us tonight.*

**29.** State a general principle that would rule out the following sentence: *\*The last six Queen of Englands had sons.*

**30.** State the principle that the following form violates: *\*the girl's down the street car*

**31.** State the principle that the following verb form violates: *\*roden*

**32.** State the word-formation process involved in the creation of the following word: *Fortran < formula translation*

**33.** State the word-formation process involved in the creation of the following word: *COBOL < common business oriented language*

**34.** State the word-formation process involved in the creation of the following word: *narc < narcotics agent*

**35.** State the word-formation process involved in the creation of the following word: *nose-bleed*

**36.** State the word-formation process involved in the creation of the following word: *pea < pease*

**37.** State the word-formation process involved in the creation of the following word: *chaise lounge* < French *chaise longue*

**38.** State the word-formation process involved in the creation of the following word: *brunch < breakfast + lunch*

**39.** State the word-formation process involved in the creation of the following word: *TB < tuberculosis*

**40.** Determine the word-formation process responsible for the following word (if you are not sure, try consulting a good dictionary): *AIDS*

**41.** Determine the word-formation process responsible for the following word (if you are not sure, try consulting a good dictionary): *quasar*

**42.** Determine the word-formation process responsible for the following word (if you are not sure, try consulting a good dictionary): *Dacron*

**43.** You hear a speaker use the term *French eyes* for *franchise*. Which of the following word-formation processes accounts for this permutation?

a. compounding
b. root creation
c. clipped form
d. blend
e. none of the above

**44.** Frederic Cassidy, editor of the *Dictionary of American Regional English*, states that the form *eaceworm* has been replaced by *East worm* in some parts of Rhode Island. This illustrates which of the following word-formation processes?

a. compounding
b. proper name
c. folk etymology
d. blend
e. none of the above

**45.** Columnist Jack Smith describes a woman who says *token pole* for *totem pole*. This illustrates which of the following word-formation processes?

a. back formation
b. folk etymology
c. clipped form
d. root creation
e. none of the above

**46.** Columnist Jack Smith describes a man who says *Mount Sinus Hospital* for *Mount Sinai Hospital.* This illustrates which of the following word-formation processes?

a. back formation
b. folk etymology
c. clipped form
d. root creation
e. none of the above

**47.** A guest on a *Donahue* television show exhibited the following slip of the tongue: *He never came and see me* (rather than *came and saw me* or *came to see me*). Explain this slip of the tongue using a principle from English word formation.

**48.** A flight instructor told a student to check that all the *Carter pins* were in place. (A *cotter pin* is a small metal rod that holds a nut to a bolt.) What word-formation process accounts for the flight instructor's misunderstanding?

**49.** Consider the following word: *convincingly* (as in *He argued convincingly*). Try to construct an argument that the {ing} in this word *is* functioning as the inflectional suffix {PRES PART}, even though it's followed by the derivational suffix {ly}. (Hint: category shift.)

**50.** A college professor was overheard incorrectly saying *Most AIDS are transmitted by . . .* rather than *Most AIDS is transmitted by. . . .* What word-formation process best accounts for the professor's error?

# *Chapter* **6**

# *Phonology*

**Phonology** is the study of the sound system of language: the rules that govern pronunciation. (The word *phonology* itself comes from the Greek word *phōnē*, which means 'voice.') The study of phonology in the Western tradition goes back almost 200 years, to the early 1800's, when European linguists began studying sound change by comparing the speech sounds in a variety of related languages. However, the emphasis in modern phonology, as it has developed over the last 35 years, has been primarily on the *psychological system* that underlies production, and only secondarily on the actual physical articulation of speech.

In order to see how phonology works, let's begin by considering some observations we can make about the sound system of English.

(1)  The first sound in the word *fight* is produced by bringing together the top teeth and the bottom lip, and then blowing air between them.

(2)  The word *war* is produced with one continuous motion of the vocal tract (lungs, tongue, lips, and so on), yet we interpret this motion as a series of three separate speech sounds, *w-a-r*.

(3)  The words *pea*, *see*, *me*, and *key* all have the same vowel, even though the vowel in each word is spelled differently.

(4)  *p* and *b* are alike in that they are both pronounced with the lips; *p* and *k* are different in that *k* is not pronounced with the lips.

(5)  The vowels in the words *cab* and *cad* are longer than the same vowels in *cap* and *cat*.

Observation (1) illustrates the fact that we use our **vocal tract** to produce speech. Observation (2) illustrates the fact that words are physically one continuous motion but are psychologically a series of discrete units called **segments**. Observation (3) illustrates that a single segment can be represented by a variety of spellings. Observations (2) and (3) can, in turn, be used to justify a **phonemic alphabet**, a system of transcription in which one symbol uniquely represents one segment.

Observation (4) illustrates the fact that segments are composed of smaller units called **distinctive features**. Thus "labial" (referring to the lips) is a distinctive feature shared by *p* and *b*, but not by *p* and *k*. Observation (5) illustrates that two segments can be the same on one **level of representation** but different on another. Thus, the vowels in *cab, cad, cap,* and *cat* are the same on one level (the vowel *a*), but different on another level (long *a* in *cab* and *cad*; short *a* in *cap* and *cat*). (Note that the terms *long* and *short* are not used here in the same way as they are in phonics. In phonology, they indicate differences in duration.) These systematic variations between levels of representation can, in turn, be stated in terms of **phonological rules** (e.g., vowels are lengthened in a particular context).

All of the phenomena in (1–5) are essentially phonological in nature, in that they have to do with the system underlying the pronunciation of words. We will make the familiar assumption that these phenomena are governed by a system of rules. What we will do now is attempt to develop a set of concepts and principles to help us explain the observations in (1–5). Bear in mind that what follows is an (unobservable) theory designed to account for the (observable) data in (1–5).

## Vocal Tract

The vocal tract consists of the passageway between the lips and nostrils on one end and the larynx, which contains the vocal cords, on the other. The vocal tract is important to the study of phonology for two reasons. First, human beings use the vocal tract to produce speech. Second, and more importantly, terms which refer to physical properties of the vocal tract are used to describe the psychological units of phonology. A cross-section of the vocal tract is given in Figure 6–1.

Let's go over the landmarks in this figure one by one: (1) **lips**; (2) **teeth**; (3) **tongue**; (4) **alveolar ridge**, the bony ridge right behind the upper teeth; (5) **palate**, the bony dome constituting the roof of the mouth; (6) **velum**, the soft tissue immediately behind the palate; (7) **uvula**, the soft appendage hanging off the velum (you can see it if you open your mouth wide and look in a mirror); (8) **pharynx**, the back wall of the throat behind the tongue; (9) **epiglottis**, the soft tissue which covers the vocal cords during eating, thus protecting the passageway to the lungs; (10) **esophagus**, the tube going to the stomach; (11) **larynx**, containing the vocal cords; and (12) **trachea**, the tube going to the lungs.

Speech is produced by pushing air from the lungs up through the vocal tract and manipulating several variables at the same time. These variables include whether or not the vocal cords are vibrating; whether the velum is raised (forcing all of the air through the mouth) or lowered (allowing some of the air to escape through the nose); and whether or not the air flow is stopped or impeded at some point between the lips and the larynx. In short, the vocal tract is a tube which produces sound when air from the lungs is pumped through it. Different speech sounds are produced by manipulating the lips, tongue, teeth, velum, pharynx, and vocal cords, thus changing the shape of this tube. For our purposes, however, the primary importance of the

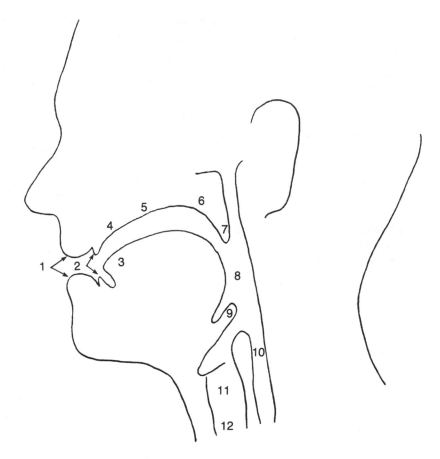

**FIGURE 6–1. Cross-section of the vocal tract.**

vocal tract is the fact that phonological units and rules are described in terms of these physical properties of the vocal mechanism.

## Segments

When we listen to someone talk, we *hear* speech but we *perceive* segments, psychological units which correspond more or less to "speech sounds." It is necessary to make this distinction because the sound waves produced by the vocal tract are *continuous* (not divided neatly into individual sounds); however, our interpretation of these sound waves is *discrete* (we perceive distinct sounds, one following the other). For example, if someone utters the word *war* within our hearing, what we actually hear is a sound that gradually changes shape through time. What we perceive, however, is a series of three discrete segments: *w-a-r*. This distinction between hearing and perceiving is fundamental to an appreciation of phonology, although it is not an easy concept to grasp. In particular, it is not immediately evident that speech is a gradually changing sound. In order to grasp this concept, you might try a simple experiment: take some recorded speech (e.g., an audio tape) and play it at half speed. You'll notice that the "speech sounds" blur one into the other. An experiment such as this illustrates quite dramatically that what we perceive as discrete segments is actually a continuous, gradually changing, physical signal.

Thus, the main point to keep in mind is that when we talk, we are actually producing a continuous set of movements within the vocal tract, which result in a continuous set of sound waves; what we think we are doing (unconsciously, of course) is producing a series of discrete segments. Likewise, when we listen to someone talk, we hear a continuously changing set of sound waves; what we perceive are segments. **Speech** refers to what we are actually doing when we talk and listen; **phonology** refers to the segments and rules in terms of which we organize our interpretation of speech. Put another way, speech refers to physical or physiological phenomena, and phonology refers to mental or psychological phenomena.

## *Phonemic Alphabet*

One type of segment that we perceive when we hear speech is termed the **phoneme**. As we have already seen, however, conventional orthography (i.e., spelling) does not provide an adequate means of representing the phonological structure of words. For example, *pea* and *key* both contain the same vowel, but in *pea* the vowel is spelled *ea* and in *key* it is spelled *ey*. In order to get around this problem, linguists have developed a phonemic alphabet, in which one symbol always corresponds to a single phoneme. So, for example, in our phonemic alphabet we might choose to represent the vowel in *pea*, *see*, *me*, and *key* as /i/. (Phonemic transcription is always enclosed in slashes to distinguish it from conventional orthography.) Thus, we can capture the fact that we perceive all of these words as having the same vowel by transcribing them as follows: *pea* /pi/, *see* /si/, *me* /mi/, and *key* /ki/.

Now that we've established this principle, let's consider the entire phonemic alphabet of English.

### *Vowels*

| *Phonemic Symbol* | *Example* |
|---|---|
| /i/ | s*ea*t |
| /ɪ/ | s*i*t |
| /e/ | s*ay* |
| /ɛ/ | s*ai*d |
| /æ/ | s*a*d |
| /ʌ/ (unstressed = /ə/ ) | s*u*ds (sod*a*) |
| /a/ | s*o*d |
| /u/ | s*ui*t |

| | |
|---|---|
| /ʊ/ | s*oo*t |
| /o/ | s*ew*ed |
| /ɔ/ | s*ough*t |
| /aɪ/ | s*igh*t |
| /aʊ/ | s*ou*th |
| /ɔɪ/ | s*oy* |

These vowel phonemes (which, remember, are percepts—psychological units) are described in terms of the following physical dimensions.

**Tongue Height.** For any articulation corresponding to one of these vowel phonemes, the tongue is either relatively *high* in the mouth (/i,ɪ,u,ʊ/), *mid* (/e,ɛ,ʌ (ə),o/), or *low* (/æ,a,ɔ/). Compare *see* /si/ (high) and *say* /se/ (mid).

**Frontness.** For any articulation corresponding to one of these vowel phonemes, the tongue is either relatively *front* (/i,ɪ,e,ɛ,æ/) or *back* (/ʌ(ə),a,u,ʊ,o,ɔ/). Compare *see* /si/ (front) and *sue* /su/ (back).

**Lip Rounding.** For any articulation corresponding to one of these vowel phonemes, the lips are either relatively *round* (/u,ʊ,o,ɔ/) or *spread* (/i,ɪ,e,ɛ,æ,ʌ(ə),a/). Compare *so* /so/ (round) and *say* /se/ (spread).

**Tenseness.** For any articulation corresponding to one of these vowel phonemes, the vocal musculature is either relatively *tense* (/i,e,u,o,ɔ/) or *lax* (/ɪ,ɛ,æ,ʌ(ə),a,ʊ/). Compare *aid* /ed/ (tense) and *Ed* /ɛd/ (lax).

Figure 6–2 charts the vowel phonemes of English in terms of these four physical dimensions. Thus, for example, /i/ in the upper left-hand corner is high, front, tense, and spread. On the other hand, /ɔ/ in the lower right-hand corner is low, back, tense, and round. And so on.

Viewed from this perspective, it becomes apparent that each of these vowel phonemes is not really an indivisible unit, but rather a composite of values (+ or –) along several dimensions. Each such dimension constitutes a **distinctive feature**. The vowel chart in Figure 6–2 can be broken down into the following distinctive features: [±high], [±low], [±back], [±tense], and [±round]. Thus, for example, /i/ and /ɔ/ are not really units in themselves, but rather each is a bundle of features, as follows.

$$/i/ \ = \ \begin{bmatrix} +\text{high} \\ -\text{low} \\ -\text{back} \\ +\text{tense} \\ -\text{round} \end{bmatrix} \qquad /ɔ/ \ = \ \begin{bmatrix} -\text{high} \\ +\text{low} \\ +\text{back} \\ +\text{tense} \\ +\text{round} \end{bmatrix}$$

If you have tried to articulate words containing these vowels while you were reading the chart, you may have noticed that it is hard to determine the exact configuration of your vocal tract during any particular articulation. For example, is /i/

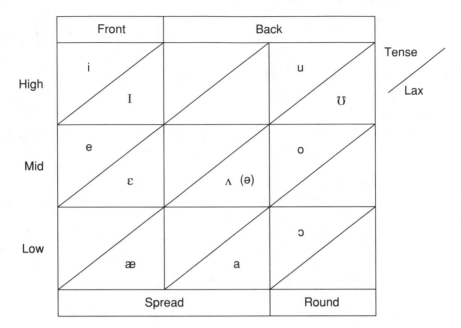

**FIGURE 6–2. Vowel phonemes of English.**

really tense and is /ɪ/ really lax? Actually, this is of no great importance. Keep in mind that phonemes and distinctive features are theoretical constructs within a theory of phonology. Phonemes are abstract entities postulated to account for the fact that speakers of English perceive the vowels in *seat* and *sit*, for example, as different. Likewise, distinctive features are postulated to account for the fact that these segments are different along a particular dimension, here what we have somewhat arbitrarily decided to call [±tense]. The fact that phonemes and distinctive features are described in physical terms is of no real consequence. It results from the fact that modern phonology developed from the study of sound change, which in turn was thought to be a direct function of the vocal tract. In short, even though phonemes and distinctive features are described in physical terms, they are actually psychological entities: *no one has ever uttered a phoneme or a distinctive feature.* Rather, when we talk, we utter a physical speech signal which we *interpret* as containing phonemes, which in turn consist of distinctive features.

## Consonants

For each consonant phoneme in the following table, there are three examples: one each for the occurrence of the phoneme in word-initial, word-medial, and word-final position. A blank indicates that the phoneme does not occur in that position in English.

| Phonemic Symbol | Example |
|:---:|:---|
| /p/ | *p*at, zi*pp*er, ca*p* |
| /b/ | *b*at, fi*bb*er, ca*b* |
| /t/ | *t*ab, ca*tt*y, ca*t* |
| /d/ | *d*ab, ca*dd*y, ca*d* |
| /k/ | *c*ap, di*ck*er, ta*ck* |
| /g/ | *g*ap, di*gg*er, ta*g* |
| /f/ | *f*at, sa*f*er, belie*f* |
| /v/ | *v*at, sa*v*er, belie*v*e |
| /θ/ | *th*in, e*th*er, brea*th* |
| /ð/ | *th*en, ei*th*er, brea*th*e |
| /s/ | *s*ue, la*c*y, pea*c*e |
| /z/ | *z*oo, la*z*y, pea*s* |
| /š/ | *sh*oe, thre*sh*er, ru*sh* |
| /ž/ | —, trea*s*ure, rou*ge* |
| /h/ | *h*am, a*h*ead, — |
| /č/ | *ch*ain, ske*tch*y, besee*ch* |
| /ǰ/ | *J*ane, e*dg*y, besie*ge* |
| /m/ | *m*itt, si*mm*er, see*m* |
| /n/ | *kn*it, si*nn*er, see*n* |
| /ŋ/ | —, si*ng*er, si*ng* |
| /l/ | *l*ight, te*ll*er, coa*l* |
| /r/ | *r*ight, te*rr*or, co*r*e |
| /w/ | *w*et, lo*w*er, — |
| /y/ | *y*et, la*y*er, — |

(Note: English words which appear to end in /w/ and /y/ are analyzed as ending in vowels in this system. For example, *cow* = /kaʊ/ and *sky* = /skaɪ/.)

As was the case with vowels, these consonant phonemes (which, once again, are percepts—psychological units) are described in terms of physical dimensions, as follows.

**Place of Articulation.** For any articulation corresponding to one of these consonant phonemes, the vocal tract is constricted at one of the following points.

(a) **Bilabial** (from *bi* 'two' + *labial* 'lips'). The primary constriction is at the lips (/p,b,m,w/). Compare *pea* /pi/ (bilabial) and *tea* /ti/ (non-bilabial).

(b) **Labiodental** (from *labio* 'lip' + *dental* 'teeth'). The primary constriction is between the lower lip and upper teeth (/f,v/). Compare *fee* /fi/ (labiodental) and *see* /si/ (non-labiodental).

(c) **Interdental** (from *inter* 'between' + *dental* 'teeth'). The primary constriction is between the tongue and the upper teeth (/θ,ð/). Compare *thigh* /θaɪ/ (interdental) and *shy* /šaɪ/ (non-interdental).

(d) **Alveolar** (from *alveolar ridge*). The primary constriction is between the tongue and the alveolar ridge (/t,d,s,z,n,l/). Compare *tea* /ti/ (alveolar) and *key* /ki/ (non-alveolar).

(e) **Palatal** (from *palate*). The primary constriction is between the tongue and the palate (/š,ž,č,ǰ,r,y/). Compare *shoe* /šu/ (palatal) and *sue* /su/ (non-palatal).

(f) **Velar** (from *velum*). The primary constriction is between the tongue and the velum (/k,g,ŋ/). Compare *coo* /ku/ (velar) and *two* /tu/ (non-velar).

(g) **Glottal** (from *glottis*, which refers to the space between the vocal cords). The primary constriction is at the glottis (/h/). Compare *hoe* /ho/ (glottal) and *so* /so/ (non-glottal).

**Manner of Articulation.** For any articulation corresponding to one of these consonant phonemes, the vocal tract is constricted in one of the following ways.

(a) **Stops.** Two articulators (lips, tongue, teeth, etc.) are brought together such that the flow of air through the vocal tract is completely blocked (/p,b,t,d,k,g/). Compare *tea* /ti/ (stop) and *see* /si/ (non-stop).

(b) **Fricatives.** Two articulators are brought near each other such that the flow of air is impeded but not completely blocked. The air flow through the narrow opening creates friction, hence the term *fricative* (/f,v,θ,ð, s,z,š,ž,h/). Compare *zoo* /zu/ (fricative) and *do* /du/ (non-fricative).

(c) **Affricates.** Articulations corresponding to affricates are those that begin like stops (with a complete closure in the vocal tract) and end like fricatives (with a narrow opening in the vocal tract) (/č,ǰ/). Compare *chew* /ču/ (affricate) and *shoe* /šu/ (non-affricate). Because affricates can be described as a stop plus a fricative, some phonemic alphabets transcribe /č/ as /tš/ and /ǰ/ as /dž/.

(d) **Nasals.** A nasal articulation is one in which the airflow through the mouth is completely blocked but the velum is lowered, forcing the air through the nose (/m,n,ŋ/). Compare *no* /no/ (nasal) and *doe* /do/ (non-nasal).

(e) **Liquids and Glides.** Both of these terms describe articulations that are mid-way between true consonants (i.e., stops, fricatives, affricates, and nasals) and vowels, although they are both generally classified as consonants. *Liquid* is a cover term for all *l*-like and *r*-like articulations (/l,r/). Compare *low* /lo/ (liquid) and *doe* /do/ (non-liquid). The term *glide* refers to an articulation in which the vocal tract is constricted, but not enough to block or impede the airflow (/w,y/). Compare *way* /we/ (glide) and *bay* /be/ (non-glide).

Consonants can be divided into **obstruents** (stops, fricatives, and affricates) and **sonorants** (nasals, liquids, and glides).

**Voicing.** For any articulation corresponding to one of these consonant phonemes, the vocal cords are either vibrating (/b,d,g,v,ð,z,ž,ǰ,m,n,ŋ,l,r,w,y/) or not (/p,t,k,f,θ,s,š,č,h/). Compare *zoo* /zu/ (voiced) and *sue* /su/ (voiceless). Stops, fricatives, and affricates come in voiced and voiceless pairs (except for /h/); nasals, liquids, and glides are all voiced, as are vowels.

Figure 6–3 plots the consonant phonemes of English in terms of these three physical dimensions: place of articulation, manner of articulation, and voicing. Thus, for example, /p/ is a voiceless bilabial stop; /v/ is a voiced labiodental fricative; /č/ is a voiceless palatal affricate; /ŋ/ is a voiced velar nasal; and so on.

As was the case with vowels, each consonant phoneme is not really an indivisible unit, but rather a composite of values along these three dimensions. Once again, each such dimension constitutes a **distinctive feature**. For example, from one perspective /p/ and /ŋ/ are not really units in themselves, but rather each is a bundle of feature values, as follows.

$$/p/ \quad = \quad \begin{bmatrix} +\text{bilabial} \\ +\text{stop} \\ -\text{voice} \end{bmatrix} \qquad /\eta/ \quad = \quad \begin{bmatrix} +\text{velar} \\ +\text{nasal} \\ +\text{voice} \end{bmatrix}$$

Once again, it is important to keep in mind that phonemes and distinctive features are theoretical constructs within a theory of phonology. Phonemes are postu-

| | | Bilabial | Labiodental | Interdental | Alveolar | Palatal | Velar | Glottal |
|---|---|---|---|---|---|---|---|---|
| **Stops** | voiceless | p | | | t | | k | |
| | voiced | b | | | d | | g | |
| **Fricatives** | voiceless | | f | θ | s | š | | h |
| | voiced | | v | ð | z | ž | | |
| **Affricates** | voiceless | | | | | č | | |
| | voiced | | | | | ǰ | | |
| **Nasals** | voiceless | | | | | | | |
| | voiced | m | | | n | | ŋ | |
| **Liquids** | voiceless | | | | | | | |
| | voiced | | | | l | r | | |
| **Glides** | voiceless | | | | | | | |
| | voiced | w | | | | y | | |

**FIGURE 6–3.   Consonant phonemes of English.**

lated to account for the fact that the consonants in *pea* and *bee*, for example, are perceived as different. Likewise, distinctive features are postulated to account for the fact that they differ along a particular dimension, namely [±voice].

Before leaving this section, it may be useful to clear up several points of potential confusion. First, the specific symbols used in a phonemic alphabet are of no particular theoretical importance. For example, the symbols /p/ and /b/ in English could, in theory, be replaced by /1/ and /2/. All that is necessary is that one symbol be used to represent each segment that is perceived as unique by speakers of the language in question.

Second, a number of phonemic alphabets for English are currently in use. Thus, for example, you will see the initial phoneme in *yes* sometimes transcribed as /y/ and other times transcribed as /j/. Likewise, you will see the vowel phoneme in *pea* sometimes transcribed as /i/ and other times transcribed as /iy/. Similarly, you will see the second syllable in *mother* sometimes transcribed /ðər/ and other times transcribed as /ɚ/. This is simply a fact of life that anyone who deals with phonology has to get used to. (Actually, with a little practice, it is quite easy to go from one transcription system to another.) Similarly, there are several different distinctive feature systems in current use. The one we have discussed for vowels ([±high], [±low], [±back], [±round], and [±tense]) is fairly standard. The one for consonants ([place], [manner], and [±voice]) is somewhat oversimplified, but is adequate for our purposes here. The "best" set of distinctive features for describing segments found in human languages is a matter of debate and need not concern us here.

Third, you will see some of the phonemes of English charted slightly differently (recall the vowel and consonant charts discussed earlier), depending upon who you read. Thus, the phoneme /h/, which we have characterized as a fricative, is sometimes classified as a glide. Likewise, the phoneme /ɔ/, which we have characterized as a low vowel, is sometimes classified as a mid vowel. And so on. Again, for our purposes these differences are of no great theoretical consequence. What is important is that each phoneme be given a *unique* representation in terms of distinctive features. After all, by calling something a phoneme, we are saying that it is different from any other segment in the language in question.

Fourth, the phonemic representation of the words in a language is not identical for every speaker of that language. For example, the vowels in *cot* and *caught* are different for some speakers of English (*cot* has /a/ and *caught* has /ɔ/) but the same for others (both *cot* and *caught* have /a/). Likewise, some speakers of English perceive the final consonant in *garage* as /ž/, while others perceive it as /ǰ/. Such differences between speakers, however, are more noticeable among the vowels. For example, in the word *think*, some speakers have /ɪ/, others have /i/, and still others have /e/! When such differences are found, they typically involve phonemes that are near each other in articulatory terms. Note, for instance, that /i/, /ɪ/, and /e/ are adjacent on the vowel chart.

Fifth, different languages have different sets of phonemes. English contains phonemes not found in some other languages; and, conversely, English lacks phonemes which are found in other languages. For example, English contains the interdental fricatives /θ/ and /ð/, which are relatively rare among the world's languages. Modern

Greek has them, but French, German, Italian, Persian, and Russian (among others) do not. On the other hand, English entirely lacks front rounded vowels. French, however, has three: /ü/ (high) as in *sucre* 'sugar,' /ö/ (mid) as in *jeu* 'game,' and /œ/ (low) as in *oeuf* 'egg.' (To pronounce the vowel in *sucre*, for example, try to say the vowel in *see* while rounding your lips.)

## Levels of Representation

At the beginning of this chapter, we discussed the idea that two segments might, at the same time, be both the same and different. In order to reconcile this apparent paradox, linguists have developed the notion of **level of representation**. By recognizing more than one such level, we are able to say that two segments are identical on one level of representation, yet different on another. As an illustration of this concept, let's take the fact that specific properties of a phoneme vary according to its position in a word. This variation is sometimes referred to as **allophonic variation**. Consider, for example, the following English words and phrases, each of which contains an instance of the phoneme /t/: *Tim, stem, hit, hit me,* and *Betty.* Each of these instances of /t/ differs systematically from the others. These systematic variations of /t/ are called **allophones** of /t/ and are transcribed in square brackets ([ ]).

The /t/ in *Tim* is aspirated; that is, there is a puff of air following the release of the /t/. (You can test this by holding the palm of your hand about three inches from your lips and saying *Tim*. Feel the rush of air as you release the /t/?) Aspirated /t/ is transcribed [t$^h$].

The /t/ in *stem* is released, but not aspirated; that is, there is no puff of air following the release of the /t/. (You can test this by using the "palm" test just described; say *Tim* and *stem* alternately. Note that there is no rush of air with the /t/ in *stem*.) Released /t/ is transcribed [t].

The /t/ in *hit* can be released or unreleased. If it is unreleased, the tip of the tongue stops at the alveolar ridge. (You can test this by saying *hit* and leaving your tongue at the alveolar ridge after the word is pronounced.) Unreleased /t/ is transcribed [t˺].

The /t/ in *hit me* may be unreleased or it may be a glottal stop. If it is a glottal stop, there is no contact between the tip of the tongue and the alveolar ridge; instead, the vocal cords are brought together and the airflow is stopped momentarily. (You can test this by saying *hit me* without ever raising your tongue to the alveolar ridge. The /t/ you perceive is actually a stop formed with the vocal cords.) A glottal stop is transcribed [ʔ].

The /t/ in *Betty* is an alveolar flap; that is, it is formed by raising the tip of the tongue to the alveolar ridge very rapidly and releasing it. An alveolar flap is more rapid than either [t] or [d]. (You can test this by saying *Betty* with an alveolar flap, which sounds like the normal pronunciation; then with a [t], which sounds British, like Cary Grant; and then with a [d], which sounds like *beddy*.) An alveolar flap is transcribed [ɾ].

Each of these allophones of /t/ is predictable, in that it typically occurs in a particular position within a word or phrase. For example, [tʰ] as in *Tim* occurs when /t/ begins a syllable and is followed by a stressed vowel. [t] as in *stem* occurs when /t/ is followed by a vowel, but does not begin a syllable. [t˺] as in *hit* occurs when /t/ occurs at the end of an utterance. [ʔ] as in *hit me* occurs when /t/ follows a vowel and precedes a consonant. [ɾ] as in *Betty* occurs when /t/ follows a stressed vowel and precedes an unstressed vowel.

Notice the consequences of what we have done. We have essentially justified two levels of phonological representation: the **phonemic**, where phonemes are described, and the **phonetic**, where allophones (i.e., systematic variants) of phonemes are described. This situation is summarized in Figure 6–4, which illustrates the fact that speakers of English perceive the words *Tim, stem, hit, hit me,* and *Betty* as containing instances of the same phoneme, /t/. Yet each instance of /t/ differs on the phonetic level, depending on the context in which /t/ occurs. Thus, by using the concept **level of representation**, we are able to capture the fact that two segments can be both the same (i.e., phonemically) and different (i.e., phonetically).

This discussion raises the issue of how to tell whether two segments are allophones of different phonemes or allophones of the same phoneme. The basic test is to substitute one phone for another. If the substitution changes one word into another, then the two phones **contrast** and are allophones of different phonemes. If they do not, then they are in **free variation** and are allophones of the same phoneme. Consider, for example, *hit* [hɪt˺]. If we substitute [d˺] for [t˺], we get a different word, *hid*. Thus, [t˺] and [d˺] contrast, and therefore are allophones of different phonemes, namely /t/ and /d/, respectively. On the other hand, if we substitute [t] for the [t˺] in [hɪt˺], we are left with the same word, *hit*. Thus, [t˺] and [t] are in free variation, and therefore are allophones of the same phoneme, namely /t/.

There is one other possibility: namely, one in which two phones are not interchangeable because they never occur in the same environment (i.e., position within a word). Consider, for example, the phones [tʰ] and [ɾ]. These never occur in the same context; [tʰ] always occurs before a stressed vowel and [ɾ] always occurs before an unstressed vowel. Thus, in the word *tatter* /tǽtər/ (an accent mark indicates stress), the first /t/ is always [tʰ] and the second /t/ is always [ɾ]. Note that if we try to substitute one phone for the other, we get something that is not even pronounceable in English, namely *[ɾǽtʰər]. Two such phones that never occur in the same

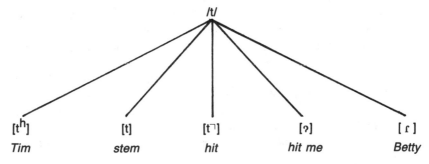

**FIGURE 6–4. Phonemic and phonetic levels of representation.**

context are said to be in **complementary distribution** and are allophones of the same phoneme. In this case, [tʰ] and [ɾ] are allophones of /t/.

Let's summarize the main points made in this section. Linguists have posited the phonemic and phonetic levels of representation to account for the fact that two segments may be both alike (i.e., the same phoneme, e.g., /t/) and unalike (i.e., different allophones, e.g., [tʰ] and [ɾ]) at the same time. If two phones contrast (i.e., substituting one for the other causes a change in meaning), they are allophones of different phonemes. On the other hand, if two phones are either in free variation (i.e., if substituting one for the other does not cause a change in meaning) or in complementary distribution, they are allophones of the same phoneme. The main point to keep in mind is that both the phonemic and phonetic levels and the segments that comprise them are psychological in nature and should not be confused with the speech production mechanism or the speech signal.

## Phonological Rules

Because levels of phonological representation are not always identical to one another, part of phonology consists of rules that essentially translate segments on one level into segments on another level. We will now look at some common phonological rules or processes in English, working from the data to the rules themselves.

### Aspiration

Let's begin with a phonological process that we have already discussed informally, namely Aspiration. Consider the following English words, each of which is accompanied by its phonemic and phonetic representations.

| | | |
|---|---|---|
| *sip* | /síp/ | [síp] |
| *appear* | /əpír/ | [əpʰír] |
| *pepper* | /pépər/ | [pʰépər] |
| *space* | /spés/ | [spés] |
| *papaya* | /pəpáɪyə/ | [pəpʰáɪyə] |

In these data, /p/ has two allophones, [pʰ] and [p]. Our task is to determine under what conditions (i.e., in what environments) /p/ becomes [pʰ]. We might begin by trying to determine what all of the occurrences of [pʰ] have in common. One thing we observe is that all instances of [pʰ] occur immediately before a stressed vowel. Thus we can hypothesize the following rule: /p/ becomes [pʰ] when it occurs before a stressed vowel. This rule, however, will not account for the fact that the [p] in *space* [spés] is not aspirated, even though the following [é] is stressed. Since our rule is not 100 percent accurate, we will have to revise it. We might ask how the [p] in *space* is different from the [pʰ]'s in *appear* [əpʰír], *pepper* [pʰépər], and *papaya* [pəpʰáɪyə]. Note that the [pʰ]'s in *appear*, *pepper*, and *papaya*, in addition to preceding a stressed vowel, also begin a syllable, whereas the [p] in *space* does not. Now we are in a position to hypothesize a revised version of our rule: /p/ becomes [pʰ] when it both begins a syllable and is followed by a stressed vowel. This rule accurately predicts those cases where /p/ becomes [pʰ]; and, by exclusion, it also predicts where /p/ remains unchanged.

We might leave our Aspiration Rule as it stands, in a simple prose statement: /p/ becomes aspirated when it begins a syllable and is followed by a stressed vowel. However, since informal prose statements can often be (unintentionally) vague or ambiguous, phonologists have adopted the practice of stating rules in formal notation. The standard notation for writing phonological rules is as follows.

$$W \rightarrow X \ / \ Y \ \underline{\quad} \ Z$$

This rule states that segment W becomes segment X when it follows Y and precedes Z. (Read the arrow as "becomes" and the slash as "in the following environment.")

The next step is to formalize our Aspiration Rule using this format. Before doing so, however, we need some way of indicating a syllable boundary. One symbol that is often used for this purpose is $. Now we can formalize our rule as follows.

$$\text{/p/} \rightarrow \text{[+aspirated]} \ / \ \$ \ \underline{\quad} \ \underset{\text{[+stress]}}{V}$$

This rule states that the phoneme /p/ becomes aspirated when it begins a syllable (i.e., when there is a syllable boundary to its left) and is followed by a stressed vowel (V). There are several variations on this notation; for example, you might also see this rule written as follows.

$$\text{/p/} \rightarrow \text{[pʰ]} \ / \ \$ \ \underline{\quad} \ \acute{V}$$

The two notations mean exactly the same thing.

Before leaving this example, it is worthwhile to point out that if we were to go beyond the data on which this rule is based and include examples containing the allophones of /t/ and /k/ as well as those of /p/, we would see that /p/, /t/, and /k/ all become aspirated under identical conditions, namely when they begin a syllable and are followed by a stressed vowel. Since /p/, /t/, and /k/ constitute the set of voiceless stops in English, we could state the Aspiration Rule for them all as follows.

$$\begin{bmatrix} +\text{stop} \\ -\text{voice} \end{bmatrix} \rightarrow \text{[+aspirated]} \ / \ \$ \ \underline{\quad} \ \underset{\text{[+stress]}}{V}$$

Note the advantage of stating the rule in terms of distinctive features rather than segments. If we were to use segments, then we would miss the generalization that this rule applies not to /p/, /t/, and /k/ individually, but rather to the intersection of their common properties: [+stop] and [−voice].

## *Vowel Lengthening*

Consider the following English words, each of which is accompanied by its phonemic and phonetic representations.

| *heat* | /hit/ | [hit] |
| *seize* | /siz/ | [siːz] |
| *keel* | /kil/ | [kʰiːl] |
| *leaf* | /lif/ | [lif] |
| *heed* | /hid/ | [hiːd] |
| *cease* | /sis/ | [sis] |
| *leave* | /liv/ | [liːv] |

In these data, /i/ has two allophones, [i] and [iː] (a colon after a vowel indicates that it is lengthened). Once again, our task is to determine under what conditions /i/ becomes [iː]. We might begin by hypothesizing that some property of the consonant to the *left* of the vowel causes it to lengthen. This hypothesis, however, must clearly be wrong. Consider, for example, *seize* [siːz] and *cease* [sis]. The former has a long vowel and the latter has a short vowel, yet in both cases the vowel is preceded by [s]. Thus, the consonant to the left of the vowel obviously has no effect upon the length of the vowel, since here the same consonant precedes both a long vowel and a short vowel.

Alternatively, we might hypothesize that some property of the consonant to the *right* of the vowel causes it to lengthen. Here we have more luck. Note that the vowels in *heat*, *leaf*, and *cease* are short, and each one is followed by a voiceless consonant ([t], [f], and [s] are [−voice]). In contrast, the vowels in *heed*, *leave*, *seize*, and *keel* are long and each one is followed by a voiced consonant ([d], [v], [z], and [l] are [+voice]). Now we are in a position to propose a rule: /i/ becomes [iː] when it precedes a voiced consonant. This rule accurately accounts for our data. It predicts exactly those cases where /i/ becomes [iː] and, by exclusion, it also predicts where /i/ remains unchanged.

Let's go one step further and formalize our rule as follows.

$$/i/ \rightarrow [+long] / \_\_\_ \; \underset{[+voice]}{C}$$

This rule states that the phoneme /i/ becomes lengthened when it precedes a voiced consonant (C). As in our Aspiration Rule discussed earlier, there are variations on this notation. You might also see this rule written as follows.

$$/i/ \rightarrow [iː] / \_\_\_ \; \underset{[+voice]}{C}$$

In addition, if we were to go beyond the data on which we have based this rule and include examples containing allophones of the other vowels in English, we would see that *all* vowels become lengthened under the same conditions, namely when they precede a voiced consonant. Thus, we can state the Vowel Lengthening Rule as follows.

$$V \rightarrow [+\text{long}] \: / \: \underline{\hspace{1.5em}} \quad \underset{[+\text{voice}]}{C}$$

Once again, we can see that phonological rules apply to *classes* of segments (e.g., vowels) rather than to individual segments (e.g., /i/, /e/, /æ/, and so on).

## Vowel Nasalization

Consider the following English words, each of which is accompanied by its phonemic and phonetic representations.

| | | |
|---|---|---|
| *map* | /mæp/ | [mæp] |
| *pan* | /pæn/ | [pæ̃n] |
| *pad* | /pæd/ | [pæd] |
| *Pam* | /pæm/ | [pæ̃m] |
| *gnat* | /næt/ | [næt] |
| *pang* | /pæŋ/ | [pæ̃ŋ] |

In these data, /æ/ has two allophones, [æ] and [æ̃]. (A tilde over a vowel indicates that it is nasalized. A nasalized vowel is perceived as being pronounced with the velum lowered.) As before, our task is to determine under what conditions /æ/ becomes [æ̃]. Before getting started, however, note that the vowels in *pan, pad, Pam,* and *pang* should be long (i.e., [æː]), since they each precede a voiced consonant; yet the phonetic transcription does not indicate this. Pay this no mind; it is common practice in phonology to ignore phonetic details irrelevant to the particular task at hand. In this case, vowel lengthening has nothing to do with vowel nasalization, so it has been ignored. Likewise, the aspiration notation in this data has been omitted, since aspiration has nothing to do with vowel nasalization.

Let's now return to the problem of determining under what conditions /æ/ becomes [æ̃]. First of all, we might assume, naturally enough, that since English has no nasalized vowel phonemes, a phonetically nasalized vowel is the result of being adjacent to a nasal consonant, /m/, /n/, or /ŋ/. Thus, our task is simplified. Is it the preceding or the following nasal consonant that is causing the vowel to become nasalized? The answer is straightforward. Since *map* [mæp] and *gnat* [næt] both contain a preceding nasal consonant but no nasalized vowel, vowel nasalization must not be caused by a preceding nasal consonant. On the other hand, since *pan* [pæ̃n], *Pam* [pæ̃m], and *pang* [pæ̃ŋ] each contain a nasalized vowel followed by a nasal consonant, it must be the following nasal consonant that is causing the vowel nasalization. We are now in a position to propose a rule: /æ/ becomes [æ̃] when it is followed by a nasal consonant. This rule accurately predicts exactly the cases where /æ/ becomes [æ̃]; and, by exclusion, it also predicts where /æ/ remains unchanged.

We can formalize this rule as follows.

$$/æ/ → [+nasal] / \_\_\_ \; C$$
$$[+nasal]$$

Or, alternatively, as follows.

$$/æ/ → [\tilde{æ}] / \_\_\_ \; C$$
$$[+nasal]$$

Once again, if we were to go beyond the data on which our rule is based, we would see that *all* vowels in English become nasalized when they precede a nasal consonant. Thus, we could state the Vowel Nasalization Rule for English as follows.

$$V → [+nasal] / \_\_\_ \; C$$
$$[+nasal]$$

Again, we see that phonological rules apply to classes of segments, rather than to individual segments. It is also worth mentioning that this type of rule, in which a segment becomes more like a neighboring segment in some way, is called an **assimilation** rule. In this case, a vowel becomes more like an adjacent nasal consonant by becoming nasalized itself.

## *Flapping*

Consider the following English words, each of which is accompanied by its phonemic and phonetic representations.

| | | |
|---|---|---|
| *ride* | /ráɪd/ | [ráɪd] |
| *dire* | /dáɪr/ | [dáɪr] |
| *rider* | /ráɪdər/ | [ráɪɾər] |
| *write* | /ráɪt/ | [ráɪt] |
| *tire* | /táɪr/ | [táɪr] |
| *writer* | /ráɪtər/ | [ráɪɾər] |
| *lender* | /lɛ́ndər/ | [lɛ́ndər] |
| *Easter* | /ístər/ | [ístər] |
| *attack* | /ətǽk/ | [ətǽk] |
| *adobe* | /ədóbi/ | [ədóbi] |

In these data, both /t/ and /d/ become [ɾ] (an alveolar flap) under certain circumstances. Our task is to determine under what conditions /t/ and /d/ become [ɾ]. We might begin by noting that /t/ and /d/ never become [ɾ] when they begin or end a word. Thus, the relevant alveolar stops (/t/ and /d/) must be those that occur somewhere in the middle of the word. This narrows the field to *rider, writer, lender, Easter, attack,* and *adobe.* Of these, only the alveolar stops in *rider* and *writer* become [ɾ]. What is different about the environment of /t/ and /d/ in these words? First of all, they occur between vowels. (Compare *lender* and *Easter,* where the stop occurs between a consonant and a vowel.) Second, the vowel to the left is stressed and that to the right is unstressed. (Compare *attack* and *adobe*, where the vowel to the left of the stop is unstressed and that to the right is stressed.) Now we are in a position to propose a rule: /t/ and /d/ become [ɾ] when they occur between two vowels, the first of which is stressed and the second of which is unstressed. This rule accurately accounts for all of the [ɾ]'s in our data. That is, it predicts exactly those cases where /t/ and /d/ become [ɾ]; and, by exclusion, it also predicts where they remain unchanged.

The Flapping Rule, in turn, can be formalized as follows.

$$\begin{bmatrix} +\text{stop} \\ +\text{alveolar} \end{bmatrix} \rightarrow [\text{ɾ}] \; / \; \underset{[+\text{stress}]}{V} \; \underline{\quad} \; \underset{[-\text{stress}]}{V}$$

As usual, there are variations on this notation. You might also see this rule written as follows.

$$\begin{Bmatrix} /t/ \\ /d/ \end{Bmatrix} \rightarrow [\text{ɾ}] \; / \; \acute{V} \underline{\quad} \breve{V}$$

A breve ( ˘ ) above a vowel indicates that it is unstressed.

Flapping is a special case of **neutralization**, a process that obliterates the contrast between two segments in a particular environment.

### Nasal Deletion

Consider the following English words, each of which is accompanied by its phonemic and phonetic representations.

| | | |
|---|---|---|
| *can* | /kæn/ | [kæ̃n] |
| *cad* | /kæd/ | [kæd] |
| *canned* | /kænd/ | [kæ̃nd] |
| *cat* | /kæt/ | [kæt] |
| *can't* | /kænt/ | [kæ̃t] |

In these data, two phonological rules apply. First, the Vowel Nasalization Rule applies in *can* [kæ̃n], *canned* [kæ̃nd], and *can't* [kæ̃t]. Second, a rule deleting a nasal consonant applies, so that *can't* /kænt/ becomes [kæ̃t]. What we need to do is determine (a) under what conditions Nasal Deletion applies, and (b) in what order Vowel Nasalization and Nasal Deletion must apply. (It should be noted that not all speakers have the Nasal Deletion Rule.)

Consider first the Nasal Deletion Rule itself. Note that the /n/ in *can't* is deleted, but that in *can* and *canned* is not. How can we differentiate the /n/ in *can't* from that in *can* and *canned*? One difference is that the /n/ in *can't* is followed by a /t/, while the /n/ in the other two words is not. We are now in a position to propose a rule: delete /n/ when it precedes /t/. This rule accounts for the absence of [n] in *can't*; and, by exclusion, it also accounts for the presence of [n] in *can* and *canned*.

We can formalize this rule as follows.

$$/\text{n}/ \rightarrow \varnothing / \underline{\quad} /\text{t}/$$

The symbol ø indicates the null set; thus, the rule reads: /n/ is deleted (i.e., "becomes nothing") when it occurs before a /t/. As in our other cases, if we were to go beyond the data on which we have based this rule, we would see that *any* nasal (/m,n,ŋ/) is deleted in English when it occurs before *any* voiceless stop (/p,t,k/) within the same syllable. Thus, we can state the Nasal Deletion Rule for English as follows.

$$\begin{matrix} \text{C} \\ [+\text{nasal}] \end{matrix} \rightarrow \varnothing / \underline{\quad} \begin{bmatrix} +\text{stop} \\ -\text{voice} \end{bmatrix} \$$$

This brings us to our second question. To transform a phonemic form such as *can't* /kænt/ into the phonetic form [kæ̃t], which rule must apply first: Nasal Deletion or Vowel Nasalization? The most straightforward way of answering this question is to try both orders. The one that accurately maps the phonemic representation into the phonetic representation is correct. First, let's try Nasal Deletion before Vowel Nasalization, as illustrated in the following diagram.

| | |
|---|---|
| Phonemic Level | /kænt/ |
| Nasal Deletion | kæt |
| Vowel Nasalization | cannot apply |
| Phonetic Level | [kæt] |

This ordering is obviously wrong; it yields [kæt], which is the phonetic representation of *cat*, not *can't*. The problem is that the nasal /n/ must be present at the point at which Vowel Nasalization applies. In this case, Nasal Deletion has removed the /n/ before Vowel Nasalization has had a chance to apply, thus blocking the application of the Vowel Nasalization Rule.

Now let's try Vowel Nasalization before Nasal Deletion, as follows.

| | |
|---|---|
| Phonemic Level | /kænt/ |
| Vowel Nasalization | kæ̃nt |
| Nasal Deletion | kæ̃t |
| Phonetic Level | [kæ̃t] |

This ordering is correct; it yields [kæ̃t], which is the phonetic representation of *can't*. In this case, the /n/ is present to trigger Vowel Nasalization. After Vowel Nasalization applies, the /n/ is deleted via Nasal Deletion. Thus, the correct ordering between the two rules is Vowel Nasalization first and then Nasal Deletion.

Thus, in this section we have seen that phonological rules are necessary for mapping (or translating) one level of phonological representation into another. Moreover, we have seen that more than one such rule may apply in this mapping process, in which case the rules may have to apply in a particular order. Before leaving this section, however, let's return to one of the forms in our last example: *can't.* Our discussion of this form assumed the following phonemic and phonetic representations.

Phonemic            /kænt/
Phonetic            [kæ̃t]

We then proposed two phonological rules, Vowel Nasalization and Nasal Deletion, to account for the relationship between these two levels of representation.

What we want to focus on now is the claim that there is no phonetic nasal segment in *can't* [kæ̃t]. In other words, what evidence do we have for assuming that the nasal segment /n/ in *can't* is deleted phonetically? There is one approach to this question that linguists characteristically do *not* take, namely inspection of the physical speech signal itself. Under this approach, we might make a recording of a speaker uttering the word *can't* and then make a spectrogram (i.e., voiceprint) of the utterance. A spectrogram is essentially a picture of the acoustic characteristics of an utterance. Since nasals typically display certain acoustic characteristics, we might look at the spectrogram and try to determine if these specific acoustic properties are present. If they are, then we might conclude that the nasal segment has *not* been deleted; if they are not, then we might conclude that the nasal segment *has* been deleted. A number of researchers have tried this approach and have not come to any unequivocal conclusions. Sometimes physical evidence of the nasal segment is found; other times it is not. This state of affairs, however, should not come as too much of a surprise. As we have already seen, segments are psychological units which a speaker *imposes* on the speech signal; they are not part of the physical signal itself.

Linguists, on the other hand, would approach the problem from an entirely different perspective, namely by examining the hypothesized *psychological* system. That is, linguists would compare what they could explain by assuming the nasal *has* been deleted to what they could explain by assuming the nasal has *not* been deleted. To see how this line of reasoning works, consider the following English words: *caddy, catty, candy,* and *canty.* (*Canty* means 'cheerful' and can be pronounced exactly like the phrase *can't he.*) Each of these words is given in the following chart, along with its phonemic and phonetic representations.

| | | |
|---|---|---|
| *caddy* | /kǽdi/ | [kǽɾi] |
| *catty* | /kǽti/ | [kǽɾi] |
| *candy* | /kǽndi/ | [kǽndi] |
| *canty* | /kǽnti/ | [kǽɾi] |

Note, first, that the /d/ and /t/ in *caddy* and *catty,* respectively, become [ɾ]'s. This, of course, is predicted by our Flapping Rule, which states that an alveolar stop between a stressed vowel and an unstressed vowel becomes a flap. Note, second, that the /d/ in *candy* does not become [ɾ]. (To check this claim, try to pronounce *candy* with a flap; it comes out sounding like *canty*.) This, too, is predicted by our Flapping Rule: since the /d/ in *candy* does not occur between two vowels (but rather between a consonant /n/ and a vowel /i/), it does not become [ɾ] but instead remains [d] on the phonetic level of representation. So far, so good.

Now, however, note that the /t/ in *canty* does become [ɾ]. (This is not to say the word *must* be pronounced with a flap—certainly [kǽnti] is possible—only that it *may* be pronounced with a flap.) This fact has no transparent explanation. That is, the /t/ in *canty* occurs between a nasal /n/ and a vowel /i/ on the phonemic level of representation. Thus, the Flapping Rule should not be able to apply to /kǽnti/. This leaves us with an unexplained fact: the /d/ in *candy* does not become [ɾ], but the /t/ in *canty* does!

One way out of this bind is to *assume* that the phonology of English contains a rule of Nasal Deletion which deletes nasal consonants before voiceless stops. Once we make this assumption, then we have a ready explanation for the flap in *canty* but not in *candy*. The mapping between the phonemic representation and the phonetic representation for these two words is given here.

|  | *canty* | *candy* |
| --- | --- | --- |
| Phonemic Level | /kǽnti/ | /kǽndi/ |
| Vowel Nasalization | kǽnti | kǽndi |
| Nasal Deletion | kǽti | cannot apply |
| Flapping | kǽɾi | cannot apply |
| Phonetic Level | [kǽɾi] | [kǽndi] |

Since Nasal Deletion cannot apply to *candy* (Nasal Deletion applies only when the nasal consonant precedes a voiceless stop), there is no way that Flapping can apply.

It is important to understand that this difference in behavior between *candy* and *canty* is not just an isolated example in English. There are numerous parallel cases where Flapping can apply to /t/ after a nasal consonant but not to /d/: for example, *Mindy* [mĩndi], *minty* [mĩɾi]; *candor* [kǽndər], *canter* [kǽɾər], *pander* [pǽndər], *panter* [pǽtər] 'one who pants'; *plunder* [plʌ̃ndər], *punter* [pʌ̃ɾər]; *bandy* [bǽndi], *panty* [pǽɾi]; and so on.

## Summary

Let's review what we have done. We started with five observations about the pronunciation of words. However, we had no unified explanation for these phenomena. Thus, we constructed a theory of phonology to account for our original observations. This theory is based (indirectly) upon the physiology of the vocal tract and makes use of such concepts as segment, distinctive feature, allophonic variation, levels of representation, and phonological rules. These theoretical constructs were developed by linguists in order to help explain the observations in (1–5). This theory may turn out to be incorrect in part, but it is the best working hypothesis of the internal structure of phonology that we have at the present time.

In addition, it is important to understand that there is more to the study of phonology than we have covered in this one short chapter. However, you have now been exposed to the basic ideas in the field; if you want to learn more about the subject, consult the supplementary readings. Also, you may want to check your understanding of the material in this chapter by working through the practice problems and solutions that follow the readings. As usual, we've added 50 exercises for you to do on your own.

## Supplementary Readings

### Primary

Anderson, S. R. (1985). *Phonology in the twentieth century.* Chicago: University of Chicago Press.

Chomsky, N., and Halle, M. (1968). *The sound pattern of English.* New York: Harper and Row.

Jakobson, R., Fant, G., and Halle, M. (1963). *Preliminaries to speech analysis.* Cambridge, MA: MIT Press.

### Secondary

Schane, S. (1973). *Generative phonology.* Englewood Cliffs, NJ: Prentice-Hall.

Schane, S., and Bendixen, B. (1978). *Workbook in generative phonology.* Englewood Cliffs, NJ: Prentice-Hall.

Wolfram, W., and Johnson, R. (1982). *Phonological analysis: Focus on American English.* Washington, DC: Center for Applied Linguistics.

Hogg, R., and McCully, C. B. (1987). *Metrical phonology: A coursebook.* Cambridge, England: Cambridge University Press.

It may be best to approach these works in the following order. Wolfram and Johnson is an introductory text dealing solely with American English. Schane and the accompanying workbook provide an excellent introduction to "doing" phonology; they deal primarily with non-English data. Hogg and McCully is a textbook dealing with word stress in English. It represents the current interest in "multi-tiered" phonology, which treats the syllable as hierarchically structured rather than as simply a string of linear segments.

Anderson is an excellent reference book dealing with the development of phonology as a field and its key figures. Chomsky and Halle is the classic statement of linear generative phonology (the theory discussed in this chapter), and Jakobson, Fant, and Halle is one of the earliest comprehensive treatments of distinctive feature theory. These last two works, however, are difficult going and are now mainly of historical interest.

## Practice

1. Give the English phonemic symbol that corresponds to each of the following articulatory descriptions.
    a. low front spread lax vowel
    b. voiced velar nasal
    c. voiced interdental fricative
    d. high back round lax vowel

e.  voiced palatal glide

2.  Give the English phonemes that correspond to the following feature specifications.

a. $\begin{bmatrix} -\text{back} \\ +\text{tense} \end{bmatrix}$

b. $\begin{bmatrix} +\text{fricative} \\ -\text{voice} \end{bmatrix}$

c. $\begin{bmatrix} +\text{bilabial} \\ +\text{voice} \end{bmatrix}$

d. [+glide]

e. $\begin{bmatrix} +\text{back} \\ +\text{round} \end{bmatrix}$

3.  Write the following English words in phonemic transcription.

a.  thrush
b.  breathe
c.  they
d.  fox
e.  choose

4.  Identify the following English words.

a.  [ǽtʼ]
b.  [sǽrərn]
c.  [ǰɔːz]
d.  [ətʰɛ́ːnčə̃ːn]
e.  [óʔmiːl]

5.  Identify the error (omission, wrong segment, or extra segment) in the transcriptions of the following words:

a.  fine        /faɪne/
b.  took        /tuk/
c.  correct     /kərrékt/
d.  finger      /fíŋər/
e.  sigh        /saɪh/

6.  In English, the phoneme /g/ has two allophones: the voiced velar stop [g] and the voiced palatal stop [ɟ]. Based on the following phonetic representations, (a) determine the conditions under which /g/ becomes [ɟ]; and then (b) try to formalize the rule using the notation developed in this chapter.

| god   | [gaːd]  | gone | [gɔ̃ːn] |
| geese | [ɟis]   | gain | [ɟẽːn]  |
| ghoul | [guːl]  | good | [guːd]  |
| gab   | [ɟæːb]  | gear | [ɟɪːr]  |

7.  Like /g/, the phoneme /k/ in English exhibits exactly the same sort of allophonic variation between [k] (velar) and [c] (palatal): [c] occurs before /i,ɪ,e,ɛ,æ/ and [k] occurs before

other vowels. (a) State the rules for the allphones of both /k/ and /g/ and (b) put the rule into formal notation.

8. Consider the following data from Droolingua, a hypothetical language attributed to employees of the Pentagon. There are no voiced stop phonemes in Droolingua, only voiceless ones. Each one has three allophones: a voiceless stop, a voiceless aspirated stop, and a voiced stop.

| | |
|---|---|
| [pʰiːk] | 'cornflake' |
| [padan] | 'Mr. Shekel' |
| [loban] | 'oil of olay' |
| [piga] | 'bleat' |
| [suːbu] | 'Waring blender' |
| [tʰaːp] | 'larvae' |
| [kʰaːgot] | 'wooden teeth' |
| [kap] | 'McNeese State University' |
| [pibu] | 'cortex' |
| [setnok] | 'variorum edition' |
| [kʰuːdan] | 'friends of the library' |
| [lupnot] | 'special hat' |
| [tuknes] | 'processed cheese food' |

a.  Under what conditions does a stop become aspirated?

b.  Formalize the rule in (a).

c.  Under what conditions does a stop become voiced?

d.  Formalize the rule in (c).

9. In the fifteenth century, English underwent what is known as the Great Vowel Shift, which entailed a change in the quality of Middle English long vowels.

| | *Middle English* | *Modern English* |
|---|---|---|
| ride | /i/ | /aɪ/ |
| feet | /e/ | /i/ |
| bade | /æ/ | /e/ |
| house | /u/ | /aʊ/ |
| goose | /o/ | /u/ |
| boat | /a/ | /o/ |

a.  In what general direction did the vowels move?

b.  Assuming this direction of movement, what relative height do the diphthongs /aɪ/ and /aʊ/ have in Modern English?

10. A few years ago in the Baton Rouge *Morning Advocate*, a headline appeared stating *Nurses Demand More Imput* (instead of *Input*).

a.  What feature change occurs when *input* becomes *imput*?

b.  What phonological property of the /p/ in *input* might cause this change?

c.  Why would this change ordinarily not occur in forms like *input*, even though it regularly occurs in forms like *impossible*? (Hint: stress.)

# Answers

The following answers are in some cases not the only ones possible. Discussion of alternative answers is part of the practice.

**1.** a. /æ/  
   b. /ŋ/  
   c. /ð/  
   d. /ʊ/  
   e. /y/

**2.** a. /i,e/  
   b. /f,θ,s,š,h/  
   c. /b,m,w/  
   d. /w,y/  
   e. /u,ʊ,o,ɔ/

**3.** a. /θrʌš/  
   b. /brið/  
   c. /ðe/  
   d. /faks/  
   e. /čuz/

**4.** a. aunt/ant  
   b. Saturn  
   c. jaws  
   d. attention  
   e. oatmeal

**5.** a. extra segment    /faɪn/  
   b. wrong segment    /tʊk/  
   c. extra segment    /kərɛ́kt/  
   d. omitted segment    /fíŋgər/  
   e. extra segment    /saɪ/

**6.** a. /g/ becomes [ɟ] when it is followed by a front vowel. (Note: /g/, a velar segment, becomes "fronted" to a palatal segment when it is followed by a "front" vowel.)

   b. $\begin{bmatrix} +stop \\ +velar \\ +voice \end{bmatrix} \rightarrow [+palatal] / \underline{\quad} \begin{matrix} V \\ [-back] \end{matrix}$

**7.** a. Velar stops become palatal stops when they occur before front vowels.

   b. $\begin{bmatrix} +stop \\ +velar \end{bmatrix} \rightarrow [+palatal] / \underline{\quad} \begin{matrix} V \\ [-back] \end{matrix}$

**8.** a. Stops become aspirated when they occur before long vowels.  
   b. [+stop] → [+aspirated] / ___ V  
                  [+long]  
   c. Stops become voiced when they occur between two vowels.  
   d. [+stop] → [+voice] / V ___ V

**9.** a. up  
   b. the highest

**10.** a. [+alveolar] becomes [+bilabial]  
   b. [+bilabial]  
   c. Change does not occur in stressed syllables (*ínput*) but does occur in unstressed syllables (*impóssible*).

## *Exercises*

1. For each group, identify the segment that differs in manner of articulation from the other segments.
   a. /n/, /f/, /s/, /z/
   b. /v/, /ð/, /g/, /ž/
   c. /l/, /r/, /d/

2. For each group, identify the segment that differs in place of articulation from the other three.
   a. /s/, /č/, /t/, /n/
   b. /k/, /n/, /g/, /ŋ/
   c. /θ/, /p/, /b/, /m/

3. For each group, identify the segment that differs in voicing from the other three.
   a. /m/, /g/, /ǰ/, /s/
   b. /n/, /f/, /θ/, /p/
   c. /b/, /p/, /r/, /v/

4. Describe each of the following consonant phonemes of English in terms of voicing, and place and manner of articulation.
   a. /ð/
   b. /h/
   c. /l/
   d. /f/
   e. /d/
   f. /ž/

5. Describe each of the following vowel phonemes of English in terms of tongue height, frontness, lip rounding, and tenseness.
   a. /æ/                  e. /a/
   b. /o/                  f. /ɔ/
   c. /ɛ/                  g. /ʊ/
   d. /ʌ/                  h. /i/

6. The transcription /pʌr/ represents the word
   a. pair                 d. pear
   b. peer                 e. purr
   c. par

7. The transcription /taɪp/ represents the word
   a. tap          b. tape          c. tip          d. type

8. The transcription /ič/ represents the word
   a. edge         b. each          c. etch          d. itch

9. The transcription /θaɪ/ represents the word
   a. thy          b. thou          c. thigh         d. thee

**10.** The transcription /rɪč/ represents the word

    a.  reach        b.  rich        c.  ridge        d.  reich

**11.** The transcription /ðiz/ represents the word

    a.  thighs        b.  these        c.  this        d.  tease

**12.** Which transcription represents the word *look*:

    a.  /lʌk/                d.  /lok/
    b.  /luk/                e.  /lak/
    c.  /lʊk/

**13.** Which transcription represents the word *fleece*:

    a.  /flaɪz/             d.  /flɪz/
    b.  /fles/              e.  /flis/
    c.  /flɪs/

**14.** Match each of the following words with its phonemic transcription.

    a.  case               ___ /kiz/
    b.  keys               ___ /kɔz/
    c.  cause            ___ /kyuz/
    d.  cues              ___ /kes/

**15.** Match each of the following words with its phonemic transcription.

    a.  sues               ___ /sɔs/
    b.  sews              ___ /siz/
    c.  cease            ___ /sis/
    d.  sighs            ___ /suz/
    e.  sees             ___ /sɪs/
    f.  says              ___ /sɛz/
    g.  Sis                ___ /saɪz/
    h.  sauce            ___/soz/

**16.** Match each of the following words with its phonemic transcription.

    a.  course          ___ /karz/
    b.  cures            ___ /kʌrs/
    c.  cars              ___ /kyurz/
    d.  cares           ___ /kɛrz/
    e.  curse            ___ /kʊrz/
    f.  Coors            ___ /kors/

**17.** Match each of the following words with its phonemic transcription.

    a.  thigh              ___ /ðaʊ/
    b.  thou              ___ /θaɪ/
    c.  thee               ___ /ðe/
    d.  they              ___ /ði/
    e.  though          ___ /θɔ/
    f.  thaw              ___ /ðo/

**18.** Match each of the following words with its phonemic transcription.

a. cough      ___ /koč/
b. cuff      ___ /kag/
c. cog      ___ /kɔf/
d. couch      ___ /kaʊ/
e. coach      ___ /kʌf/
f. cow      ___ /kaʊč/

19. Identify the error (omission, wrong segment, or extra segment) in the following transcriptions; then correct each transcription.

    a. mother      /mʌ́ðər/
    b. speed      /sped/
    c. receipt      /rəsípt/
    d. ankle      /ǽŋəl/
    e. crate      /cret/

20. A "linguistics" teacher once explained that the misspelling *would of* for *would have* is caused by Final Devoicing, a rule which changes a word-final obstruent from voiced to voiceless. Explain how the teacher was fooled into making this faulty analysis.

21. Consider the following rule:

$$\begin{bmatrix} /t/ \\ /d/ \end{bmatrix} \rightarrow [\mathrm{ɾ}] \ / \ \acute{V} \_\_\_ \ \check{V}$$

Which of the following statements corresponds to this rule?

    a. A /t/ or a /d/ is unreleased when it occurs between a stressed vowel and an unstressed vowel.
    b. A /t/ or a /d/ becomes a glottal stop when it occurs between a stressed vowel and an unstressed vowel.
    c. A /t/ or a /d/ becomes an /r/ when it occurs between a stressed vowel and an unstressed vowel.
    d. A /t/ or a /d/ is unreleased when it occurs word-finally.
    e. none of the above.

22. Choose the formal statement that is equivalent to the following informal statement: A vowel is lengthened when it occurs at the end of a word. (# indicates a word boundary.)

    a. V → [V:] / # ___          c. V → [V:] / ___ C #
    b. V → [V:] / # ___ C        d. V → [V:] / ___ #

23. Identify the formal statement that is equivalent to the following informal statement: A voiceless consonant becomes voiced when it occurs between two vowels.

    a. C → [+voice] / $\check{V}$ ___ $\acute{V}$        c. C → [+voice] / V ___ V
    b. C → [+voice] / VV ___          d. C → [+voice] / ___VV

24. Identify the formal statement that is equivalent to the following informal statement: A voiceless stop becomes aspirated when it begins a stressed syllable.

    a.    C → [+asp] / $ ___ $\check{V}$        c. C → [+asp] / # $\acute{V}$ ___

$$\begin{bmatrix} -\text{voice} \\ +\text{stop} \end{bmatrix}$$               $$\begin{bmatrix} -\text{voice} \\ +\text{stop} \end{bmatrix}$$

b.    C → [+asp] / \$ ___ V́      d.   C → [+asp] / ___ V́ #
$$\begin{bmatrix} -\text{voice} \\ +\text{stop} \end{bmatrix}$$                      $$\begin{bmatrix} -\text{voice} \\ +\text{stop} \end{bmatrix}$$

25. Which informal statement is equivalent to the following formal statement: V → Ṽ / ___ N (N indicates any nasal consonant.)

   a. A vowel becomes nasalized when it occurs after a nasal consonant.
   b. A vowel becomes stressed when it occurs after a nasal consonant.
   c. A vowel becomes nasalized when it occurs before a nasal consonant.
   d. A nasal consonant is replaced by a nasalized vowel when it occurs before another nasal consonant.
   e. A nasalized vowel is inserted before a nasal consonant.

26. Correct the error in the following phonological rule of English.

   V → [−nas] / ___ C
                [+nas]

27. Correct the error in the following phonological rule of English.

        C → [ɾ] / V́ ___ V̆
   $$\begin{bmatrix} +\text{alv} \\ +\text{fric} \end{bmatrix}$$

28. Correct the error in the following phonological rule of English.

   V → [+long] / ___ C
                   [−vce]

29. Correct the error in the following phonological rule of English.

       C → [+asp] / \$ ___ V́
   $$\begin{bmatrix} +\text{vce} \\ +\text{stop} \end{bmatrix}$$

30. Correct the rule below so that it corresponds to the following informal statement: A voiced stop becomes voiceless when it occurs word-finally.

       C → [−vce] / # ___
   [+stop]

31. Correct the rule below so that it corresponds to the following informal statement: A nasal segment is deleted when it occurs before a voiceless stop.

   ø → C / ___ C
     [+nas]     $$\begin{bmatrix} +\text{stop} \\ -\text{vce} \end{bmatrix}$$

32. Consider the English word *prove*. Which of the following words is related to it phonologically and semantically? (You may need to consult a dictionary.)

   a. prawn               d. poor
   b. proverb            e. poverty
   c. probation

33. Consider the following pairs: *wife-wives, knife-knives, elf-elves*. Which of the following rules is most likely to account for the differences betweeen the members of each pair?

a. Flapping
b. Vowel Nasalization
c. Aspiration

d. Nasal Deletion
e. none of the above

**34.** Consider the following forms:

| cloth | /klɔθ/ | clothing | /kloðɪŋ/ |
|-------|--------|----------|----------|
| north | /nɔrθ/ | northern | /nɔrðərn/ |
| south | /sauθ/ | southern | /sʌðərn/ |
| bath | /bæθ/ | bathing | /beðɪŋ/ |

In what environment does /θ/ show up as /ð/?

What type of phonological process accounts for this change?

**35.** German contains both a palatal fricative [ç] and a velar fricative [x]. Consider the following forms (from Hyman [1975: 63]):

| siech | [ziːç] | 'sickly' | Buch | [buːx] | 'book' |
|-------|--------|----------|------|--------|--------|
| mich | [mɪç] | 'me' | hoch | [hoːx] | 'high' |
| Pech | [pɛç] | 'pitch' | noch | [nɔx] | 'still' |
| | | | Bach | [bax] | 'brook' |

Based on these data, what vowel feature determines whether the following fricative is palatal or velar?

**36.** Spanish contains both voiced stops [b,d,g] and the corresponding voiced fricatives [β,ð,ɣ]. Consider the following forms (from Hyman [1975: 62] and Halle [1985: 241]):

| [baŋka] | 'bench' | [la βaŋka] | 'the bench' |
|---------|---------|------------|-------------|
| [baho] | 'low' | [a βaho] | 'below' |
| [demora] | 'delay' | [la ðemora] | 'the delay' |
| [donde] | 'where' | [a ðonde] | 'where to' |
| [gana] | 'desire' | [la ɣana] | 'the desire' |
| [gwardar] | 'to watch' | [a ɣwardar] | 'to wait for' |

Based on these data, write a phonological rule for Spanish stating when a voiced stop becomes the corresponding voiced fricative.

**37.** Consider the following Swahili data (from Schane & Bendixen [1978:50]):

| [ubao] | 'a plank' | [ukuni] | 'a stick' |
|--------|-----------|---------|-----------|
| [wayo] | 'a footprint' | [ugwe] | 'a string' |
| [wimbo] | 'a song' | [wembe] | 'a razor' |

In each form, the initial segment represents a prefix indicating singular number.

a. What phonological property do [u] and [w] have in common?
b. How do [u] and [w] differ phonologically?
c. What determines whether the singular prefix shows up as [u] or [w]?

**38.** Consider the following pairs of words:

divine/divinity     serene/serenity     opaque/opacity

a. Transcribe the stressed vowel in each of these words.
b. How do the members of each pair differ? (Hint: assume /aɪ/ is higher than /i/.)

**39.** Consider the following two sets of correspondences between non-Germanic and Germanic languages.

|   | *Non-Germanic* | *Germanic* |
|---|---|---|
| A. | *p*ater (Latin) | *f*ather |
|   | *t*res (Spanish) | *th*ree |
|   | *c*ardiac (Greek) | *h*eart |
| B. | kanni*b*is (Greek) | hem*p* |
|   | *d*os (Spanish) | *t*wo |
|   | *g*ynecologist | *q*ueen |

These data indicate that Germanic languages have undergone two phonological changes that non-Germanic languages have not experienced.

a. For each set, transcribe the phonemic change from non-Germanic to Germanic.

b. How can the change in set A be characterized in terms of classes of segments? (Hint: assume /h/ is a velar fricative.)

c. How can the change in set B be characterized in terms of classes of segments?

d. Which change (i.e., that in set A or set B) had to occur first? Why?

**40.** Consider the following data:

| inaccurate | [ɪnækyərət] | indirect | [ɪndərɛkt] |
|---|---|---|---|
| impossible | [ɪmpasəbəl] | imbalance | [ɪmbæləns] |
| incomplete | [ɪŋkəmplit] | ingrate | [ɪŋgret] |
| intolerable | [ɪntalərəbəl] | inept | [ɪnɛpt] |

a. What three phonetic forms does the prefix take in these words?

b. What determines the phonetic form of the prefix?

c. Which of the three forms of the prefix appears to be the most basic? Which words serve as evidence for your answer?

**41. Phonotactics** is the study of the permissible sequences of segments allowed in a language. For example, English has phonotactic restrictions on the sequence of consonants that can begin a word. Consider the following data.

| step | /stɛp/ | *sdep | */sdɛp/ |
|---|---|---|---|
| skip | /skɪp/ | *sgip | */sgip/ |
| spot | /spat/ | *sbot | */sbat/ |

State the phonotactic restriction that rules out the ungrammatical sequences.

**42.** Consider the following Yoruba data (adapted from Schane & Bendixen [1978: 49]):

|   | *Stem* | *Present Progressive* |
|---|---|---|
| 'stop' | [kuro] | [ŋkuro] |
| 'press sand' | [tɛyɔnrin] | [ntɛyɔnrin] |
| 'spoil' | [baǰɛ] | [mbaǰɛ] |

Assume that [ŋ,n,m] are variants of /n/.

a. State the morphological rule for forming the present progressive form of the verb.

b. State the phonological rule for determining the shape of the present progressive affix.

Now consider the following Yoruba data:

|   |   |   |
|---|---|---|
| 'say' | [wi] | [ŋwi] |
|   |   | *[mwi] |

c. What is the most accurate way of describing the place of articulation of [w] in Yoruba?

**43.** Consonants are often subdivided into obstruents (i.e., stops, fricatives, and affricates) and sonorants (nasals, liquids, and glides). Now consider the following English data.

| /fɔlt/ | /its/ | /paint/ | /ist/ |
|--------|-------|---------|-------|
| */nɪds/ | /old/ | */isd/ | /izd/ |
| /lænd/ | /nidz/ | */izt/ | */itz/ |

    a.  What English word does each non-starred form represent?

    b.  What phonotactic generalization can be stated using the category "obstruent" that cannot be stated using the category "consonant"?

**44.**  a.  Consider the speech error *cuff of coffee* for *cup of coffee* (from Fromkin [1971: 30]). This is known as an **anticipation** error, where a segment that occurs later in a series is repeated in an earlier position. What segment is anticipated in this example?

    b.  Consider the speech error *gave the goy* for *gave the boy* (from Fromkin [1971: 30]). This is known as a **perseveration** error, where a segment that occurs earlier in a series is repeated in a later position. What segment is perseverated in this example?

    c.  Consider the speech error *the nipper is zarrow* for *the zipper is narrow* (from Fromkin [1971: 31]). This is known as a **metathesis** error, where two segments in a series switch places. What segments are metathesized in this example?

**45.** Consider the speech error *pig and vat* for *big and fat* (from Fromkin [1971: 36]). This example involves the metathesis of the values of a feature rather than two segments. What feature is involved in this example?

**46.** Consider the speech error *piss and stretch* for *pitch and stress* (from Fromkin [1971: 33]).

    a.  Does this error involve anticipation, perseveration, or metathesis?

    b.  Does it involve an entire segment or a feature specification?

    c.  What are the segments or feature specifications that are involved?

**47.** Consider the speech error *Cedars of Lemadon* for *Cedars of Lebanon* (from Fromkin [1971: 35]).

    a.  Does this error involve anticipation, perseveration, or metathesis?

    b.  Does it involve an entire segment or a feature specification?

    c.  What are the segments or feature specifications that are involved?

**48.** Syllables are composed of a **nucleus** (i.e., the vowel), an **onset** (i.e., the consonant(s) preceding the nucleus), and a **coda** (i.e., the consonant(s) following the nucleus).

    a.  Consider the speech error *one swell foop* for *one fell swoop*.

       (i)  Does this error involve anticipation, perseveration, or metathesis?

      (ii)  Does it involve a feature specification, a segment, or a larger unit?

     (iii)  What is the unit that is involved?

    b.  Consider the speech error *the hags flung out* for *the flags hung out*.

       (i)  Does this error involve anticipation, perseveration, or metathesis?

      (ii)  Does it involve a feature specification, a segment, or a larger unit?

     (iii)  What is the unit that is involved?

**49.** English contains numerous singular/plural pairs such as *goose/geese, foot/feet, mouse/mice*. These plurals were formed historically by a process known as **umlaut**, whereby the vowel in a plural suffix had an effect on the vowel in the root. Then the suffix was lost. The vowel in the root was subsequently changed by the Great Vowel Shift. For example, the form *geese* developed as follows:

### *Root*        *Plural Suffix*

/gos/    + /i/
/ges/    + /i/ – via umlaut
/ges/    + ø  – via loss of suffix
/gis/    + ø  – via Great Vowel Shift

a.  What feature changes are required to turn /o/ in English into /e/?

b.  How might the vowel suffix /i/ have caused the change from /o/ to /e/?

**50.** Assume the following division among all English vowels.

| [+long] | [–long] |
|---------|---------|
| /i/ | /ɪ/ |
| /e/ | /ɛ/ |
| /u/ | /æ/ |
| /o/ | /ʌ,ə/ |
| /aɪ/ | /a/ |
| /aʊ/ | |
| /ɔɪ/ | |

a.  Consider the following data, adapted from Hogg & McCully (1987:11):

| design | /dəzaɪn/ | cocaine | /koken/ |
|--------|----------|---------|---------|
| balloon | /bəlun/ | domain | /domen/ |

(i)  Indicate the primary stress in each word by placing an acute accent (´) over the appropriate vowel.

(ii) State in words the rule assigning primary stress to the correct vowel in these words.

b.  Consider the following data, adapted from Hogg & McCully (1987: 11):

| museum | /myuziəm/ | fluid | /fluɪd/ |
|--------|-----------|-------|---------|
| aroma | /əromə/ | stupid | /stupɪd/ |

(i)  Indicate the primary stress in each word by placing an acute accent (´) over the appropriate vowel.

(ii) State in words the rule assigning primary stress to the correct vowel in these words.

c.  Consider the following data, adapted from Hogg and McCully (1987: 11):

| polygamy | /pəlɪgəmɪ/ | precipice | /prɛsɪpɪs/ |
|----------|------------|-----------|------------|
| elephant | /ɛləfənt/ | leviathan | /ləvaɪəθən/ |

(i)  Indicate the primary stress in each word by placing an acute accent (´) over the appropriate vowel.

(ii) State in words the rule assigning primary stress to the correct vowel in these words.

d.  Consider the following data:

| design | /dəzaɪn/ |
|--------|----------|
| museum | /myuziəm/ |
| elephant | /ɛləfənt/ |

(i) Indicate the primary stress in each word by placing an acute accent (′) over the appropriate vowel.

(ii) State a rule that will assign the correct primary stress to each of these words. [Hint: Assume stress is assigned from the right.]

e.  Consider the following data, adapted from Hogg & McCully (1987:11):

| ellipsis | /əlɪpsɪs/ | republic | /rəpʌblɪk/ |
| inspector | /ɪnspɛktər/ | propaganda | /prapəgændə/ |

(i) Indicate the primary stress in each word by placing an acute accent (′) over the appropriate vowel.

(ii) Is the stress pattern in these words most like that in *design, museum,* or *elephant*?

(iii) Assume that stress is assigned in terms of a [+long] syllable. A [+long] syllable can be defined as one containing a [+long] vowel or one containing a ___ vowel followed by ___ consonants.

# Chapter 7

# *Language Variation*

**Language variation** is the study of those features of a language that differ systematically as we compare different groups of speakers or the same speaker in different situations. Rather than comparing features of two different languages (say, English and French), language variation studies **regional** varieties of the same language (e.g., English as spoken by natives of Mississippi and by natives of Massachusetts); **social** varieties of the same language (e.g., the English of upper-middle class New Yorkers and that of lower-working class New Yorkers); and **stylistic** varieties of the same language (e.g., how a speaker uses language during a job interview and during a casual conversation with a close friend). In this chapter we will look at some examples of these three types of variation: regional, social, and stylistic.

Within each of these categories, we can further note several sources of linguistic variation. Consider the following observations.

(1)  In some regions of the United States, a large container used to carry water is called a *pail*; in others, the same item is called a *bucket*.

(2)  In some regions of the United States, the word *greasy* is pronounced with medial [s]; in others, it is pronounced with a [z].

(3)  Among some groups in the United States, words such as *this, that, these,* and *those* are pronounced with initial [ð]; among others, they are pronounced with initial [d].

(4)  For some groups of speakers in the United States, a sentence such as *He walks home every day* would be phrased as *He walk home every day.*

(5)  For some groups of speakers in the United States, the question *What is it?* would be phrased as *What it is?*

(6)  Men are more likely than women to use *ain't.*

(7)  A person being interviewed for a job might say *In which department will I be working?* The same speaker, in a more informal situation, might say *Which department will I be working in?*

Observations (1) and (2) illustrate the fact that particular lexical (i.e., vocabulary) items and phonological forms are associated with specific geographical areas of the United States. Observations (3), (4), and (5) illustrate the fact that particular phonological, morphological, and syntactic forms are associated with specific social groups. Observation (6) illustrates the fact that men and women use language differently. Observation (7) illustrates the fact that any one speaker commands a variety of styles appropriate for a variety of situations.

All of these phenomena involve language variation, in that they reflect the way language varies regionally, socially, and stylistically. Moreover, we will assume that the phenomena in observations (1–7) are governed by a system of principles. What we will do now is try to elucidate these principles. Bear in mind that what follows is a theory designed to explain observations (1–7).

## Language Universals, Languages, Dialects, And Idiolects

In Chapters 3 through 6, we have looked at language from the perspective of different components of the grammar—semantics, syntax, morphology, and phonology. From another perspective, the study of linguistics can be divided into a different set of domains, depending on what group of speakers we are looking at. One such domain is **language universals**, those properties (i.e., categories and rules) that all human languages, past and present, have in common. For example, all known languages make use of the categories noun and verb. Another domain concerns the properties of a particular **language** (e.g., Classical Latin, Russian, Modern English, and so forth). Still another domain is a **dialect**, a systematic variety of a language specific to a particular region or social group (e.g., American English, British English, Appalachian English, Black English, and so on). A final domain is the **idiolect**, the specific linguistic system of a particular speaker (e.g., the linguistic system of Oprah Winfrey, Phil Donahue, or Geraldo Rivera). All but the last of these domains are of primary interest to linguists, although different linguists tend to focus on different domains. The reason that most linguists are not especially interested in idiolects is that individual variations from speaker to speaker are thought to be idiosyncratic rather than systematic. Figure 7–1 summarizes the relationship among these different domains.

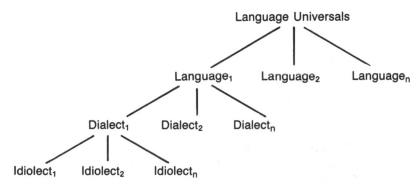

**FIGURE 7–1. Domains of language study, by groups of speakers.**

Since the topic of this chapter is language variation and since one domain of language variation is a dialect, we can start by differentiating a dialect from a language. One useful rule of thumb is that different languages are not mutually intelligible, whereas different dialects generally are. For example, if you are a monolingual speaker of English and you encounter a monolingual speaker of Norwegian, the two of you will have a great deal of difficulty communicating through language alone, since English and Norwegian are two different languages. On the other hand, if you are a native Texan and you encounter a native Bostonian, the similarities between your linguistic systems will far outweigh any differences; you will have (relatively) little trouble communicating with each other, since Texan and Bostonian represent two different dialects of the same language. The relationship between languages and dialects is represented in Figure 7–2.

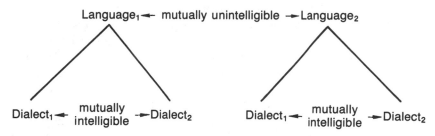

**FIGURE 7–2. Relationship between languages and dialects.**

One point that must be made at the outset of our discussion is that a dialect is an abstraction, a theoretical construct hypothesized by linguists to account for subsystems of regularities within a particular language. Informally, we might say that each subsystem is a dialect. Keep in mind, however, that in reality every native speaker of a language speaks his or her own idiolect, one shading into another. When a significant number of idiolects share a common set of features not shared by other idiolects, then we might say that this group of idiolects forms a dialect.

Let's now take a look at three types of variation within a language: **regional variation** (or regional dialects), **social variation** (or social dialects—typically referred to as standard or nonstandard dialects), and **stylistic variation**.

## Regional Variation

Regional varieties of a language result from a number of political, geographical, and cultural factors. First, the early population of an area leaves its linguistic heritage. For example, a paper napkin is sometimes called a *serviette* in modern Canadian English, because of the early French settlement of Quebec. Second, migration routes tend to demarcate dialect boundaries. For example, the United States has traditionally been thought to have three major dialect areas running horizontally from the east coast to the Mississippi River: Northern, Midland, and Southern. This pattern resulted because the east coast was colonized by settlers from different parts of England, who then migrated west rather than north or south. Third, political and ecclesiastical divisions contribute to regional dialect differences. For example, the equivalent of a county in Louisiana is called a *parish*, reflecting the early influence of the Catholic Church. Fourth, physical geographical boundaries can contribute to regional dialects by segregating groups of speakers. For example, the language variety known as Gullah or Sea Island Creole has not been absorbed into mainstream American English because its speakers live on islands off the coast of mainland South Carolina. In short, regional varieties of a language are primarily a function of settlement history and physical geography.

The study of regional variation, at least in the modern Western tradition, began in 19th-century Europe. By the early 20th century, dialect dictionaries or regional atlases had been begun or completed for England, Germany, France, and Italy. A **dialect atlas** is essentially a series of maps, each of which plots the geographical distribution of a particular linguistic feature. Following the lead of the Europeans, a group of American linguists established the American Dialect Society in 1889, intending to develop an American dialect dictionary. Over the next 50 years they published their research in a journal called *Dialect Notes*. (The organization now sponsors *American Speech*, a quarterly journal about language variation.) In 1965 Frederic Cassidy was named chief editor of the *Dictionary of American Regional English* (*DARE*). Two volumes of *DARE*, covering letters A-H, have been published since 1985. The final volumes of *DARE* will not be published until the 21st century.

In 1928, the Modern Language Association's Present-Day English Language group inaugurated a large-scale project entitled The Linguistic Atlas of the United States and Canada (LAUSC) under the direction of Hans Kurath. The work for this study was subdivided into a number of smaller regional projects. Research on the New England area was carried out from 1931 to 1933 and published in several volumes as the *Linguistic Atlas of New England* (*LANE*) from 1939 to 1943. This atlas included a handbook describing the informants and the method of data collection and a series of maps, each indicating the geographical distribution of one or more dialect terms. For example, the map in Figure 7–3 shows the distribution of *creep* and *crawl* (as in *The baby* _____ *on all fours*) in North Dakota, South Dakota, Nebraska, and Iowa.

Such data can be used to define an **isogloss**, a line that demarcates the area in which some phonological, lexical, morphological, or syntactic feature can be found. For example, the isoglass in Figure 7–4 demarcates the southern limit, within the Upper Midwest states, of *(Devil's) darning needle* as a variant for *dragonfly*. Below this boundary, *snake feeder* is more common as a variant.

A **bundle of isoglosses** delineates a dialect area: a geographic region whose language is characterized by a distinct set of phonological, lexical, morphological, and syntactic features. For example, if you were to superimpose Figures 7–3 and 7–4, you would find that both *crawl* and *snake feeder* predominate over other variants in Nebraska and southern Iowa. If a number of other linguistic features were found to coincide in this region, but not in adjacent ones, then we would be justified in treating this region as a distinct dialect area. And, in fact, such a bundle of isoglosses does exist, as shown in Figure 7–5. As a result, this area has been identified as one of the boundaries between the Northern and Midland dialects.

Fieldwork on the Middle and South Atlantic States was begun in 1933 and completed in 1949. (World War II interrupted the collection of data.) From this fieldwork

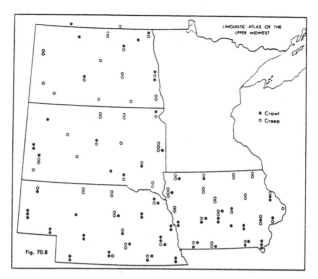

**FIGURE 7–3.** Geographical distribution of
*creep* and *crawl*, from Allen
(1973: 393).

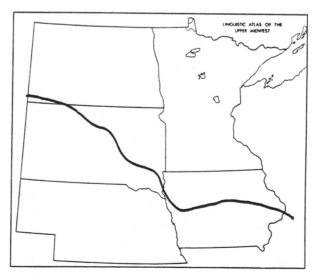

**FIGURE 7–4.** Isogloss for *(Devil's) darning
needle* in the Upper Midwest.
Based on Allen (1973: 318).

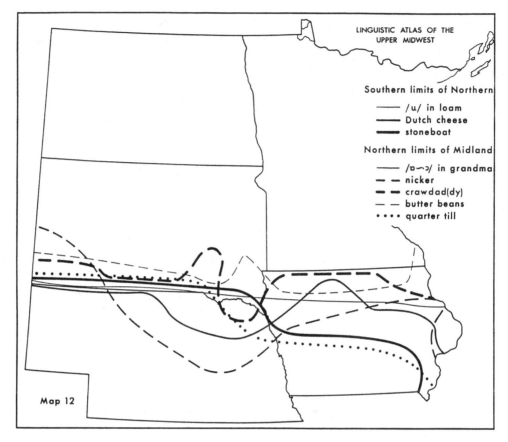

**FIGURE 7–5.  Bundle of isoglosses, reflecting one boundary between the Northern and Midland dialect regions. From Allen (1973: 128).**

came a number of important studies. In 1949 Kurath published *A Word Geography of the Eastern United States*, which divided the east coast into the Northern, Midland, and Southern dialect areas. In 1953 E. Bagby Atwood published *A Survey of Verb Forms in the Eastern United States*, and in 1961 Kurath and Raven McDavid published *The Pronunciation of English in the Atlantic States*.

These derivative works aside, however, the publication of the regional atlases has been slow and sporadic since the end of World War II. Even though countless hours of fieldwork have been invested in the Middle and South Atlantic States, the North Central States, and the Gulf States, most of the results still await publication. In fact, the only other atlas projects that have been published in complete and final form since *LANE* are the *Linguistic Atlas of the Upper Midwest*, published in three volumes between 1973 and 1976, and the *Linguistic Atlas of the Gulf States*, published in seven volumes in 1992. Nonetheless, even though progress on the regional atlases has been slow, dialectologists have a reasonably accurate picture of the major regional dialects in the United States, as illustrated in Figure 7–6. Note that Kurath's

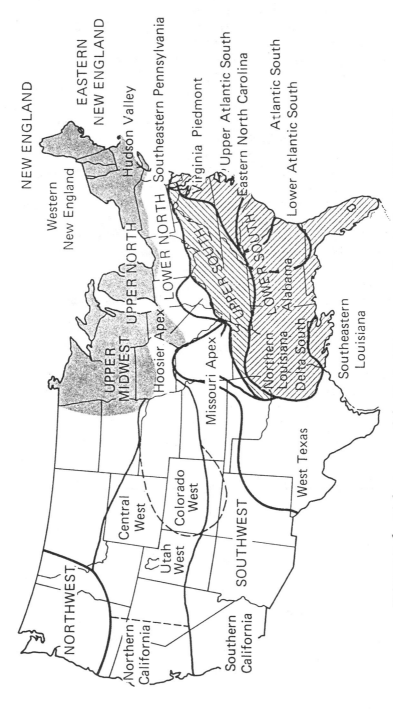

**FIGURE 7–6. Dialect areas of the United States, according to Carver (1987: 248).**

divisions of Northern, Midland, and Southern have been realigned into four areas: Upper North, Lower North, Upper South, and Lower South.

A number of factors account for the slow progress of the LAUSC since World War II. Any project covering more than half a century (1931 to the present), more than 3,500,000 square miles (the area of the United States alone), and involving hundreds of fieldworkers and thousands of informants is fraught with inherent logistical problems. The LAUSC also lost financial support and personnel to the Depression and World War II. Moreover, recall that American regional dialectology was modelled on the European studies, which dealt with relatively immobile populations and small, well-defined dialect areas. North America, on the other hand, is vast in comparison to Europe; and the population, especially since World War II, has become increasingly mobile. Regional dialect areas also become less well defined as we move away from the east coast. Under such circumstances, massive regional studies become increasingly difficult. Finally, the arrival of Chomsky's generative grammar in 1957 attracted the attention of many younger linguists, as did the shifting emphasis within dialect studies from regional to social variation. Consequently, the study of regional dialects has experienced competition for people entering the linguistics profession.

Having briefly gone over some of these background issues, let's now take a look at a representative sampling of some of the lexical and phonological dialect characteristics of North America.

## Regional Lexical Variation

As mentioned earlier, Northern and Southern varieties constitute two of the main regional dialects in the United States. Following are some of the characteristic lexical (i.e., vocabulary) differences between these two varieties.

| Northern U.S. | Southern U.S. |
| --- | --- |
| pail | bucket |
| bag | sack |
| faucet | spigot |
| quarter of four | quarter till four |
| dove | dived |
| sick to my stomach | sick at my stomach |
| (cherry) pit | (cherry) seed |

Lexical differences also exist between United States and Canadian English. The following are representative.

| United States | Canada |
| --- | --- |
| sofa | chesterfield |
| napkin | serviette |
| huh? | eh? |
| faucet | tap |

Frederic Cassidy, in his research for the *Dictionary of American Regional English*, found thousands of examples of more exotic regionalisms: for instance, *eaceworm* 'earthworm' (Rhode Island); *democrat bug* 'box-elder bug' (Kansas and Iowa, Republican strongholds!); *snoose* 'snuff' (Wisconsin and Minnesota); *hooftie* 'hippie' (Pennsylvania; from *hooft* 'hip' in Pennsylvania German); *black Christmas* 'Christmas without snow' (Alaska); and *peach-limb tea* 'a whipping administered to a child' (Arkansas).

Lexical differences between British and American English are so numerous that we can cover only a few examples here. Some common British terms, with their American equivalents, include the following:

| *American English* | *British English* |
|---|---|
| photo | snap |
| pedestrian underpass | subway |
| exit | way out |
| 7-Up (or other lemon-lime drink) | lemonade |
| mobile home | caravan |
| ground beef | mince |
| stove | cooker |
| public housing project | council estate |
| costume/masquerade | fancy dress |
| popsicle | ice lolly |
| passing lane | crawler lane |
| traffic circle | circus/roundabout |
| dead end | close |
| advice columnist | agony aunt |

## Regional Phonological Variation

The following are representative examples of regional phonological variation in North American English.

**Linking [r].**  This feature, which is associated with eastern New England and New York City, refers to a phenomenon whereby a vowel-vowel sequence between words is "linked" with an [r]. For example, consider a phrase like *That idea is crazy.* Note that *idea* ends with a vowel, and the following word *is* begins with a vowel. For a speaker whose dialect contains the "linking [r]" feature, this phrase would be pronounced as if *idea* ended in an [r] (*idear*). Speakers of this dialect presumably have a rule in their phonological systems which inserts an [r] between a word ending in a vowel and another word beginning with a vowel, as follows.

$$\varnothing \rightarrow [r] \; / \; V \; \underline{\quad} \; \# \; V \; (\# \text{ indicates a word boundary})$$

In contrast, this rule would not insert the "linking [r]" in the phrase *That idea sounds crazy*, since there are no vowel-vowel sequences between words (*idea* ends in a vowel, but *sounds* begins with a consonant).

This type of process, whereby a consonant is inserted to break up a series of two vowels, is called **consonant epenthesis**. The mirror-image process, whereby a vowel (typically [ə]) is inserted to break up a series of two consonants, is called **vowel epenthesis** (e.g., *athlete* [ǽθəlit]). Both processes reflect the fact that languages gravitate toward CVCV syllable structure.

**Vowel Neutralization before Nasals.** For many speakers of Southern dialects, the phonemes /ɪ/ and /ɛ/ are both represented phonetically as [ɪ] before a nasal consonant. This process, whereby two segments lose their contrast in a particular phonetic environment, is known as **neutralization**. So, for example, the words *pen* and *pin* would both be represented phonologically as [pʰɪn] for speakers of this dialect. Such speakers apparently have a rule in their phonological systems which changes /ɛ/ to [ɪ] before a nasal consonant, as follows.

$$/ɛ/ \rightarrow [ɪ] / \_\_\_ \; C$$
$$[+nasal]$$

Thus, for speakers of this regional dialect, the pairs *ten-tin* and *hem-him* are phonetically identical. On the other hand, the words *pet* and *pit* would be represented phonetically as [pʰɛt] and [pʰɪt], respectively, since no nasal occurs after the vowels in these words. Likewise, *net* and *knit* would be represented phonetically as [nɛt] and [nɪt], respectively, since the nasal in each of these words comes before, rather than after, the vowel.

Before leaving this rule of Vowel Neutralization, we can give you a concrete example which illustrates the practical effects of such dialect differences. During the summer of 1985, one of the authors, Frank Parker, was visiting the National Zoo in Washington, D.C., which attracts tourists from all over the country. Because this zoo was displaying the famous pandas Hsing-Hsing and Ling-Ling (now deceased), it predictably sold quite a lot of "panda paraphernalia"—shirts, postcards, and so on. A man approached the clerk at a souvenir shop and asked for a "panda [pʰɪn]." The clerk brought him a panda pin (i.e., a button designed to be worn on a shirt). The man promptly said, "No, I want a [pʰɪ̃n], like a ball point pen," and the clerk responded, "Oh, you want a [pʰɛ̃n]." Finally, the man got what he wanted: a pen decorated with panda pictures. However, neither the man nor the clerk, it appeared, ever did understand the cause of the confusion. We, on the other hand, can explain this interchange by assuming a rule of Vowel Neutralization, which is a feature of Southern dialects but not of others. The man (presumably from the South) pronounced *pen* as [pʰɪ̃n], which the clerk (presumably not from the South) interpreted as *pin*.

**Vocalization.** This rule, common among speakers in the deep South, substitutes [ə] for a post-vocalic liquid (i.e., an /l/ or /r/ following a vowel). In other words, the rule "vocalizes" the liquid (i.e., turns it into a vowel). For example, *there* /ðɛr/ may be pronounced [ðɛə].

**Voicing Assimilation.** This rule changes the voicing feature of an obstruent (i.e., a stop, fricative, or affricate) to match that of an adjacent segment. This rule, for example, accounts for the difference between *greasy* with an [s] in the North and a [z] in the South. In the Southern dialect, the [s] assimilates the voicing of the adjacent vowels to yield [z].

**Other Regional Phonological Features.** There are many examples of phonological variation too numerous to discuss in detail here. The following, however, constitute a representative sample: *bottle* [baʔɛl] (New York City); *wash* [warš] (Washington, D.C. area); *cot* and *caught* [a] (Pennsylvania); *shone* [ɔ] (Canada); and *out* [əʊ] (Canada, eastern Virginia, and South Carolina).

Several patterns also distinguish British and American English pronunciations. First of all, stress patterns may differ, resulting in a different pattern of full and reduced (/ə/) vowels. This pattern is evident in the following pairs.

|  | *American English* | *British English* |
| --- | --- | --- |
| *laboratory* | /lǽb(ə)rətɔri/ | /ləbɔ́rətri/ |
| *garage* | /gəráž/ | /gǽraž/ |
| *massage* | /məsáž/ | /mǽsaž/ |
| *cervical* | /sʌ́rvɪkəl/ | /sərváɪkəl/ |

Second, the vowel used within a stressed syllable may differ. This pattern is illustrated in the following pairs.

|  | *American English* | *British English* |
| --- | --- | --- |
| *process* | /prásɛs/ | /prósɛs/ |
| *patent* | /pǽtənt/ | /pétənt/ |
| *migraine* | /máɪgren/ | /mígren/ |
| *path* | /pæθ/ | /paθ/ |

We should point out that these examples illustrate differences between American English and only one variety of British English, the dialect often referred to as RP (for Received Pronunciation). This variety is actually more of a social dialect, since it is associated with educated, upper-class speakers rather than with one region of England. In reality, a number of regional dialects exist within British English as well.

Several additional points should be made before leaving this section on regional variation. First, regional dialects, at least in North America, differ primarily in vocabulary and pronunciation (i.e., lexically and phonologically). As we will see in the next section, social dialects may differ in pronunciation, word formation, and sentence structure (i.e., phonologically, morphologically, and syntactically). Second, many of the regional dialect differences detected by fieldworkers in the 1930's and 1940's are not as clear-cut as they once were. As a result, you may have noticed that some of the dialect features ascribed to your particular area of the country do not match the way you speak. For example, you may say *faucet* (Northern) rather than *spigot* (Southern), even though you're from Alabama! This should come as no great surprise; as we've already seen, the mobility of the American population since World War II has blurred, if not obliterated, what were earlier distinct limits on a particular dialect feature. Third, as we discussed earlier, a dialect is a theoretical construct devised to account for certain linguistic patterns. That is, a dialect boundary exists solely by virtue of the fact that the limits of a number of different dialect features coincide there. For example, the fact that the boundaries of *bucket, sack, spigot, dived*, and so on coincide (or at least formerly did) constitutes evidence for hypothesizing a Southern dialect area. A dialect area does not (and, in fact, cannot) exist apart from these individual dialect features.

# Social Variation

In the preceding section we discussed data drawn from studies in regional dialectology. While many researchers still maintain an interest in this field, much research in language variation has shifted, over the past 30 years or so, to **sociolinguistics**. This field is concerned with the interrelationship between the language of a group and its social characteristics (especially socioeconomic status and ethnicity). For example, working-class New Yorkers "drop their r's" (i.e., delete post-vocalic [r] in words like *forty-four* more often than middle-class New Yorkers do. It would be misleading, however, to say that regional dialectology and sociolinguistics are mutually exclusive fields of study. On the contrary, researchers in regional dialectology often include sociological information about their informants (e.g., age and education). Likewise, researchers in sociolinguistics must often take into account regional influences on the social dialects they are studying. Nevertheless, we can draw a few generalizations about why research in language variation has expanded from regional dialectology to include sociolinguistics, and about the different types of phenomena that sociolinguistics emphasizes.

Several trends developed in the United States during the late 1950's and early 1960's that focused more and more attention on social variation. First, since regional dialectologists had categorized information all along according to such social variables as age and education, it was a natural step for linguists to become interested in social variables for their own sake. The one person who did the most to bring sociolinguistics to prominence was William Labov. His doctoral dissertation, completed in the mid-1960's, dealt with the social stratification of English in New York City. In particular, Labov correlated several different phonological variables (e.g., the deletion of post-vocalic [r]) with different social classes (i.e., upper-middle, lower-middle, upper-working, and lower-working). Among his innovations was the use of a pre-existing sociological classification system for his informants. That is, he used a model of social stratification developed independently within the field of sociology, whereas most regional dialectologists had classified their informants using more or less subjective criteria. Moreover, he attempted to collect data from four different styles of speech: casual, careful, reading, and formal. Finally, he tried to use the results of his studies to develop both linguistic and sociological theory, whereas many regional dialectologists were working without any particular attention to fundamental issues in linguistic theory.

Second, linguists found it impossible to deal with language variation without acknowledging the fact that listeners judge a speaker according to characteristics of the speaker's dialect. For example, someone who says *I ain't working this afternoon* may be judged as socially inferior to another person who says *I'm not working this afternoon*. Thus arose an interest in **standard** and **nonstandard** dialects. It is no simple matter to define the difference between a standard and a nonstandard variety of language. However, for our purposes, we can define a standard dialect as one that draws no negative attention to itself; that is, educated people would not judge a person speaking such a dialect as socially inferior, lacking education, and so forth. On the other hand, a nonstandard dialect does draw negative attention to itself; that is, educated people might judge the speaker of such a dialect as socially inferior, lacking education, and so on. A nonstandard dialect can thus be characterized as having **socially marked** forms, such as *ain't* in the example cited earlier. A socially marked form is one that causes the listener to form a negative social judgment of the speaker.

It is important to understand that identifying a dialect as standard or nonstandard is a sociological judgment, not a linguistic one. If we say that Dialect X is nonstandard, we are saying that the educated members of the society in which X is spoken judge the speakers of X as inferior in some way, and associate this negative judgment with certain linguistic characteristics of X. We are not, however, saying that X is inferior linguistically in the sense that it is cruder, less well developed, and so forth than the standard. All dialects of all natural languages are rule governed and systematic. None is more or less developed than another; all are equally complex.

Let's look at a concrete example of the difference between a sociological and a linguistic judgment. Consider the reflexive pronouns in the following sentences.

(a)   John fed *himself.*
(b)   John fed *hisself.*
(c)   *John fed *heself.*

First of all, observe that (a) and (b) are used by speakers of English, but (c) isn't. In other words, (a) and (b) are part of English, but (c) isn't. This is a linguistic fact. Second, the pronominal forms in (a) and (b) are used by different groups of speakers. That is, they belong to different dialects. This, too, is a linguistic fact. Third, the utterance of sentence (a) goes unnoticed by educated speakers of the language; it draws no negative attention to the speaker; it is not socially marked. On the other hand, the utterance of (b) does not go unnoticed; it does draw negative attention to the speaker; it is, in fact, socially marked. These and the judgments that follow from them (e.g., (a) is standard, (b) is nonstandard) are sociological facts.

Third, this interest in nonstandard dialects and socially marked forms led quite naturally to an interest in Black English (BE), a nonstandard dialect spoken primarily by low-income, inner-city blacks. There were several reasons that BE became the focus of interest in the study of nonstandard dialects. For one thing, the civil rights movement and the integration of the public schools brought the language differences between lower-class blacks and middle-class whites into noticeable contrast. This led to concerns about how best to administer public education. Also, BE is thought to be the nonstandard dialect most different from standard English. Thus, it seemed reasonable for linguists to begin their description of nonstandard dialects with the one most distinct from standard English. In addition, the interest in BE was fueled by the controversy surrounding its origin. Some scholars maintained the traditional position that BE was no different from the dialect spoken by poor Southern whites. Others, however, who were studying Caribbean creoles pointed out creole forms in modern-day BE and suggested that BE itself developed from a creole. (A **creole** is the native language of a group of speakers which has evolved from a **pidgin**, a mixture of two existing languages brought into contact by trade or colonization.) Until recently, these factors focused attention on BE to the virtual exclusion of other nonstandard dialects of American English (for example, those of the deep South and Appalachia).

Fourth, research on nonstandard dialects in general and BE in particular led quite naturally to its application to practical problems in mass education. The relevance of such research is obvious. For example, a teacher is less likely to be concerned with a student who uses *sack* instead of *bag* (a purely regional distinction) than with a student who uses *Can't nobody tell me what to do* instead of *Nobody can tell me what to do* (a socially marked distinction). Likewise, nonstandard variations may result in a child's being diagnosed for language therapy or failing a standardized test. For example, a student who pronounces *these* with initial [d] instead of [ð] may be judged as having an "articulation problem." Because social variations in language are, rightly or wrongly, so strongly linked to how students are tested and evaluated, many sociolinguists have focused their efforts on communicating with teachers, test developers, and speech-language pathologists about the nature of nonstandard dialects.

Finally, while regional dialects are largely characterized by lexical variation, nonstandard dialects are more likely to be characterized by grammatical variation (i.e., variations in phonology, morphology, and syntax). Many linguists find grammatical variation of more interest than lexical variation because it tends to be more systematic and predictable. For example, given a form such as *submarine*, referring to a sandwich made on an oblong loaf of bread, no amount of linguistic theorizing would enable an observer to predict that other speakers might call the same object a *hero*, *hoagie*, *grinder*, or *poboy*! On the other hand, grammatical forms are more likely to reflect predictable variations, as we will see in the next three sections.

## *Nonstandard Phonological Variation*

As we have seen, not all phonological variation carries social weight. For example, a speaker who pronounces *caught* as [kʰɔt] would probably not form any negative social judgments about a speaker who pronounces the same word as [kʰat], at least not on the basis of this single form. Similarly, a speaker from New England whose dialect contains the Linking [r] Rule would probably not form a social judgment about a speaker whose dialect lacks this feature. However, some phonological variation is socially marked. Let's now look at some examples.

**Substitution of [d] for [ð].** Consider the pronunciation of *this, that, these, those*, and so on with initial [d] instead of [ð]. From a social perspective, a listener may associate such forms with speakers from, say, working-class sections of New York City. If the listener holds this group in low social esteem, he or she may label such forms as "bad" or "incorrect" English. As pointed out earlier, however, it is essential to try to separate social judgments from linguistic ones. Let's concentrate on examining such forms from a linguistic standpoint: that is, with the purpose of discovering, from a phonological perspective, *why* these particular forms are used by some speakers.

First, in what sense is the pronunciation of *these* as [diz] a predictable and systematic phonological variation? In order to answer this question, we can begin by comparing the features for /ð/ and /d/. The phoneme /ð/ is a voiced interdental fricative; /d/ is a voiced alveolar stop. Intuitively, it would seem more plausible for a substitution to occur between similar segments than between dissimilar segments. At first glance, /ð/ and /d/ seem to have little in common, since they differ in place and manner of articulation. On the other hand, both segments are voiced consonants. Note, moreover, that /ð/ and /d/ are very close in their places of articulation. (To confirm this, consult the consonant chart in Chapter 6.) Therefore, the place of articulation contrast between these two segments is not so great as it may initially seem.

But what about the contrast in the manner of articulation? In order to understand why a dialect might substitute [d], a stop, for [ð], a fricative, some additional background is required. Several pieces of evidence suggest that stops are more "natural" than fricatives, especially interdental fricatives such as /ð/. One such piece of evidence comes from language acquisition, which studies the order in which children acquire linguistic forms. Evidence from this field suggests that children acquire stops before they acquire fricatives, indicating that stops are somehow more "basic" consonants than fricatives. A second piece of evidence comes from language change, the study of how languages evolve historically. As a rule, the likelihood of finding a language which had alveolar stops in its consonant inventory and then later added interdental fricatives is much greater than that of finding a language which had interdental fricatives and then later added alveolar stops. Again, this indicates that alveolar stops are more basic than interdental fricatives. A third, related piece of evidence is the fact that languages without interdental fricatives are relatively easy to find—French, German, and some dialects of Spanish are a few examples—whereas languages without at least one alveolar stop are extremely rare. All of these facts, then, support the hypothesis that a dialect which substitutes a stop such as [d] for a fricative such as [ð] is following a "natural" linguistic trend. This process, whereby a stop is substituted for a corresponding fricative, is termed **stopping**. (Having gone through this argument, try to determine, as an exercise, why words such as *think* and *throw* might be pronounced with initial [t] rather than [θ] in some dialects of American English.)

**Consonant Cluster Reduction.** Consonant Cluster Reduction is a phonological rule that reduces a series of two or more word-final consonants by deleting one of the consonants. More specifically, the second member of a consonant cluster (typically a stop) is deleted if the following word starts with a consonant. For example, *iced tea* /aɪst ti/, which contains the cluster /st/ followed by another consonant /t/, would become [aɪs ti] by the rule of Consonant Cluster Reduction. (Note that *iced tea* is, not surprisingly, often spelled *ice tea*.) Such reduction occurs in the running speech even of speakers of standard dialects. This can be confirmed through introspection—try saying *iced tea* at a normal rate of speech—or by listening to another person say it at a normal rate of speech. It is very difficult to enunciate the final [t] of *iced* without pausing between words, thereby creating an artificial speaking style.

Nonstandard dialects, however, often create socially marked forms by extending the environment of a rule that applies in the standard dialect, so that the rule applies in contexts where it did not previously apply. In order to see how such things occur, consider the sentence *He pushed the car* /hi pʊšt ðə kar/. Note that *pushed* ends in a consonant cluster /št/ and the next word starts with a consonant /ð/; thus Consonant Cluster Reduction can apply and delete the /t/. This rule can be formalized as follows:

$$C \rightarrow \emptyset \: / \: C \underline{\quad} \# \: C$$

This rule would delete the /t/ in *pushed the car* (since the cluster /št/ is followed by a word-initial consonant, /ð/), but it would not delete the /t/ in *pushed a car* (since the cluster /št/ is followed by a word-initial vowel, /ə/).

There are, however, nonstandard dialects of English in which *both* of the forms just mentioned would undergo Consonant Cluster Reduction. These dialects have generalized the Consonant Cluster Reduction rule so that it deletes the second member of a word-final consonant cluster, regardless of what kind of segment begins the next word. This rule can be formalized as follows:

$$C \rightarrow \emptyset / \: C \underline{\quad} \#$$

This rule in the nonstandard dialect applies in the same contexts as the rule in the standard dialect. However, it also applies in contexts that the standard dialect rule does not, namely where the consonant cluster is followed by a word beginning with a vowel (e.g., *He pushed a car* → *He push a car*) or by nothing at all (e.g., *He got pushed* → *He got push*).

**Other Nonstandard Phonological Features.** There are many examples of socially marked phonological variation too numerous to mention here; the following, however, constitute a representative sample. One is the substitution of [t] for [k], and vice-versa: [kémark] for *K-Mart*, [krédɪk] for *credit*, [rɪsk] for *wrist*, [ot] for *oak*, [dɛst] for *desk*, and so on. The segments [t] and [k] are very similar acoustically, especially when they occur before another consonant, as in *K-Mart Plaza*. A speaker who is only semiliterate (i.e., unfamiliar with the spelling of a word) might understandably perceive a word like *K-Mart* as ending in the phoneme /k/.

Another nonstandard phonological process is the substitution of [f] for [θ]: [maʊf] for *mouth*, [smɪf] for *Smith*, and so on. Like [t] and [k], [f] and [θ] are very similar acoustically. Moreover, the phoneme /f/ is much more common among the world's languages than is /θ/. Thus, a semiliterate speaker is likely to perceive the final segment in *Smith* as the more common /f/ than the less common /θ/. However, such a misinterpretation is not restricted to semiliterates. LSU's football stadium has been nicknamed *Death Valley* (presumably out of wishful optimism for the "death" of the opposing team); the nickname, however, has been misperceived by some as *Deaf Valley*. Those who call it this claim that the name refers to the "deafening" noise during football games.

Another example is the reversal of two segments, one of which is typically a liquid (i.e., /l/ or /r/): [číldərn] for *children*, [kǽlvəri] for *cavalry*, and so on. The process by which two segments, features, or parts of a syllable are reversed is called **metathesis**.

Another example is the deletion of a liquid following a vowel: [hɛp] for *help*, [hod] for *hold*, and so on. This process is commonly known as **post-vocalic liquid deletion** and applies optionally in some nonstandard dialects. This process is responsible for the variant pronunciations of, for example, *Carol* /kǽrəl/: [kǽrə] (/l/ deleted), [kǽəl] (/r/ deleted), and [kǽə] (both /l/ and /r/ deleted).

A final example of socially marked phonological variation is the devoicing of a word-final obstruent (stop, fricative, or affricate): [kɪlt] for *killed*, [əhólt] for *ahold*, [hɛt] for *head*, and so on. The process of **final devoicing** is quite common among the world's languages. It applies (in one form or another) in both German and Russian, and has applied selectively in English earlier in its history, as can be seen in the pairs *spilled/spilt, dreamed/dreamt, learned/learnt, burned/burnt*, and so on.

## Nonstandard Morphological Variation

Morphological variation refers to differences in word formation, especially those related to the inflection of nouns and verbs. Whereas many phonological processes are common to all spoken dialects of English, variations in morphology tend to be restricted to particular social dialects. In general, morphological variation is more socially marked in speech than is phonological variation. However, morphological variation, like phonological variation, is also predictable and systematic. In fact, nonstandard morphological forms often reflect more regular treatments of the noun and verb systems of English than their standard counterparts do, as we will see in the following examples.

**Reflexive Pronouns.** One example of nonstandard morphological variation was given in the exercises for Chapter 5. In one exercise, we observed that some nonstandard dialects of English use the following system of reflexive pronouns.

|              | *Singular*        | *Plural*     |
|--------------|-------------------|--------------|
| 1st person   | myself            | ourselves    |
| 2nd person   | yourself          | yourselves   |
| 3rd person   | herself/hisself   | theirselves  |

This system is identical to the standard English system, with two exceptions: the third-person singular form *hisself* is used, instead of the standard English form *himself*; and the third-person plural form *theirselves* is used, instead of the standard English form *themselves*.

Again, if we set aside any social judgments that we may have about the nonstandard forms, we can see that these forms are highly systematic from a linguistic perspective (and, in fact, are more predictable than the standard English forms *himself* and *themselves*). Note that the first- and second-person reflexive pronouns have as their base a possessive pronoun: *my*, *our*, or *your*. (The third-person singular feminine form, *herself*, can be interpreted as either possessive + *self* or objective + *self*.) In other words, given the first- and second-person forms, the principle for forming a reflexive pronoun in English appears to be the following: add -*self* or -*selves* to the possessive form. Following this rule would give us *hisself* and *theirselves* for the third-person forms. Therefore, from a linguistic perspective, the nonstandard forms *hisself* and *theirselves* are actually more systematic than the standard forms *himself* and *themselves*. The reflexive pronoun system illustrates quite pointedly the systematic nature of nonstandard morphological variation.

**Omission of Final -s on Verbs.**  Consider the sentence *He walk home every day*. We can begin by comparing this sentence to its standard English counterpart, *He walks home every day*. One way to account for the nonstandard form *walk* is to hypothesize that a morpheme has been deleted, namely the {PRES} inflection that occurs in standard English as -*s* on the third-person singular form of present tense verbs. In order to understand why this morpheme is omitted in some nonstandard dialects, we need to look at the standard English system for the inflection of present tense verbs.

|              | *Singular*     | *Plural*   |
|--------------|----------------|------------|
| 1st person   | I walk         | We walk    |
| 2nd person   | You walk       | You walk   |
| 3rd person   | He/She walks   | They walk  |

Upon examining the standard English system, we can see immediately that most present tense verbs have no overt inflection for {PRES}. If we substitute the nonstandard forms (*He/She walk*) for the corresponding standard forms, we come out with a perfectly regular system (i.e., no present tense forms have an overt inflection). This regularization of the third-person present tense verb forms generalizes to all main verbs and auxiliaries in some nonstandard dialects of English, yielding forms like *He do* for *He does*, *He don't* for *He doesn't*, and *He have* for *He has*.

**Other Nonstandard Morphological Features.**  Once again, more examples exist than can be detailed here. The following, however, are representative. One feature is the use of nonstandard past tense and past participial verb forms: for example, *see, seed,* or *seen* for *saw; come* for *came;* and *rid* for *rode.* (Atwood's *Survey of Verb Forms* is filled with such examples, owing primarily to older and relatively uneducated informants.) Another feature is the omission of *-s* on plural nouns (the morpheme {PLU}) and possessive NP's (the morpheme {POSS}): for example, *girl* for both *girls* and *girl's.* It is significant that in BE the *-s* endings representing {PRES}, {POSS}, and {PLU} are omitted with different frequencies. Specifically, {PRES} is omitted more frequently than {POSS}, and {POSS} is omitted more frequently than {PLU}. This indicates that the omission of *-s* is morphological rather than phonological. If it were phonological, all three morphemes would be omitted with equal frequency, since they are phonologically identical.

Another nonstandard morphological feature is the extension of one inflected form of *be* to all forms. Unlike other present tense verbs in English, which have a predominant form (without *-s*) and an exceptional form (with *-s*), *be* has three forms, all of which appear to be exceptional: *am, are,* and *is.* Thus, speakers of some nonstandard dialects regularize all present tense forms of be to one single form: for example, *I is, You is, We is,* and *They is.* Note that when this happens *be* is no longer an "irregular" verb (i.e., one with exceptional forms). The point is that nonstandard morphological variations, like nonstandard phonological variations, tend to reflect a highly systematic treatment of English.

## Nonstandard Syntactic Variation

Like morphological variations, syntactic variations tend to be more socially marked than phonological variations, some of which are regional as well as social. Let's take a look at some specific nonstandard syntactic constructions.

**Inversion in *wh*-Interrogatives.**  In some nonstandard dialects of English, an interrogative such as *What is it?* may be phrased as *What it is?* In order to demonstrate the relation between these two syntactic forms, we will need to make use of several concepts discussed in Chapter 4 (Syntax), namely underlying structure, surface structure, and transformation. With these concepts at hand, we can begin by analyzing the **derivation** of the standard English form *What is it?;* that is, by making some observations about the transformations that relate its underlying and surface structures.

Let us assume that, in the underlying structure of this interrogative, we have a sequence of elements like the following:

it - is - what

Note that this underlying structure differs from the surface form in two ways. First, the verb (*is*) follows the subject (*it*) in the underlying structure, but precedes it on the surface. Second, the *wh*-word (what) is in final position in the underlying structure, but in initial position on the surface. Each of these differences involves a transformation. Inflection Movement (I-Movement) moves the verb-form inflected for tense to the left of the subject. *Wh*-Movement moves the *wh*-word to clause-initial position. Applying each of these transformations yields the standard English form *What is it?*, as shown in the following derivation.

| | |
|---|---|
| Underlying structure: | it - is - what |
| I-Movement: | is - it - what |
| *wh*-Movement: | what - is - it |
| | *What is it?* |

How can we account for the nonstandard English structure, *What it is?* Let's assume that this form has the same underlying structure as its standard counterpart: it - is - what. What transformational rules are needed to relate this underlying structure to the surface form *What it is?* Only one: *wh*-Movement. Applying this transformation to the underlying structure would yield the surface form *What it is?*

Let's compare the standard and nonstandard derivations side by side. As we have seen, the difference between them can be explained by assuming that I-Movement applies in the standard derivation but not in the nonstandard derivation. This situation is summarized here.

| | *Standard English* | *Nonstandard English* |
|---|---|---|
| Underlying structure: | it - is - what | it - is - what |
| I-Movement: | is - it - what | (does not apply) |
| *wh*-Movement: | what - is - it | what - it - is |
| | *What is it?* | *What it is?* |

At this point, it should be clear that the nonstandard derivation omits a step (I-Movement) that appears in the standard derivation. This should not be interpreted to mean that the nonstandard derivation is "deficient" or "incomplete" in some way. Rather, a dialect containing this nonstandard feature is perfectly rule governed and differs from standard English in a systematic and predictable way.

**Double Negatives.** Let's now take a look at the infamous double negative construction, exemplified by sentences such as *I don't have no money* (cf. standard English *I don't have any money*). This construction is significant not so much because it is socially marked (which of course it is in Modern English), but because of the faulty reasoning usually associated with its prohibition.

Every school child is familiar with the following rule: double negatives are incorrect because two negatives make a positive. This statement of the rule can largely be traced to a highly influential book written by Robert Lowth in 1762, *A Short Introduction to English Grammar.* Lowth's work was one of many similar collections of "do's and don't's" about the English language which appeared during the 18th-century prescriptive grammar movement. Unfortunately, many of these proclamations were based on personal prejudices against certain structures (for example, Jonathan Swift objected to verb forms such as /dɪstɪ́rbd/ instead of /dɪstɪ́rbəd/ for *disturbed*) and on the notion that new forms (including words such as *banter, bully*, and *mob*) would corrupt the language. Moreover, many leaders of this movement believed that English should emulate Greek, Latin, and other systems which were perceived as more authoritative and rational than English.

Lowth's prohibition against double negatives illustrates this latter tendency, in that it attempted to make English conform to mathematical logic. According to Lowth, "Two Negatives in English destroy one another, or are equivalent to an Affirmative." Here Lowth was apparently generalizing the principle that the product of two negative numbers is a positive number: for example $(-2) \times (-2) = 4$. (Interestingly enough, Lowth could likewise have *defended* the double negative by analogy to mathematics, arguing that the sum of two negative numbers is itself a negative number: that is, two negatives reinforce, rather than cancel, each other.) The point is that Lowth proclaimed the double negative in English to be "illogical" not because it violates our linguistic system, but because it violates a principle from another system—mathematics.

If Lowth's reasoning were correct, we would expect certain things to follow from it. First, we would expect a sentence such as *I don't have no money* to mean 'I have some money.' Contrary to Lowth's prediction, however, this sentence means 'I don't have any money,' as any native speaker of English can point out. Second, we would expect human languages in general to shun double negative constructions. This, however, is not the case. If we turn to the present-day forms of languages other than English, we find that double negatives appear as a matter of course. For example, the standard English sentence *I don't want anything*, which contains one negative (the contracted form of *not*), has as its Spanish equivalent *No quiero nada*, where both *no* and *nada* indicate negation. Thus, there is nothing inherently deviant about the double negative construction. Moreover, if we look back at earlier stages of the English language, we find double negatives in the language of quite a few highly esteemed writers. The double negatives in the following passages have been italicized.

> Old English (King Alfred, the *Orosius*, ca. 880–890): "*ne* bið ðær *nænig* ealo gebrowen mid Estum" (literally 'not is there not-any ale brewed among Estonians'; Modern English 'no ale is brewed among the Estonians').
>
> Middle English (Chaucer, the *Canterbury Tales*, ca. 1390): "he that is irous and wrooth, he *ne* may *nat* wel deme" (literally 'he that is angry and wrathful, he not may not well judge'; Modern English 'he cannot judge well').
>
> Early Modern English (Shakespeare, *2 Henry IV*, ca. 1600): "There's *never none* of these demure boys come to any proof" (literally 'Not one of these young boys amounts to anything').

From a historical perspective, then, it is difficult to say that the double negative construction was either socially or linguistically marked in earlier forms of English.

If, then, Lowth's analysis of double negatives is inaccurate, what actually led to the socially marked status of double negatives in Modern English? Briefly, here's what seems to have happened. In Old English, the double negative construction was obligatory, as it is in Modern Spanish. That is, the Old English equivalent of *I don't have no money* would have been grammatical, and the equivalent of *I don't have any money* would have been ungrammatical. By Shakespeare's time, the double negative construction had become optional. That is, the Early Modern English equivalents of *I don't have no money* and *I don't have any money* existed side by side, both fully grammatical. Apparently, however, the single negative construction somehow became associated with educated speakers, while the double negative became associated with uneducated speakers. This, of course, eventually led to the double negative construction being socially marked in Modern English. The point to keep in mind, however, is that sociolinguistic phenomena are a function of the interaction of linguistic and sociological forces; mathematical and logical systems have no bearing on them whatsoever.

**Other Nonstandard Syntactic Features.** There are many other socially marked syntactic constructions too numerous to detail here. The following, however, constitute a representative sample. Labov has determined that BE speakers can omit an inflected form of *be* only where standard English can contract it. Thus, in standard English *be* can be contracted in a construction such as *Do you know if it is his?* → *Do you know if it's his?*, but not in *Do you know what it is?* → *\*Do you know what it's?* Similarly, in BE *be* can be omitted in *Do you know if it is his?* → *Do you know if it his?*, but not in *Do you know what it is?* → *\*Do you know what it?*

Another nonstandard syntactic feature involves the treatment of main verb *be* in interrogatives such as *Do they be sick?* In standard English, I-Movement applies to auxiliaries to form an interrogative: *John has seen Mary* → *Has John seen Mary?* On the other hand, I-Movement never applies to main verbs: *John saw Mary* → *\*Saw John Mary?* Instead, when there is no auxiliary verb, a form of *do* takes the place of the missing auxiliary: *John saw Mary* → *John did see Mary* → *Did John see Mary?* Thus, standard English has a general rule for forming interrogatives: I-Movement applies to auxiliaries but not to main verbs; *do* appears when there is no overt auxiliary. There is, however, a major exception to this rule in standard English: main verb *be* behaves like an auxiliary rather than a main verb, in that it undergoes I-Movement. For example, *They are sick* → *Are they sick?*

Now consider what form we would get if main verb *be* behaved like all other main verbs, that is, not undergoing I-Movement and consequently triggering the appearance of *do*: *They be sick* → *They do be sick* → *Do they be sick?* This is the nonstandard counterpart of standard English *Are they sick?* In this case, the nonstandard dialect has regularized an exception in standard English, namely the treatment of main verb *be*. The nonstandard dialect treats main verb *be* exactly like all other main verbs.

A final example of a socially marked syntactic feature involves moving a negative auxiliary to sentence-initial position when the subject is an indefinite NP (e.g., *everyone*, *nobody*, and so on), as in *Everybody can't win* → *Can't everybody win*.

To summarize this section, socially marked grammatical variations are highly systematic from a linguistic perspective. They reflect predictable variations of standard English forms and are by no means "illogical" from the standpoint of how language actually works. Any negative judgments that we may have about nonstandard forms are based more on our social biases about the speakers who use them than on their linguistic structure.

Does this mean that linguists take an "anything goes" attitude toward language? That is, do linguists advocate the use of double negatives and other socially marked forms? We cannot speak for all linguists, of course, but our own point of view is that social judgments are just as real as linguistic judgments. That is, a form like *What it is?* is likely to elicit a negative social judgment from many listeners, even though they understand the meaning of the sentence. It would be foolhardy to pretend that such social judgments are nonexistent or unimportant. On the other hand, it would be just as misguided to claim that a structure like *What it is?* constitutes an illogical or inferior linguistic form. We believe that anyone who is in the business of teaching language and evaluating the language of others should understand the distinction between social and linguistic judgments, as well as the underlying regularity of many socially marked forms.

## Language and Gender

So far we have dealt with linguistic variation that correlates with socioeconomic status and ethnicity. In addition to these social variables, however, linguists have also investigated the relation between language and **gender**: the social and psychological roles, attitudes, and traits associated with biological sex. The field of language and gender has focused on two questions. First, what correspondences can be drawn between a speaker's language and gender? (Can we generalize, for example, about the degree to which males and females use indirectness?) Second, is language sexist? That is, do certain linguistic forms (such as the use of *mankind* to refer to all people) reflect, or perhaps promote, an anti-female bias? In this section we will focus on issues that have been raised by investigations of the first question, referring the reader to supplementary readings for discussions of the second question.

### Gender as a Social Variable

We have already seen that socioeconomic status and ethnicity are related to the use of standard and nonstandard linguistic forms. For instance, suppose we were to study two groups of 30-year-old white males: one upper-middle class and one lower-working class. A typical finding would be that lower-working class speakers are more likely than upper-middle class speakers to omit the -*s* on the third-person singular form of the verb (e.g., *He don't* for *He doesn't*). This is the expected result: other things being equal (in this example, age and ethnicity), the use of nonstandard forms increases among speakers of lower socioeconomic status.

What happens, though, when gender is introduced as an additional variable? A number of studies have found that, within a given socioeconomic class, female speakers are more likely to use standard forms than male speakers. For example, lower-working class women are more likely than lower-working class men to retain third-person singular *-s* (e.g., *He doesn't* rather than *He don't*). In some cases, in fact, the language of women patterns more like that of the men in the next-highest class.

This general tendency for women to use standard forms more often than men (or, stated conversely, for men to use nonstandard forms more often than women) has emerged in studies of a number of linguistic variables. For example, Labov found that New York City men were more likely than women to employ stopping (i.e., substitution of [t] and [d] for [θ] and [ð], respectively). Other forms that have been studied, with similar findings, include post-vocalic [r] deletion, the use of medial and word-final [ʔ] for /t/ (e.g., [baʔəl] for *bottle*), Consonant Cluster Reduction, omission of the {POSS} and {PLU} morphemes, and multiple negatives.

Researchers such as Peter Trudgill have offered several explanations for gender differences in the frequency of standard and nonstandard forms. The greater use of standard forms may reflect women's traditional role as caregivers to children and a concern with transmitting more highly valued forms to the next generation. The use of standard forms may also offer women a way of achieving or signalling a higher social status when other paths (such as greater earning power) have been closed off to them. Along other lines, Trudgill has proposed that middle- and working-class men attach "covert prestige" to their use of nonstandard forms, which may reflect their association of these forms with masculinity and strength. This theory is supported by the fact that men tend to over-report their use of nonstandard forms; that is, they claim to use even more nonstandard forms than they actually do.

## Gender Patterns Within Standard English

In addition to differences in the use of standard and nonstandard forms, other differences between men and women's language have also been investigated, many of them as the result of Robin Lakoff's influential work *Language and Women's Place* (1975). Lakoff proposed that there is a set of traits which distinguish women's language from men's language, among them a greater use of tag questions, hedges (e.g., *sort of, you know, I guess*), question intonation on declarative structures, indirect speech acts, euphemisms (e.g., *powder room* for *toilet*), "empty" adjectives and intensifiers (e.g., *that is SUCH an ADORABLE puppy!*), and specialized vocabularies in domains such as color terms (e.g., *magenta* and *periwinkle* for shades of purple and blue).

Lakoff based her claims on her own impressions and personal observations rather than on empirical study. Consequently, much subsequent research has attempted to test the accuracy of her perceptions. One finding has been that Lakoff's claims do reflect common stereotypes about women's language. For example, people presented with a cartoon caption (minus the cartoon) like *That is SUCH an ADORABLE puppy!* and asked to guess the speaker's gender will usually identify the speaker as a woman. Other research has been more concerned with confirming whether or not women's language actually displays the traits proposed by Lakoff. This research has borne out some of her claims to varying degrees. In some studies, for example, women have been found to use comparatively more hedges, fewer taboo terms for sexual and bodily functions, and more indirect speech acts. On the other hand, studies of question intonation and tag questions have yielded mixed results, with some studies finding gender differences but others not.

In addition to the linguistic traits proposed by Lakoff, other patterns have also been studied, such as those involving conversation and other interaction. For example, a number of studies of classroom behavior have found that boys talk more than girls and that teachers are likely to give more attention (both positive and negative) to boys. Such differences persist to adulthood, when men tend to dominate situations such as question-and-answer periods after lectures. Studies of conversations between men and women have also revealed that men tend to take longer "turns" throughout the conversation and have a greater tendency to interrupt women than vice versa. Women, on the other hand, tend to ask more questions and provide frequent "support indicators" for the other speaker—expressions like *yeah*, *um-hm*, and *right*.

Gender patterns, where found, have naturally given rise to attempts at their explanation. Following Lakoff, some analysts have associated the (purported) traits of women's language with powerlessness, uncertainty, and deference. Under this view, for example, hedging is seen as a sign of the speaker's tentativeness. In fact, one extension of this view is that "women's" language is actually the language used by powerless speakers of either gender; "women's" language reflects the fact that women have tended to occupy less powerful positions. This hypothesis is reinforced by studies that have discovered "women's" language used by men in subordinate roles and "men's" language used by women in powerful roles.

Other analysts have taken a different approach, arguing that women's language reflects a social interaction style that is different from, but not inferior to, that of men. Under this view, women's language reflects their concern with building cooperation, showing empathy, and facilitating communication. This approach, for example, treats the more frequent use of questions among women not as a sign of deference and uncertainty, but instead as a strategy for showing interest in and engaging the other speaker. Similarly, studies of children playing have revealed that boys tend to give each other direct orders (*Put that piece here!*), while girls tend to use more indirect, "inclusive" language (*Why don't we see if this piece fits here?*). From a social interaction perspective, these linguistic differences may reflect differences between a more individualistic, competitive mode more typical of males and a more communal, cooperative mode more typical of females.

Some interest has developed in applying findings about language and gender to solving problems in cross-gender communication at the personal, institutional, and professional levels. For example, as discussed in Deborah Tannen's work *You Just Don't Understand*, many misunderstandings between couples can be traced to differences in male and female conversational styles. Similarly, language and gender studies have been applied in the teaching profession to promote more egalitarian treatment of male and female students. Differences in male and female communication styles have also been used to analyze communication problems encountered by females entering traditionally male fields such as management.

## Stylistic Variation

Earlier in this chapter, we looked at linguistic features that vary from one group to the next. In this section, we will look at stylistic variation—that is, systematic variations in the language of any one speaker, depending upon the occasion and the participants in the interchange. Different styles or **registers** range from extremely formal to quite informal.

An analogy can be drawn between stylistic variation in language and variation in dress. For example, if Professor Smith goes on a job interview for a teaching position—a fairly formal encounter with an unfamiliar audience—he is likely to wear a dark suit, a conservative tie, and black dress shoes. If he gets the job, however, it is unlikely that he will continue to dress in this same manner while teaching from day to day. Rather, he is likely to dress more informally, perhaps in a sweater, trousers, and loafers. And, if he goes to a backyard barbecue at the house of one of his colleagues, he is likely to wear shorts, a tee-shirt, and tennis shoes.

Although Smith's manner of dress changes according to the situation and the participants, these changes have in common the fact that they reflect what is appropriate for his role in each situation, the activities he expects to participate in, and the impression he wants to make on the other participants. In this regard, his navy blue suit is not "better" than his Bermuda shorts in any absolute sense. Rather, the suit is more appropriate for the job interview, while the Bermuda shorts are more appropriate for the backyard barbecue. (Anyone who has ever looked into a closetful of clothes and declared, "I don't have a thing to wear" was actually saying, "I don't have anything to wear that is appropriate for this particular occasion.") Moreover, variations in dress are largely automatic; that is, they do not require a lot of conscious thought. For example, while Smith might decide to wear sandals instead of tennis shoes to the barbecue, it probably would never occur to him to wear his sandals on his hands. Likewise, while he may have to make a conscious decision about which suit to wear to the job interview, the decision to wear some suit is relatively unconscious. In other words, we move from one style to another without giving it a lot of conscious thought, so long as we are familiar with the conventions of each style.

Similar observations can be made about stylistic variation in language. First of all, linguistic style is a matter of what is **appropriate**. Like variation in our manner of dress, stylistic variations in language cannot be judged as appropriate or not without reference to the participants in the interchange (i.e., speaker and listener or reader and writer). For example, you would not speak to a 5-year-old child, an intimate friend, and a professor using the same style of speech. Using the term *eleemosynary* 'charitable' would probably be inappropriate for the child and the friend, while using *number one* 'urinate' would probably be inappropriate for the friend and the professor. Moreover, stylistic variations in language are largely automatic, in that we do not normally have to stop and think about which style to shift into next. For example, even though many Americans are given to peppering their conversations with "four-letter words" occasionally, very few speakers have to consciously suppress such forms when they are talking to their mother, the president of their company, or a store clerk. In short, shifting styles is essentially automatic and unconscious, and is governed by the concept of appropriateness.

Differences in formality tend to form a continuum rather than a discrete set of categories. Therefore, even though it is fairly easy for an observer to determine when two styles are different, it is sometimes difficult to draw a clear boundary between two styles. The best we can do is identify the relative formality of a particular form (i.e., state the circumstances in which it would be appropriate) and determine the type of variation it represents: lexical, phonological, morphological, or syntactic. With these points in mind, let's take a look at some different types of stylistic variation.

## Stylistic Lexical Variation

One rather obvious stylistic dimension that speakers vary from one situation to another is vocabulary. When speaking or writing in a more formal register, our word choice may lean toward polysyllabic words rather than their shorter equivalents. For example, someone writing a letter of application for a job may close with a phrase like *Thank you for your consideration.* In more informal correspondence, the same person may use *Thanks for your time* to express the same idea. In the same way, a person may use connectives such as *however, therefore,* and *thus* in a more formal register, and use *but* and *so* in a less formal one. Similarly, idiomatic expressions such as *let the cat out of the bag, kick the bucket, make the grade,* and *give me a break* are characteristic of more informal registers. Likewise, words borrowed from Latin and Greek tend to be more formal than native Germanic lexical items: for example, *canine* (from Latin) rather than *dog; thermal* (from Greek) rather than *heat; dental* (from Latin) rather than *tooth;* and *lexical* (from Greek) rather than *word.*

## Stylistic Phonological Variation

The application (or nonapplication) of various phonological rules also correlates with changes in register. In particular, neutralization rules (i.e., those that obliterate the distinction between segments) and deletion rules tend to be suppressed in more formal types of speaking. For example, Flapping, which reduces both /t/ and /d/ to [ɾ], may be suppressed, so that *latter* is pronounced with a [t] and *ladder* with a [d] (rather than both being pronounced [lǽɾər]). Likewise, English has a rule of Vowel Neutralization that reduces all unstressed vowels to [ə], so that *affect* /æfέkt/ and *effect* /ifέkt/ are both ordinarily pronounced [əfέkt]; speakers often suppress this rule in very formal registers. Likewise, Consonant Cluster Reduction may be suppressed, so that the /t/ in *soft drink* is pronounced. Finally, the **deletion of unstressed syllables** (e.g., [mέmbər] for *remember*) may be suppressed, resulting in "hypercorrect" pronunciations such as [ɛləmέntəri] for *elementary* or [mæθəmǽrɪks] for *mathematics.*

The suppression of such rules in informal settings, however, can have unintended effects. One of the authors, Frank Parker, had a colleague whom he first encountered in an informal conversation in the hallway. After listening to him speak for a few minutes, Parker inferred that he was not a native speaker of English. Later, after learning that this fellow was a native of Chicago, Parker realized what had given him his initial impression: the colleague systematically (and quite unnaturally) suppressed rules like Flapping, Consonant Cluster Reduction, and Vowel Neutralization in *all* styles of speech.

These examples illustrate two points worth emphasizing. First, pronunciations characterized by phonological neutralization and deletion do not reflect "careless" speech; on the contrary, they reflect a style of speech appropriate for informal registers. Second, it is easy to make the mistake of thinking that informal styles are appropriate only for informal occasions, but that formal styles are appropriate for all occasions. The latter half of this proposition is false, as we have seen from the example of the colleague from Chicago. Using a formal register in casual situations is just as inappropriate as using a casual style on formal occasions.

## Stylistic Morphological Variation

The formation of words can also exhibit stylistic variation. One of the features most commonly associated with more informal registers is contraction: for example, *I'm* for *I am* and *you're* for *you are*. Note, however, that contraction of a lexical NP (e.g., *John'll* for *John will* ) seems to be more informal than contraction of a pronoun (e.g., *he'll* for *he will* ). Moreover, contraction in speech is characteristic of all but the most formal styles. For example, even when being interviewed for a job, you might be more likely to say *I'll do it immediately* rather than *I will do it immediately.* In fact, most people would have to concentrate very carefully in order to block contraction in speech.

Another morphological characteristic of informal registers is the use of clipped forms: for example, *psych* for *psychology, econ* for *economics,* and *comp lit* for *comparative literature.* Note that in an academic treatise on compulsive behavior you might find the term *sports fanatic,* but in the sports section of the newspaper you would see *sports fan.* Once again, contracted and shortened forms are no more "careless" than their lengthier counterparts; rather, they are perfectly appropriate in more informal speech and writing.

## Stylistic Syntactic Variation

Changes in syntax may also occur as a function of changes in register. For example, a speaker in a job interview might ask *In which department will I be working?* Having gotten the job, however, the same speaker might ask a colleague *Which department do you work in?* Notice that in shifting from a relatively formal to a more informal register, the speaker has placed the preposition *in* at the end of the clause, rather than at its beginning. The more formal structure, with *in* in initial position, may reflect the speaker's awareness of a prescriptive rule: don't end a sentence with a preposition. This prohibition originated with the 18th-century prescriptive grammarians; it was based on an attempt to model English after Latin, a language in which prepositions cannot appear in sentence-final position. (In fact, the word *preposition* comes from a combination of Latin morphemes meaning 'put before [NP's].') Likewise, the use of *whom* for *who* in the objective case is characteristic of more formal styles. These two variables (moving a preposition to initial position and substituting *whom* for *who*) interact to form a continuum from formal to casual: for example, *For whom do you work?* → *Whom do you work for?* → *Who do you work for?*

Another informal syntactic pattern is omission in interrogatives. Such omission forms another continuum from relatively formal to more informal: for example, *Do you want another drink?* → *You want another drink?* → *Want another drink?* The rule here seems to be (a) omit the auxiliary (in this case *do*) and (b) omit *you*. It is clear, however, that these omissions are absolutely rule governed, since the subject *you* cannot be omitted unless the auxiliary has been omitted (cf. *\*Do want another drink?*). Once again, the more informal syntactic constructions discussed in this section do not constitute "careless," "sloppy," or "incorrect" English. The key to their use is appropriateness. Suppose, for example, that you knock on a friend's door and a voice from inside asks *Who's there?* You respond with *It is I* (rather than *It's me*). The use of this extremely formal construction (with a nominative case pronoun following an uncontracted form of *be*) is clearly inappropriate in this case.

Before leaving these examples of stylistic variation, we want to make one final point concerning the central concept of appropriateness. All of the examples we have covered in this section on stylistic variation involve standard English. The only difference between, say, *Who did you speak to?* and *To whom did you speak?* is a matter of register. There are times, however, when the use of even nonstandard forms is appropriate. For example, a black adolescent from the inner city would in all likelihood be ostracized by his friends on the street if he were to address them in standard English, no matter how informal the style. He would be better off speaking BE under the circumstances, because anything else would be inappropriate. Roger Shuy, a well known sociolinguist, has told a similar story about his experiences. While in college, he got a summer job working on a loading dock in his home town. At first, he was shunned by his co-workers, lower-working class men who worked on the dock year round. The fact that he was excluded from their circle bothered him and pretty soon he figured out the problem: he was speaking standard English, which was inappropriate in this situation. Once he started using some nonstandard forms (e.g., *ain't, he don't, me and him went*, etc.), he was accepted into the group.

## Summary

Let's review what we have covered in this chapter. We began with seven observations about language variation. However, we had no transparent explanation for these phenomena. Thus, we constructed a (partial) theory of variation to account for our observations. This theory makes use of such concepts as regional, social, and stylistic variation; dialect; social markedness; standard and nonstandard forms; gender; and register. We have also seen that one variety of language can differ from another in terms of its lexicon, phonology, morphology, and syntax. Perhaps most importantly, we have seen that language variation is highly systematic.

As usual, we want to point out that there is much more to the study of language variation than what has been presented in this one short chapter. However, you have now been exposed to some of the basic ideas in the field; if you want to learn more, the supplementary readings will introduce you to additional information about language variation. In the meantime, the practice problems and exercises can be used to check your understanding of the principles we have covered.

## Supplementary Readings

Cassidy, F. (1985, 1992). *Dictionary of American regional English*, 2 vols. Cambridge, MA: Harvard University Press.

Dillard, J. (1972). *Black English: Its history and usage in the United States.* New York: Random House.

Fasold, R. (1981). The relation between black and white speech in the south. *American Speech, 56,* 163–189.

Fasold, R. (1984). *The sociolinguistics of society.* New York: Blackwell.

Fasold, R. (1990). *The sociolinguistics of language.* Cambridge, MA: Blackwell.

Graddol, D., and J. Swann. (1989). *Gender voices.* Oxford: Blackwell.

Labov, W. (1972). Academic ignorance and black intelligence. *The Atlantic* (June), 59–67.

McDavid, R. I. (1958). The dialects of American English. In W. N. Francis (Ed.), *The structure of American English* (pp. 480–543). New York: Ronald Press.

Wolfram, W. (1991). *Dialects and American English.* Englewood Cliffs, NJ: Prentice-Hall.

Wolfram, W., and D. Christian. (1989). *Dialects and education: Issues and answers.* Englewood Cliffs, NJ: Prentice-Hall.

You are now prepared to read all of these works. Wolfram is the most recent introductory textbook on variation in American English, including treatments of regional, social, and gender variation. McDavid is an accessible overview of early regional dialectology in the United States. Cassidy is the result of almost 30 years of research and contains over 23,000 regional expressions found in the United States. These two volumes, which are the first of five, cover only those regional terms beginning with the letters A-H. The books by Fasold are in-depth texts covering the sociology of language (where linguistic factors are brought to bear on the study of society) and sociolinguistics (where social factors are brought to bear on the study of linguistics), respectively. Dillard is a thorough account of the purported creole origins of BE. Labov is a brief popular discussion of the issues involved in the relationship between BE and education. Fasold's article compares non-standard forms peculiar to BE and those also found in dialects spoken by Southern whites. Wolfram and Christian is an excellent discussion of dialect issues that concern professionals in the language arts, reading, and speech-language pathology. Graddol and Swann discusses research in language and gender, looking both at differences in male and female language and the question of sexist language.

# *Practice*

**1.** True-False. [tʰɪs] is a possible pronunciation for *this* in nonstandard English.

**2.** Determine what phonological process is responsible for the following misspelling. Target: *char-broiled*. Misspelling: *cha-broiled*.

**3.** The phonetic representations of words such as *absorb* and *Mrs.* contrast for some Northern and Southern speakers in the United States as follows.

| **Northern** | **Southern** |
|---|---|
| [əbsɔ́rb] | [əbzɔ́rb] |
| [mísɪz] | [mízɪz] |

What systematic contrast occurs between the Northern and Southern dialects? How does the phonological environment account for the Southern forms?

**4.** One prescriptive rule states that the nominative case of a pronoun should be used after a form of main verb *be*: hence, *It is I, That is he*, and so on. However, most speakers, at least in an informal register, tend to use the objective case of a pronoun in these structures: *It's me, That's him*. Given the following data (where an asterisk marks an ungrammatical structure), what general principle do speakers appear to be following when they use the objective case pronoun following *be* instead of the nominative case?

A.1.  The girl hit him.
A.2.  *The girl hit he.

B.1.  Please call me.
B.2.  *Please call I.

C.1.  I don't know her.
C.2.  *I don't know she.

**5.** Some nonstandard forms actually fill gaps or regularize exceptions in the standard English system, as was the case with *hisself* and *theirselves*. Now consider another case: all but one of the following phrases can be contracted in two different ways; the exceptional case has only one contracted form.

A.  I am not
B.  We are not
C.  You are not
D.  He/She is not
E.  They are not

a.  Which phrase has only one contracted form in standard English?
b.  By analogy with the other four phrases, how would the "missing" contracted form for this phrase be constructed? Give a phonological representation for this form.
c.  Assume, first, that two consecutive nasals cannot occur in the same syllable in English (e.g., *mnemonic* is represented phonemically as /nimánɪk/ and, second, that in some dialects of English the vowel before a nasal is raised (e.g., *can't* is pronounced as

[kʰēt] rather than as [kʰǣt]). Apply these principles to the form you constructed for (b). What nonstandard form seems to fill the role of the "missing" contracted form?

6. Based on exercise (5), it appears that *ain't* fills a gap in the standard English system by providing an alternative contracted form for the phrase *I am not*. However, the use of *ain't* is not restricted to the first person subject in nonstandard dialects. Given the following data, in what sense is the nonstandard system more regular than the standard one?

| *Standard System* | | *Nonstandard System* | |
|---|---|---|---|
| (no form) | we aren't | I ain't | we ain't |
| you aren't | you aren't | you ain't | you ain't |
| he/she/it isn't | they aren't | he/she/it ain't | they ain't |

7. When a speaker attempts to emulate a stylistic register that he or she is not completely familiar with, a phenomenon known as **structural hypercorrection** may result. This term describes the use of a structure associated with a more formal register in a linguistic environment where it is not typically used. Now consider the following data.
   A. To whom should I speak?
   B. Whom did you see?
   C. Whom is taking you to dinner?
   a. Which sentence illustrates structural hypercorrection?
   b. What principle has the speaker of these sentences apparently learned?
   c. What principle has the speaker failed to learn?

8. In one of her comedy routines, Lily Tomlin introduced the character of Ernestine, a rather obnoxious telephone operator. A typical utterance from Ernestine might be *Is this the party to whom I was just speaking to?*
   a. How would you render this utterance in a more informal style?
   b. Which forms and constructions does Tomlin use to help characterize Ernestine's personality?

9. Consider the following sentence: *That is not where they are now.* Which occurrences of inflected *be* could be omitted in BE?

10. Weasel Podowski handed in the following paragraph to his English teacher, Miss Moveable Feast.
    Muffy pulled out her overnight case. She plan to go to her frien's house the nex day. She had been there before. She walked a mile to get there. She wish she did not have to walk all the way.
    Miss Feast, who is a friend of yours, claims that Weasel has no sense of time, because he makes so many "tense errors." You realize Miss Feast's mistake.
    a. What part of Weasel's grammatical system is responsible for these errors?
    b. Write a rule (in formal notation) that accounts for these errors.

## Answers

The following answers are, in some cases, not the only possible ones. Discussion of other possibilities is part of the practice.

1. False. [dɪs] is.

**2.** Post-vocalic liquid deletion.

**3.** In the Northern forms, [s] (a voiceless consonant) appears between vowels; in the Southern forms, however, [z] (a voiced consonant) appears. The occurrence of [z] for [s] in the South may arise from the fact that the surrounding segments are vowels, which are also voiced.

**4.** After other verbs in English (e.g., *hit*, *call*, and *like*), the objective case of a pronoun is used; the nominative case results in an ungrammatical sentence. Speakers who use the objective case pronoun after a form of main verb *be* are following the general pattern associated with all other verbs. They are essentially regularizing an exception.

**5.** a. Two contracted forms are readily apparent for phrases (B–E)—*We're not, We aren't*, and so on. Phrase (A), though, has only one contracted form in standard English, *I'm not*, and so violates the overall pattern for contracting phrases of this type.
  b. On analogy with phrases (B-E), the "missing" form for (A) would be *amn't* ([ǽmnt]).
  c. Deleting one of the nasals in [ǽmnt] and raising the vowel from [æ] to [e] would yield [ẽnt] = *ain't*.

**6.** The nonstandard system is more regular in that it uses one contracted negative verb form (*ain't*) for all persons and numbers, whereas the standard system uses two (*aren't* and *isn't*), which vary according to person and number.

**7.** a. Sentence (C).
  b. Substitute *whom* for *who*, regardless of its function.
  c. *Whom* can substitute for *who* only when it is an object of a verb or preposition. Note, incidentally, that the only environment in which *who* cannot occur in standard English is when it immediately follows a preposition: *To who did you speak?* (cf. *Who did you speak to?*).

**8.** a. Something like *Is this the person I was just speaking to?*
  b. By using overly formal forms (*the party*) and constructions (*to whom*), Tomlin characterizes Ernestine as somewhat self-important. Note that the two occurrences of the preposition *to* (one fronted and the other not fronted) suggest that Ernestine doesn't have complete mastery of the formal style "to which she aspires to."

**9.** *Is* but not *are* (i.e., *That not where they are now*). Note: *are* can't undergo deletion, since it can't be contracted with *they* in this sentence.

**10.** a. phonology
  b. C → ø / C ___ C

# Exercises

**1.** The term *idiolects* refers to _____.
  a. relic areas in which older forms of a language are still used
  b. mutually unintelligible language variations
  c. variations by individual speakers of the same dialect
  d. Chomsky's innate constraints on language

2. Identify three regions of the United States where neighboring or immigrating ethnic groups have influenced the local vocabulary, and give an example for each.

3. Look up *black Christmas* in the *Dictionary of American Regional English*.
   a.  What does it mean?
   b.  Where is it most common in the United States?

4. Look up *choppies* in the *Dictionary of American Regional English*.
   a.  What does it mean?
   b.  Where is it most common in the United States?

5. Look up *choupique* in the *Dictionary of American Regional English*.
   a.  What does it mean?
   b.  Where is it most common in the United States?

6. Certain regional dialects of English (e.g., eastern New England and the deep South) contain the following rule:

   /r/ → ø / V ___

   Which of the following words would not be affected by this rule?
   a. *forty*      c. *pretty*      e. both (a) and (b)
   b. *four*       d. *free*        f. both (c) and (d)

7. Many Southern varieties of English contain the following rule:

   V → [+high] / ___ C
   $$\begin{bmatrix} -high \\ -low \\ -back \\ -tense \end{bmatrix} \qquad [+ nas]$$

   Based on this rule, indicate the vowel that would occur in the phonetic form corresponding to each of the following phonemic forms.
   a.  hem       /hɛm/        e.  strength   /strɛŋkθ/
   b.  pin       /pɪn/        f.  teen       /tin/
   c.  pant      /pænt/       g.  net        /nɛt/
   d.  pen       /pɛn/        h.  neat       /nit/

8. Many dialects of the northeastern seaboard contain the following rule:

   ø → [r] / V ___ # V

   Indicate how each of the following phrases would be affected by this rule (if at all):
   a.  Anna asked Neal
   b.  Neal asked Anna
   c.  Anna told Neal
   d.  Neal told Anna

9. How must the rule in (8) be restricted in order to correctly predict the following data?
   Cuba is        [kyubər ɪz]
   Tahiti is      *[təhitirɪz]
   Martha ate     [marθəret]

Linda ate        [lɪndəret]
Roscoe ate       *[raskoret]

10. In all varieties of English, certain consonants are deleted phonetically in certain environments. Consider the following data.

|  | *Phonemic* | *Phonetic* |
|---|---|---|
| most people | /most pipəl/ | [mos pipəl] |
| most of us | /most əv əs/ | [most əv əs] |
| iced tea | /aɪst ti/ | [aɪs ti] |
| iced a cake | /aɪst ə kek/ | [aɪst ə kek] |
| eight people | /et pipəl/ | [et pipəl] |
| six people | /sɪks pipəl/ | [sɪks pipəl] |

a. Which forms show a systematic change between the phonemic and phonetic levels?

b. What do these forms have in common?

c. State in words the rule that describes this change.

d. Write the rule in formal notation.

11. Consider the following vowel contrasts between General American English and certain South Midland dialects (southern Indiana down to northern Alabama, Maryland over to Arkansas).

|  | *General American* | *South Midland* |
|---|---|---|
| fish | [fɪš] | [fiš] |
| fifth | [fɪfθ] | [fifθ] |
| measure | [mɛžər] | [mežər] |
| left | [lɛft] | [lɛft] |
| push | [pʊš] | [puš] |
| itch | [ɪč] | [ič] |
| fresh | [frɛš] | [freš] |
| butcher | [bʊčər] | [bučər] |
| puss | [pʊs] | [pus] |

a. What generalization can you state about the difference between the vowels in these two dialects?

b. Construct a formal rule that would change the relevant vowels in the General American dialect to those in the South Midland dialect.

12. Consider the following dialects of English.

|  | *Dialect A* | *Dialect B* |
|---|---|---|
| police | /pəlís/ | /pólis/ |
| hotel | /hotél/ | /hótɛl/ |
| July | /jəláɪ/ | /júlaɪ/ |
| insurance | /ɪnšúrəns/ | /ínšərəns/ |
| Detroit | /dətrɔ́ɪt/ | /dítrɔɪt/ |

a. Construct a rule for assigning stress in Dialect A. (Assume stress is assigned from the right.)

b.  Construct a rule for assigning stress in Dialect B. (Assume stress is assigned from the left.)

c.  Which rule is simpler?

d.  Which dialect is more socially marked?

**13.** Some dialects of Appalachian English use the prefix {a} on certain forms. Based on the following data (adapted from Wolfram [1982]), state five constraints on the use of this prefix. (Some are phonological; others are morphological.)

A.  She kept *a-callin'* my name.

B.  She woke up *a-screamin'*.

C.  The bear come *a-runnin'* out of the woods.

D.  She kept *a-waterin'* the lawn.

E.  *She kept *a-forgettin'* my name.

F.  *She kept *a-askin'* my name.

G.  *She woke up *a-screaming*.

H.  *They like *a-sailin'*.

I.  *They shot the *a-runnin'* bear.

a.  _____

_____

b.  _____

_____

_____

c.  _____

_____

d.  _____

_____

e.  _____

_____

**14.** Assume that the rule of Consonant Cluster Reduction in English deletes the second member of a consonant cluster. What restrictions must be placed on this general rule so that it predicts the following data?

hand /hænd/ → [hæn]          help /hɛlp/ → *[hɛl]

lamp /læmp/ → *[læm]         hold /hold/ → [hol]

last /læst/ → [læs]               bulk /bʌlk/ → *[bʌl]

bent /bɛnt/ → *[bɛn]

**15.** Wolfram and Fasold (1974: 208–211) point out that some tests used to diagnose articulation problems in children contain items that may be biased against speakers of certain regional or social dialects. For example, if a child is asked to name a picture of a pie and says [pa] rather than [paɪ], this response may be scored as an error. Analyze the way that each of the following forms might lead to similar problems if used on an articulation test.

a.  death

b.  felt

c.  they

d.  Ken

e.  test

16. What criterion would a linguist use to determine that a language should be classified as a creole rather than as a pidgin?

17. Which of the following phonological variations is not typically found in nonstandard English?
    a. [kemark] for *K-Mart* /kemart/
    b. [dɛst] for *desk* /dɛsk/
    c. [saʊf] for *south* /saʊθ/
    d. [hæθ] for *half* /hæf/

18. Cassidy (1981) notes that in the South and Southwest *nother* is a separate word meaning 'other' as in *That's a whole nother thing*. Explain the origin of the form *nother*.

19. Explain how the nonstandard form *tesses* /tɛ́səz/ occurs for *tests*.

20. True - False. [dɪŋk] is a possible form of *think* in some nonstandard dialects.

21. True - False. Consonant Cluster Reduction is found only in nonstandard spoken dialects.

22. True - False. [pʰæf] is a possible pronunciation of *path* in nonstandard English.

23. Identify the process reflected by the following.
    arithmetic /əríθmətɪk/ → /ríθmətɪk/

24. What phonological process is responsible for the following misspelling? Target: *spiritualist reader*. Misspelling: *spiritualis reader*.

25. What phonological process is responsible for the following misspelling? Target: *athlete*. Misspelling: *athelete*.

26. What phonological process is responsible for the following spelling? Sign in the parking lot of the East Baton Rouge school board: *Handicap Parking*.

27. What phonological process is responsible for the following misspelling? Sign in front of a clothing store: *bran new*.

28. What phonological process is responsible for the following misspelling? Sign in a bakery window: *Fresh Pasteries*.

29. What phonological process is responsible for the following misspelling? Roadside billboard: *Truck Stop and Restraunt*.

30. What phonological process is responsible for the following misspelling? Sign on tavern in Savannah: *Cold Draugh Beer*.

31. What phonological process is responsible for the following misspelling? Target: *suppose*. Spelling: *spose*.

32. What phonological process is responsible for the following misspelling? Hand-painted sign advertising carpentry work: *Carpentery work done*.

33. A handpainted sign on a building in Baton Rouge reads exactly as follows: *No loitᵉring*. Explain.

34. The following sign was seen in a driveway in front of a Halls, Tennessee store: *There Is No Turn Aroun*. What phonological process is responsible for this misspelling?

**35.** Consider the following forms, found in some nonstandard dialects of English.

| | *Standard* | *Nonstandard* |
|---|---|---|
| business | [bíznɪs] | [bídnɪs] |
| wasn't he | [wʌ́zni] | [wʌ́dni] |
| Disney | [dízni] | [dídni] |

What phonological process accounts for the nonstandard forms?

**36.** A bar in Baton Rouge has a sign over the jukebox which reads *Don't use nickels in judebox.* Explain how *jukebox* becomes *judebox* phonologically.

**37.** Cassidy (1981) states that in some dialects *bronical* /bránɪkəl/ is substituted for *bronchial* /bráŋkiəl/. Which of the following processes best describes this substitution?

    a. voicing assimilation
    b. deletion of an unstressed syllable
    c. vocalization
    d. metathesis
    e. both (a) and (d)
    f. all of the above

**38.** Consider Figure 7–7, showing the percentage of times that ain't was substituted for other verb forms during casual conversation. The results are broken down by both socioeconomic status and gender.

    a. Based on this graph, what generalization can be made about the relative use of nonstandard forms among males and females?
    b. Among speakers of different socioeconomic status?

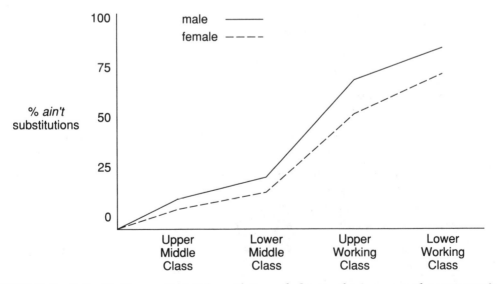

**FIGURE 7–7. Substitutions of *ain't* for other verb forms during casual conversation.**

**39.** The following is taken from a church bulletin: *The deacon wives will be meeting on Thursday, April 11, 1991 in the uptown location.* Explain how the socially marked form in this passage arises. (Hint: the wives are not deacons.)

**40.** The terms on the left are used in the United States, while those on the right are used in other English-speaking countries (e.g., England, Australia). Try to match each term on the left with its non-American counterpart.

| *United States* | *Other English-speaking Countries* |
|---|---|
| _____ biscuit | a. tomato sauce |
| _____ bag (as of potato chips) | b. crisps/chips |
| _____ candy | c. green mealies |
| _____ canned | d. scone |
| _____ cookie | e. packet |
| _____ corn meal | f. sweets |
| _____ cornstarch | g. serviettes |
| _____ ears of corn | h. icing sugar |
| _____ flavoring (as in vanilla) | i. cream cracker |
| _____ french fries | j. biscuit |
| _____ Jello™ | k. corn flour |
| _____ ketchup | l. tinned |
| _____ molasses | m. chips |
| _____ napkins | n. maize meal |
| _____ potato chips | o. essence |
| _____ powdered sugar | p. treacle |
| _____ soda cracker | q. jelly |

**41.** Assume a speaker has been told to say *running* instead of *runnin'*. The speaker then extends this treatment to forms like *mountain* and *button*.

a. What forms will result?
b. What principle has the speaker misinterpreted?
c. What general phenomenon do the forms in (a) illustrate? (Hint: see the Practice Problems.)

**42.** What forms might result from structural hypercorrection of the following forms?
a. two children
b. Bob Johnson's car
c. I want a cookie.

**43.** The morphemes {PRES}, {PLU}, and {POSS} are omitted with different frequencies in Black English. Thus, given the different frequencies of omission, the standard English sentence *Sam hates his sister's boyfriends* is most likely to show up in Black English as _____.

a. Sam hate his sister's boyfriends.
b. Sam hate his sister boyfriends.
c. Sam hates his sister boyfriends.
d. Sam hates his sister's boyfriend.
e. both (a) and (b)

**44.** When two morphemes are combined into a compound, they tend to undergo changes in stress which trigger segmental changes. Originally, both morphemes have primary stress (´); then the second morpheme reduces first to secondary stress (`) and then to zero stress; finally, the unstressed vowel reduces to schwa. Thus, for example, *cupboard* /kʌ́pbórd/ becomes /kʌ́pbòrd/ and finally /kʌ́bərd/. Which of the following compounds has been in the language longer: *mailman* or *fireman*? Explain.

**45.** A freshman composition teacher corrects a student's sentence from *I asked her what did she want* to *I asked her what she wanted.* What syntactic rule of English accounts for the difference between the original version of the sentence and the revised version?

a. I-Movement
b. *wh*-Movement
c. NP Movement

d. Extraposition
e. none of the above

**46.** In a study reported by Fasold (1984: 258–59), college freshmen were tested to see whether they would use *is* or *are* in the frame *There _____ about five minutes left.* Following this performance test, they were asked to self-report on which verb they had used and also to judge one of the verbs as more "correct." The following graph shows the results (P = performance test, R = self-report, and C = judgment as correct):

Based on the graph, answer the following questions.

a. T - F   The form judged "correct" by most speakers is the same one actually used by most speakers.
b. T - F   Most speakers think that they actually use an "incorrect" form.
c. T - F   The form judged "correct" is more formal than the form actually used by most speakers.
d. T - F   It appears that most speakers are able to give a reliable report of the forms that they themselves use.

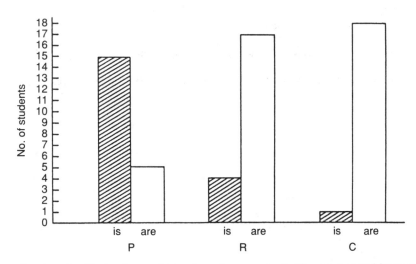

Number of subjects who used *is/are* in performance tests (P), who reported *is/are* as the form they used (R), and who considered *is/are* correct (C).

**FIGURE 7–8.   Results of performance test, self-reported usage, and judgments as correct.**

**47.** One goal of prescriptive grammar was to

    a.  make English conform to classical languages such as Latin
    b.  objectively describe the actual language of speakers
    c.  indicate the geographical distribution of certain dialects
    d.  show how creole languages evolve from pidgin languages

**48.** Consider the following data:

    A.  *Are they sick?* (standard)
    B.  *Do they be sick?* (nonstandard)
    C.  *Are they going?* (standard)
    D.  *Do they be going?* (nonstandard)
    E.  *Do they have a car?* (both dialects)
    F.  *Do they need money?* (both dialects)

Label the following generalizations about *yes-no* questions as true or false.

    a.  T - F   SE treats main verb *be* like other main verbs.
    b.  T - F   NSE treats main verb *be* like other main verbs.
    c.  T - F   NSE treats auxiliary *be* like a main verb.
    d.  T - F   SE treats main verb *have* like an auxiliary verb.

**49.** The phrase *What can I do you for?* is sometimes used facetiously for *What can I do for you?* Explain how the underlying structure of the facetious phrase differs from that of its Standard English counterpart.

**50.** Consider the following interchange between a judge and the foreman of a jury on a recent episode of *L. A. Law*.

Judge:     Have you reached a verdict?
Foreman: We have, Your Honor.
Judge:     What say you?

How does the judge's grammar differ from that of Modern English?

# Chapter *8*

# *First-Language Acquisition*

**Language acquisition** is the study of how human beings acquire a grammar: a set of semantic, syntactic, morphological, and phonological categories which underlie their ability to speak and understand the language to which they are exposed. For example, a normal child born to English-speaking parents in the United States obviously is not born knowing English. By the age of 5, however, the child can speak and understand English with relative facility. Language acquisition is the study of how this transformation takes place—from a mental state in which the child does not possess a grammar of a particular language to a mental state in which the child does. As defined here, language acquisition does not include the process by which a person learns a language other than his or her native tongue. This process is called second-language acquisition and is discussed in Chapter 9. Keeping this distinction in mind, let's consider some observations we can make about the acquisition of a first language.

(1)   A child acquiring English might form the plural of *foot* first as *foots*, then as *feets*, then as *feetses*, and finally as *feet*.
(2)   A child acquiring English might form an interrogative such as *Why can't I go?* as *Why I can't go?*
(3)   All normal children acquire a language, but not all children learn to read and write.
(4)   Many children gain a fairly sophisticated facility with language before they master tasks such as tying their shoes, telling time, or adding numbers.

Observation (1) illustrates the fact that language is acquired in stages. Observation (2) illustrates the fact that language is not acquired through simple imitation (adults don't say *Why I can't go?*, so the child cannot simply be mimicking the adult).

Instead, the child infers a system of rules (i.e., a grammar) for forming sentences, based upon the samples of the language to which he or she is exposed. Observation (3) supports the hypothesis that human beings are genetically programmed to acquire a language. That is, children do not *learn* a language in the way they learn to read and write, through conscious effort and instruction; rather they *acquire* a language in the same way they acquire their ability to walk, effortlessly and without instruction. Observation (4) supports the hypothesis that language acquisition is subserved by a mental faculty designed specifically and solely for that purpose. In other words, language acquisition is not thought to be a function of intelligence or general intellectual abilities.

All of these phenomena have to do with language acquisition, the way we acquire the grammar of our first language. As usual, we will assume that the phenomena in observations (1–4) are systematic; that is, they are governed by a system of principles. What we will now try to do is construct a set of concepts that will account for these phenomena. Keep in mind that what follows is a theory designed to account for the data in observations (1–4).

## Prelinguistic Stages

In the first year of life, infants go through three stages generally thought to have nothing directly to do with the acquisition of language. The **crying** stage lasts from birth to around 2 months. The **cooing** stage, characterized by vowel-like sounds, lasts from about 2 months to 5 months. And the **babbling** stage, characterized by syllable-like consonant-vowel sounds, lasts from about 5 months to 12 months. Note that these sounds are described as language-*like*; they are not thought to be either an early form of language or necessary prerequisites to language acquisition. For example, even babies born deaf babble as infants, but they cease at about 6 months. The fact that deaf babies babble just as hearing infants do suggests that such behavior is not "practice" for language acquisition. However, the linguistic status of these stages is still best regarded as an open question for the present time.

If, however, language-like behaviors such as cooing and babbling are not actually "practice" for language acquisition, what are they? One hypothesis is that they are simply genetically determined stages that the human organism goes through as it matures. In fact, there is evidence that much of what appears to be "practice" for a specific skill is actually just a genetically encoded stage and may not be necessary for the acquisition of that skill. For example, young birds go through a stage of flapping their wings before they actually begin to fly. Years ago a scientist named Grohmann decided to test the hypothesis that wing flapping is "practice" for flying. He studied two groups of newly hatched pigeons. One group (the control group), he simply left alone. The other group (the experimental group), he encased in open-ended tubes that restrained the young pigeons from flapping their wings. Otherwise, both groups were allowed complete freedom to follow the dictates of nature. After several weeks, the control group quite naturally began to fly. When Grohmann removed the tubes from the experimental group, they too immediately began to fly, just as well as the control group. The point, of course, is that wing-flapping does not appear to be "practice" for flying at all; rather, it seems to be a genetically encoded stage in maturation. Likewise, cooing and babbling do not appear to be "practice" for language acquisition.

This is not to say that nothing goes on during the first year of life that has to do with language acquisition. For example, infants generally exhibit the beginnings of comprehension at around 9 months. Also, intonational patterns emerge late in the first year. Likewise, infants begin to exhibit meaningful gestures around 9 to 10 months, which has been interpreted by some linguists as an early stage in the acquisition of pragmatics.

It is also worth noting that infants are able to perceive differences between pairs of stimuli such as [ba] and [pa] or [ba] and [ga]. Several ingenious methods have been devised for testing the perception of infants as young as 1 month old. One method involves having the child suck on a pacifier which is connected by wire to a monitoring device. The child hears a repeated stimulus for several minutes (e.g., [ba-ba-ba-ba-ba]) and gradually attains a steady sucking rate (e.g., 25 sucks per minute). Then a new stimulus is presented (e.g., [pa-pa-pa-pa-pa]). The infant's sucking rate typically increases significantly at the onset of the new stimulus (e.g., to 50 sucks per minute). From this change, the experimenter can infer that the infant perceived the change from [ba] to [pa] and thus is capable of discriminating between [b] and [p].

The apparently innate ability of infants to perceive at least some such auditory contrasts may partially contribute to the relatively rapid pace at which language acquisition proceeds (a point discussed further toward the end of this chapter). At the same time, it would be misguided to conclude that infants can comprehend language; instead, it would be more accurate to say that they can discriminate between acoustic stimuli that also happen to be linguistically significant. For example, researchers have found that chinchillas are capable of perceiving these same contrasts, but we would not want to conclude from this that chinchillas can understand human language.

## Linguistic Stages

In this section, we will look at the stages of language acquisition from the perspective of the four components of grammar: phonology, morphology, syntax, and semantics, in that order. However, before getting into details, we want to clarify several potential points of confusion.

First, in acquiring language, children go through more or less the same stages at more or less the same time. These stages, however, represent general trends, and every child does not follow them in lock-step fashion. For example, a child will typically acquire stops (e.g., /p,b,t,d,g,k/ in English) before liquids (e.g., /l,r/ in English). This does not mean, however, that every normal child will acquire all of the stops, completely and correctly, before any of the liquids. Likewise, a child will typically acquire grammatical morphemes (e.g., inflectional affixes, prepositions, articles, and so on in English) by the age of 5. Again, this does not mean that no normal child will acquire them earlier or later; rather, it is simply a general pattern.

Second, in this chapter we will deal solely with the acquisition of English. However, the principles discussed here typically apply, where they are relevant, to the acquisition of other first languages as well. For example, children tend to correctly interpret complex sentences in which the order of the clauses reflects the order of events before they correctly interpret sentences in which this ordering relation does not hold. As a result, a child exposed to English will typically be able to correctly interpret *John ate before he came home* at an earlier stage than *Before John came home, he ate*. This general principle, however, seems to apply to children acquiring any first language.

Third, it is much more difficult to draw inferences about first-language acquisition than it is to study almost any other area of linguistics. This is because language acquisition is the only area of linguistics that requires investigators to deal with immature informants (i.e., infants and children). One problem for investigators is interpreting the structure underlying a child's utterance. For example, a child acquiring English may utter *wear shirt no* rather than, for example, *I don't want to wear that shirt*. Is such an utterance a structured sentence or just an unstructured string of words? Is *wear shirt* a verb-object construction or just a memorized phrase? Is the placement of *no* at the end of the utterance the result of a rule or simply an afterthought? It is often impossible to answer such questions conclusively. Another problem is that investigators cannot question a child like they can an adult speaker. For example, a linguist can ask an adult informant such questions as "Is sentence X an acceptable sentence in English?" and "Are sentences X and Y paraphrases of each other?" In the example just mentioned, however, it would be quite difficult (to say the least) to elicit from the child whether *wear shirt no* and *no wear shirt* are equivalent in meaning.

Thus, a primary concern for anyone studying language acquisition is to avoid overinterpreting a child's productions. Let's consider an actual example from the literature. In "The Acquisition of Language," Breyne Moskowitz cites an interchange between Ronald Scollon, a language acquisition researcher at the University of Hawaii, and a 19-month-old girl named Brenda.

| | |
|---|---|
| BRENDA: [kʰa] (4 times) | SCOLLON: What? Oh, bicycle? Is that what you said? |
| SCOLLON: What? | BRENDA: [na] |
| BRENDA: Go. Go. | SCOLLON: No? |
| SCOLLON: (undecipherable) | BRENDA: Not. |
| BRENDA: [baɪš] (9 times) | SCOLLON: No. I got it wrong. |

Now consider how Moskowitz interprets this exchange: "Brenda was not yet able to combine two words syntactically to express 'Hearing that car reminds me that we went on the bus yesterday. No, not on a bicycle.' She could express that concept, however, by combining words sequentially" (1979: 91). However, when we compare Brenda's productions to Moskowitz's interpretation, it is clear that Moskowitz may be attributing more linguistic structure to Brenda's utterances than they actually have. In short, keep in mind the inherent problems involved in using infants and children as informants.

## *Acquisition of Phonology*

Let's take a look at some representative examples of the stages a child goes through in acquiring the phonology of his or her language. Note that here and throughout, when we say that a child *acquires* such-and-such a segment, we don't mean simply that he or she produces a sound that an adult observer perceives as that segment. Rather, we mean that the child has actually incorporated that segment into his or her phonological system. Such a judgment, of course, requires interpretation by the analyst—which, as we saw in the last section, is a tricky business.

**Vowels.** Children exposed to English typically acquire /a,i,u/ at an early stage. This tendency reflects two principles. First, extreme values in the vowel system tend to be acquired before intermediate values. In this instance, the child is filling in the end points of the vowel triangle as shown in Figure 8–1. (For reference, see the vowel chart in Chapter 6.) Note that /a,i,u/ are maximally distinct from each other: /i/ and /u/ are maximally distinct from each other along the horizontal dimension [±back]; and both /i/ and /u/, in turn, are maximally distinct from /a/ along the vertical dimensions [±high] and [±low]. Second, children typically acquire segments common among the world's languages before they acquire those that are relatively rare. For example, /a/ is universal (i.e., it occurs in all languages), and /i,u/ are nearly universal (i.e., they occur in the vast majority of languages). Thus, the interaction of both principles predicts that /a,i,u/ will be acquired early, and the other intermediate vowels will come later.

**Consonants.** Children exposed to English typically acquire /p,b,m,w/ at an early stage. This tendency reflects several principles. First, **place of articulation** tends to be acquired from the front of the mouth to the back. In particular, labials are generally acquired before alveolars, palatals, and velars. (For reference, consult

|          | [−back] | [+back] |
|----------|---------|---------|
| [+high]  | i       | u       |
| [+low]   |         | a       |

**FIGURE 8–1.  The child's first vowels.**

the consonant chart in Chapter 6.) For example, the labial stop /p/ would be expected to appear before the velar /k/. Second, **manner of articulation** tends to be acquired from most consonant-like to least consonant-like. In particular, stops and nasals (both of which require complete closure of the oral cavity) are generally acquired before liquids and fricatives. For example, among the alveolar consonants in English, we would expect /t/ before /l/. The fact that liquids are acquired extremely late is evidenced by the phonological process of **gliding**, which substitutes a glide (typically [w]) for a liquid. For example, *room* may be pronounced [wum] and *love* [wʌv]. The interdental fricatives /θ,ð/ are also acquired at a relatively late stage. (They are also rare segments among the world's languages.) Thus, it is not suprising to find the phonological process of **stopping** (the substitution of a stop consonant for a fricative) in child forms such as [dæt] for *that*.

Let's now consider some of the forms predicted by the interaction of the principles governing the acquisition of vowels and consonants. Variations on *ma* /ma/ and *pa* /pa/ are extremely widespread as early forms for male and female parents, respectively. This is no accident: as we have just seen, /m,p,a/ are all acquired very early. Another predictable form is Dennis the Menace's *telebision* (with a /b/) for *television* (with a /v/). Even though Dennis is a fiction of Hank Ketchum's imagination, this example of stopping is based on fact. Our principles governing child phonology predict that the stop /b/, which is acquired early, will substitute for the fricative /v/, which is acquired somewhat later. Note, incidentally, that our theory predicts that /b/ alone (not just any stop) will substitute for /v/. The phoneme /b/ is the only stop in English that agrees with /v/ in both place of articulation ([+labial]) and voicing ([+voice]).

Likewise, these principles are often reflected in children's productions which become "lexicalized" into proper names. One child, for example, referred to his mother with a form perceived as /bámbi/, presumably for *mommy* /mámi/. This child had apparently acquired /b/ and was in the process of acquiring /m/, thus substituting the voiced labial stop for the voiced labial nasal in /mámi/, which became /bámbi/. In fact, the child's family began to refer to the mother as *Bombi*. Another example is the name *Teeter* /titɛr/ from *sister* /sɪstər/. In this case, the child had an aunt whom the mother called *Sister*, a nickname common in the South. The child, who apparently had acquired the stop /t/ but not the fricative /s/, substituted /t/ for /s/, since both are [+alveolar] and [–voice]. This resulted in a production that the adults perceived as /titɛr/, and the aunt from then on was known in the family as *Teeter*.

**Syllable Structure.** The simplest type of syllable found among the world's languages is CV, where C = consonant and V = vowel. All languages contain words made up of CV syllables. In fact, Japanese words, with a few predictable exceptions, are all of this form: for example, *Fujiyama* and *Hasegawa*. English, however, has a quite complex syllable structure; for example, we have words like *spy* (CCV), *ask* (VCC), *spry* (CCCV), *asked* (VCCC), and even *splints* (CCCVCCC). Thus, it comes as no surprise that a child will go through several stages in acquiring the full range of syllable types in English. This acquisition generally proceeds in the following order:

| (C)V | (initial C is optional) |
| CV | (initial C) |
| CVC | (final C) |
| CCVC | (initial cluster) |
| CCVCC | (final cluster) |

For example, a child trying to pronounce *stoves* might proceed through the following stages: [o] or [tʰo], [tʰov], [stov], and then [stovz]. Likewise, **simplification** of initial consonant clusters is common. For example, we get [skǽmbəl] for *scramble* [skrǽmbəl], [dɪ̄k] for *drink* [drɪ̄k], and so on. Another example of a child's production becoming "lexicalized" as a new word is *tummy* /tʌ́mi/ for *stomach* /stʌ́mɪk/. Note, first, that *stomach* begins with a cluster /st/. A child who has not yet acquired clusters will simplify /st/ to /t/. (Recall that stops are generally acquired before fricatives.) Note also that the second syllable of *stomach* ends in a final consonant /k/. If the child has not yet acquired syllable-final consonants, the /k/ will be omitted, resulting in /tʌ́mɪ/. Finally, English has a rule that tenses a lax vowel in word-final position. (Note, for example, that *said* contains the lax vowel /ɛ/ followed by a consonant; *say*, however, contains the tense vowel /e/, since it is in word-final position.) This vowel-tensing rule changes /ɪ/ to /i/, yielding /tʌ́mi/. Again, the point is that a child's acquisition of phonology is rule governed and predictable.

Another common syllable process, especially among the child's first 50 words, is **reduplication** (syllable repetition). This process can be seen in forms like *mama, papa, peepee,* and so on. Partial reduplication (the repetition of part of a syllable) may also occur; very often an /i/ is substituted for the final vowel segment, as in *mommy* and *daddy*. Note that both types of reduplication result in CVCV word structure, which is based on the universal CV syllable structure. Other phonological processes may also act to create basic CV syllable structure. **Final consonant reduction**, for example, deletes a post-vocalic, word-final obstruent, turning CVC into CV (e.g., *good* /gʊd/ pronounced [gʊ]). Likewise, **blending** combines features of two adjacent segments into a single segment, turning CCV into CV (e.g., *snow* /sno/ pronounced [n̥o]; an open circle under a segment indicates voicelessness).

The tendency toward CV syllable structure also reflects the fact that a particular consonant phoneme is not typically acquired in all word positions at the same time. For example, a child may acquire /t/ in initial position by age 3½, but not acquire /t/ in final position until age 4½. Generally speaking, segments are first acquired in word-initial position.

## *Acquisition of Morphology*

We will now examine a few representative examples of the stages a child goes through in acquiring the morphology of his or her language. Around the age of 2, the child begins to form two-word utterances; around the age of 3, these gradually increase to more than two words. Grammatical morphemes gradually begin to appear during this multiword stage, although their acquisition is not usually complete until around age 5. The class of grammatical morphemes includes inflectional and derivational affixes, among other things. (See Chapter 5 for a review of these concepts.)

**Inflectional Affixes.** In general, the {PRES PART} affix, spelled *-ing*, is acquired fairly early, presumably because this affix shows little phonological variation; that is, it always appears as /ɪŋ/ or /ɪn/. The morphemes {PAST}, {PLU}, {POSS}, and {PRES}, on the other hand, are all acquired somewhat later, presumably because they exhibit more phonological variation. For example, {PAST} shows up variously as /t/ (as in *walked* ), /d/ (as in *hugged* ), and /əd/ (as in *added* ). The rule governing this alternation involves three simple principles.

- If a verb ends in a voiceless segment other than /t/, add the voiceless segment /t/; *walk* ends in the voiceless segment /k/, so {PAST} shows up as /t/.
- If the verb ends in a voiced segment other than /d/, add the voiced segment /d/; *hug* ends in the voiced segment /g/, so {PAST} shows up as /d/.
- If the verb already ends in /t/ or /d/, add /əd/; *hate* ends in /t/, so {PAST} shows up as /əd/.

Note that the third principle is purely functional. If we were to simply add /t/ to *hate*, we would get /hett/, which is indistinguishable from the uninflected form /het/. The insertion of /ə/, however, breaks up the two /t/'s and we get /hétəd/.

Because of this phonological variation, it makes sense that a child acquiring English will take some time to infer the rules governing the various forms of {PAST}, which can be summarized as follows.

| Final Segment of Root | Phonological Form of {PAST} | Example |
|---|---|---|
| [–voice] (other than /t/) | /t/ | walk-walked |
| [+voice] (other than /d/) | /d/ | hug-hugged |
| /t,d/ | /əd/ | hate-hated |

However, the fact that the child is inferring rules is unarguable. This can be seen by examining the acquisition of irregular {PAST} forms in English. A child might first use adult irregular forms (e.g., *went* or *broke*). These, however, are apparently just memorized forms, since the child quickly moves to a second stage in which the past tense is formed following the rule just outlined. At this stage, the child often overgeneralizes the regular {PAST} morpheme to irregular verbs, resulting in forms like *goed*, *breaked*, and even *wented*. The point to note is that these are phonologically well-formed. For example, *go* ends in the voiced segment /o/; thus the past tense should be formed by the addition of /d/, yielding /god/. Finally, the child learns that verbs like *go* and *break* are exceptional in that they have irregular past tense forms, and his or her usage begins to conform to the adult's.

The acquisition of {PLU}, generally spelled *-(e)s*, follows the same progression as that of {PAST}. The morpheme {PLU} shows up variously as /s/ (as in *ducks*), /z/ (as in *dogs*), and /əz/ (as in *horses*). The rule governing this alternation involves three principles.

- If the noun ends in a voiceless segment other than /s,š,č/, add the voiceless segment /s/; *duck* ends in /k/, so {PLU} shows up as /s/.
- If the noun ends in a voiced segment other than /z,ž,ǰ/, add the voiced segment /z/; *dog* ends in /g/, so {PLU} shows up as /z/.
- If the noun ends in /s,z,š,ž,č,ǰ/, add /əz/; *horse* ends in /s/, so {PLU} shows up as /əz/.

As was the case with {PAST}, the third principle is purely functional. If we were to simply add /z/ to *horse*, we would get /hɔrzz/, which is indistinguishable from the uninflected form /horz/. The insertion of /ə/, however, breaks up this sequence and we get /hɔrzəz/.

Once again, it makes sense that a child exposed to English would take some time to infer the rules governing the various phonological forms of {PLU}, which are summarized here.

| Final Segment of Root | Phonological Form of {PLU} | Example |
|---|---|---|
| [–voice] (other than /s,š,č/) | /s/ | duck-ducks |
| [+voice] (other than /z,ž,ǰ/) | /z/ | dog-dogs |
| /s,z,š,ž,č,ǰ/ | /əz/ | horse-horses |

As with {PAST}, the fact that the child is acquiring rules is clear from examining the acquisition of irregular plural forms. For example, a child acquiring the plural of *foot* might first use the adult form *feet*. Once again, this seems to be simply a memorized form, since the child moves rapidly to a second stage in which he or she forms the plural following the rule just outlined, namely as *foots* or *feets*. Note that *foot* ends in a voiceless segment; thus the plural should be formed by adding /s/, resulting in /fʊts/. A third stage often follows in which the child treats *foots* or *feets* as an uninflected form, thus constructing the plural following the rule, namely as *footses* (or *feetses*). Note that *foots* (and *feets*) ends in /s/; thus the plural should be formed by adding /əz/, yielding *footses* /fʊtsəz/ (or *feetses*). Finally, the child learns that *foot* is exceptional in English in that it has an irregular plural form, and his or her usage begins to conform to the adult's.

The morphemes {POSS} and {PRES}, generally spelled *-'s* and *-(e)s*, respectively, exhibit the same phonological variation as {PLU}. This is illustrated in the following chart.

| | {PLU} | {POSS} | {PRES} |
|---|---|---|---|
| /s/ | cats | Bart's | waits |
| /z/ | cads | Bud's | wades |
| /əz/ | cases | Bess's | winces |

What is interesting, however, is that these three morphemes are not acquired at the same time. Instead, a child exposed to English typically acquires them in the following order: {PLU}, {POSS}, and then {PRES}. This indicates that the child acquires them as a function of their morphological, rather than their phonological, structure. The late Roman Jakobson, a Harvard linguist, proposed a sensible explanation for this progressive acquisition: the smaller the domain of application of an affix, the earlier the affix is acquired. Thus, {PLU} is acquired first because it affixes to nouns (e.g., *kids*). {POSS} is acquired next because it affixes to NP's (e.g., *the kid next door's dog*). (See Chapter 5 for a detailed discussion of this distinction.) {PRES} is acquired last because, even though it is affixed to verbs, it is a function of the entire sentence. That is, the affixation of {PRES} to a verb depends on its subject, and a subject plus a verb is essentially a sentence. Only a third-person singular subject takes an overt affix on a present tense verb (e.g., *The kid plays there* versus *The kids play there*). The distinctions among {PLU}, {POSS}, and {PRES} are summarized in the following chart.

| Order of Acquisition | Morpheme | Domain |
|---|---|---|
| 1 | {PLU} | N |
| 2 | {POSS} | NP |
| 3 | {PRES} | S |

**Derivational Affixes.** The acquisition of derivational affixes is not as well understood as the acquisition of inflectional affixes. This is because English has many more derivational affixes than inflectional affixes. (You may recall from Chapter 5 that English has only eight inflectional affixes.) Moreover, many derivational affixes in English have been borrowed from Latin and Greek, whereas all inflectional affixes are native to English. Thus, derivational affixes are associated with more advanced vocabulary, which is acquired relatively late; for example, the word *inconsolable* (from Latin) will typically come later than *unhappy* (native English). Nonetheless, we can make one generalization concerning the acquisition of derivational affixes: the more productive they are, the earlier they are acquired. A more productive affix is one that can be attached to a relatively large number of roots. For example, the *-ly* suffix, which forms an adverb from the corresponding adjective, is very productive, yielding forms such as *quick-quickly*, *careful-carefully*, and *intelligent-intelligently*. Likewise, the agentive suffix *-er*, which forms a noun from the corresponding verb, is quite productive: *love-lover*, *farm-farmer*, *drive-driver*, and so on. A less productive affix is one that can be attached to relatively few roots. For example, the suffix *-hood*, which typically forms an abstract noun from a concrete noun, is relatively unproductive: we have *father-fatherhood* and *mother-motherhood*, but not *uncle-\*unclehood*, *aunt-\*aunthood*, or *cousin-\*cousinhood*.

We can close this section by stating simply that a child's acquisition of morphology is for the most part systematic and rule governed, even though some domains, such as the acquisition of derivational morphology, are not well understood.

## Acquisition of Syntax

Let's now look at some representative examples of the stages a child goes through in acquiring the syntax or his or her language.

**Length of Utterance and Word Order.** Somewhere between the ages of 1 and 2 years, every child enters the **one-word** or **holophrastic stage**. This stage normally lasts between 3 and 9 months and is characterized by one-word utterances, where each word typically refers to some concrete object in the child's environment (e.g., *shoe, milk, eye, ball, car, Mommy, Daddy*). Around age 2, children typically enter the **two-word stage**, characterized by utterances containing a maximum of two words. These utterances are usually interpreted by adults as subject-verb (e.g., *doggie run*), verb-modifier (e.g., *push bike, sit there*), or possessor-possessed (e.g., *Mary chair*). At this stage, word order is not always consistent; thus *doggie run* might be expressed as *run doggie*, or *push bike* as *bike push*. Moreover, utterances in the two-word stage tend to lack bound and free grammatical morphemes, including auxiliary verbs. For example, *doggie run* for *The doggie's running* omits the article (*the*), the auxiliary verb (*is*), and the present participle affix (*-ing*). Instead, the child's strategy appears to be one of focusing on "content" words (i.e., lexical morphemes). As a result, the absence of grammatical morphemes may result in some surface ambiguity. For example, *Mary chair* could, at various times, indicate possession ('Mary's chair'), location ('Mary is in the chair'), or a request ('Put Mary in the chair'). However, contextual clues would typically enable a listener to interpret the intended meaning.

Next comes the **multiword stage**, which is characterized by utterances of more than two words. Harvard researcher Roger Brown has referred to this as **telegraphic speech**, since it is open-ended in length but generally lacks many grammatical morphemes, just like a telegram (e.g., *That Mary chair* 'That's Mary's chair'). The absence of grammatical morphemes also renders many forms ambiguous; for example, *Mary sit on chair* might mean 'Mary is sitting on the chair' or even 'Mary wants to sit on the chair.' It is in this stage that word order starts to become fixed. As we would expect, the most common word orders are those acquired earliest. Thus, in English, adjective-noun order (e.g., *big boy*) and subject-verb-object order (e.g., *Mary want teddy*) are acquired relatively early. Systematic permutations found in questions, negatives, and passives generally come later.

**Questions.** Stages in the acquisition of questions by children acquiring English have been studied quite extensively by language acquisition researchers. As we look at these stages, keep in mind that English has two basic interrogative structures: *yes-no* interrogatives (e.g., *Has Biff seen Tammy?*) and *wh*-interrogatives (e.g., *Who has Biff seen?*). The formation of *yes-no* interrogatives involves the rule of I-Movement, a transformation which moves the tensed auxiliary verb to the left of the subject: for example, *Biff has seen Tammy* → *Has Biff seen Tammy?* The formation of *wh*-interrogatives involves both I-Movement and *wh*-Movement, which moves a *wh*-word to clause-initial position: for example, *Has Biff seen who?* → *Who has Biff seen?*

A child exposed to English first signals questions simply by **intonation**. A declarative in English typically has falling intonation ( ⟍ ), whereas a *yes-no* interrogative has rising intonation ( ⟋ ). Thus, a child will first form *yes-no* interrogatives simply by adding a rising intonation contour to a declarative structure (e.g., *Daddy going* = 'Daddy is going' and *Daddy going?* = 'Is Daddy going?'). In the second stage, *wh*-interrogatives appear with the *wh*-word in clause-initial position (e.g., *Where Daddy going?*). At this stage, *yes-no* interrogatives are still marked only by intonation (e.g., *Daddy going?*) In the third stage, *yes-no* interrogatives are formed by I-Movement (e.g., *Is Daddy going?*). In this stage, however, *wh*-interrogatives are formed without I-Movement, even though an auxiliary may be present (e.g., *Where Daddy's going?*). In the fourth stage, the child finally forms *wh*-interrogatives with both *wh*-Movement and I-Movement (e.g., *Where's Daddy going?*). These stages may be summarized as follows.

| *Stage* | *Question Type* | *Rules* | *Example* |
|---|---|---|---|
| 1 | *yes-no* | Intonation | Daddy going? |
|   | *wh* | — | — |
| 2 | *yes-no* | Intonation | Daddy going? |
|   | *wh* | WHM | Where Daddy going? |
| 3 | *yes-no* | IM | Is Daddy going? |
|   | *wh* | WHM | Where Daddy's going? |
| 4 | *yes-no* | IM | Is Daddy going? |
|   | *wh* | WHM + IM | Where's Daddy going? |

Progression through these stages makes perfect sense. First, the earliest linguistic structure acquired by a child seems to be the intonation contours of the language to which he or she is exposed, regardless of what that language may be. In fact, intonation seems to be acquired by about the age of 12 months. Second, *wh*-Movement is a structurally simpler rule than I-Movement. *Wh*-Movement moves any *wh*-item to clause-initial position, regardless of category (NP, PP, ADVP, and so on). I-Movement, on the other hand, is less general; it moves one specific category (tensed auxiliary) to the left of another specific category (subject NP). Thus, it makes some sense that *wh*-Movement would be acquired before I-Movement. Third, *yes-no* interrogatives are formed by applying one rule (I-Movement), whereas *wh*-interrogatives are formed by applying two rules (I-Movement and *wh*-Movement). Thus, it is predictable that the adult form of *yes-no* interrogatives would appear in a child's speech before the adult form of *wh*-interrogatives.

**Negatives.**  As was the case with questions, stages in the acquisition of negative structures have been studied extensively. As we look at these stages, keep in mind that negative declarative sentences in the adult grammar place *not* immediately to the right of the first auxiliary: for example, *Biff has not seen Tammy, Biff might not have seen Tammy*, and so forth.

The use of negation begins fairly early. During the one- and two-word stages, at around age 2, the child may express negation with *no* or *not* as well as with semantically related terms like *all gone*. Negation at this stage involves juxtaposing the negative element and the term being negated (e.g., *no milk, all gone milk, no eat pudding, wear hat no*). At this stage it is typical for the subject to be omitted from the negative utterance. As the child's utterances become longer, the negative element gradually becomes incorporated into the sentence. Around age 2½–3, the contracted forms *can't* and *don't* (but not their uncontracted counterparts) may be added to the repertoire of negative elements. The exact semantic distinctions among *no, not, can't*, and *don't* may not be evident from the child's usage. At this stage the negative element typically appears between the subject and the predicate (e.g., *It not hot* or *I don't like that*).

During the final stage in the acquisition of negatives, the negative element is consistently incorporated into the sentence. (The onset of this stage varies a great deal; some children may attain it as early as age 2, while others may be closer to 3½.) This stage corresponds to a further increase in the length of the child's utterances; other auxiliary verbs, such as *can't, won't*, and *didn't*, are also added. It is important to note that the child at this stage may not have acquired other auxiliary elements that are necessary for truly adult-like negatives. In particular, forms such as *wasn't, couldn't, wouldn't*, and *shouldn't* may be acquired relatively late. At this point we may also hear forms like *I didn't told him*, indicating that the child has not yet internalized the principle for {PAST} inflection (note that both *didn't* and *told* are inflected for {PAST}, whereas in the adult grammar only the first verb form is inflected for {PAST}). The main point, though, is that the child has mastered the basic principle for negation in the adult grammar, which places *not* in sentence-internal position.

Again, this progression makes sense. If the child's early positive utterances form some sort of nucleus, then we would expect their negative counterparts to be formed by simply appending a negative item before or after this nucleus. Once a child begins to analyze utterances into subject and predicate, we would expect the negative item to appear between them, since this is its basic position within the adult grammar. Finally, since acquisition of the auxiliary system is relatively late (compared to major sentence constituents such as subject, object, and verb), we would expect relatively late acquisition of the adult rule for negatives, namely put *not* after the first auxiliary.

Once again, the point of this section is that a child's acquisition of syntactic categories and rules proceeds through orderly, systematic, and predictable stages.

## *Acquisition of Semantics*

As we saw in Chapter 3, semantics is probably the most poorly understood component of grammar. Likewise, the way that children acquire semantics is also not well understood. Nonetheless, we can still draw some generalizations concerning this process. In doing so, it is convenient to distinguish between **lexical semantics** (meanings of individual words) and **sentence semantics** (the interpretation of entire sentences). Let's look at a few representative examples within each area.

**Lexical Semantics.** Two fairly clear processes that children go through in acquiring the meaning of individual words are **overgeneralization** and subsequent **narrowing.** These processes can best be seen in the acquisition of concrete nouns. At first, the child will overgeneralize a word by using it to refer to more things than it does in the adult's lexicon. For example, *cookie* might be used to refer to anything round: a cookie, a cracker, a coin, a wheel, the moon, and so on. Over time, however, the meaning of *cookie* is narrowed so that it refers to only those items that an adult would call a *cookie.* Moreover, this narrowing often occurs in stages. For example, *dog* might be used at first to refer to any animal, then only to four-legged animals, then only to four-legged animals with fur, then only to relatively small four-legged animals with fur, and so on. (Note, incidentally, how well this process lends itself to analysis in terms of semantic features, which we discussed in Chapter 3.)

In addition, overgeneralization may affect the child's productions without affecting comprehension. For example, a child may use the term *daddy* to refer to any adult male, such as Uncle Fred or the mailman. However, if asked *Where's Daddy?* with other males present, the child may correctly point to his or her father. This is not as paradoxical as it sounds. It is a general characteristic of language acquisition that comprehension outdistances production; that is, a child can perceive distinctions that he or she cannot yet produce.

Consider another systematic stage that children seem to go through. In acquiring the meaning of individual words, children tend to acquire so-called **basic-level terms** like *house* before terms such as *building* or *cabin. House* is intermediate between a very general term such as *building* and a relatively specific term such as *cabin.* Along the same lines, children would be expected to acquire *bird* (basic-level) before *animal* (too general) or *robin* (too specific). Although the notion of "basic-level term" appeals to our intuitions, it is difficult to define exactly what distinguishes a basic-level term from one that is not "basic."

A third principle is that children typically acquire the **positive member** of a pair of opposites before the **negative member**. For example, when 3-year-olds are presented with two sticks of different lengths, they give more correct responses to questions like *Which stick is longer?* than to *Which stick is shorter?* The positive term of a pair of opposites is the unmarked member of the pair; that is, the one which carries the fewest presuppositions. For example, if a friend says that he just saw a new movie, you might ask *How long was it?* You would ask *How short was it?* only if you had some reason in advance for believing it was short. In this example, *long* is the positive term and *short* is the negative term. Likewise, we would expect a child exposed to English to acquire *tall* before *short, big* before *little, wide* before *narrow,* and *deep* before *shallow.*

**Sentence Semantics.** The way a child acquires the ability to interpret sentences is not purely a semantic phenomenon; it is inextricably bound up with syntax. Even our example concerning the acquisition of positive terms depends upon the child's ability to interpret an entire sentence: *Which stick is longer?* Thus, throughout this section, keep in mind that it is virtually impossible to keep the acquisition of sentence semantics completely separate from syntax.

One interesting case is the acquisition of the ability to interpret **passive** sentences. At one time, linguists thought that children acquired their entire linguistic system (except for vocabulary) perfectly and completely by about the age of 5. More recent research, however, indicates that some structures such as passives may not be acquired fully by some children until as late as 6 to 10 years of age. Some children as old as 4 and 5 interpret passive sentences as if they were active. For instance, sentences such as *John pushed Mary* (active) and *John was pushed by Mary* (passive) are both interpreted as 'John pushed Mary.' In such cases, it appears that the child is responding to the order of the major sentence constituents (*John, pushed,* and *Mary*) and ignoring the grammatical morphemes (*was* and *by*). In other words, the child seems to be interpreting the first NP (*John*) as the **agent**, the volitional actor, and the second NP (*Mary*) as the **patient**, the thing acted upon.

An interesting method has been developed for testing a child's ability to interpret such sentences. In this method a child is given a sentence and a set of toys, and is instructed to "act out" the sentence using the toys. Thus, for example, a child might be given two dolls, one "John" and the other "Mary." Then the child is presented with a sentence like *John was pushed by Mary* and asked to demonstrate what was said with the aid of the dolls. If the child acts out the sentence by having "John" push "Mary," then the experimenter concludes that the child interprets the sentence as 'John pushed Mary.'

A child exposed to English must also acquire the ability to interpret **bare infinitives**. Like the interpretation of passives, this ability may be acquired relatively late. A bare infinitive is a subordinate clause containing an infinitive verb and no overt subject (thus, the infinitive is said to be "bare"). For example, the sentence *I told you where to sit* contains a subordinate clause *where to sit*, which has no overt subject NP; thus, *where to sit* is a bare infinitive clause. The strategy for interpreting the subject of such bare infinitives is called the **Minimum Distance Principle** (MDP), which can be stated as follows: interpret the subject of a bare infinitive as the closest NP to the left. Note that our sample sentence, *I told you where to sit,* has two NP's to the left of the bare infinitive: *I* and *you.* The closest NP to the left of the bare infinitive is *you.* Thus, the MDP predicts that the subject of the bare infinitive *where to sit* will be the closest NP to the left, *you.* This is exactly how speakers of English interpret this sentence: 'I told you where *you* should sit,' not 'I told you where *I* should sit.' In general, the MDP seems to work fairly well in the interpretation of English.

There are, however, exceptions. Consider, for example, the analogous sentence *I asked you where to sit.* The MDP predicts that the subject of the bare infinitive *where to sit* should be the closest NP to the left, *you.* This, however, is not the way speakers of English generally interpret this sentence. For most speakers, it is interpreted as 'I asked you where *I* should sit' rather than 'I asked you where *you* should sit.' Not surprisingly, Carol Chomsky, in her research on children's interpretation of such structures, found that children acquiring English can correctly interpret sentences that conform to the MDP earlier than sentences that don't. Consequently, a child will typically go through a stage in which *I told you where to sit* will be correctly interpreted as 'I told you where *you* should sit,' but *I asked you where to sit* will be incorrectly interpreted as 'I asked you where *you* should sit.'

A final ability that children acquire in systematic stages involves the interpretation of sentences containing the temporal connectives *before* and *after*. Consider, for example, the following synonymous sentences: *He came home before he ate lunch*, *Before he ate lunch he came home*, *He ate lunch after he came home*, and *After he came home he ate lunch*. Researcher Eve Clark found that children typically go through four different stages in learning to interpret such sentences. In the first stage, they interpret all the sentences according to the **order of mention** principle: the event reported in the first clause is interpreted as happening before the event reported in the second clause. Thus, *He came home before he ate lunch* will be interpreted correctly ('First he came home, then he ate lunch'), but *Before he ate lunch, he came home* will be interpreted incorrectly ('First he ate lunch, then he came home'). In the second stage, children interpret all sentences containing *before* correctly; however, they continue to interpret sentences containing *after* according to the order-of-mention strategy. Thus, *After he came home, he ate lunch* will be interpreted correctly ('First he came home, then he ate lunch'), but *He ate lunch after he came home* will be interpreted incorrectly ('First he ate lunch, then he came home'). In the third stage, they interpret both *before* and *after* as 'before.' Thus, *Before he ate lunch, he came home* will be interpreted correctly ('First he came home, then he ate lunch'), but *After he came home, he ate lunch* will be interpreted incorrectly ('First he ate lunch, then he came home'). In the fourth and final stage, the children interpret all four sentence types correctly; that is, *before* as 'before' and *after* as 'after.' This progression is summarized in the following chart.

### Stages

1    All sentences interpreted via order of mention (i.e., event in first clause happened first; event in second clause happened second).
2    *Before* interpreted correctly; *after* interpreted via order of mention.
3    *Before* and *after* interpreted as 'before.'
4    All sentences interpreted correctly.

### Examples

|  | Stages (+ = correct; 0 = incorrect) | | | |
|---|---|---|---|---|
|  | 1 | 2 | 3 | 4 |
| He came home *before* he ate lunch. | + | + | + | + |
| *Before* he ate lunch, he came home. | 0 | + | + | + |
| He ate lunch *after* he came home. | 0 | 0 | 0 | + |
| *After* he came home, he ate lunch. | + | + | 0 | + |

One further point to note in this example is that children interpret more sentences correctly at stage 2 than at stage 3. This illustrates the fact that a child acquiring a native language may appear to be regressing at certain points in his or her development. However, once language acquisition is seen as a series of rule-governed and systematic stages, it is clear that the child is not regressing at all, but simply revising his or her set of rules. Note the parallel between this example and the acquisition of the plural of *foot*, discussed earlier: *feet* → *foots/feet* → *footses/feetses* → *feet*. The child appears to be regressing, but actually is simply acquiring a rule.

After this discussion of the acquisition of phonology, morphology, syntax, and semantics, one point should be clear. The acquisition of a first language involves more than simply imitating and memorizing samples of the language to which a child is exposed. Rather, it involves constructing a grammar of the language. This grammar, in turn, is a system composed of categories and rules which essentially constitute a definition of that language. Moreover, this grammar is acquired in stages, each of which more and more closely resembles the adult system.

## Issues in Language Acquisition

In the first half of this chapter, we looked at some representative stages a child goes through in acquiring a first language, or, more specifically, a grammar of that language. In other words, we have considered how a child passes from an initial mental state through intermediate states until he or she reaches a final mental state (possessing a grammar more or less equivalent to an adult's). One thing we have not dealt with so far is the **initial state**. The second half of this chapter briefly discusses some positions that various researchers have held concerning this initial state.

### Nativism and Empiricism

In general terms, there are basically two schools of thought on the nature of the initial mental state. On one side, we have what might be called **nativism**. Extreme nativism would hold that human beings are born with all of the knowledge that they will eventually have as adults. With respect to language, this position would hold that a child is born knowing a language and this knowledge manifests itself during the first few years of life. On the other hand, we have what might be called **empiricism**. Extreme empiricism would hold that human beings are born with none of the knowledge that they will have as adults. With respect to language, this position would hold that a child is born with no linguistic knowledge whatsoever and that all language ability is somehow learned throughout life by making associations among events in the environment. These two positions are mutually exclusive.

It is fairly easy to see that the extreme nativist position cannot be correct. If human beings were born knowing, say, English, it would be impossible to explain the fact that most people in the world do not acquire English as a first language. The same, of course, could be said of Russian, Chinese, or any other language. On the other hand, it is not quite as easy to see that the extreme empiricist position is wrong, as indeed it is. The problem with this view is that it cannot explain how human beings ever acquire a language at all (or for that matter, any knowledge whatsoever). If human beings are born with absolutely nothing in their minds, how can they make even the simplest "associations" among events in their environment? Consequently, it should not come as a surprise that no serious researcher today could hold either of these extreme positions. Instead, most students of language and language acquisition hold a position of either modified nativism or modified empiricism. From now on we will refer to these modified positions as nativism and empiricism, respectively.

The nativist position (sometimes referred to as **mentalism**) focuses on the fact that much of human behavior is **biologically determined**. That is, much of our behavior is a function of the fact that we are human beings and our genes are structured in characteristic ways. Our ability to walk is an example of biologically determined behavior: we do not learn to walk, no one teaches us to walk; as normal human beings, we simply **acquire** the ability to walk because such ability is dictated by our genes. To use one of Chomsky's favorite examples, we do not "learn" to have arms any more than birds "learn" to have wings; rather, different species develop different attributes as a function of their different genetic structures.

The person most often associated with the nativist view of language acquisition is Chomsky. Quite simply, Chomsky holds the view that human beings are born already "knowing" something about the structure of human language. That is, human beings, by virtue of their characteristic genetic structure, are born in an initial mental state in which general properties of human language are already specified. (Note that this is different from saying that humans are born with properties of one particular human language already specified.) Candidates for this innate knowledge would be those characteristics common to all human languages: for example, the fact that the phonology of every human language appears to operate in terms of segments, distinctive features, levels of representation, and phonological rules. In other words, according to this view, human beings are born with part of their grammar already in place. For example, they "know" that whatever language they are exposed to, they will have to organize the phonological component for that language in terms of segments, distinctive features, levels of representation, and phonological rules. It would probably safe to say that the nativist position is the dominant (although certainly not exclusive) view of language acquisition among American linguists today. We will discuss the motivation for this position in more detail later on.

On the other hand, the empiricist position (sometimes referred to as **behaviorism**) focuses on the fact that much of human behavior is **culturally determined**. That is, much of our behavior is a function of specific environmental factors. The ability to write (among literate societies) is an example of culturally determined behavior. We **learn** to write by going through specific training; we do not simply acquire this ability spontaneously and naturally the same way we learn to walk. Witness the fact that all normal human beings learn to walk, just as they all acquire a first language; there are entire cultures, however, which do not use any writing system at all. A more transparent example of culturally determined knowledge would be learning the rules of, say, football. This game is played by two teams of 11 players each, on a field 100 yards long, and so on and so forth. (Note, incidentally, that in Canada the game is played with 12 players on each team on a field 110 yards long.) Knowledge of the game of football is obviously culturally determined. Human beings are clearly not born with any sort of knowledge of football. Instead, the rules of the game must be learned in the same way we learn to tie our shoes or to drive on the proper side of the road: by conscious attention, specific training, and trial and error.

The person most often associated with the empiricist view of language acquisition is the late B. F. Skinner. In 1957, Skinner published *Verbal Behavior,* in which he set out his views in detail. In greatly oversimplified terms, Skinner proposed that language is learned essentially through vaguely defined powers of "association" and that human linguistic communication is a stimulus-response chain. That is, a stimulus in a person's environment causes him or her to speak (a response). In turn, this utterance (now a stimulus) causes another person to speak (a response), and so on. Under this view, the initial state has some innate structure (perhaps general powers of association and abstraction), but not much. Moreover, this view holds that language is not necessarily a human-specific capacity. That is, adherents to this position would not automatically assume that human languages are qualitatively different from animal communication systems (e.g., those found among bees, dolphins, and chimpanzees). However, since empiricism has been largely discredited within linguistics (see, for example, Chomsky's review of *Verbal Behavior*), at least in its present form and for the present time, there is little point in pursuing it here.

The main points of these two views are summarized in Figure 8–2. Keep in mind, however, that this represents a greatly oversimplified view. In reality, there are probably as many different views, representing points between what we have been calling nativism and empiricism, as there are people who have thought about the subject. Moreover, the controversy surrounding these views is still very much alive; Chomsky's position is by no means universally held.

| NATIVISM | EMPIRICISM |
|---|---|
| • Mentalism<br>• Chomsky<br>• Mind has more innate structure<br>• Language acquisition is primarily biologically determined<br>• Language is acquired | • Behaviorism<br>• Skinner<br>• Mind has less innate structure<br>• Language acquisition is primarily culturally determined<br>• Language is learned |

**FIGURE 8–2.  Nativism versus empiricism.**

## Language-Specific and General Cognitive Capacities

Even though both nativists and empiricists disagree on how much structure the human mind comes equipped with, they agree that there must be at least some innate structure in the initial state. This in turn raises another question: is any of this innate structure specifically designed to facilitate language acquisition? In other words, does the initial state contain **language-specific capacities** or does it contain only **general cognitive capacities**? Chomsky makes it quite clear that he believes the initial state to contain language-specific information. For example, the Subjacency Constraint, which essentially limits movement to adjacent clauses, has no known analog in any other domain of human knowledge. In contrast, others who have addressed this question, most notably the late French psychologist Jean Piaget, have held that the initial state does not contain language-specific information. Rather, language acquisition results from the interaction of various general cognitive capacities, such as memory, intelligence, motivation, and so on. If these "general cognitive capacities" sound vague, it is because they are. The state of the human mind as it enters the world is very poorly understood. This question of what kind of innate structure (i.e., language-specific versus general) is even harder to debate than that of how much structure (i.e., nativism versus empiricism). Here we will present one of the most clearly articulated positions on the subject, namely Chomsky's.

## Chomsky's Position

As we have seen, Chomsky is essentially a nativist. He is convinced that human beings are born with a very rich fabric of mental structure already in place. Moreover, he is convinced that part of this mental structure is language-specific in nature. Chomsky has arrived at this position through what we might call a "what else" argument. That is, he starts with a number of observations about language and language acquisition and argues that the simplest way to explain them is to assume that human beings are born with a certain amount of language-specific knowledge already in place. In other words, according to Chomsky, if linguistic ability is not due to innate, language-specific knowledge, "what else" could explain it? Let's now consider some of the observations that have led Chomsky to this conclusion.

**The Complexity of Acquired Structures.**   As we have seen throughout this chapter (indeed, throughout this entire book), the acquisition of a language is essentially the acquisition of a grammar: that is, a set of categories and rules for characterizing all and only the sentences of that language. By hypothesis, the semantic component consists of knowledge organized in terms of sense relations (e.g., antonymy, hyponymy, etc.), reference relations (e.g., anaphora, coreference, etc.), and logical relations (e.g., entailment and presupposition). The syntactic component consists of knowledge organized in terms of categories (e.g., NP, VP, etc.), constituent structure (i.e., bracketing of categories into higher units), and transformations (e.g., *wh*-Movement, NP-Movement, etc.). The morphological component consists of knowledge organized in terms of different types of morphemes (e.g., lexical or grammatical, free or bound, and inflectional or derivational). The phonological component consists of knowledge organized in terms of segments, distinctive features, levels of representation, and phonological rules. If this is a reasonably accurate representation of a grammar, then the final state achieved by a human being (i.e., an adult grammar) is exceedingly complex. From Chomsky's point of view, it is difficult to explain how human beings acquire such a complex system, unless we assume that they are genetically predisposed to do so.

**Fixed Onset and Development.**   As we have seen in the first half of this chapter, the acquisition of language begins at about the same time for all normal children (i.e., it has a "fixed onset") and progresses through predictable stages, regardless of each child's particular environment or the specific language to which he or she is exposed. For example, a child typically acquires the intonational patterns of a language around the end of his or her first year. Efforts to speed up language acquisition are generally in vain. Specific studies have found that it is generally impossible to "teach" a child a detail of language until the child is ready to acquire it spontaneously. A case often cited in the literature concerns a little boy who told his mother *Nobody don't like me.* She tried to correct this double negative by responding with *Nobody likes me.* They repeated this interchange eight times, until the boy finally said *Oh! Nobody don't likes me.* Presumably, the boy eventually acquired the adult rule for forming negatives as well as the {PRES} morpheme, but only when he reached the appropriate stage of development.

In order to appreciate the systematic and uniform progression of language acquisition, it is useful to consider the errors children do *not* make in acquiring their native language. For example, part of the experience of a child exposed to English might be utterances such as *She is cooking dinner* and *Is she cooking dinner?* From these and many other such examples, a child might be expected to form a rule for forming interrogatives as follows: move the first occurrence of *is* to the beginning of the sentence. However, this rule would predict that at some stage in the child's acquisition of English syntax, he or she would make an error of the following sort. Given a sentence with two occurrences of *is* (e.g., *The spoon she is using is broken*), the child would form the interrogative by moving the first occurrence of *is* to the beginning of the sentence. This would yield *\*Is the spoon she using is broken?* rather than the correct form *Is the spoon she is using broken?*

The significant point is that children acquiring English (or any other language with such a rule) seem never to make such mistakes. It appears that children are constrained from forming a syntactic rule which is independent of structure; that is, a rule of the form: move the first, second, or *n*th word to, say, the beginning of the utterance. Rather, all syntactic rules for all languages seem to be structure-dependent; that is, they must be framed in structural terms, with reference to units such as NP, auxiliary, subject, main clause, and so forth. In our example, the rule would be something like the following: move the first occurrence of *is* following the subject NP of the main clause to initial position in that clause. Thus, in our sample structure, the rule would identify and move the occurrence of *is* in the main clause, while completely ignoring the occurrence of *is* in the subordinate clause. Details of this analysis aside, Chomsky argues that it is difficult to account for the uniform onset and quite narrowly constrained development of language unless we assume that children are genetically predisposed to acquire a grammar that meets certain predetermined criteria.

**Rapidity of Acquisition.** A child acquires his or her first language in remarkably rapid fashion. Even though some structures are acquired later than researchers had originally thought, the fact remains that a normal child acquires the majority of his or her grammar by about 5 years of age. This is amazing when you consider the nonlinguistic tasks that many children do not master until later (e.g., tying their shoes, telling time, learning the basic conventions of etiquette, throwing a ball, snapping their fingers, riding a bicycle, and so on). Moreover, the rapidity of first-language acquisition is brought into relief by considering the painstaking labor involved in learning a second language as an adult. Approximately half of the Americans who attend college are required at some time in their careers to take a foreign language. Very few, however, ever actually gain facility in it.

Such facts suggest a genetic predisposition among humans that begins to dissipate around the age of puberty and falls off dramatically at the onset of adulthood. This view is supported by the fact that children who are exposed to two languages seem to acquire both of them with equal ease and rapidity. Another piece of evidence comes from Genie, an abused girl discovered in Los Angeles in 1971 at the age of 13. Because her father isolated her from the rest of the family, Genie had reached puberty without being exposed to language. Subsequent attempts to teach English to Genie indicated that, although she was intelligent, she was unable to acquire English in the same way or as completely as a normal child. (See Susan Curtiss's book, *Genie.*) Once again, in Chomsky's view, it is difficult to explain both the rapidity of language acquisition and the rapid decline in this ability unless we assume that language acquisition is part of a human being's genetically programmed biological development.

**Features Common to All Languages.**    On the face of things, it appears that human languages are wildly divergent. English and Japanese, for example, seem so different that it would be hard to find anything that they have in common. In fact, as recently as the late 1950's, many linguists believed that languages could differ without limit and in unpredictable ways. If, however, we look below the surface, we find that human languages are remarkably similar. As we discussed earlier, the grammars of all languages can be characterized in terms of four components—semantics, syntax, morphology, and phonology—each of which is organized in terms of the same types of categories and rules. Of course, it could be that grammars of all languages share these components and subcomponents because linguists analyze languages in terms of them; that is, linguists find what they are looking for. However, if we accept as inevitable the fact that theorists in any field must necessarily look at the subject through a theory of their own construction, languages still exhibit certain common properties that are by no means logically necessary. You may recall from the beginning of Chapter 7 that such common properties are called **language universals**.

During the past 30 years an enormous number of language universals have been proposed. Consider just a few examples. From the standpoint of phonology, all languages have at least one voiceless stop (e.g., /p,t,k/ in English), but not all languages have a voiced stop (e.g., /b,d,g/). Similarly, all languages have syllables of the form CV, but not all languages have syllables of the form VC. From the standpoint of morphology, if a language inflects nouns for gender (i.e., masculine and feminine), it always inflects them for number (i.e., singular and plural). For example, Spanish inflects nouns are inflected for gender, as in *hermano* 'brother' versus *hermana* 'sister' (*-o* = masculine, *-a* = feminine). Thus, nouns in Spanish are necessarily inflected for number, as in *hermano* 'brother' versus *hermanos* 'brothers.' On the other hand, a language that inflects for number does not necessarily inflect for gender. For example, English inflects nouns for number, as in *brother* versus *brothers*, but not for gender. From the standpoint of syntax, if a language moves *wh*-items (e.g., *who, what*, etc. in English), it moves them leftward to clause-initial position, never rightward to clause-final position. Similarly, in simple declarative sentences, the vast majority of languages (approximately 99 percent) order the subject before the object. And the list goes on and on.

Even though some of these universals are absolute (i.e., all languages have property X) and others are implicational (e.g., if a language has property X, then it will also have property Y), the fact is that none of these universals is logically necessary. For example, there is no logical reason that inflectional suffixes must follow derivational suffixes. It is perfectly possible to imagine a human language in which the opposite situation holds. Likewise, there is no logical reason that languages move *wh*-items to the left; they could just as easily move them to the right. Chomsky's view is once again straightforward: it is difficult to explain the vast number of common (but not logically necessary) features among languages unless we assume that such properties are specified by the genetically determined initial state.

**Independence of Instruction.** A normal child acquires the bulk of his or her first language (other than vocabulary) before ever starting school; thus, it is clear that teachers do not "teach" a child language. Indeed, children who never attend school in their lives acquire language. Likewise, parents do not "teach" their children language. In fact, most parents have no conscious knowledge of the rules of their language. What parent (other than one who has studied syntax) would be able to state, say, the rule of I-Movement? Even for those few adults who have conscious knowledge of (some of) the rules of their own language, it is hard to imagine how they could convey such information to a child. Consider an extremely simple example, often cited by Chomsky. Every native speaker of English knows that in the sentence *Bob proved that he is incompetent*, the pronoun *he* can refer either to Bob or to someone else. Likewise, every such speaker knows that in the sentence *Bob proved him to be incompetent*, the pronoun *him* must refer to someone other than Bob. This knowledge is clear-cut and acquired without training; yet imagine trying to explain the principle involved here to a 5- or even a 10-year-old child!

Moreover, much of our grammatical knowledge is acquired without appropriate experience; that is, we know things about our language for which we apparently have no relevant experience. A favorite example of Chomsky's involves what he calls **parasitic gaps**. In such constructions, a pronoun can be omitted without affecting the interpretation of the sentence—for example, *Who did you insult by ignoring him?* versus *Who did you insult by ignoring?* (Most speakers prefer one or the other of these sentences, but the point is that both of them can be interpreted as identical in meaning.) These parasitic gap constructions, however, are extremely rare in English. Compare, for example, the sentences *Who insulted Bob by ignoring him?* and *\*Who insulted Bob by ignoring?* In this pair, which is the typical case in English, the pronoun *him* cannot be optionally omitted. Chomsky's point is that constructions containing parasitic gaps are so uncommon that it is unlikely that a child would ever be exposed to one while acquiring the syntax of English. Nevertheless, all native speakers of English know exactly when a pronoun may and may not be omitted, and they apparently know this without training and without relevant experience.

From Chomsky's point of view, it is difficult to explain how such subtle grammatical distinctions are acquired independently of instruction and experience, unless we assume that the basic grammatical principles that underlie these distinctions are biologically determined and present in the initial state.

**Independence of Intelligence and Motivation.** Acquiring a first language does not seem to be a direct function of intelligence. The individual with an IQ of 70 acquires the grammar of the language to which he or she is exposed just as the individual with an IQ of 130 does. Even children with Down syndrome acquire a grammar. Likewise, language acquisition does not seem to be a function of motivation. Normal children do not "try" to acquire language; they do not have to work at it; they simply acquire it—effortlessly and spontaneously. In fact, it is impossible to interrupt or retard language acquisition short of isolating the child from language completely (as in the case of Genie mentioned earlier). Again, from Chomsky's perspective it is virtually impossible to explain the fact that language acquisition is independent of intelligence and motivation, unless we assume that it is a biologically determined process.

Since there has been so much controversy and misunderstanding over this line of reasoning, let us reiterate this argument in point form. Chomsky first makes the following observations.

- The final state achieved (i.e., an adult grammar) is extremely complex.
- Language acquisition is characterized by a fixed onset and uniform stages of development.
- Language acquisition is comparatively rapid (i.e., it is accomplished almost totally by age 5 or 6).
- All languages have numerous features in common—features which are not the product of logical necessity.
- Human language is not taught.
- Language acquisition is independent of intelligence and motivation.

Chomsky then concludes that these observations are difficult (if not impossible) to explain unless we make the following assumptions. First, human beings acquire a language because they are genetically programmed to do so. Second, this genetic endowment contains (among other things) language-specific capacities, present at birth. The only requirement for language acquisition external to the individual is exposure to a human language. In other words, language acquisition is both biologically and culturally determined. The biologically determined linguistic capacities present in the initial state interact with the culturally determined experience of the child (i.e., the particular language spoken around the child) to set off the acquisition of a human language.

This position, of course, may turn out to be either totally or partially incorrect. And, in fact, there is widespread controversy over its details. It is, however, the most clearly articulated and (for us, at least) the most convincing theory presently available to explain commonplace observations about language acquisition.

# Summary

Let's review what we have done. We started with four observations about the acquisition of a first language. However, we had no ready explanation for these phenomena. Thus, we constructed a (partial) theory of language acquisition to account for our original observations. This theory makes use of such concepts as prelinguistic and linguistic stages, the latter of which constitute grammars (i.e., systems of categories and rules) that more and more closely correspond to the adult's. We have also seen that the acquisition of language can be subdivided into the acquisition of phonology, morphology, syntax, and semantics. Moreover, we have looked at some of the fundamental philosophical issues surrounding language acquisition. These issues reflect two positions regarding the initial mental state of the human organism: nativism (more innate structure) and empiricism (less innate structure). Furthermore, controversy exists over whether the initial state contains language-specific capacities or only general cognitive capacities.

As usual, it is worth pointing out that there is much more to the study of language acquisition than what has been presented in this one short chapter. However, you have now been exposed to some of the basic ideas in the field; if you want to learn more about the subject, see the readings listed below. In the meantime, the practice problems and answers may be beneficial in checking your understanding of the material presented here. Following them are 50 exercises without answers for you to do on your own.

# Supplementary Readings

## Primary

Chomsky, N. (1959). A review of B. F. Skinner's *Verbal behavior*. Language, 35, 26–58.

Chomsky, N. (1980). *Rules and representations*. New York: Columbia University Press.

Curtiss, S. (1977). *Genie: A psycholinguistic study of a modern-day "wild child."* New York: Academic Press.

Flanagan, O. J. (1984). *The science of the mind*. Cambridge, MA: MIT Press.

Lightfoot, D. (1982). *The language lottery*. Cambridge, MA: MIT Press.

Newmeyer, F. (1983). *Grammatical theory*. Chicago: University of Chicago Press.

Skinner, B. F. (1957). *Verbal behavior*. New York: Appleton-Century-Crofts.

## Secondary

Chomsky, N. (1983). Interview. *Omni* (November), 113–118, 171–174.

Clark, H., and Clark, E. (1977). *Psychology and language* (Chapters 8–10). New York: Harcourt Brace Jovanovich.

Ingram, D. (1988). *First language acquisition: Method, description, and explanation*. Cambridge: Cambridge University Press.

Lenneberg, E. (1964). The capacity for language acquisition. In J. Katz and J. Fodor (Eds.), *The structure of language* (pp. 579–603). Englewood Cliffs, NJ: Prentice-Hall.

Moskowitz, B. A. (1979). The acquisition of language. *Scientific American* (November), 82–96.

You are now prepared to read all of the secondary works. Clark and Clark and Moskowitz provide good discussions of the stages a child goes through in acquiring a language. Ingram provides a comprehensive review and synthesis of research on the acquisition of phonology, morphology, syntax, and semantics; it assumes familiarity with basic concepts in these areas. Lenneberg distinguishes between biologically determined and culturally determined behavior, and discusses the characteristics of each. Chomsky (1983) provides a straightforward rendering of his views on the biological basis of language acquisition.

An introductory course in linguistics is probably necessary to fully appreciate the primary works. Chomsky (1980), Lightfoot, and Newmeyer are excellent discussions of Chomsky's views. Curtiss is a classic study in the effects of depriving a child of linguistic stimuli. Flanagan provides a rich discussion of the intellectual traditions from which Skinner, Piaget, and Chomsky operate. Skinner and Chomsky (1959), however, are difficult going and are now primarily of historical interest. The former is the classic statement of the empiricist view of language, and the latter is Chomsky's detailed rejection of it.

# Practice

1. For each set of structures (a–g), which construction would children exposed to English be most likely to acquire first?

   a. /ɪ/           /a/           /æ/
   b. /k/           /č/           /p/
   c. /t/           /s/           /r/
   d. VC            CV            CVC
   e. {POSS}        {PRES}        {PLU}
   f. V-Movement    *wh*-Movement    Intonation
   g. *not*         *don't*        *do not*

2. True/False
   a. Intelligence seems to play a major role in a child's ability to acquire a language.
   b. It will generally take a child longer to acquire Japanese than to acquire English.
   c. It is generally impossible for a parent to speed up the process of language acquisition.
   d. To support the empiricist point of view, a researcher would be more likely to cite second-language acquisition by an adult rather than first-language acquisition by a child.
   e. The babbling stage seems to be a necessary prerequisite for normal language acquisition.
   f. Before a child exposed to English has acquired the ability to interpret passives, he or she would be likely to interpret *Tommy petted Bozo* and *Bozo was petted by Tommy* as having different meanings.
   g. A child exposed to English would be likely to acquire the meaning of *old* before *young*.

3. Consider the following interchange between 4-year-old Muffin and her mother.
   MUFFIN:  Why you don't eat?
   MOTHER:  What?
   MUFFIN:  Why don't you eat?

These data illustrate that Muffin is in the process of acquiring a particular syntactic rule of English. Which one?

4. A child exposed to English might go through the following stages in acquiring the rule for forming the past tense of verbs. At which stage has the child actually acquired a *rule* similar to that in the adult grammar?

   Stage I:     eat
   Stage II:    ate
   Stage III:   eated
   Stage IV:    ate

5. Assume a child is acquiring English. Which of the following representations of *stick* would be most likely to appear first: [tʰɪk] or [stɪ]?

6. The empiricist approach to language acquisition would claim that children must base their grammar only on the language they hear spoken around them. Chomsky would say that this view is not entirely correct. What additional information would he claim that the child brings to the task of language acquisition?

7. A child acquiring English who says *feetses* for *feet* has apparently misanalyzed the root form to which the {PLU} suffix is attached. What is the root of *feetses* for this child?

8. Consider the following sentences.

   A. I promised Mary to go.
   B. I persuaded Mary to go.

   a. Which of these sentences would be correctly interpreted first by a child acquiring English?
   b. What principle accounts for this?

9. Forms such as *comed* (for {come} + {PAST}), *wented* (for {go} + {PAST}), and *foots* (for {foot} + {PLU}) are common in child language. How do such forms bear on the views of language acquisition held by Skinner and Chomsky?

10. A 3-year-old imitated a Folgers coffee commercial as follows: *The best part of waking up is SOLDIERS in your cup.* What word-formation process is the child utilizing? (Hint: see Chapter 5. )

## Answers

The following answers are, in some cases, not the only possible ones. Discussion of other possible answers is part of the exercises.

**1.** a. /a/                          e. {PLU}
    b. /p/                          f. Intonation
    c. /t/                          g. *not*
    d. CV

**2.** a. F                           e. F
    b. F                           f. T

c. T                               g. T
d. T

**3.** I-Movement

**4.** Stage III

**5.** [tʰɪk]

**6.** Genetically encoded universal properties of language (sometimes called **universal grammar**).

**7.** *feets*

**8.** a.  sentence (B)
b.  Minimum Distance Principle

**9.** They support Chomsky's views at the expense of Skinner's, since none of these forms could be the result of imitation.

**10.** Folk etymology.

# Exercises

**1.** In terms of syllable structure alone, which word would a child exposed to English be expected to acquire earliest?

a.  dog            b.  dough         c.  slow          d.  March

**2.** In terms of syllable structure alone, which of the following words would typically be acquired earliest by children exposed to English?

a.  train          b.  play          c.  kick          d.  past

**3.** A child acquiring English produces the following forms:

|       | Adult Form | Child's Form |
|-------|-----------|--------------|
| stop  | /stap/    | [tap]        |
| slide | /slaɪd/   | [laɪd]       |
| Sue   | /su/      | [su]         |
| Casey | /kési/    | [kési]       |
| house | /haʊs/    | [haʊs]       |

Which rule describes the way that the child's forms differ from the adult's?

a. /s/→ø/ ___ C              d. /s/→ø/ ___ V
b. /s/→ø/ C ___              e. /s/→ø/ C ___
c. /s/→ø/ V ___                   [-vce]

**4.** How would the child described in question (3) be expected to pronounce *smoke*?

a.  [mok]          b.  [smok]        c.  [smo]         d.  [mo]

**5.** Consider the forms /wiwi/, /pupu/, and /kaka/. These forms illustrate _____.
a.  reduplication
b.  the three earliest vowels acquired by children

c.  blending
d.  all of the above
e.  (a) and (b) only

6.  According to Clark & Clark (1977: 399), the following rules are common in child language:

A.  fricative + stop → stop (e.g., *stop* → [tʰɔp])
B.  nasal + stop → stop (e.g., *lamp* → [læp])
C.  fricative + liquid → fricative (e.g., *free* → [fi])

a.  How does the order in which segments are acquired appear to relate to the order in which segments are omitted?

b.  Explain in particular why the fricative is deleted in rule A. but retained in rule C.

7.  Smith & Wilson (1985) report the case of a 3-year-old who produced the following forms:

| | | | |
|---|---|---|---|
| [rətǽk] | 'attack' | [rəd͡ʒɔ́ɪ] | 'enjoy' |
| [rəstʌ́rb] | 'disturb' | [rətár] | 'guitar' |
| [rəlǽstɪk] | 'elastic' | [rədʌ́ktər] | 'conductor' |

What property of the first syllable of these words might explain why it is the one replaced by [rə]?

8.  Identify the phonological process(es) illustrated by the following form: [síwi] for *silly*.

9.  Identify the phonological process(es) illustrated by the following form: [tíbí] for *T.V.*

10.  Identify the phonological process(es) illustrated by the following form: [blǽŋki] for *blanket*.

11.  Identify the phonological process(es) illustrated by the following form: [bɛ́wi] for *very*.

12.  Identify the phonological process(es) illustrated by the following form: [l̥o] for *slow*.

13.  Identify the phonological process(es) illustrated by the following form: [dɔ] for *dog*.

14.  Identify the phonological process(es) illustrated by the following form: [kwézi] for *crazy*.

15.  Consider the childhood form [skéti] for *spaghetti* /spəgéti/. Explain where the /k/ comes from.

16.  The article "Say Rabbit, Not Wabbit" (1971) describes the following hypothesis put forth by Robert Ringel of Purdue University: "persons with functional speech disorders [e.g., who say *wabbit* for *rabbit*] have faulty sensory perception in their mouths . . . they lack the oral sense of touch."

a.  Name one piece of evidence that this hypothesis is false. (Hint: if the hypothesis were true, what "mistakes" would you expect such people to make?)

b.  How are /r/ and /w/ similar? (Hint: lips.)
c.  How are /r/ and /w/ different? (Hint: tongue.)

17.  Consider the following riddles.

Q: How do you catch a unique rabbit?
A: "Unique" up on him.
Q: How do you catch a tame rabbit?

A: The "tame" way.

Explain how regular phonological processes account for the "humor" in these riddles.

18. A child acquiring English systematically produces [tap] for *stop* rather than [tʰap].

    a. What can you conclude about the child's phonemic representation of *stop*?
    b. Explain your reasoning.

19. Brown (1973: 358), in a longitudinal study of three children, tracked their acquisition of 14 grammatical morphemes as well as the relative frequency with which their parents used the same morphemes. One of his findings was that the articles *a* and *the* were among the morphemes most frequently used by the parents, yet they were acquired eighth out of fourteen by the children. How does this finding constitute a problem for the behaviorist view of first-language acquisition?

20. In experiments conducted by Warden (1976), subjects of different ages were asked to look at drawings and construct a story from them. Over half of the 3-year-olds began their stories with structures like the following:

    A. *The* cat was chasing *the* bird. *The* bird flew away from *the* cat.

    In contrast, over 80 percent of the 9-year-olds and 100 percent of the adults began their stories with structures like the following:

    B. *A* cat was chasing *a* bird. *The* bird flew away from *the* cat.

    Note the way that the 3-year-olds differ from the older stubjects in their use of definite and indefinite articles. What pattern do the older subjects follow that the 3-year-olds have not acquired yet? (Hint: "old" information is that known to the hearer, and "new" information is not.)

21. Consider the following exchange reported by Aitchison (1985: 96):

    CHILD: My teacher holded the baby rabbits and we patted them.
    ADULT: Did you say your teacher held the baby rabbits?
    CHILD: Yes.
    ADULT: What did you say she did?
    CHILD: She holded the baby rabbits and we patted them.
    ADULT: Did you say she held them tightly?
    CHILD: No, she holded them loosely.

    a. What does this exchange illustrate about the relative processes of acquiring regular and irregular verbs?
    b. About the disjunction between comprehension and production?
    c. About the role of imitation in language acquisition?

22. Which of the following forms would a child acquiring English be expected to produce first? Second? Third?

    A. Why he's crying?
    B. Why he crying?
    C. Why's he crying?

23. According to Limber (1973: 181), children first learning to produce sentences with relative clauses produce sentences like (A) before those like (B):

    A. I want the doll *Mary's got*.
    B. The doll *Mary's got* is pretty.

What structural difference between the placement of the relative clause in (A) and (B) might explain why the (A) structure is acquired earlier?

**24.** Judy Reilly of UCLA (cited in Moskowitz [1979: 94]) recorded the following interchange between 6-year-old Jamie and his mother.

| | |
|---|---|
| JAMIE: | Why are you doing that? |
| MOTHER: | What? |
| JAMIE: | Why are you writing what I say down? |
| MOTHER: | What? |
| JAMIE: | Why are you writing down what I say? |

These data illustrate that Jamie has mastered a syntactic principle of English. Considering only these data, name the principle. (Hint: consult the practice problems at the end of Chapter 4. )

**25.** A child learns the meaning of *chair* before that of *recliner, rocker,* or *furniture.* This illustrates which principle:

a. minimum distance principle
b. overgeneralization
c. basic-level terms
d. order of mention
e. none of the above

**26.** Clark (1975: 83) describes a child who used the word [bɔ] to refer to a ball, an apple, an egg, and a bell clapper. What semantic property appears to be the basis for this over-generalization?

**27.** Clark (1975: 84) describes a child who used the word *fly* to refer to a fly, a speck of dust, crumbs of bread, and her own toes. What semantic property appears to be the basis for this overgeneralization?

**28.** Clark (1975: 83) describes a child who used the word [kotibaɪz] to refer to the bars of his cot, a large toy abacus, a toast rack, and a picture of a building with a columned facade. What semantic property appears to be the basis for this overgeneralization?

**29.** A child was observed saying *the UPMOST importance* for *the UTMOST importance.* What word-formation process is the child using here? (Hint: see Chapter 5. )

**30.** Why would children exposed to English be expected to learn the meaning of the prepositions *in* and *on* before *behind* and *in front of*? (Hint: perspective.)

**31.** A child uses *car* to refer to cars, trucks, and buses, but not to bicycles or airplanes. What semantic features does the child appear to associate with *car* at this stage?

**32.** Consider the following sentences:

A. Tommy kicked Mary.
B. Mary was kicked by Tommy.

a. Which sentence would a child typically interpret correctly at an earlier stage?
b. Explain why.

**33.** For the following set of sentences, identify the one that a child would be expected to interpret correctly at the earlier stage, and state the principle that accounts for your answer.

A. Which tree is taller?
B. Which tree is shorter?

**34.** For the following set of sentences, identify the one that a child would be expected to interpret correctly at the earlier stage, and state the principle that accounts for your answer.

A. We'll go to the movie as soon as we go to the store.

B. As soon as we go to the store, we'll go to the movie.

**35.** According to Clark & Clark (1977: 355–56), children acquiring relative clauses find them easier to interpret if the relative pronoun cannot be deleted and if the relative clause does not interrupt the main clause. Based on these principles, which of the following sentences should be easiest for a child to interpret? Most difficult?

a. The girl that ran after the boy caught the dog.

b. The girl that the boy ran after caught the dog.

c. The girl caught the dog that ran after the boy.

d. The girl caught the dog that the boy ran after.

**36.** Carol Chomsky (1969: 24–32) conducted research on the ability of 5- to 10-year-olds to interpret certain syntactic structures. She showed the subjects a blindfolded doll and then asked *Is this doll hard to see or easy to see?* Nearly all of the 5-year-olds (and some of the 6-, 7-, and 8-year-olds) responded *hard to see*, as in the following exchange:

| CHOMSKY: | Is this doll easy to see or hard to see? |
| LISA: | Hard to see. |
| CHOMSKY: | Will you make her easy to see? |
| LISA: | If I can get this untied. |
| CHOMSKY: | Will you explain why she was hard to see? |
| LISA (TO DOLL): | Because you had a blindfold over your eyes. |
| CHOMSKY: | And what did you do? |
| LISA: | I took it off. |

Explain how the children's interpretation of these structures differs from an adult's.

**37.** In research conducted by Bates (1976: 295–326), pairs of sentences like the following were presented to 3-year-olds and 6-year-olds and they were asked to choose the more polite form:

A. Give me a candy.

B. Would you give me a candy?

The 3-year-olds judged (B) as more polite only about 50 percent of the time, while the 6-year-olds judged (B) as more polite about 80 percent of the time. What concept from pragmatics do the 6-year-olds appear to be more sensitive to?

**38.** Clark & Clark (1977: 364–65) describe a study in which 7-year-olds were tested on their ability to produce speech acts for asking, ordering, and promising another child to do something. Over 90 percent of the children produced appropriate utterances for asking and ordering, but only 55 percent produced appropriate utterances for promising. Try to explain these results, using a principle from either pragmatics or semantics.

**39.** At an amusement park, a child and his parents are arguing about the child riding on the roller coaster. The child says *I promise I won't throw up if you let me go on the ride.* The parents protest that the child cannot make such a promise. The child continues to scream *I promise . . . I promise.* What felicity condition on promises has the child not yet learned?

**40.** A child says to his parent, *If you don't let me stay up and watch T.V., you'll be sorry.* The parent, however, may interpret this as a nonfelicitous threat.

a. If so, what felicity condition on performatives does the parent assume it violates?

b. On the other hand, what might the child do to make the threat felicitous?

**41.** A mother says to her child *Why don't you stop sucking your thumb?* in order to get the child to stop sucking his thumb. The child replies *Because I don't want to.*

a. What pragmatic distinction has the child failed to learn (or is at least ignoring)?

b. Explain how the child interprets the mother's utterance so he can respond to it as he does.

**42.** In an early study by Berko & Fraser (cited in Ingram [1988: 441–43]), 2- to 3-year olds were asked to imitate sentences like the following:

A. I showed you the book.
B. I will read the book.
C. Do I like to read books?
D. Where does it go?

Some of the different children's responses to each sentence are given below.

A1.  I show book.
A2.  I show you the book.

B1.  Read book.
B2.  I will read book.
B3.  I read the book.

C1.  To read book?
C2.  I read books?
C3.  I read book?

D1.  Go?
D2.  Does it go?
D3.  Where do it go?

What generalizations can you draw about the types of morphemes that tend to be omitted in the children's repetitions? Retained?

**43.** Consider the following exchange between a father and his 3-year-old daughter about nursery school.

FATHER:  What is the name of the dog at your school?
CHILD:  Way.
FATHER:  Way?
CHILD:  No, Way.
FATHER:  Did you say Way?
CHILD:  No. (Angrily) I said WAY!
FATHER:  (Suddenly catching on) Oh, you mean Ray?
CHILD:  Yes, that's what I said—Way!

This exchange illustrates the developmental relationship between comprehension and production. What is that relationship?

**44.** Aitchison (1985: 93–94) compares the case of Genie to that of Isabelle, the child of a deaf mute, who was isolated from language until age 6½. Isabelle exhibited normal language behavior by age 8½, two years after her discovery. In contrast, Genie, who was nearly 14 when discovered, has never exhibited normal language behavior. What hypothesis about language acquisition might explain the different outcomes of these two cases?

**45.** On an episode of the TV show *Family Feud*, host Ray Coombs asked the contestants, "Besides walking and talking, name something else parents teach their children to do."

  a. Would Chomsky agree or disagree with the premises of this question?

  b. Why would Chomsky agree or disagree?

**46.** Moscowitz (1979) makes a number of claims concerning language acquisition. Which of the following claims is consistent with the *nativist* view of language acquisition?

  a. "The child is confronted with the task of learning a language about which she knows nothing."

  b. First-language acquisition involves "intense effort."

  c. "Any language specialization that exists in the child is only one aspect of more general cognitive capacities."

  d. "People who learn at least two languages in early childhood appear to retain a greater flexibility of the vocal musculature."

  e. none of the above

**47.–50.** In the article "How Genes Shape Personality" (1987), Stanford psychiatrist Herbert Leiderman is quoted as saying "The pendulum is definitely swinging toward the side of the biologists and away from the environmentalists." The article explains that "scientists are turning up evidence that heredity has a greater influence on one's personality and behavior than either one's upbringing or the most crushing social pressure."

**47.** In terms of this passage, would Chomsky be more of a "biologist" or an "environmentalist"? How about Skinner?

**48.** According to the article, the science of sociobiology claims that the mind is not a *tabula rasa* (blank slate) "to be filled in from birth by family and society," but rather "is 'hard wired' before birth with a predisposed personality. This predisposition can be enhanced or suppressed, but not eliminated." Which of the following persons and concepts would be in basic agreement with the tenets of sociobiology?

  a. mentalism          d. Skinner

  b. nativism           e. "environmentalists"

  c. Chomsky            f. "biologists"

**49.** The article quotes Harvard zoologist Edward O. Wilson as saying "Genes hold the culture on a leash." Which of the following terms best describes Wilson?

  a. behaviorist        d. Skinnerian

  b. empiricist         e. "environmentalist"

  c. nativist

**50.** Assume that it turns out that the "biologists" turn out to be correct and that the "environmentalists" are wrong. The article says that some people fear that this might have an adverse effect on education. What would drive this fear?

# Chapter 9

# Second-Language Acquisition

**Second-language acquisition** is the study of how native speakers of one language acquire another language. (Hereafter, the native or source language will be referred to as the L1, and the second or target language as the L2.) In particular, second-language acquisition is concerned with explaining phenomena like the following:

(1) Norwegian forms negatives by placing the negative after the main verb (analogous to *He wrote not the book*). However, a speaker of Norwegian learning English may produce forms like *He not wrote the book*, even though such a construction never occurs in Norwegian or English.

(2) A speaker of Spanish learning English may pronounce *Spain* with an initial vowel [ɛspén], much as it would be pronounced in Spanish.

(3) A speaker of English learning German will have relatively little difficulty pronouncing *Tag* [tak] 'day' with a final [k], as native German speakers do. However, a speaker of German learning English will have relatively more difficulty pronouncing *bag* with a final [g], as native English speakers do.

(4) A speaker of Spanish learning English may produce *wh*–questions such as *Where she went?*, just as children acquiring English as an L1 do.

Observation (1) suggests that speakers acquiring an L2 go through stages during which they construct a grammar different from that of both L1 and L2. Observation (2) suggests that some properties of this intermediate grammar reflect the influence of rules in the L1. Observation (3) suggests that apparent mirror-image differences between two languages are not equally easy to acquire. Observation (4) suggests that speakers acquiring an L2 go through stages similar to those that native speakers go through when acquiring that language as an L1.

The remainder of this chapter discusses research of two types. First, it reviews some basic issues in second-language acquisition, focusing on the intermediate grammar of the language learner and how it is formed. Second, it describes some specific patterns in phonology, morphology, syntax, and semantics that have been observed in speakers acquiring a second language. This chapter does not discuss classroom methods for facilitating second-language acquisition; however, the reader should be aware that a large body of research exists on teaching both foreign languages and English as a second language.

## Issues in Second-Language Acquisition

To learn a second language is more than just to unlearn by trial and error the habits of one's native language. Between L1 and L2 the learner constructs a rule-governed **interlanguage**, arising from several different influences besides **language transfer**, that is, forms from the native language imposed on the second language. These include **language universals**, **markedness** relationships between L1 and L2, and **developmental processes** typical of first- (i.e., child) language acquisition. This section discusses each of these basic concepts needed to understand current issues in second-language acquisition.

### Interlanguage Theory

The term *interlanguage*, first used by Selinker, refers to an intermediate grammar (i.e., linguistic system) that evolves as a learner acquires an L2. The interlanguage is characteristically distinct from both the L1 and the L2. A procedure known as **error analysis** attempts to identify regularities in interlanguage forms. These forms are viewed as reflecting the learner's hypotheses about the L2 and are believed to be rule-governed, just as the L1 and L2 are. For example, the learner may go through a stage of producing English negatives of the type *He not wrote the book.* Even though this is not a pattern found in the L1 or L2, the learner is forming negatives in a systematic way, by putting *not* before the main verb. At the same time, more recent studies of interlanguage have acknowledged that it has variation, just as variation exists in any natural language. For example, a learner may exhibit more native-like pronunciation of an L2 when reading a word list than when engaged in casual conversation. An English speaker learning Russian, for instance, might pronounce *czar* [tsar] as [dzar] in a word list but as [zar] in conversation.

### Language Transfer

The degree to which the L1 influences interlanguage is still subject to debate. During the 1950's and 1960's, an approach known as **contrastive analysis** attempted to account for learner errors by examining similarities and differences (i.e., contrasts) between the L1 and L2. These contrasts were used to construct **hierarchies of difficulty**, predictions about the ease with which a particular L2 structure could be acquired, given facts about the L1. The most difficult type of contrast was predicted to be one in which the learner has to acquire a form that is nonexistent in the L1, as for example when a speaker of English must learn Spanish [β] (a voiced bilabial fricative) as an allophone of /b/ after a vowel, as in *cabeza* [kaβesa] 'head.' At the other end of the hierarchy, the contrastive analysis hypothesis predicted that the least difficulty would be encountered when a form or structure could be transferred with no change from L1 to L2; for example, both Spanish and English require that an /sw/ cluster be followed by a vowel.

Despite the common-sense appeal of contrastive analysis, its predictions of difficulty were not always borne out. For example, neither /ŋ/ nor /ž/ occurs word-initially in native English words. Yet speakers of English have much greater difficulty acquiring initial /ŋ/ (as in the Vietnamese name *Ngo*) than initial /ž/ (as in the French name *Jacques*). In some cases, in fact, it was found that similar forms in L1 and L2 presented *more* difficulties than dissimilar forms did. For example, Japanese contains the phoneme /r/, yet Japanese speakers have difficulty acquiring the distinction between the English phonemes /r/ and /l/, despite their similarity (i.e., both are voiced liquids). More generally, the contrastive analysis approach viewed language as a set of "habits," some of which must be "unlearned" during second-language acquisition. This essentially empiricist view was incompatible with subsequent nativist approaches that also took into account other forces, such as the learner's active contribution and the role of developmental processes in language acquisition and, by extension, second-language acquisition. (See Chapter 8 for a brief discussion of issues in first-language acquisition.)

At the same time, the influence of L1 on L2 acquisition cannot be ignored. The language learner may exhibit either **negative transfer** (also known as **interference**), in which some property of the L1 impedes acquisition of the L2, or **positive transfer**, in which some property of the L1 promotes the acquisition of the L2. An example of negative transfer would be a native speaker of English who, while acquiring French as an L2, transfers English subject-verb-pronominal object word order to French, as in *Il veut les* (he-wants-them) for *Il les veut* (he-them-wants). An example of positive transfer would be a native speaker of French who, while acquiring English as an L2, transfers French subject-verb-nominal object word order to English, as in *He wants the books.* The degree of L1 influence may also vary according to linguistic domain. For example, it is much easier to identify a non-native speaker from pronunciation errors than from syntactic errors. That is, negative transfer from the L1 may be more apparent in phonology that in syntax: when we think of a "foreign accent," it is phonological interference that we are typically responding to.

## *Other Linguistic Factors*

Other factors that cannot be attributed to language transfer from the L1 also affect second-language acquisition and the form of the interlanguage.

**Language Universals.** Language universals are those properties (i.e., categories and rules) that (nearly) all human languages have in common. (See Chapter 8.) The theory of language universals is intended primarily to explain first-language acquisition: universal properties of language are attributed to the child's initial state, thus relieving the child from having to learn these properties as idiosyncratic facts about the particular language to which he or she is exposed. Not surprisingly, researchers in second-language acquisition have also become interested in language universals. For one thing, L2 learners apparently face a **projection problem** similar to that faced by L1 learners: namely, they must acquire grammatical knowledge that cannot be inferred solely from the data they are exposed to. Language universals provide an explanation for this ability. In addition, controversy exists over the critical period hypothesis (i.e., the notion that language-acquisition abilities atrophy with age). This leaves open the possibility that adults may have access to language universals when acquiring an L2.

Universals can be classified as implicational or non-implicational. An **implicational** universal is a property whose presence implies some other property. A commonly cited example concerns the distribution of voiced and voiceless stops among the world's languages. Some languages have only voiceless stops (e.g., Paiute and many other American Indian languages); other languages have both voiced and voiceless stops (e.g., English and most Western European languages); but no languages have only voiced stops. Based on this distribution, we can state that the presence of voiced stops in a language implies the presence of voiceless stops, but not vice versa. On the other hand, some universals are **non-implicational**. For example, all languages have stop consonants, but this property alone does not imply the presence or absence of any other property.

Likewise, language universals can be classified as absolute or statistical. Universals are **absolute** if they are without exception. For example, all languages have syllables of the form CV, all languages have pronominal categories that include three persons and two numbers, and *wh*-movement always moves the *wh*-item leftward to clause-initial position. On the other hand, **statistical** universals, or tendencies, are properties that occur frequently but that do have exceptions. For example, verb-initial languages *generally* have prepositions (e.g., *in there*), while verb-final languages generally have postpositions (e.g., *therein*).

Finally, language universals can also be **parametric**, meaning that languages can vary according to the value they assign to a parameter. For example, languages vary in their setting for the so-called Pro-Drop Parameter, that is, in whether or not they allow the omission of subject pronouns in tensed clauses. For example, Spanish allows Pro-Drop, whereas English does not. The Spanish sentence *Está enfermo* translates literally as 'Is sick'; the referent of the subject is identified from the linguistic and nonlinguistic context. The English counterpart of this sentence, however, must have an overt subject, as in *He/She/It is sick*.

**Markedness.** The concept of **markedness** follows naturally from the concept of universals. Structures that are consistent with universals are considered **unmarked**, and those that are inconsistent with universals are considered **marked**. Marked structures are thought to be more difficult to acquire than are unmarked structures. Markedness can be viewed in an implicational sense: since voiced stops imply the presence of voiceless stops, but not vice versa, voiced stops are considered marked and voiceless stops are considered unmarked. Markedness may also be viewed in a statistical sense: property X is more marked than property Y if X is rarer than Y. Under this definition, the interdental fricative /θ/ is more marked than the alveolar fricative /s/, since /θ/ occurs in fewer of the world's languages. Markedness can also be viewed in a parametric sense: for example, heads of phrases (N is the head of NP, V the head of VP, etc.) tend to come at either the beginning or the end of each phrase in a given language. Thus, a language containing a VP made up of V-NP and a PP made up of P-NP is unmarked since both phrases are head-initial. In contrast, a language containing a VP made up of NP-V and a PP made up of P-NP is marked since one phrase is head-final and the other is head-initial.

The theory of markedness has been used to refine the contrastive analysis hypothesis and the notion of language transfer in general. As mentioned earlier, contrastive analysis in its initial form did not always make accurate predictions about second-language acquisition. For example, English and German differ in that English allows both voiced and voiceless obstruents (i.e., stops, fricatives, and affricates) word-finally (e.g., *tack/tag*), but German allows only voiceless obstruents word-finally (e.g., *Tag* 'day' is pronounced [tak]). Contrastive analysis would predict that English speakers learning German would have as much difficulty suppressing the voicing contrast as German speakers learning English would have mastering it. In fact, however, it is the L1 speakers of German who have the greater problem.

In order to predict more accurately when language differences will cause difficulty in second-language acquisition, Eckman proposed a **Markedness Differential Hypothesis** consisting of the following principles:

- Those properties of the L2 which differ from the L1 and are more marked than the L1 will be difficult.
- Among properties of the L2 that are more marked than the L1, the relative degree of difficulty will correspond to the relative degree of markedness.
- Those properties of the L2 which differ from the L1 but are not more marked than the L1 will not be difficult.

Evidence from language universals suggests that a word-final voicing contrast among obstruents, such as that found in English, is more marked than no such contrast. Therefore, the Markedness Differential Hypothesis correctly predicts the direction of difficulty between English and German for this particular property: L1 speakers of German will have relatively more difficulty learning the *marked* word-final voicing contrast in English; L1 speakers of English will have relatively less difficulty learning the *unmarked* word-final devoicing of obstruents in German.

**Developmental Processes.** It appears that an L2 learner may go through stages similar to those that speakers go through when acquiring their native language. For example, as discussed in Chapter 8, children acquiring English as an L1 break up or simplify consonant clusters (e.g., *tay* for *stay*); they acquire lexical morphemes before grammatical ones (e.g., *dog* before *the*) and inflectional affixes before derivational ones (e.g., tall*er* before sing*er*); in forming questions, they acquire *wh*-Movement before I-Movement (e.g., *Why I can't go?*); and they employ over-generalization in the acquisition of lexical items (e.g., *Daddy* for all men). Speakers acquiring English as an L2 appear to go through these same stages and employ these same processes.

# Patterns in Second-Language Acquisition

This section looks at four areas of linguistic theory—phonology, morphology, syntax, and semantics—and examines some specific L2 acquisition patterns within each area. It is important to emphasize that each of these areas has a different pattern of influence on interlanguage forms. In particular, interlanguage phonology shows perhaps the strongest L1 transfer influence. On the other hand, interlanguage morphology shows strong developmental influence, with clear resistance to transfer. Interlanguage syntax demonstrates a complex interaction of transfer (affected by universals and markedness) and developmental influences. Interlanguage semantics is strongly developmental, with some negative transfer; semantics is also influenced by developing cultural knowledge in ways that no other domain of interlanguage is.

## Phonology

Speakers may transfer the segmental structure of L1 to L2. One situation in particular in which L1 interference is noticeable is when the L2 makes a phonemic distinction that does not exist in the L1. For example, Japanese has one phoneme /r/ with allophones [l] and [r]; thus, there is no phonemic distinction between [l] and [r]. In contrast, English maintains a phonemic distinction between /l/ and /r/. Therefore, the native speaker of Japanese learning English as an L2 would be expected to experience greater difficulty than an English speaker learning Japanese. The Japanese speaker has to learn to make a phonemic distinction not found in his or her native language. On the other hand, the English speaker's distinction between [l] and [r] will go unnoticed by Japanese listeners.

Speakers may also transfer phonological rules from L1 to L2. One example that we have already looked at is the rule of Final Devoicing in German, which states that word-final obstruents must be voiceless. Obstruents may display a voicing contrast in medial position (e.g., [p] in [lumpən] 'rascals' but [b] in [šterbən] 'to die'), but this contrast is neutralized in word-final position (e.g., [p] in [lump] 'rascal' and [p] in [štarp] 'died'). Consequently, it is common for native speakers of German to devoice final obstruents when they are learning English, pronouncing both *back* and *bag*, for example, as [bæk].

Speakers may also transfer **phonotactic constraints** (i.e., conditions on permissible sequences of segments) from their L1 to the L2. For example, English permits syllable-initial clusters of up to three consonants, as long as the first consonant is /s/, the second is a voiceless stop, and the third is a liquid (e.g., *street* /strit/, *splash* /splæš/). A speaker whose native language does not permit such initial clusters may insert a vowel that breaks up the cluster, making it conform to a syllable structure acceptable in the speaker's L1. For example, Broselow (1987) reports that native speakers of Egyptian Arabic and Iraqi Arabic produced the following forms:

| *English Target* | | *Egyptian Arabic* | *Iraqi Arabic* |
|---|---|---|---|
| floor | [flor] | [filor] | [iflor] |
| three | [θri] | [θiri] | [iθri] |
| Fred | [frɛd] | [firɛd] | [ifrɛd] |
| children | [čɪldrɛn] | [čildirɛn] | [čilidrɛn] |

Note that native speakers of the two Arabic dialects employ different strategies for breaking up the unacceptable clusters. Egyptian Arabic speakers insert [i] between members of a consonant-liquid cluster, while Iraqi Arabic speakers insert [i] before a consonant-liquid cluster, allowing resyllabification (e.g., [flor] → [iflor]). Both of these strategies, however, achieve a similar end: they allow the consonant and liquid to be analyzed as members of *different* syllables. The resultant forms thus reflect an acceptable syllable structure in the L1.

Interference from the L1 and developmental processes may also interact during second-language acquisition. Research by Major (1987) suggests that L1 interference takes precedence during the earlier stages of phonological acquisition, and then developmental processes may predominate for a time. Finally, these processes are suppressed, yielding a form approximating that of the native speaker. For example, a Brazilian Portuguese speaker learning English as an L2 went through the following stages in producing the word *dog*:

[dɔgi]
[dɔgə]
[dɔk]
[dɔg]

The first form, [dɔgi], reflects the transfer of a phonotactic constraint from the L1. Portuguese does not permit any word-final obstruents except /s/; thus, the addition of [i] removes [g] from word-final position. The second form, [dɔgə], reflects a developmental process: reduction of unstressed vowels to [ə]. This cannot be a transfer from the L1, since Portuguese does not allow word-final [ə]. The third form, [dɔk], also reflects a developmental process: devoicing of word-final obstruents. The fourth form, [dɔg], approximates the pronunciation of a native English speaker.

## *Morphology*

Developmental processes play a major role in the acquisition of L2 morphology. For example, several studies have found similarities among both child and adult learners of English as an L2, in the order in which certain grammatical morphemes are acquired. For example, the {PLU} morpheme is acquired by both groups relatively early, whereas the {PRES} and the {POSS} morphemes are acquired later. The point to note is that these morphemes seem to be acquired in much the same way that they are acquired by native speakers. First, they are acquired in the same order—{PLU} first, then {POSS} and {PRES}. Second, they are acquired according to their morphological function rather than their phonological form. If they were acquired according to form, they would all be acquired at the same time.

Other research also indicates that L2 learners may exhibit developmental processes in expressing temporality, in the absence of verb morphology. Among these devices are temporal markers such as *yesterday* and *last night,* locatives such as *in Vietnam* and *at work,* calendar expressions such as *January* and *Tuesday,* and clause sequencing as in *I go to school Vietnam. [Then] I come U.S.* Once again, children acquiring English as an L1 go through similar stages.

Likewise, Dulay & Burt (1983) found that native speakers of Spanish employed strategies that are not found in Spanish but that do occur when children are acquiring English as their native language. Examples include the following:

> *He took her teeths off.* Here the irregular plural form *teeth* is misanalyzed as a root form and inflected again with the regular plural suffix.

> *I didn't weared any hat.* Here both verb forms are inflected for tense, rather than just the first verb form.

> *Me need crayons now.* Here the objective case pronoun is generalized to nominative position.

> *He didn't come yesterday* (*He* = a little girl). Here the masculine pronoun is generalized to a female referent.

> *He say he bring it to school.* Here the tense inflection is omitted from the first verb form in both the main clause and the subordinate clause.

Less research has been done on the acquisition of derivational morphology by L2 learners. However, Laufer (1990) reports that derivational complexity may be both a help and a hindrance to the non-native speaker. For example, a learner's knowledge that {pre} means 'before' (as in *preview* and *premature*) may help the learner to understand the meaning of a newly encountered word such as *prenuptial.* On the other hand, the L2 learner also has to deal with "deceptive transparency"—morphemes that lead to a misinterpretation of a word. For example, Laufer describes non-native speakers of English who interpreted *outline* as meaning 'out of line' and *discourse* as meaning 'without direction.'

## Syntax

Along with phonology, syntax is one of the domains that has been studied the most by researchers in second-language acquisition, largely because of the concurrent interest in syntax which Chomsky generated within linguistics in general. Researchers have found transfer, markedness, and developmental processes to play a role in interlanguage syntax.

One area in which transfer commonly occurs is subcategorization—that is, restrictions on the syntactic categories that can co-occur with a particular lexical item. Consider the example of English speakers learning French as an L2. In English, the verb *listen* is subcategorized for a preposition (*listen to NP*); however, the equivalent French verb is not (*écouter NP*). Conversely, the English verb *obey* is not subcategorized for a preposition (*obey NP*); however, the equivalent French verb is (*obéir à NP*). Adjémian (1983) reports that English speakers commonly transfer English subcategorization restrictions to French, producing interlanguage forms like the following:

| *Interlanguage Form* | *English Gloss* | *Correct French Form* |
|---|---|---|
| écouter à | 'listen to' | écouter |
| obéir | 'obey' | obéir à |

Negative transfer errors may also result when the L1 and L2 share a rule, but apply the rule under different circumstances. For example, Dulay & Burt (1983) report the following productions by Norwegian speakers learning English as an L2:

*Like you* me not, Reidun?
*Like you* ice cream?
*Drive you* car yesterday?

They account for these data by observing that English inverts the subject and first *auxiliary verb* in questions, whereas Norwegian inverts the subject and the first *verb*, whether auxiliary or main verb.

It is important to remember that transfer between an L1 and L2 is not a simple bidirectional phenomena, indicating that factors other than simply "difference" come into play. For example, consider the case of English speakers learning French or Spanish as an L2. (The following data and analysis are drawn from Anderson [1983].) French and Spanish adhere to a subject-object-verb (SOV) order when the object is a pronoun:

| French: | Je *les* vois | (I-*them*-see) | 'I see them' |
|---|---|---|---|
| Spanish: | Yo no *la* vi | (I-not-*her*-see) | 'I didn't see her' |

However, English speakers learning Spanish or French often place the pronoun after the verb, reflecting English word order (SVO):

| *Interlanguage Form* | *Correct Target* | |
|---|---|---|
| Je vois *les* | Je les vois | 'I see them' |
| Yo no vi *a ella* | Yo no *la* vi | 'I didn't see her' |

Conversely, one might predict that native speakers of French and Spanish learning English would reverse the process, producing forms like *I them see* and *I not her see*. However, forms like these do not appear in the interlanguage of Spanish or French speakers. That is, in sentences with pronominal objects, English speakers transfer SVO order, but French and Spanish speakers do not transfer SOV order.

One principle that accounts for this asymmetrical transfer is markedness. Consider the permissible word orders in English and in French and Spanish:

|  | *English* | *French/Spanish* |
|---|---|---|
| Nominal object | SVO | SVO |
| Pronominal object | SVO | SOV |

With no alternative order, SVO is clearly unmarked in English. Thus, English speakers can be expected to transfer SVO to the L2. On the other hand, SOV is marked in French and Spanish. (Pronominal objects are the only elements of VP in French and Spanish that precede the verb, thus representing the exceptional or "marked" case.) Consequently, French and Spanish speakers would not be expected to transfer SOV to the L2.

Sometimes transfer and developmental processes appear to interact. For example, Anderson (1983) reports a study of two children learning English: one a native speaker of Spanish, the other a native speaker of Japanese. The native speaker of Spanish acquired English articles quite quickly, which can be attributed to positive transfer from Spanish, which also has articles. In contrast, the Japanese child went through a stage where articles were omitted, a stage which is also found among children acquiring English as their native language. However, this stage was prolonged for the Japanese child, since Japanese does not have articles. Thus negative transfer from the L1 may prolong an interlanguage feature associated with a developmental process.

The role of language universals in the acquisition of L2 syntax is still a controversial one. Some research indicates that L2 learners are able to acquire knowledge about the L2 which is derivable from neither L1 nor L2 input. For example, research reported by White (1989) investigated the ability of native Japanese speakers to recognize the Right Roof Constraint in English. This constraint on rightward movement prevents an element from being extraposed out of its original clause. For example, the Right Roof Constraint permits (b), but not (c), as a paraphrase of (a).

(a)    That [a book *by Chomsky* has just come out] is not surprising.
(b)    That [a book has just come out *by Chomsky*] is not surprising.
(c)    *That [a book has just come out] is not surprising [*by Chomsky*].

Japanese speakers of English as an L2 were, in most cases, able to recognize sentences like (c) as ungrammatical. This ability is significant because the Right Roof Constraint does not operate in Japanese, which is verb-final and does not allow rightward movement. What is even more significant, however, is that this constraint cannot be directly inferred from merely listening to English, since no violations of it ever occur. (Just because something *does not* occur in a corpus of data doesn't mean it *cannot* occur.) Thus, it may be that the Japanese speakers are able to infer the Right Roof Constraint from the putatively universal Subjacency constraint on movement, which essentially states that all movement must be within one clause or between adjacent clauses.

## *Semantics*

Semantics has received somewhat less attention in research on second-language acquisition than have phonology and syntax. Nonetheless, it is possible to draw some generalizations about processes that occur when speakers attempt to acquire the vocabulary of an L2. The following phenomena are based on studies by Laufer (1990) and Zughoul (1991); all deal with speakers learning English as a second language.

One developmental strategy such speakers employ is the overgeneralization of superordinates, much as children overgeneralize in acquiring the lexicon of their native language. Because of their limited vocabulary, speakers may rely on superordinate terms (e.g., *animal* where native speakers would use the hyponym *dog*). The learner's strategy here seems to be to use words that are generalizable to more contexts. In addition, some speakers may rely heavily on the modifiers *good*, *bad*, *big*, *small*, *very*, and *many*, generalizing their use to inappropriate contexts (e.g., *I have small money* for *I have little money*).

Another common developmental strategy is the inappropriate use of synonyms. Two or more words may have similar meanings, but differ in their selectional restrictions (i.e., in the semantic features of the words with which they co-occur), in their subcategorization restrictions (i.e., in the categories of words with which they co-occur), in their connotations (i.e., in the emotional associations of the word), and in their register restrictions (i.e., in their level of formality). The non-native speaker may use a word whose literal meaning is appropriate but which violates one of the restrictions just described. Sometimes this use may reflect the fact that two synonyms are equivalent to one word in the speaker's L1. For example, *tall* and *long* are subsumed by one Arabic word, *tawīl*. Consequently, an Arabic speaker learning English may produce a sentence like *My father is a long thin man*, not realizing that *long* is not used with [+human] nouns. Or the learner may rely on a bilingual dictionary that simply lists synonyms (e.g., *career, job, occupation, work*) without explaining their restrictions. This strategy may lead the L2 learner to produce sentences like *There are not many occupations in the village* or *There are many works in the city*. Similarly, the non-native speaker who says *I want to grow my knowledge* may have found *grow* as a synonym for *develop* in a dictionary or thesaurus.

Another semantic relation that may cause difficulty has to do with converses: a pair of words that express a reciprocal relation. For example, *teach* and *learn* are converses: if X teaches Y, Y learns from X. It is not unusual for a non-native speaker to confuse the members of a pair of converses, producing sentences like *It learns them independence*. This phenomenon appears to be developmental and is similar to the stages a child goes through in acquiring the positive member of a pair of opposites (e.g., *long*) before the negative member (e.g., *short*).

Yet another developmental strategy is the use of **circumlocutions**, which involve substituting a descriptive phrase for a word that the learner has not yet acquired or cannot retrieve: for example, a student who did not know the word *pregnant* wrote *Smoking cigarettes has a bad effect, especially on a lady who is carrying an infant.*

Another common problem in the semantic domain is difficulty with **idioms**, expressions whose meaning cannot be derived from their component words—for example, *kick the bucket* for 'die,' *pull one's leg* for 'joke,' and *blow one's top* for 'get angry.' Not surprisingly, idioms are often incomprehensible for the non-native speaker, who may also prefer to use nonidiomatic equivalents in expressive tasks. The difficulty seems to be compounded by the degree of mismatch between the literal and figurative meanings of the idiom. For example, an idiomatic expression like *flying high* 'exuberant' would probably present fewer difficulties than *chewing the fat* 'talking.' Related problems may arise with the numerous phrasal verbs in English. For example, we have *run up* 'incur,' *run down* 'find,' and *run out* 'expire.' Here again, the non-native speaker may prefer the one-word equivalent to the phrasal verb.

Finally, confusion of words with similar sounds or spelling may also occur. For example, in the following sentences the target words are in brackets: *People are unable to work and earn efficient [sufficient] money*; *They are reasonable [responsible] for the loss of our land.* A related problem may arise with **polysemes** (one form with related meanings, e.g., *mouth* 'orifice for eating' and *mouth* 'opening of a river into another body of water') and **homonyms** (one form with unrelated meanings, e.g., *swallow* 'ingest' and *swallow* 'small, long-winged bird'). For example, a learner may mistakenly interpret *state* in a sentence like *He is in a critical state* in its geopolitical sense, rather than as 'situation.'

## Nonlinguistic Influences on Second-Language Acquisition

While this chapter has focused on the role of linguistic variables in second-language acquisition, other forces are believed to play a role as well. A few of these are treated briefly here.

**Age.** The traditional view of the role of age in second-language acquisition has been that acquiring an L2 is more difficult for an older (i.e., post-pubescent) learner than for a younger one. This view derives largely from the Critical Period Hypothesis, developed by the neurobiologist Eric Lenneberg. According to Lenneberg, the critical period for language acquisition is between years 2 and 12, after which plasticity of the brain's left hemisphere declines. However, the Critical Period Hypothesis in general and its implications for second-language acquisition in particular are not universally agreed upon by researchers. For example, Hatch (1983) reviews findings which suggest that adult L2 learners actually achieve higher levels of proficiency than younger learners, at least initially, and learn more efficiently than younger learners (i.e., with relatively less exposure). It is generally agreed, however, that phonology is the one domain where adult learners lag behind younger learners, in that a native-like accent is difficult to acquire if L2 acquisition begins beyond the age of puberty.

The role of age is a complex issue because age interacts with other nonlinguistic variables that may also affect second-language acquisition. For example, length of exposure has been shown to correlate positively with proficiency. Thus, if two learners started studying an L2 at different ages, the learner who started at an earlier age may display superior proficiency simply because of having studied the L2 for a longer period of time, not necessarily because of having begun at an earlier age. Also, younger learners may be less self-conscious about learning an L2, which can promote acquisition. On the other hand, older learners bring to the acquisition process more mature cognitive skills in analysis and problem-solving—skills which, though not strictly linguistic, may be profitably applied to the task of language acquisition.

**Cognitive Style.**  Cognitive style reflects the learner's approach to problem-solving and to conceptualizing and organizing information. There are two types of cognitive style. **Field independence** is a relatively analytical style in which the learner imposes structure on individual parts, distinguishing the irrelevant from the essential. **Field dependence** is a relatively global or holistic style in which the learner does not differentiate individual parts. Field independence has been found to correlate somewhat with success in second-language acquisition (although this may reflect the fact that most teaching techniques emphasize analysis).

**Personality Traits.**  Traits found to correlate with success in second-language acquisition include extroversion and a willingness to take risks. Extroversion has been found to be more of an advantage in naturalistic settings than in formal learning settings. Risk-taking may be both social (e.g., a willingness to engage in conversations) and linguistic (e.g., a willingness to try new vocabulary).

**Social-Psychological Forces.**  Factors such as the learner's motivation and attitude toward the L2 have also been hypothesized to play a role in second-language acquisition. Two types of motivation have been identified. **Integrative motivation** reflects the language learner's desire to become part of the community or culture represented by the L2. **Instrumental motivation** reflects the language learner's desire to learn the language for practical purposes, such as getting a job. Integrative motivation is seen as the more important component in second-language acquisition.

## *Summary*

Let's go over what we have covered. We began with four observations about the acquisition of a second language. However, we had no ready explanation for these phenomena. Therefore, we constructed a (partial) theory of second-language acquisition to account for our original observations. This theory makes use of such concepts as interlanguage, language transfer (both positive and negative), language universals, markedness, and developmental processes. We have also seen that second-language acquisition can be subdivided into the acquisition of phonology, morphology, syntax, and semantics. Moreover, we have looked briefly at some of the non-linguistic influences on second-language acquisition, including age, cognitive style, personality, and other social-psychological forces such as motivation and attitude.

As usual, it's worth pointing out that there is much more to the study of second-language acquisition than what has been covered in this one short chapter. However, you have now been exposed to some of the basic ideas in the field; if you want to learn more about the subject, see the readings at the end of this chapter. Following the readings are practice problems and answers to test your understanding of the chapter. After that are 50 exercises for you to do on your own.

## Supplementary Readings

Beebe, L. (Ed.) (1988). *Issues in second language acquisition.* New York: Newbury House.

Gass, S., and Schachter, J. (1989). *Linguistic perspectives on second language acquisition.* Cambridge, England: Cambridge University Press.

Hatch, E. (1983). *Psycholinguistics: A second language perspective.* Rowley, MA: Newbury House.

Ioup, G., and Weinberger, S. (1987). *Interlanguage phonology: The acquisition of a second language sound system.* Cambridge, MA: Newbury House.

McLaughlin, B. (1987). *Theories of second language learning.* London: Edward Arnold.

White, L. (1989). *Universal grammar and second language acquisition.* Amsterdam: John Benjamins.

You are now prepared to read the Hatch, Beebe, and McLaughlin works. Hatch, the most accessible of these, reviews basic concepts in linguistics and demonstrates their applicability to second-language acquisition. Beebe is a collection of essays by researchers in five areas—psycholinguistics, sociolinguistics, neurolinguistics, classroom research, and bilingual education—each offering a different perspective on issues in second-language acquisition. McLaughlin also examines different theoretical perspectives on second-language acquisition, for example interlanguage theory and universal grammar theory.

The other works are more advanced and would therefore be more accessible to readers with additional coursework in syntax or phonology. Gass and Schachter is a collection of studies on second-language acquisition, most of them experimental, by researchers in syntax, semantics, and phonology. Ioup and Weinberger is a collection of essays on phonology and second-language acquisition, many of them reprinted from journals. White investigates the role of universal grammar in second-language acquisition.

## *Practice*

**1.** Consider the following forms produced by non-native speakers acquiring English as an L2. Classify the errors by domain of linguistics (i.e., phonology, morphology, syntax, or semantics).

    a. Why you gave him your paper?
    b. She caught two fishes.
    c. Hand me the pincers (i.e., pliers).
    d. Do you play any [ɛspórts] (i.e., sports)?

**2.** Languages with front round vowels, like French, also have front unround vowels; but languages with front unround vowels, like English, don't necessarily have front round vowels. According to markedness theory, would the vowel system of French or English be harder for a speaker of the *other* language to learn? Explain.

**3.** The cluster [ts] is not permitted in word-initial position in English. Thus, the form [tsitsi] *tsetse* may be modified to [titsi] or [sitsi]. What developmental process(es) is involved?

    a. metathesis
    b. consonant cluster simplification
    c. devoicing
    d. consonant epenthesis
    e. both (b) and (c)
    f. both (b) and (d)

**4.** Morphological information is missing from each of the following sentences. In each case, state how the speaker signals temporal information in the absence of relevant verb morphology.

    a. I eat MacDonald last night.
    b. I say prayer, I go bed.
    c. Already I fly San Francisco.

**5.** A French speaker acquiring English as an L2 uses the form *Look that plane* for *Look at that plane*. The French verb that corresponds to *look at* is *regarder*. Explain the error.

**6.** All languages allow relativization of the subject (e.g., *the teacher <u>who</u> taught me*). However, not all languages allow relativization of the object of a preposition (e.g., *the teacher <u>to whom</u> I talked*); even fewer allow relativization of the possessive (e.g., *the teacher <u>whose course</u> I took*). Which of these constructions is most marked? Explain.

**7.** Speakers acquiring English as an L2 often make *wanna*-contraction errors such as *\*Who do you wanna go?* Based on the following examples, determine the circumstances under which *wanna*-contraction is blocked.

    A.1   Who do you *want to* go?
    A.2   *Who do you *wanna* go?
    A.3   Who do you *want to* go with?
    A.4   Who do you *wanna* go with?

    (Hint: where does *who* originate in the underlying structure of each sentence?)

**8.** Consider the following putative universal: I-Movement occurs in *yes-no* questions only if it occurs in *wh*-questions. This universal is _____.

    a.  implicational  
    b.  statistical  
    c.  parametric  

    d.  both (a) and (b)  
    e.  none of the above  

9. In an example cited by Adjémian (1983), French speakers acquiring English as an L2 produced forms like the following:

He stopped *to defend* himself. (Target [apparent from context]: *defending*)  
We just enjoyed *to move* and *to play*. (Target: *moving* and *playing*)

What can be inferred about French from such errors?

10. Some researchers have noticed that L2 learners of English prefer *decide* to *make up your mind*, *postpone* to *put off*, and *reprimand* to *tell off*. What principle from semantics appears to explain this preference?

# Answers

The following answers are, in some cases, not the only possible ones. Discussion of other possibilities is part of the practice.

**1.** a.  syntax            c.  semantics  
    b.  morphology      d.  phonology

**2.** French, because the front round vowels are marked.

**3.** b.  consonant cluster simplification

**4.** a.  *last night* = past time  
    b.  sequencing of clauses  
    c.  *already* = past time

**5.** *regarder* is subcategorized for an NP (not a preposition); this restriction is transfered to English.

**6.** Relativization of a possessive, because it's the rarest.

**7.** *wanna*-contraction is blocked across a movement site (e.g., *who* in (A.1) originates between *want* and *to*; *who* in (B.1) originates to the right of *with*).

**8.** a.  implicational

**9.** Verbs in French can take infinitive complements, but not gerund complements.

**10.** Non-native speakers avoid idioms.

# Exercises

**1.** In English, [p] and [pʰ] are allophones of one phoneme, /p/. In contrast, Hindi maintains a phonemic distinction between /p/ and /pʰ/: [p] is an allophone of /p/, while [pʰ] is an allophone of /pʰ/. Who will have more difficulty—a native English speaker learning Hindi, or a native Hindi speaker learning English? Explain.

**2.** A native speaker of English learning German as an L2 may produce [kənɔf] for German /knɔpf/. What developmental process(es) is involved?

    a. final devoicing
    b. vowel epenthesis
    c. consonant cluster simplification
    d. consonant epenthesis
    e. both (a) and (b)
    f. both (b) and (c)

**3.** There is a tendency for speakers acquiring English as an L2 to produce forms such as [pe] or [pəle] for play /ple/, even when attempting clusters that appear in their L1. Is this phenomenon an example of _____ .

    a. positive transfer
    b. negative transfer
    c. a developmental process
    d. a statistical universal
    e. none of the above

**4.** Consider the following error produced by a native speaker of Arabic acquiring English as an L2: *Did you sail your boat?* for *Did you sell your boat?* What can be inferred about the phonology of Arabic from this error?

**5.** Consider the following error produced by a native speaker of Vietnamese acquiring English as an L2: *Did you forget your code?* for *Did you forget your coat?* What can be inferred about the phonology of Vietnamese from this error?

**6.** In the movie *Murder on the Orient Express*, the protagonist is a Belgian detective, Hercule Poirot. Poirot, a native speaker of French, speaks excellent English but regularly pronounces the word *pipe* as /pip/. Explain Poirot's pronunciation of this word.

**7.** Assume the following hierarchy of markedness (> = "is more marked than"): final voicing contrast > medial voicing contrast > initial voicing contrast. How does this hierarchy explain the relative ease with which L1 speakers of English are able to acquire the initial /ž/-/š/ contrast in French, as in *jais* [žɛ] 'jet' vs. *chez* [še] 'at'?

**8.** Based on the markedness hierarchy in question (7) , arrange the following patterns from least marked to most marked.

    a. a voicing contrast among obstruents in all syllable positions (i.e., initial, medial, final)
    b. a voicing contrast among obstruents in initial position only
    c. a voicing contrast among obstruents in initial and medial position only

**9.** Hungarian has the following rule of Regressive Voicing Assimilation:

$$[\text{+obstruent}] \rightarrow [\text{-voice}]/\_\_\_\_ \ (\#) \begin{bmatrix} \text{+obstruent} \\ \text{-voice} \end{bmatrix}$$

How might an L1 speaker of Hungarian pronounce the following English phrases:

    a. said that                b. have tried

**10.** Korean has the following phonological rule:

$$C \rightarrow [+\text{palatal}] \: / \: \_\_\_ \: V$$

[+alveolar]
$\begin{bmatrix} +\text{hi} \\ -\text{back} \end{bmatrix}$

Assume a native speaker of Korean is learning English. How might this speaker pronounce the word *seat*?

**11.** Languages with back unround vowels, like Chinese, also have back round vowels; but languages with back round vowels, like English, don't always have back unround vowels. According to markedness theory, would the vowel system of Chinese or English be harder for a speaker of the *other* language to learn? Explain.

**12.** Assume that languages with affricates also have stops and fricatives, but that not all languages with stops and fricatives have affricates. Which type(s) of consonants should be easiest to learn, according to markedness theory?
   a. affricates
   b. stops
   c. fricatives
   d. both (a) and (b)
   e. both (b) and (c)

**13.** Assume that languages with nasalized vowels also have non-nasalized ones, but that not all languages with non-nasalized vowels have nasalized ones. Which type of vowel should be easier to learn, according to markedness theory?
   a   non-nasalized vowels
   b. nasalized vowels
   c. both (a) and (b)
   d. none of the above

**14.** Native speakers of Spanish learning English often produce forms like the following:

| | | | |
|---|---|---|---|
| school | [ɛskúl] | spell | [ɛspél] |
| stop | [ɛstáp] | Spanish | [ɛspǽnɪš] |
| sell | [sɛl] | soup | [sup] |

   a. These data illustrate that Spanish has a phonotactic constraint not found in English. State the constraint.
   b. What is the function of the epenthetic /ɛ/ in some of these forms?

**15.** Consider the following pronunciations by native speakers of Japanese acquiring English as an L2.

| | | | |
|---|---|---|---|
| bus | [basu] | baby | [bebi] |
| bath | [basu] | gum | [gamu] |

   a. What can be inferred about the basic syllable structure of Japanese?
   b. What English consonant phoneme(s) does Japanese lack?
   c. What English vowel phoneme(s) does Japanese lack?

**16.** Consider the following forms used by a speaker acquiring English as an L2.
   A. Gimme that pencil to me.
   B. Gimme that pencil to her.

What can be inferred about the morphological structure of *gimme* in this person's lexicon?

**17.** An English speaker acquiring French as an L2 uses the form *entrer* 'enter' for *entrer dans* 'enter into.' Explain the error.

**18.** An English speaker learning French as an L2 produces the form *Le chien a mangé les* (the dog-ate-them) for *Le chien les a mangé* (the dog-them-ate). This error is caused by _____.

    a. the positive transfer of an L1 feature to L2
    b. the negative transfer of an L1 feature to L2
    c. a subcategorization restriction in L1
    d. a developmental process
    e. a universal

**19.** Dulay & Burt (1983) report that Spanish speakers produce forms like *I finished to watch TV when it was four o'clock* instead of *I finished watching TV when it was four o'clock.* What can be inferred about Spanish from this error?

**20.** Which of the following words exhibits "deceptive transparency"? For those that do, how would a non-native speaker of English be likely to misinterpret them?

    a. upbraid            e. uncooperative
    b. reanalyze         f. disability
    c. discover           g. uproar
    d. underhanded

**21.** Consider the following forms, produced by a native speaker of German acquiring English as an L2.

    A. Can you go with me?
    B. Has he drunk the beer?
    C. Came you home early?

What can be inferred about the syntax of German from these examples?

**22.** Speakers of English as an L2 tend to go through the same stages as native English speakers do in acquiring negatives. Put the following forms in the order in which non-native speakers are most likely to acquire them.

    A. I no eat meat.
    B. I don't eat meat.
    C. No eat meat.

**23.** Speakers of English as an L2 tend to go through the same stages as native English speakers do in acquiring questions. Put the following forms in the order in which non-native speakers are most likely to acquire them.

    A. Where do you come from?
    B. You come from where?
    C. Where you come from?

**24.** In question (23), what rule has applied in (C) that has not applied in (B)?

**25.** In question (23), what rule has applied in (A) that has not applied in (C)?

**26.** Consider the following structures:

    A. The door was closed.
    B. The door was closed by the janitor.

All languages with agentive passives like (B) have agentless passives like (A). However, some languages have structures like (A) but not like (B).

    a. Which structure is more marked?
    b. Arabic has structures like (A) but not like (B). Japanese has structures like (A) and (B). Which language learner is likely to have greater difficulty: an L1 Arabic speaker learning Japanese as an L2, or an L1 Japanese speaker learning Arabic as an L2? Explain.

**27.** Some languages adhere to the Adjacency Principle, which requires noun phrases to be next to the item (e.g., verb or preposition) that assigns them case. Other languages do not adhere to this principle. Now consider the following data:

French:    A.1  Marie a mangé le dîner rapidement. [Marie-ate-the dinner-quickly]
            A.2  Marie a mangé rapidement le dîner. [Marie-ate-quickly-the dinner]
English:   B.1  Mary ate her dinner quickly.
            B.2  *Mary ate quickly her dinner.

    a. Which language, French or English, adheres to the Adjacency Principle?
    b. If you assume negative transfer from L1, who is likely to make more errors: an English speaker acquiring French, or a French speaker acquiring English? Explain.

**28.–34.** Consider the following table from Eckman (1987), which describes the use of pronominal reflexes in five different languages. A pronominal reflex is an item that marks the underlying position of a relativized NP. (If English had pronominal reflexes, it would have structures like *the boy that he came* for *the boy that came* and *the boy that John hit him* for *the boy that John hit*.) Relativization without a pronominal reflex is more marked than relativization with a pronominal reflex.

| | Subject | Direct Obj. | Indirect Obj. | Obj. of a Preposition |
|---|---|---|---|---|
| Persian | (+) | + | + | + |
| Arabic | (+) | (+) | + | + |
| Chinese | − | − | + | + |
| Japanese | − | − | − | (+) |
| English | − | − | − | − |

[+ = relativization with obligatory reflex, (+) = relativization with optional reflex, − = relativization without reflex.]

**28.** Which of these languages is most marked with respect to relativization? Least marked? Explain.

**29.** Given this table, would Persian speakers or Chinese speakers be expected to make more errors in producing relative clauses in English?

**30.** How does the Markedness Differential Hypothesis account for your analysis in question (29)?

**31.** Across languages, which position (e.g., subject, direct object, etc.) is most likely to allow relativization without a pronominal reflex?

**32.** Native speakers of which of these languages would be expected to have difficulty with a relative clause like *He's the person that I was counting on?*

**33.** Native speakers of which of these languages would be expected to have difficulty with a relative clause like *She's the one that told me?*

**34.** Native speakers of which of these languages would be expected to have difficulty with a relative clause like *He's the one that I saw?*

**35.** Spanish forms negatives as follows: *pienso* 'I think' → *No pienso* 'I don't think.' Dulay & Burt (1983) report the following negative forms by Spanish speakers learning English:

He no wanna go.
It no cause too much trouble.
He look like a glass, but no is a glass.

These errors are due to _____.

  a.  positive transfer
  b.  negative transfer
  c.  a universal
  d.  a developmental process
  e.  either (b) or (d)

**36.** Speakers acquiring English as an L2 often make subject-verb contraction errors such as *Do you know where she's today?* Based on the following examples, determine the circumstances under which subject-verb contraction is blocked.

A.1  Do you know where *she is* today?
A.2 *Do you know where *she's* today?

B.1  You've eaten more than *I have.*
B.2 *You've eaten more than *I've.*

C.1  You've eaten more than *I have* eaten.
D.2  You've eaten more than *I've* eaten.

**37.** Justin Wilson, a Cajun comedian from Louisiana, is famous for the greeting *How y'all are?* (instead of *How are y'all?*). Wilson's greeting suggests that English has a syntactic rule not found in Cajun French. What is the rule?

**38.** There is a putative universal that heads of phrases tend to occur either first in the phrase or last in the phrase. Now consider four languages, each of which has a different combination of adjective-noun (AN) order within NP and verb-object (VO) order within VP.

Japanese:    AN + OV
Modern Irish:  NA + VO
English:      AN + VO
Persian:      NA + OV

  a.  Which combinations, if any, are marked?
  b.  Which combinations, if any, are unmarked?
  c.  In the unmarked languages, where would prepositions/postpositions be expected to occur with respect to their objects? (A postposition is essentially a preposition that *follows* its object.)

**39.** Consider the following putative universal: the subject occurs before the object in the vast majority of the world's languages. This universal is _____ .

    a. implicational
    b. statistical
    c. parametric
    d. both (a) and (b)
    e. none of the above

**40.** Forms like the following were produced by Spanish speakers learning English.

In my country isn't army, navy and air force.
The fountain of work in Venezuela is petroleo; is our principle fountain of work.
In Venezuela is holiday both days.

What principle might explain the common error found in all of these examples?

**41.** Speakers acquiring English as an L2 often make subject-verb agreement errors such as *Where does the spiders go?* for *Where do the spiders go?* These same speakers, however, typically produce correct forms such as *The spiders go* and *The spider goes.* How might the incorrect forms be explained?

**42.** Consider the following riddle:

Q: What do you call the jelly beans that get left in the bottom of your Easter basket because they're a flavor you didn't like?
A: "Has beans."

The "humor" here might escape someone acquiring English as an L2. (a) What concept from semantics would help explain the non-native speaker's failure to "get" it? (b) What phonological distinction might add to the confusion?

**43.** A non-native speaker of English produces the form *I went to the U.S. in 1975*, when he is, and has been, in the U.S. since 1975. Explain his error.

**44.** Assume that an ESL student writes *I returned the books I lent from the library.* What concept from semantics explains this error?

**45.** Speculate on the intended word in the following sentence. The word used and the one intended are covered by one form in the writer's native language: *Most works require the applicant to speak English.*

**46.** Speculate on the intended word in the following sentence. The words used and the one intended are covered by one form in the writer's native language: *I am for coeducation because of two reasons. The first is that friendship grows up among the two races. Coeducation also teaches students to improve their ability to deal with the other kind.*

**47.** Bilingual speakers sometimes engage in **code-switching**, that is, changing from one language to the other in the course of a conversation. The following excerpt, adapted from Fishman (1972: 29–32), illustrates code-switching between English and Spanish. Analyze the conversation between a boss and his secretary and form a generalization about where code-switching takes place.

Boss: Carmen . . . I have a letter to dictate to you.
Sec'y: Fine. Let me get my pen and pad. . . .

BOSS: Ah, this man William Bolger got his organization to contribute a lot of money to the Puerto Rican parade. . . . ¿Tú fuiste a la parada? [Did you go to the parade?]

SEC'Y: Sí, yo fuí. . . . [Yes, I went.]

BOSS: ¿Y cómo te estuvo? [And how did you like it?]

SEC'Y: Y, lo más bonita. [Oh, very pretty.]

BOSS: . . . . Fuí con mi señora y con mis nenes . . . . y tuve día bien agradable. Ahora lo que me molesta a mi es que las personas cuando viene una cosa así, la parada Puertorriqueña . . . corren de la casa a participar porque es una actividad festiva, . . . y sin embargo, cuando tienen que ir a la iglesia, o la misa para pedirle [secretary laughs] a Diós entonces no van.

[I went with my wife and my children . . . . And I had a pleasant day. Now what bothers me is that people when something like this comes along, the Puerto Rican parade, . . . they run from the house to participate because it is a festive activity, . . . and then, when they have to go to church or mass to ask God then they don't go.]

SEC'Y: Sí, entonces no van. [Yes, then they don't go.]

BOSS: Pero, así es la vida, caramba. [But that's life, you know.] Do you think you could get this letter out today?

SEC'Y: Oh yes, I'll have it this afternoon for you.

**48.** Consider the passage in question (47). Which of the following nonlinguistic factors seems to be the most important in this case of code-switching?

   a. age
   b. cognitive style
   c. personality traits
   d. social-psychological factors
   e. both (b) and (d)
   f. none of the above

**49.** Consider the passage in question (47). Which of the following factors seems to be most important in switching from English to Spanish?

   a. age
   b. field independence
   c. field dependence
   d. extroversion
   e. integrative motivation
   f. instrumental motivation

**50.** Consider the passage in question (47). Assume both speakers are L1 speakers of Spanish and L2 speakers of English. Which of the following factors are likely to be most important in their learning English?

   a. age
   b. field independence
   c. field dependence
   d. extroversion
   e. integrative motivation
   f. instrumental motivation

# Chapter 10

# *Written Language*

This chapter focuses on **written language**, in particular the question of how linguistic theory can elucidate problems in written discourse. Analyses of writing have come from essentially three quarters: rhetoric, psychology, and linguistics. Rhetoricians, dating from the time of Aristotle, traditionally have been interested in techniques for organizing and developing such modes of discourse as persuasion, narration, description, and so forth. Psychologists have been primarily interested in studying the process of writing. That is, they attempt to investigate experimentally the mental steps that a writer goes through in creating a piece of writing. Linguists, on the other hand, are mainly interested in using linguistic concepts to analyze the written document itself and its effects upon the reader. Let's consider some problems in writing that would interest linguists.

(1) A 9-year-old girl writes an essay in which *drowned* is spelled *deround*.
(2) A portable sign in front of a restaurant reads *Our biscuit have the majority vote*.
(3) A college freshman writes *The alarm must have been set off by myself*.
(4) A job seeker closes a letter of application with *When can we get together to discuss the position?*
(5) In a memo to tenants, an apartment manager writes *You are forbidden to smoke in the hallways*.

Observations (1–5) illustrate the fact that problems in writing may be phonological, morphological, syntactic, semantic, or pragmatic, respectively. The problems in these examples range from misspellings, as in (1), to tactless phraseology, as in (5). The point to note, however, is that problems of these types occur regularly in writing and can be accounted for by some domain of linguistic theory. What we will now do is attempt to articulate the linguistic principles that will account for these observations.

## Writing Systems

It may be useful to start by discussing the various types of writing systems in use among the world's languages. Writing systems developed from drawing, in particular from pictographs and ideographs, both of which are **iconic** (i.e., an actual depiction of an object in the real world). A **pictograph** is essentially a drawing of an object. For example, a drawing of the sun represents the sun (e.g., ✿ = sun). An **ideograph** is a drawing of an object that represents that object and other related concepts. For example, a drawing of the sun might represent not only the sun, but also heat, light, and so on. Drawing, unlike writing, is not peculiar to a specific language. Any human can interpret pictographs and ideographs regardless of the language he or she speaks. For example, the ancient Egyptians spoke a language called Coptic and left records in the form of ideographs (i.e., hieroglyphics). Modern English speakers, however, can learn to interpret these ideographs without having to learn to speak Coptic. In contrast, the symbols in a writing system are non-iconic. For example, the English word *sun* is not a depiction of the sun. Since writing is not iconic, each writing system is peculiar to a specific language. This means that in order to interpret a writing system, one must speak the language that the writing system represents.

There are essentially three types of writing systems in use today, each based on a particular linguistic unit. In **morphographic** writing, each symbol represents a single morpheme. The various Chinese languages (e.g., Cantonese and Mandarin) are written with a morphographic writing system. For example, the Chinese symbol for the word *sun* is 日 . This symbol is a single indivisible unit; no part of it represents its pronunciation. Likewise, we occasionally use morphographic symbols when writing English. For example, in a road sign saying *Deer X-ing*, the symbol *X* stands for the morpheme {cross}. In the second type of writing system, **syllabic**, each symbol represents a single syllable. Sanskrit, an ancient language of India, is written with a syllabic writing system. For example, the Sanskrit word for *sun* is pronounced /surya/ and is written with the two symbols 拘 (representing the syllable /su/) and स्र्य (representing the syllable /rya/). Each symbol is a single, indivisible unit; no part of it represents the individual segments that reflect its pronunciation. We occasionally use syllabic symbols when writing English. For example, in a personalized license plate spelled *IMMT*, the sequence *MT* stands for the syllables /ɛm/ and /ti/, which constitute the word *empty*. The third type of writing system is **alphabetic**, where each symbol of the writing system represents a single phonological segment. English is written with an alphabetic system. For example, the word *top* contains three symbols (*t*, *o*, and *p*), each representing a single segment (/t/, /a/, and /p/).

A caveat is in order before we proceed. First, the alphabetic system we use to write English only *approximates* a segmental system. In a purely segmental system, each segment would be represented by a unique symbol. However, English has about 38 phonemes, but the Roman alphabet we use has only 26 letters. This means there is not a unique match between phoneme and symbol. For example, the word *box* consists of four phonemes (/baks/), but is written with three symbols. In this case, the symbol *x* represents the two phonemes /ks/. In other words *x* represents only a single phoneme, but neither /k/ nor /s/. For example, the *x* in *xylophone* represents the phoneme /z/. This imperfect relation between segment and symbol in English has two causes. One is historical. When English writing was standardized in the fifteenth century, it was nearly perfectly segmental. For example, each letter in the word *knife* corresponded to the Middle English phonemic representation /knifə/. Over time, the phonemic representation of the word has changed from /knifə/ to /naɪf/, but the spelling has not. In addition, English has borrowed much of its vocabulary from Latin and Greek. Consequently, we have had to make these borrowings fit our writing system. For example, English borrowed its word *phone* from Greek, which has a unique symbol Φ, *phi*, to represent the initial consonant in *phone*. When brought into English, the initial consonant was spelled *ph* to indicate its Greek origin.

The writing systems we have discussed and the drawings out of which they grew are summarized in the following chart.

| Drawing | Pictographic | ☀ | = sun |
|---------|-------------|------|-------|
| Drawing | Ideographic | ☀ | = sun, heat, light |
| Writing | Morphographic | 日 | = sun |
| Writing | Syllabic | पूज | = sun |
| Writing | Alphabetic | *sun* | = sun |

Having discussed some general properties of various representational systems, let's now consider how the domains of phonology, morphology, syntax, semantics, and pragmatics can illuminate problems in writing.

## Applications of Linguistics to Writing

As we look at some applications of linguistics to writing, we will see that the different domains of linguistic theory are not equally relevant to writers of all levels of education and sophistication. For example, phonology and morphology play a larger role in analyzing the writing of grade-school children and semi-literate adults than do semantics and pragmatics. Conversely, semantics and pragmatics play a larger role in analyzing the writing of advanced high-school and college students. If you think about it, this makes sense. The productions of immature or unsophisticated writers tend to be shorter and have a meager written context. Thus, phonology and morphology, which focus on the segment and word, are likely to be more relevant in analyzing the output of such writers. On the other hand, the productions of more mature or sophisticated writers tend to be longer and have a rich written context. Thus, semantics and pragmatics, which focus on meaning and situational context, are likely to be more relevant in analyzing the output of such writers. Syntax seems to be more relevant to understanding the writing of those of intermediate ability and sophistication. On the one hand, their writing is complex enough to provide an opportunity for syntactic infelicities, yet they have not completely mastered long and complex discourse.

In short, then, as the sophistication of the writer changes, the relevant linguistic domain generally changes as well. With this in mind, let's now consider some specific applications of linguistics to writing.

## *Phonology and Writing*

The most obvious application of phonology to writing is in helping to explain spelling errors. The fundamental assumption behind this line of investigation is that at least *some* spelling errors are a direct consequence of the phonology of English. For example, **unstressed syllable deletion** deletes a completely unstressed vowel (typically [ə]) and optionally deletes the adjacent consonants in the same syllable. The deleted syllable may be in initial, medial, or final position within a word. The same process can affect spelling as well as pronunciation. For example, a six-year-old girl wrote *guvment* for *government*. Note that if the medial syllable in /gʌ́vərnmənt/ is removed, the result is [gʌ́vmənt].

Other phonological processes that can account for misspellings have been discussed in Chapter 7 (Language Variation). Among them are vowel epenthesis (e.g., *thero* for *throw*), metathesis (e.g., *Southren* for *Southern*), consonant cluster reduction (e.g., *attrac* for *attract*), post-vocalic liquid deletion (e.g., *ho* for *whole*), voicing assimilation (e.g., *haf to* for *have to*), and neutralization (e.g., *whin* for *when*).

Aside from errors caused by applying phonological rules, spelling deviations may also be caused by attaching the orthography to the wrong level of phonological representation. Earlier, we said that English orthography is alphabetic, which means that each orthographic symbol represents a single phonological segment, at least in principle. There are, however, three separate levels of phonological representation upon which the orthography can be based: morphophonemic, phonemic, or phonetic.

**Morphophonemic Spelling.** This type of orthography equates each *morpheme* with a unique symbolic representation. For example, *caps* and *cabs* would be written *caps* and *cabs*. Note that the plural morpheme has a unique representation (i.e., *s*), even though it appears as two different phonemes (i.e., /s/ and /z/) in these two words.

**Phonemic Spelling.** This type of orthography equates each *phoneme* with a unique symbolic representation. For example, *caps* and *cabs* would be written *caps* and *cabz*. Note that the spelling of the plural morpheme reflects the fact that it appears as two different phonemes in these two words.

**Phonetic Spelling.** This type of orthography equates each *phone* with a unique symbolic representation. For example, *caps* and *cabs* would be written *caps* and *caabz*. Note that the spelling of the vowel in the two words reflects the fact that the vowel in *cabs* is longer than the vowel in *caps*.

It's obvious from this example that English spelling is *primarily* morphophonemic, in that each morpheme is given a unique segmental representation. For example, consider the spelling of the three words *photo*, *photograph*, and *photography*.

Each contains an instance of the morpheme {photo}, spelled *p-h-o-t-o* in each case. Note, however, that these three instances of {photo} are phonemically different: *photo* /fóto/, *photograph* /fótə/, and *photography* /fətá/. If English spelling were phonemic rather than morphophonemic, these three words would have different spellings, say, *photo*, *photugraph*, and *phutagraphy*.

On the other hand, it is equally clear that the English spelling system is not *purely* morphophonemic. It has some phonemic elements, as for example in the spelling of *wife* and *wives*. Here the morpheme {wife} is spelled phonemically, with an *f* in the singular and *v* in the plural to reflect the fact that the singular form has undergone final devoicing (i.e., the word-final /v/ is devoiced to /f/ in the singular). If these two words were spelled morphophonemically, they would be represented as, for example, *wive* and *wives*.

Children, as well as adults just learning to spell, will often construct a phonemic rather than a morphophonemic orthography. For example, a seven-year-old wrote *u lot uv mune* for *a lot of money*. Note the consistent use of the symbol *u* for the phonemes /ə/ and /ʌ/. The point to keep in mind about such errors is that they are not the result of phonological processes but rather the result of attaching letters of the alphabet to the wrong level of phonological representation.

Note finally that some orthographic errors have nothing to do with phonology or any other domain of linguistics. **Capitalization**, for example, is not linguistically driven in English orthography; its use is strictly a convention that has nothing directly to do with the structure of English. For instance, in writing English, we capitalize the first letter of the first word in a sentence, the pronoun *I* (but, interestingly enough, not *you* or *me*), and proper nouns. That capitalization is arbitrary is evidenced by the fact that other languages written in the Roman alphabet capitalize quite differently. For example, in Spanish many proper nouns are *not* capitalized (e.g., *inglés* 'English'), whereas in German *all* nouns are capitalized, including common nouns (e.g., *Kirche* 'church').

## *Morphology and Writing*

Morphology is the study of word formation; thus, morphology is most useful in helping to explain errors whose domain is a single word. The following constitute a representative sampling of actual morphological errors in writing.

**Verb Morphology.**   Some problems in writing reflect the misanalysis of verb forms. For example, a child who writes *drownded* for *drowned* is misanalyzing the final /d/ of /draʊnd/ as part of the root of the verb rather than as a suffix representing {PAST}. Consequently, the child adds an additional past tense suffix to the root (i.e., {drownd} + {PAST} = *\*drownded*). Note, incidentally, that the additional past tense suffix is formed according to rule: since the new root ends in a /d/, the past tense suffix will be /əd/. Another common morphological deviation is the absence of the {PRES} inflection on third-person singular verb forms (e.g., *He do it without thinking*).

Many apparent verb-form errors can be analyzed as either morphological or syntactic in origin. In contrast to a morphological error, a syntactic error involves more than one word or is caused by an element outside of the word affected. Consider, for example, a student who writes *He come over here twice before. Come* is a morphological error if the target is *came*: someone who systematically substitutes *come* for *came* has internalized the incorrect past tense form. On the other hand, *come* is a syntactic error if the target is *has come*. That is, someone who systematically omits the auxiliary *have* may leave a past participial form in first position within the verb phrase, a position normally filled by a tensed verb.

**Noun Morphology.**   One type of morphological error in nouns is the treatment of a non-count noun as though it were a count noun. **Count nouns** are those that can take the {PLU} suffix (e.g., *job/jobs*); **non-count nouns** cannot. For example, a college student wrote *Machines can easily perform many manual labors. Manual labor* is non-count, but the student treated it as if it were a count noun by modifying it with *many* and pluralizing *labor.* Moreover, singular count nouns require an article (e.g., *A man appeared/*Man appeared*), whereas non-count nouns cannot take the singular indefinite article (e.g., *hail/*a hail*). Other common morphological deviations are the absence of the {PLU} inflection on a plural count noun (e.g., *two book*) and of the {POSS} inflection (e.g., *John car*).

**Adjective Morphology.**   A common error is the misformation of the comparative and superlative degrees of adjectives. Consider, for example, the form **foolishest* for *most foolish*. In general, the more syllables an adjective has, the more pressure there is to form the comparative and superlative with *more/most* rather than with *-er/-est*. Thus, we have *taller* rather than **more tall*, but *more abrupt* rather than **abrupter*. However, not all multisyllabic adjectives require *more/most* in the comparative and superlative. Consider, for example, the two-syllable adjectives ending in *-y*: *funny/funnier, silly/sillier,* and *happy/happier.* Another tendency seems to be that non-Germanic (i.e., non-native) adjectives form their comparative and superlative degrees with *more/most.* For example, *more chic* seems preferable to *chicer.*

## Syntax and Writing

Syntax is the study of the structure of phrases, clauses, and sentences. Thus, syntax is most useful in analyzing structural errors whose domain is larger than a word. Numerous problems in writing have their foundations in syntax. Some of the more common ones are as follows.

**Subject-verb Agreement.**   Subject-verb agreement applies only in present tense clauses. A singular subject requires a singular verb (*The price rises*) and a plural subject requires a plural verb (*The prices rise*). Subject-verb agreement errors are most likely to occur when the subject and verb are separated by other material that ends in a noun of a different number than the subject, as in **The point of his arguments escape me.* The singular subject (*the point*) and the plural verb (*escape*) are separated by other material (*of his arguments*) that ends in a plural noun.

**Fragments.** A sentence fragment is a series of words (typically a clause) which cannot stand alone as a sentence in writing. A clause is a structure containing a subject and a predicate. For example, *The stock fell ten points* is a clause because it contains a subject (*The stock*) and a predicate (*fell ten points*). Although most clauses can stand alone as separate sentences (as in the preceding example), there are four major clause types that cannot. In particular, noun clauses (*That the stock fell ten points*), infinitive clauses (*For the stock to fall ten points*), participial clauses (*The stock having fallen ten points*), and indirect questions (*How far the stock fell*) are all fragments.

A fragment can often be corrected by making it part of a larger sentence. Consider the following examples.

(6) It was upsetting *that the stock fell ten points.*
(7) It was completely unexpected *for the stock to fall ten points.*
(8) *The stock having fallen ten points,* Boesky started to buy.
(9) Mr. Bevins asked his broker *how far the stock fell.*

**Pronoun Reference.** Several rules govern pronoun reference in written discourse. First, a reflexive pronoun (e.g., *myself, themselves*) normally requires an antecedent, as in *I made a copy for myself/\*He made a copy for myself.* On the other hand, a personal pronoun (e.g., *me, them*) does not require an antecedent, as in *He made a copy for me*; but if it has one, the antecedent should be unambiguous. For example, in *Trump sent Dinkins a letter stating that he was going to be sued,* it is unclear who *he* refers to. This sentence can be revised as follows: *Trump sent Dinkins a letter stating that Dinkins was going to be sued.* Second, a pronoun must agree with its antecedent in person, number, and gender (e.g., *Stock prices fell slowly at first and then they/\*it took a nosedive*). Third, some readers object to masculine pronouns being used in a generic sense (e.g., *Each student must pass his exam with a grade of B or better*). This usage can be avoided by pluralizing the pronoun and its antecedent (e.g., *Students must pass their exams . . .*) or by eliminating the pronoun altogether (e.g., *Students must pass exams . . .*).

**Dangling Modifiers.** A dangling modifier is any sort of predicate which has no overt noun phrase (NP) to serve as its subject: for example, *\*Feeling a bull market coming on, stock prices were bid up.* *Feeling a bull market coming on* is a dangling modifier, because there is no NP in the rest of the sentence that can serve as its subject. The only other NP in the sentence is *stock prices,* which can't serve as the subject: *\*Stock prices felt a bull market coming on.* In contrast, the sentence *Feeling a bull market coming on, traders bid up stock prices* does not contain a dangling modifier, because the NP *traders* can serve as subject of *Feeling a bull market coming on.*

One common cause of a dangling modifier is a passive sentence without an agent. For example, *Traders bid up stock prices* is an active sentence, and the agent is *traders.* This sentence can be made passive, as in *Stock prices were bid up by traders.* Then the agent can be omitted, as in *Stock prices were bid up.* Now note how passive and agent omission can interact to create a dangling modifier:

(10a)   Feeling a bull market coming on, *traders bid up stock prices.* (Active)
(10b)   Feeling a bull market coming on, *stock prices were bid up by traders.* (Passive)
(10c)   *Feeling a bull market coming on, *stock prices were bid up.* (Passive and Agent Omission)

**Subcategorization.**  Word choice problems can arise from faulty subcategorization, in which the writer fails to use a direct object or a prepositional phrase with a verb that requires one (or, conversely, uses an object or a prepositional phrase with a verb that does not allow one). For example, *warn* requires a direct object, a principle violated by the college student who wrote *AmTech warned about the hostile takeover bid.* This violation can be corrected by adding a direct object, as in *AmTech warned their stockholders about the hostile takeover bid.*

## Semantics and Writing

Semantics is the study of linguistic meaning; but, as we have learned, this includes a range of phenomena as diverse as sense, reference, and truth. Thus, it is not surprising that semantics can help us understand problems that range from word choice to tone.

**Selectional Restrictions.**  One problem in writing derives from violating a selectional restriction: a semantic constraint on the type of subject or object a particular verb requires. For example, the verb *educate* requires a human direct object. This selectional restriction is violated by the college writer who referred to *educating a variety of disabilities.* Here, the direct object of *educating* is the non-human noun phrase a *variety of disabilities.* This particular violation is fairly easy to correct, since we can readily construct a human direct object without changing the author's intent: for example, *educating a variety of disabled people* or *educating patients with a variety of disabilities.*

**Jargon.**  Lexical problems may also result from the inappropriate use of jargon, the technical vocabulary of a particular discipline. One problem arises from the use of jargon where it is unnecessary; for example, a researcher might write *With chronicity, the effect decreased* instead of *With time, the effect decreased.* Another type of problem is the use of undefined jargon: for example, a computer might offer the message *File is READ-ONLY* without any explanation of what *READ-ONLY* means. It is important to understand, however, that jargon can be used appropriately. When both writer and reader are members of the same discipline, the jargon term essentially acts as "shorthand" for a complex of concepts. For example, if both reader and writer are familiar with desktop publishing, the term *kerning* can be used in place of the longer phraseology *adjusting the spacing between pairs of letters to create a more pleasing visual effect.*

**Connotation.**  Lexical problems may also be traced to words with inappropriate connotations. A word's connotations are those associations that many readers attach to the word, apart from its core sense (i.e., **denotation**). Thus, two words may have a similar denotation but quite different connotations. For example, consider the adjectives *slender* and *skinny.* Both denote an animate entity without much body fat. However, *slender* has a positive connotation and *skinny* has a somewhat negative connotation. Note the difference in attitude conveyed by describing someone as *slender as a reed* versus *skinny as a beanpole.*

**Thematic Roles.**  Each NP in a sentence plays a particular thematic role in relation to the verb in that sentence. For example, (11) illustrates four of these thematic roles (adapted from Campbell, Riley & Parker [1990]).

(11) *The clerk$_1$ typed the invoice$_2$ for his boss$_3$ with a typewriter$_4$.*

NP$_1$ functions as the **agent**, the volitional performer of the action described by the verb. NP$_2$ functions as the **patient**, the thing affected by the action of the verb. NP$_3$ functions as the **beneficiary**, the entity which benefits from the action. Finally, NP$_4$ functions as the **instrument**, the thing used to carry out the action.

A given thematic role (e.g., agent, patient, etc.) can occur in a number of syntactic positions (subject, object, etc.). In sentences (11a–11c), for example, the semantic role of instrument occurs in three different syntactic positions.

(11a)  Subject = *A typewriter* was used to type the invoice.
(11b)  Direct Object = The clerk used *a typewriter* to type the invoice.
(11c)  Object of Preposition = The clerk typed the invoice on *a typewriter.*

Conversely, a given syntactic position can be filled by a number of thematic roles. In sentences (11d-f), the subject is filled by three different thematic roles.

(11d)  Agent = *The clerk* typed the invoice on a typewriter.
(11e)  Patient = *The invoice* was typed by the clerk.
(11f)  Instrument = *A typewriter* was used to type the invoice.

The flow of information in a discourse is facilitated when a particular thematic role always occupies the same syntactic position. Consider passage (12), from a proposal to develop software for a bookstore. In (12) there is no consistent relationship between thematic role and syntactic position.

(12a) *The development team* will first determine the inventory functions needed in the software. (12b) A survey of the bookstore staff's computer skills will also be conducted by *the team.*

In (12a) the agent is the subject; in (12b) it is the object of the passive *by*-phrase. Compare the following revised version of the same passage.

(13a) *The development team* will first determine the inventory functions needed in the software. (13b) *The team* will also conduct a survey of the bookstore staff's computer skills.

In (13) the subject position of each sentence is filled by the agent, thereby enhancing the flow of information.

**Thematic Progression.** A sentence can be divided into two information units—**given** information (i.e., that which the addressor assumes is known to the addressee) and **new** information (i.e., that which the addressor assumes is not known to the addressee). Given information is normally expressed as the subject, and new information is normally expressed in the predicate. This ordering of given information before new is termed the Given/New Contract. For example, consider sentence (14).

(14) *Some fruits* contain more oils than others.

In (14), the subject *Some fruits* is the given information. The predicate *contain more oils than others* expresses the new information.

The arrangement of given and new information within each sentence also forms a larger organization called **thematic progression**. A **linear** progression of given and new information can be represented as AB:BC, where the new information (B) in one sentence becomes the given information (B) in the next, as in (15a) and (15b).

(15a)   The Model 101B is the result of *new processing technology.* (AB)
(15b)   *This technology* allows us to offer you a number of exciting advances. (BC)

The new information in (15a) includes *technology*, which becomes the given information in (15b), *this technology*.

In contrast, a **hierarchical** progression of given and new information can be represented as AB:AC, where the given information (A) in one sentence is retained as the given information (A) in the next, as in (16a) and (16b).

(16a)   *The Model 101B* is the result of new processing technology. (AB)
(16b)   *This product* offers a number of exciting advances. (AC)

The given information in (16a), *Model 101B*, is repeated as the given information in (16b), *this product*.

Both the linear and hierarchical varieties of thematic progression adhere to the Given/New Contract. This is evidenced by the fact that in both the linear (AB:BC) and hierarchical (AB:AC) patterns, earlier letters of the alphabet always *precede* later ones, within each pairing. Conversely, a progression violates the contract if an earlier letter follows a later one (e.g., AB:CB), as illustrated in (17a-b).

(17a)    The Model 101B is the result of *new processing technology*. (AB)
(17b)    A number of exciting advances have resulted from *this technology*. (CB)

**Presupposition.**  Writers can manipulate the tone of their writing by the use (or avoidance) of **presupposition triggers**. These triggers are either structures or words that assume, or presuppose, the truth of the proposition expressed in a sentence or the speaker's attitude about it.

One structure that serves as a presupposition trigger is a ***wh*-question**. Consider, for example, the following sentences.

(18a)    When will you type this memo?
(18b)    Will you type this memo?
(18c)    If you type this memo, send a copy to Jones.

Sentence (18a) is a *wh*-question and presupposes the truth of the proposition it expresses, 'You will type this memo.' On the other hand, sentence (18b) is a *yes/no*-question and does not presuppose the truth of the proposition. Sentence (18c), containing an *if*-clause, likewise does not presuppose the truth of the proposition 'You will type this memo.'

Such constructions can have a strong impact on tone. For example, assume a salesperson is designing a flyer to mail to clients. Closing with a *wh*-question, such as *When may I call on you to discuss product X?*, may create a presumptuous tone, since it presupposes that the call will take place whether the client wants it to or not. Instead, it may be wiser to close with a *yes/no*-question, such as *May I call on you to discuss product X?*, which carries no such presupposition.

There are also entire classes of words that serve as presupposition triggers. One such class includes **factive verbs**. Consider, for example, the following sentences.

(19a)    Brown's presentation *demonstrates* that product X is superior.
(19b)    Brown's presentation *suggests* that product X is superior.

Sentence (19a) contains the factive verb *demonstrates* and presupposes the truth of the proposition in the subordinate clause, 'Product X is superior.' On the other hand, sentence (19b) contains the non-factive verb *suggests* and does not presuppose the truth of the proposition in the subordinate clause; it does not assume that 'Product X is superior.' Here is a partial list of factive and non-factive verbs.

FACTIVE:  demonstrate, note, acknowledge, prove, show, grasp, make clear, be aware, take into consideration, take into account, bear in mind, regret, resent

NON-FACTIVE:    suggest, assert, claim, suppose, allege, assume, charge, main-
                tain, believe, think, conclude, conjecture, fancy, figure

Such verbs can have a significant effect on tone. For example, assume a writer is replying to a customer who seeks a refund for goods that were damaged during shipment. Describing the customer's position with a non-factive verb, such as *We have your letter of June 6th, claiming that goods were damaged in transit,* may create a confrontational tone, since *claim* does not presuppose the truth of the proposition that 'Goods were damaged in transit.' Rather, it may be more diplomatic to use a factive verb such as *note,* as in *We have your letter of June 6th, noting that goods were damaged in transit.*

Finally, there is another class of verbs that serve as presupposition triggers, termed **implicative verbs**. Consider the following examples.

(20a)    You *failed* to enclose your check.
(20b)    You *forgot* to enclose your check.
(20c)    You *did not* enclose your check.

All three of these express the proposition 'You did not enclose your check.' How-ever, the implicative verbs *fail* and *forget* in (20a) and (20b) further imply an unmet obligation: 'You were supposed to enclose a check but you didn't.' Moreover, although both (20a) and (20b) presuppose some unmet obligation, they differ in their other pre-suppositions. Sentence (20a), with *fail,* implies a greater degree of culpability than does (20b), with *forget.* That is, *You forgot to enclose your check* presupposes that the act was unintentional, whereas *You failed to enclose your check* carries no such presupposition. Here is a partial list of implicative verbs and their presuppositions.

| | |
|---|---|
| *fail*: unmet obligation | *avoid*: negative act |
| *neglect*: unmet obligation | *refrain*: negative act |
| *forget*: unmet obligation, but unintentional | *manage*: difficult act |
| *remember*: obligation | *happen*: accidental act |
| *bother*: no obligation | |

Such verbs can have a noticeable impact on tone. For example, assume a writer is requesting information from a client for an insurance application. A sentence con-taining an implicative verb such as *neglect,* as in *You neglected to include your Social Security number on line 3,* puts the blame on the client. Instead, it might be more tactful to use a non-implicative construction, such as *Your social security number seems to be missing from our files.*

## *Pragmatics and Writing*

Pragmatics is the study of how language is used to communicate in its situational context. Thus, it is more concerned with how the message is delivered rather than the message itself. As such, pragmatics is especially useful in helping us understand problems of tone in written discourse, especially when the message is sensitive.

**Indirectness.** It might be easier for writers if all messages could be conveyed in their most **direct** form, since that form is the clearest. For example, imagine that you want to take a vacation from your job. The most direct way of making your request would be to use the imperative form and say to your boss, *Give me a vacation in August.* Unfortunately, however, the most direct form is not the most effective. In this case, the direct request is extremely rude and would be unlikely to achieve its goal. Instead, it would be better to use an **indirect** form for making your request. For instance, you might use the interrogative form and say *Can I have a vacation in August?*

The nine strategies illustrated below (discussed in Riley [1988]) provide ways to make a request more indirect and, thus, more polite. In each case, the request on the left is a highly direct, imperative form. The revisions on the right show the more indirect effect achieved by applying each strategy.

### *Question the request*

Give me a vacation. →       *Can* you give me a vacation?
                            *I wonder if* I could have a vacation.

### *Be pessimistic about the request*

Type this memo. →       *Could/Would* you type this memo?
                        Is it *possible* for you to type this memo?

### *Minimize the imposition of the request*

Answer these questions. →       Take *a moment* to answer *a few* questions.

### *Give deference to the agent of the request*

Send me some information. →       *As a novice*, I need your *expert* opinion.
                                  *Please* send me some information.

### *Apologize to the agent of the request*

Turn in your key. →       *I'm sorry*, but you'll have to turn in your key.

### *Impersonalize the request*

Submit your report on Friday. →       Reports must *be submitted* on Friday.
                                      *It is* necessary to submit reports on Friday.

### *Generalize the request*

Wear your ID card. →       *All* personnel must wear *their* ID cards.

### *Nominalize the request*

Do not smoke at your desk. →       *Smoking* is prohibited at your desk.

### Incur a debt for the request

Speak at our next meeting.          *I would be grateful* if you could speak at our next meeting.

**Explanations for Negative Messages.**    Quite often, a writer must refuse a request for credit, adjustments, favors, and so forth. Since there are numerous practical reasons, both business and social, for the writer wanting to maintain the goodwill of the reader, controlling tone is imperative. Thus, the writer's challenge is to write a letter or memo refusing to do what the reader has requested, but also to be as polite as possible.

The five strategies below (discussed in Campbell [1990]) are based on the felicity conditions on requests. They can be used to develop an explanation for denying a request while maintaining the reader's goodwill. For example, assume you are an administrator for a philanthropic agency charged with awarding fellowships, and someone has requested an application for the Goodbody Fellowship. Each strategy below can be adapted to explain why the request is being denied.

### Existence: All or part of X doesn't exist.

I am sorry to inform you that the Goodbody Fellowship has not been funded for the current year.

### Agency: Someone else is responsible for doing X.

The ABC agency is responsible for awarding the Goodbody Fellowship.

### Timing: Now is not the time to do X.

Unfortunately, the deadline for the Goodbody Fellowship for the current year is now past, but you may apply for next year's award any time after January 1st.

### Reader benefit: You don't really want us to do X because . . .

You may not be aware that recipients of the Goodbody Fellowship are ineligible to hold other grants. If awarded a Goodbody, you would have to forgo your Dobbs Grant, which is worth considerably more than the Goodbody Fellowship.

### Ability: X can't be done because . . .

The Goodbody Fellowship is available only to those in the physical sciences; however, you may apply for the Selby Fellowship, which is open only to students in the humanities.

# Summary

Let's go over what we have covered in this chapter. We began with five common problems in writing. However, we had no obvious explanations for them. Thus, we constructed a (partial) theory of written language to account for our original observations. This theory includes different types of writing systems (morphographic, syllabic, and alphabetic) and spelling systems (morphophonemic, phonemic, and phonetic). We have also seen that all domains of linguistic theory are relevant to written discourse: phonology, morphology, syntax, semantics, and pragmatics.

As usual, keep in mind that there is much more to the study of written language than what we have covered in this one short chapter. However, you have now been exposed to some of the basic ideas in the field; to learn more about the subject, see the readings at the end of this chapter. Following the readings are practice problems and answers to test your understanding of the material in this chapter. After that are 50 exercises for you to do on your own.

# Supplementary Readings

Campbell, K. S. (1990). Explanations in negative messages: More insights from speech act theory. *Journal of Business Communication, 20,* 357–375.

Campbell, K. S., Riley, K., and Parker, F. (1990). *You*-perspective: Insights from speech act theory. *Journal of Technical Writing and Communication, 20,* 189–199.

Ferguson, K. S., and Parker, F. (1990). Grammar and technical writing. *Journal of Technical Writing and Communication, 20,* 357–367.

Gelb, I. J. (1963). *A study of writing.* Chicago: University of Chicago Press.

Katzner, K. (1975). *The languages of the world.* New York: Funk & Wagnalls.

Parker, F., and Campbell, K. S. (forthcoming). Linguistics and writing: A reassessment. *College Composition and Communication.*

Riley, K. (1988). Speech act theory and degrees of directness in professional writing. *The Technical Writing Teacher, 15,* 1–29.

Riley, K. (1993). Telling more than the truth: Implicature, speech acts, and ethics in professional communication. *Journal of Business Ethics, 12,* 179–196.

Riley, K., and Parker, F. (1988). Tone as a function of presupposition in technical and business writing. *Journal of Technical Writing and Communication, 18,* 325–343.

Sampson, G. (1985). *Writing systems.* London: Hutchinson.

Vande Kopple, W. J. (1982). Functional sentence perspective, composition, and reading. *College Composition and Communication, 33,* 50–63.

You are now prepared to read all of these works. Gelb, Katzner, and Sampson all have information on writing systems used throughout the world; Sampson, however, is the most linguistically sophisticated and up to date. Parker and Campbell provides an overview of applications of linguistics to writing. The others all deal with specific applications of linguistic theory to professional writing.

## Practice

**1.** What type of representational/writing system is illustrated by the dollar sign in *Shirts $25.00?*

   a.  pictographic              d.  syllabic
   b.  ideographic               e.  alphabetic
   c.  morphographic        f.  none of the above

2. *Cherub* and *cherubic* as spelled in standard English orthography is an example of _____ spelling.

   a.  phonetic                d.  morphophonemic
   b.  phonemic              e.  allophonic
   c.  pathetic               f.  none of the above

**3.** Consider the following interchange.

JOE:      *M R ducks.*
BOB:    *M R not ducks.*
JOE:      *O S A R.*
BOB:    *L I B, M R ducks.*

Which of the following types of representational/writing systems is being used in the italicized part of this interchange?

   a.  pictographic              d.  syllabic
   b.  ideographic               e.  alphabetic
   c.  morphograpic        f.  none of the above

**4.** Consider the misspelling *strugged* for *struggled*. State the phonological process that accounts for the error.

**5.** Consider the following sentence written by a 7-year-old from Idaho: *They haf to make bills.* (a) Identify the error that can be traced to a phonological process and (b) state the process.

**6.** Consider the following sentence written by a college student enrolled in a remedial writing course: *A child has to see and hear things as his father dids.* (a) Identify the error that can be traced to a linguistic principle and (b) state the principle.

**7.** Consider the following sentence written by a 13-year-old: *I also admire because I think that he is the type of man that is easy to get along with.* (a) Identify the error that can be traced to a linguistic principle and (b) state the principle.

**8.** The sentence *Why does Mr. Pyle regret that Acme Goobers is a stable company?* presupposes, among other things, that Acme Goobers is a stable company. The trigger for this presupposition is _____.

   a.  a factive verb           d.  a non-implicative verb
   b.  a non-factive verb     e.  a *wh*-question
   c.  an implicative verb     f.  none of the above

**9.** Identify (a) the presupposition and (b) the trigger in the following sentence: *I managed to find the information that you requested about accounting software.*

10. The following requests were phoned in to disc jockey Tom Kenny at a radio station in Baton Rouge. Identify the indirectness strategies used by each caller.

    a. If you have a chance, play *Love Will Keep Us Together.*

    b. Excuse me, can you play a song called . . .

    c. What time does the mall close today? . . . Ya'll always know everything.

    d. Yes sir, is there any way possible you could play . . . ?

# Answers

1. c. morphographic

2. d. morphophonemic

3. d. syllabic

4. Post-vocalic liquid deletion

5. a. *haf*
    b. Voicing assimilation

6. a. *dids*
    b. *did* misanalyzed as root form; third-person singular *-s* added to past tense form (hypercorrection)

7. a. *admire because*
    b. *admire* is subcategorized to take a direct object

8. a. a factive verb

9. a. It was difficult for the speaker to find the information.
    b. *managed*

10. a. *If you have a chance*—being pessimistic about the request
    b. *Excuse me*—apologizing; *can you*—questioning the request
    c. *Ya'll always know everything*—giving deference
    d. *Sir*—giving deference; *is there*—questioning the request; *possible*—being pessimistic about the request

# Exercises

1. A company in Duluth, Minnesota specializes in mailing discount coupons for local businesses out to residents of the city. The company calls itself *Q-pon Express.* What type of representational/writing system is the company's name an example of?

2. The symbol for KOA (Campgrounds of America) is a drawing of a tent. Which of the following types of representational/writing systems is being used in a roadside sign depicting a tent, standing for 'camping facilities'?

    a. pictographic            d. syllabic

    b. ideographic           e. alphabetic

    c. morphographic

**3.** Consider the following sign on the door to a women's toilet.

Which type of representational/writing system is this an example of?

**4.** Consider the *U* in the trademark *U-Haul*. Which type of representational/writing system is this an example of?

**5.** When Barry Goldwater was running for president in 1964, his campaign bumper stickers read *AUH₂O*. Which type of representational/writing system is this an example of?

**6.** You go to a steak house for dinner and discover that the men's room has a drawing of a bull on the door, while the women's room has a drawing of a cow on the door. What type of representational/writing system is being used here?

**7.** *Elf's* and *elves'* as spelled in standard English orthography is an example of _____ spelling.

    a.  phonetic                          d.  allophonic
    b.  phonemic                        e.  both (b) and (c)
    c.  morphophonemic            f.  none of the above

**8.** *Electric* and *electricity* as spelled in standard English orthography is an example of _____ spelling.

**9.** *Ladder* and *latter* spelled *laader* and *lader*, respectively, is an example of _____ spelling.

**10.** A 7-year-old boy from Washington state wrote the following sentence: *flsh is a god man becaz he savz pepl and he iz nis he diznot kil pepl*. What level of phonological representation is he basing his spelling on, in general?

**11.** The following data is from Shaughnessy (1977). In each of the following examples, state the phonological process that accounts for the misspelling.

    a.  motvation (motivation)
    b.  inaccute (inaccurate)
    c.  impluses (impulses)

**12.** The following was seen on a roadside sign in east Tennessee: *Jamboree Augest 16th*. What phonological process is responsible for this misspelling?

**13.** An advertisement for *Leg Quaters* was seen in a Piggly-Wiggly grocery store in Wallace, North Carolina. What phonological process is responsible for this misspelling?

**14.** The following sign was observed in Savannah: *Tuxsedo Rental*.

    a.  What phoneme(s) does the letter *x* represent in this sign?
    b.  What phoneme(s) does the letter *x* usually represent in English?

**15.** The following was seen on a placard worn by a woman soliciting donations in front of a Kroger's store in Knoxville, Tennessee: *HELP ABUSE CHILDREN*. What phonological process is responsible for this misspelling?

**16.** The following sign was seen in the window of a grocery store: *Hunderds of Prizes*. What phonological process is responsible for this misspelling?

**17.** In flight instruction texts, the term *certificated* appears where you would expect *certified*, as in *That plane is certificated for stunts*. Explain the evolution of the verb *certificate* from the verb *certify*. (Hint: English morphology allows the creation of nouns from verbs and verbs from nouns.)

**18.** A 6-year-old boy from Wisconsin described the comic book character Flash as having *a thunder* on his hat. What morphological principle accounts for this error?

**19.** The following data is from Shaughnessy (1977). In each of the following examples, state the linguistic principle that accounts for the italicized error.

   a. My older brothers and sisters *founded* life not very much different.
   b. They don't see and hear things the same way as *they* children do.
   c. There *is* only 97,000 openings per year.

**20.** The following message was printed on a chopsticks wrapper:

Welcome to Chinese Restaurant.
Please try your Nice Chinese Food with Chopsticks,
the traditional and typical of Chinese glorious history and cultual.
PRODUCT OF CHINA

   a. *Chinese Restaurant* should be *a Chinese Restaurant* or *this Chinese Restaurant*, or something similar. What morphological principle accounts for this error?
   b. *Cultual* should be *cultural*. What phonological process accounts for this error?

**21.** Identify the agreement problem in each of the following passages, then state what caused it.

   a. The difference in the two systems is the way that factory overhead (i.e., all other costs besides direct material and labor) are accounted for.
   b. The memory requirements for each program is listed in Table 2.

**22.** Identify the fragment in each of the following passages, then state the kind of construction it is (e.g., noun clause, etc.)

   a. Also known as stockholders' equity, book value is the difference between the company's assets and its liabilities. In other words, what the shareholders own after the company's debts have been paid.
   b. There have been a couple of new breakthroughs in the last year in cash register software. The major one being that the receipt printer can now take the place of the old rebate system.

**23.** Identify the dangling modifiers in the following passages, then re-write each one so that the modifier has a noun phrase to serve as its subject.

   a. By self-insuring one's company, doors are opened to lawsuits and even possible bankruptcy.

b. A prescribed burning prepares the land for future forests. By reducing weak competition and exposing the mineral soil, the land becomes very fertile for growth.

24. State the thematic role played by each of the noun phrases in the following examples.

   a. The Gomosaygiama Agency has launched a new advertising campaign for the Katznelson Corporation.

   b. A new advertising campaign has been launched by the Gomosaygiama Agency.

   c. The Katznelson Corporation is benefiting from a new advertising campaign.

25. Identify the type of thematic progression illustrated in each of the following examples (AB:AC, AB:BC, or neither).

   a. S&S Lighting was established in Omaha in 1968. S&S was incorporated in 1970.
   b. The annual 'Wellness Fair' will be held this Saturday. We hope everyone will attend.
   c. We apologize for the delay in shipping your books. They will be sent within two weeks.

26. The following pair of sentences conforms to the AB:AC pattern of thematic progression. Rewrite them so that the pair follows the AB:BC pattern.

   Budget reviews will now be conducted by a Budget Review Committee made up of department heads. In this way, our future budgets should better reflect the needs of each of the individual departments.

27.–29. Consider the following paragraphs, adapted from Vande Kopple (1982: 53–54). Paragraph (1) has been shown to be more readable and memorable than paragraph (2).

   (1a) Epic poems usually include a long narrative or story. (1b) This story is almost always marked by certain conventions. (1c) These conventions are normally used to enhance the stature of a great hero. (1d) Such a hero personifies the ideals of particular societies.

   (2a) A long narrative or story is usually included in epic poems. (2b) Certain conventions almost always mark this story. (2c) The stature of a great hero is enhanced through the use of these conventions. (2d) The ideals of particular societies are personified in such a hero.

27. State the thematic progression of paragraph (1).

28. State the thematic progression of paragraph (2).

29. Explain why (1) is more "readable and memorable" than (2).

30. Is the truth of the proposition in the following introductory clause presupposed? If so, what is the trigger?

   After you computerize inventory management, you will have to select one of the three available system types.

31. Is the truth of the proposition in the following introductory clause presupposed? If so, what is the trigger?

   If we make the change to C-MOS, we can begin to take advantage of the many features of C-MOS in future designs.

**32.** Identify the presupposition (and the trigger) in the following example: *We regret that your order has been lost.*

**33.** Identify the presupposition (and the trigger) in the following example: *The results of the ratio analysis make clear that WMX is a stable company.*

**34.** What presupposition is conveyed by the following example? What is the trigger? How could the passage be revised to improve its tone?

> WMX management is aware of the indiscretions of past employees and intends to change the public's perception of the company.

**35.** The following dialogue occurred between lawyer Arnie Becker and his father on an episode of the T.V. show *L.A. Law.*

> FATHER:    Is that what you told her?
> ARNIE:     That's what I tried to tell her.
> FATHER:    'Tried' means you didn't.

The father's second utterance essentially defines *try* as a particular type of verb. What type of verb is *try*?

**36.** Britain has a "Sunday Closing" law, which requires certain businesses not to open on Sunday. Accordingly, the following notice was posted in Marks and Spencer, a department store chain:

> You will have read that a number of retailers have decided to defy the current law in England, Wales, and Northern Ireland and trade on Sundays between now and Christmas. Marks and Spencer will remain closed on these Sundays.

What's interesting about this notice is that the reader suspects that Marks and Spencer is not going to open on Sunday, *before reading the last sentence*. How is the reader able to figure this out? (Hint: implicative verb).

**37. –40.** The following memo was sent to residents of an apartment building on the shore of Lake Superior from the property manager of the building. Examples of indirectness strategies are italicized.

> We have recently observed individuals out beyond the fence line below Lake View Apartments. *We ask* that you please be aware that this area is fenced off for safety reasons; *like all lakeshores*, the embankment is always changing and is not considered a safe area for walking.
> We understand that the quiet and serenity of the lakeshore draws people near, but for safety reasons, access to *this one small area* of the grounds cannot be allowed.
> We dislike imposing on the residents, but *we would be grateful* for your assistance in this matter.

**37.** *We ask* is an example of _____.

a. nominalizing the request
b. impersonalizing the request
c. giving deference to the agent of the request
d. being pessimistic about the request
e. questioning the request
f. none of the above

**38.** *like all lakeshores* is an example of _____.

    a.  generalizing the request        d.  minimizing the request
    b.  impersonalizing the request    e.  questioning the request
    c.  nominalizing the request       f.  none of the above

**39.** *this one small area* is an example of _____.

    a.  apologizing to the agent of the request
    b.  incurring a debt for the request
    c.  being pessimistic about the request
    d.  giving deference to the agent of the request
    e.  generalizing the request
    f.  none of the above

**40.** *We would be grateful* is an example of _____.

    a.  giving deference to the agent of the request
    b.  incurring a debt for the request
    c.  apologizing to the agent of the request
    d.  impersonalizing the request
    e.  questioning the request
    f.  none of the above

**41.–45.** The following memo was sent to residents of an apartment building by the property manager.

MEMO TO ALL RESIDENTS
*Smoking Policy*

    Just a reminder that there is no smoking in any of the public areas within the building. This would include the entries, stairwells, corridors, and laundry rooms. We ask that you refrain from smoking in these areas and that you advise your guests of our building policy and ask them to refrain also. The policy is in effect for the health and safety of all residents and will be strictly enforced.

    Thank you for your understanding and for not smoking.

**41.** Identify one example of the indirectness strategy of *impersonalizing the request.*

**42.** Identify one example of the indirectness strategy of *nominalizing the request.*

**43.** Identify one example of the indirectness strategy of *questioning the request.*

**44.** Identify one example of the indirectness strategy of *incurring a debt.*

**45.** Identify one example of the indirectness strategy of *minimizing the imposition of the request.*

**46.** Decide which strategy for explaining negative messages was used to deny the following request.

    BOARD OF REALTORS' REQUEST: Ms. Fetters, you have been nominated for the position of President of the Board of Realtors.
    MS. FETTERS' EXPLANATION: Although the Board is an important organization and I am flattered by the nomination to head it, I could not devote enough time to be a worthy leader.

**47.** Decide which strategy for explaining negative messages was used to deny the following request.

KEVIN CARTER'S REQUEST: Please send me a case of your BetRFlite–2 golf balls.
BETRFLITE'S EXPLANATION: Thanks for your interest in the BetRFlite–2. However, we have binding agreements with our distributors to sell our products only to retailers.

**48.** Decide which strategy for explaining negative messages was used to deny the following request.

NORMAN ELECTRICAL CONTRACTING'S REQUEST: We are interested in starting a charge account at Automation Controls.
AUTOMATION CONTROL'S EXPLANATION: We're grateful for your business; however, since you have not established a credit rating for your new company, we are unable to open a charge account for you at the present time. Please feel free to re-apply in six months.

**49.–50.** The following passage (adapted from Shaughnessy, 1977: 247) was written by a college student in a basic writing course. The numbers in parentheses indicate places where an English teacher might mark an error.

A child playing alone can become very involve (1) in a (2) animal or object. Walking through Kings (3) Park (4) I notice (5) a little boy sitting on a bench, (6) he had a bag with something in it resting between his leg. (7) A bird (8) sitting on the edge of the bench. It look (9) as though from the expression on the little boy (10) face that he was quit (11) surprise (12) at the bird. He start (13) feeding the bird something from the bag. Although the boy (14) alone, he (15) having a good time with the bird.

**49.** Identify four errors that have a principled, linguistic explanation.

**50.** Identify four errors that do not have a linguistic explanation.

# Chapter 11

# *The Neurology of Language*

The **neurology of language**, also known as **neurolinguistics**, is the study of how the brain processes language. Let's consider some observations we can make about language and the brain.

(1) Damage to the brain can affect a person's ability to process language; damage to the heart, lungs, or kidneys (short of killing the person) does not.

(2) Damage to the left side of the brain is more likely to cause language processing difficulties (e.g., being able to hear speech but unable to comprehend it) than is damage to the right side of the brain.

(3) Damage to the front part of the brain is more likely to affect the production of language through speaking and writing. Damage to the rear part of the brain is more likely to affect the comprehension of language through listening and reading.

(4) In addition to causing language processing difficulties, brain damage may disrupt a person's ability to comprehend sensations (e.g., to recognize a common object such as an orange), or to carry out voluntary actions such as licking the lips on command.

Observation (1) illustrates the fact that the physical organ underlying the ability to process language is the brain; in particular, brain damage can result in a language-specific dysfunction called **aphasia**. Observation (2) illustrates the fact that most human beings process language in the left cerebral hemisphere. This reflects the fact that human brains exhibit **hemispherical specialization**: the left hemisphere controls one set of abilities, among them language processing, while the right controls other abilities, such as orientation in space and visuospatial processing. Observation (3) illustrates the fact that different parts of each hemisphere control different mental functions. This is sometimes referred to as **localization of function**. Observation (4) illustrates the fact that, in addition to causing a language dysfunction (aphasia), brain damage may disrupt other types of comprehension and production.

Before getting into the details of neurolinguistics, we should address three points concerning the nature of research in this field. First, neurolinguists commonly observe the language of patients who have suffered brain damage (i.e., a lesion) from a stroke, a tumor, or trauma. A stroke causes damage by shutting off the blood supply, and thus the oxygen supply, to some part of the brain. A tumor causes damage by putting pressure on part of the brain from the inside, in effect "squeezing" the brain between the tumor itself and the skull. A trauma to the brain is caused by some sort of external force, such as a blow to the head. Of these three types of damage, stroke damage is typically of more interest to the neurolinguist than damage caused by tumor or trauma. This is because a stroke is capable of damaging a very specific and localized part of the brain, whereas damage caused by tumor or trauma tends to be more global, affecting a greater part of the brain.

Second, neurolinguistics is basically a correlational and statistical enterprise. It is correlational in that it tries to find correspondences between particular language functions and particular parts of the brain. The neurolinguist draws inferences of the following type: patients 1, 3, and 5 all have had strokes in area A of the brain and all exhibit language dysfunction Y; patients 2, 4, and 6 all have had strokes in area B of the brain and all exhibit language dysfunction Z; therefore, it appears that brain area A controls function Y and that brain area B controls function Z. Neurolinguistics is statistical in that the researcher cannot draw absolute correlations between a particular part of the brain and a particular language dysfunction for all human beings. For example, in a sample of 10 patients with damage to brain area A, only 8 may exhibit language dysfunction Y. On this basis, the neurolinguist would be able to hypothesize that there is an 80 percent probability that damage to brain area A will lead to language dysfunction Y. In short, then, neurolinguists essentially make statistical correlations between localized brain damage and particular language processing deficits.

Third, as was the case with first-language acquisition, the research methods used in neurolinguistics have some inherent difficulties. As we have just seen, one main avenue for studying neurolinguistics is through pathology; that is, through studying patients with brain damage. Obviously, however, the neurolinguist cannot inflict damage on a normal subject in order to see what happens, but instead must wait for a suitable subject to come along. Moreover, the patient must have relatively localized brain damage and must also exhibit fairly specific behavioral abnormalities. If the brain damage is global or if the behavioral abnormalities are too general, the analyst will have difficulty correlating a particular area of the brain with a particular behavioral deficit. In short, the neurolinguist is constrained to some extent by having to draw inferences on the basis of what nature provides.

In order to convey a better understanding of how research in neurolinguistics is carried out, this chapter is divided into four major areas: the anatomy of the central nervous system; a survey of some of the major figures who have added to our understanding of language and brain; a discussion of the different functions performed by each of the cerebral hemispheres; and a survey of brain disorders affecting language in particular, and expression and comprehension in general.

## Anatomy of the Nervous System

The basic unit of the nervous system is the **neuron**; there are about 12 billion neurons in the nervous system. Each neuron is made up of three parts: a **cell body**; an **axon**, which transmits nervous impulses away from the cell body; and **dendrites**, which receive impulses coming in to the cell body. The point at which the nervous impulse passes from the axon of one neuron to the dendrites of another is called a **synapse**. Thus, neurons communicate with each other by transmitting information through this complex of axons, dendrites, and synapses.

The part of the nervous system that is of primary interest to neurolinguists is the **central nervous system** (CNS), composed of the brain and the spinal cord. The diagram of the CNS in Figure 11–1 illustrates the major landmarks which will be of interest to us in this chapter.

The **spinal cord** (1) transmits messages between the brain and the peripheral nervous system extending throughout the rest of the body. The spinal cord transmits the message from the brain that says, for example, to cross your right leg over your left. The spinal cord, however, plays no role in language processing. The **lower brain stem** (2) consists of the **medulla oblongata** and the **pons**. These structures serve essentially as a bridge between the spinal cord and the higher brain stem. (In fact, *pons* is Latin for 'bridge.') Damage to the lower brain stem can cause a speech disorder known as **dysarthria**. This is not a language deficit, but rather the inability to produce articulate speech.

The **higher brain stem** (3) consists of the **thalamus** and **midbrain**. These structures control involuntary regulatory functions such as breathing, heart rate, and body temperature. In addition, the thalamus receives all incoming sensory stimuli (except for the sense of smell) and transmits each stimulus to the part of the brain

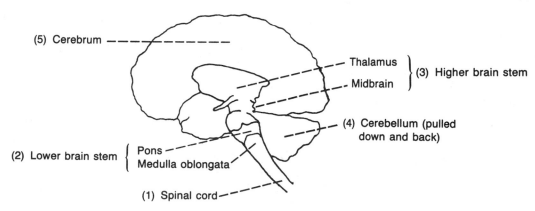

**FIGURE 11–1. Cross section of the central nervous system, facing left.**

where it is processed. The **cerebellum** (4) , which lies to the rear of the brain stem, controls equilibrium. The cerebellum plays no known role, however, in language processing.

The **cerebrum** (5) is the part of the brain on top of the brain stem and cerebellum. The cerebrum is divided into two hemispheres, the left and the right, and exhibits what is known as **contralateral control**. That is, each hemisphere controls the opposite side of the body. For example, if you raise your right arm, the message to do so originates in the left cerebral hemisphere. Likewise, if you step on a tack with your left foot, the sensation of pain is processed by your right cerebral hemisphere.

Each cerebral hemisphere consists of a mass of **white fiber tracts** covered by the **cortex**, which is approximately 0. 25 inch thick and contains about 10 billion neurons. (Recall that the entire nervous system contains only about 12 billion neurons; thus, the cortex is by far the most powerful processing center within the nervous system as a whole.) The white fiber tracts are divided into three types, according to their function. **Association fibers** connect different parts of the cortex within one hemisphere, enabling these parts to communicate with each other. **Projection fibers** connect the cortex to the brain stem and spinal cord, enabling the cortex to communicate with the peripheral nervous system. **Transverse fibers** connect the two cerebral hemispheres, enabling them to communicate with each other. The 200 million transverse fibers are known collectively as the **corpus callosum**.

Let's now turn our attention to the cortex itself, which is essentially the central storehouse of the brain and controls all voluntary activity, including the ability to process language. The diagram of the human cortex in Figure 11–2 illustrates the major landmarks which we will refer to throughout the rest of this chapter.

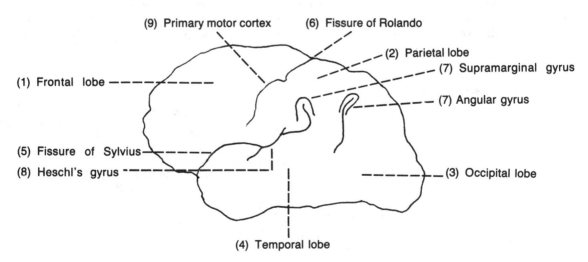

**FIGURE 11–2.  Human cortex, facing left.**

## Lobes

The cerebrum (i.e., the cortex and the white fiber tracts serving it) is divided into four lobes: the **frontal lobe** (1) in the anterior (front) part; the **parietal lobe** (2) in the superior (top) part; the **occipital lobe** (3) in the posterior (back) part; and the **temporal lobe** (4) in the inferior (bottom) part. Each lobe, in turn, subserves somewhat different functions. For example, the frontal lobe processes olfactory stimuli, the occipital lobe processes visual stimuli, and the temporal lobe processes auditory stimuli. Each cerebral hemisphere has these lobes, so we can speak of the left temporal lobe, the right occipital lobe, and so on. We will see later on that the left frontal and temporal lobes house the major language processing centers for most humans.

## Convolutions and Fissures

The cortex of the human brain has a wrinkled appearance. The indentations are called **fissures** (or sulci) and the bulges are called **convolutions** (or gyri). Certain of these fissures and convolutions serve as important anatomical landmarks. The **fissure of Sylvius** (5), also known as the lateral sulcus, separates the frontal and temporal lobes. The **fissure of Rolando** (6), also called the central sulcus, separates the frontal and parietal lobes. The **supramarginal gyrus** and the **angular gyrus** (7) lie in the inferior part of the parietal lobe. And **Heschl's gyrus** (8) , also known as the transverse temporal gyrus or the primary auditory cortex, receives all incoming auditory stimuli. One function of Heschl's gyrus is to separate different types of auditory stimuli (e.g., environmental noises such as buzzes, clicks, and whistles versus linguistic stimuli such as speech) and send them to the different parts of the cortex where they are interpreted.

The **primary motor cortex** (9) is a strip of cortex about two centimeters wide lying immediately anterior to the fissure of Rolando. Each point in the primary motor cortex controls a discrete set of muscles. For example, stimulating the superior part of the primary motor cortex will cause the leg muscles on the opposite side of the body to contract. Movements of the lips, tongue, and jaw are controlled by the inferior part of the primary motor cortex near where it meets the fissure of Sylvius. In general, the more fine-grained the movement, the larger the cortical area devoted to it. Thus, movement of the trunk has less cortex devoted to it than movement of the fingers does.

## Background of Neurolinguistics

In this section we will discuss a few of the major figures who have contributed to our modern understanding of the neurology of language.

### Broca

During the early nineteenth century, the question of whether different parts of the brain serve different mental functions was hotly debated. Scientists in the

**localizationist** camp believed that specific parts of the brain controlled different mental functions. Scientists in the **holist** camp, in contrast, believed that different mental functions were not localized in specific parts of the brain. The localization of cortical function was finally demonstrated to the satisfaction of most neuroscientists by the French physician Pierre Paul Broca (1824–1884).

Broca's evidence was based primarily on two patients. First was Leborgne, a 51-year-old male who had had brain seizures since his youth. At the age of 30, he lost his ability to produce language but not his ability to comprehend it. At the age of 40, Leborgne developed paralysis on the right side and became bedridden. (Recall that the left hemisphere controls the right side of the body.) Upon his death, an autopsy revealed extensive degeneration of the left hemisphere. Broca argued that the lesion had begun in the third convolution of the frontal lobe in the left hemisphere. In short, Broca correlated Leborgne's expressive aphasia—i.e., his inability to produce linguistic output—with (what began as) localized damage in the third frontal convolution. Based on this evidence, in 1861 Broca reported his findings in a paper later translated into English as: "Remarks on the Seat of the Faculty of Articulate Language, followed by an Observation of *Aphemia.*" (The term *aphasia* was later introduced by Trousseau.) The case of Leborgne, however, was not completely conclusive since the patient's condition had degenerated slowly over the years and since he had numerous, diffuse brain lesions at his death.

Broca offered additional evidence based on a second patient, Lelong, an 84-year-old male who had had expressive aphasia for the past 9½ years. The only words he could utter were his name and the French words for *yes, no, three,* and *always.* Moreover, he was unable to write, although he knew how. His motor power, however, was intact: in other words, his inability to speak and write was not due to paralysis. After his death, an autopsy revealed localized damage to the third convolution of the frontal lobe in the left hemisphere, the same general area that Broca had argued was the site of Leborgne's original lesion. Later in 1861, Broca reported the case of Lelong.

Shortly thereafter, several other neurologists reported a total of ten cases of aphasia with damage to the third frontal convolution in the left hemisphere, essentially replicating Broca's findings. At the same time, a patient was reported with damage to the third frontal convolution in the right hemisphere, without any sort of language disturbance. Based on such cases, Broca contended a few years later that the left frontal lobe is specialized for language. The type of disorder described by Broca has come to be known alternatively as **Broca's aphasia**, **expressive aphasia** (because it affects linguistic output rather than comprehension), or **motor aphasia** (because the damage site is near the primary motor cortex).

In summary, Broca was the first to substantiate convincingly the localizationist theory of cortical function. Moreover, he was the first to propose the idea that the left hemisphere is specialized for language.

## *Wernicke*

The next major step in our understanding of aphasia was put forward by the German Carl Wernicke (1848–1904). Wernicke was the first to differentiate the expressive aphasia described by Broca from sensory aphasia. Wernicke studied patients whose language disorders differed markedly from those described by Broca. In general terms, Broca's patients could comprehend speech but could not produce it; moreover, they displayed varying degrees of right-sided paralysis. In contrast, patients with sensory aphasia could not comprehend speech, but they could produce it (although it was characterized by errors); moreover, they exhibited a general absence of paralysis. Wernicke correlated this type of sensory disturbance with damage to the first convolution of the temporal lobe in the left hemisphere.

Wernicke published his theories in 1874 as *Der aphasische Symptomenkomplex* (*The Aphasic Complex*). Consequently, the type of disorder described by Wernicke has come to be known alternatively as **Wernicke's aphasia**, **receptive aphasia** (because it affects linguistic comprehension rather than output), or **sensory aphasia** (because the damage site is near the sensory cortex).

In sum, whereas Broca localized language in the left hemisphere, Wernicke subdivided that hemisphere as subserving two different language functions: the frontal lobe controls expression, and the temporal lobe controls comprehension. Moreover, Wernicke's division of the left hemisphere into two different linguistic centers makes perfect sense anatomically. The expressive aphasia described by Broca results from damage near the motor cortex, which in turn controls outgoing motor movements, including the articulation of speech. The receptive aphasia described by Wernicke results from damage near the sensory cortex, in particular the primary auditory cortex (Heschl's gyrus), which processes incoming auditory stimuli, including speech. Broca's area and Wernicke's area are shown in Figure 11–3.

## Penfield and Roberts

More recently, research in the neurology of language has been advanced by Wilder Penfield and LaMar Roberts, two neurologists working at the Montreal Neurological Institute in the 1940's and 1950's. Penfield and Roberts were treating patients for epilepsy, a disorder characterized by abnormal electrical discharges in the brain. One method they used for treating this was to remove those areas

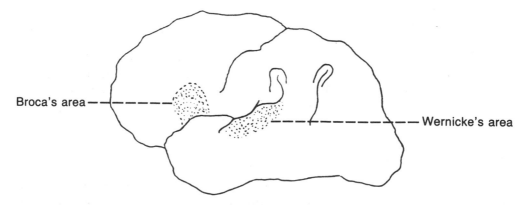

**FIGURE 11–3. Broca's area and Wernicke's area.**

of the brain that served as the sources for these discharges. However, they did not want to remove a part of the brain that subserved some necessary mental function such as language. In other words, they didn't want the cure for epilepsy to be worse than the disease itself.

In order to determine the function of different parts of the brain, Penfield and Roberts stimulated specific parts of the exposed cortex with a weak electrical current transmitted through silver probes. Since the cortex itself cannot feel pain, it was possible for them to remove part of the patient's skull under a local anesthetic and have the patient remain conscious throughout the procedure. During stimulation they would have the patient perform such tasks as naming an object in a picture. When they stimulated an area of the cortex subserving language, the patient would experience some sort of linguistic difficulty such as total arrest of speech, halting and slurred speech, repetitions, confusions of numbers while counting, or inability to name. Penfield and Roberts describe some responses as follows.

> An example is . . . . "Oh, I know what it is. That is what you put in your shoes." After withdrawal of the stimulating electrodes, the patient immediately said "foot." Still another example is the inability to name a comb. When asked its use, he said, "I comb my hair." When asked again to name it, he couldn't until the electrode was removed. (1959: 123–124)

It is interesting to note in passing that this last patient was apparently able to access the verb *comb* (as in *I comb my hair*), but not the noun *comb*.

Using this technique on numerous patients, Penfield and Roberts "mapped" the entire cortex, publishing their results in 1959 as *Speech and Brain Mechanisms*. They were able to identify three discrete language centers in the brain. Their findings coincided, in general, with the earlier theories of Broca and Wernicke, except that they identified language centers in the cortex surrounding Wernicke's area and extending up to the supramarginal and angular gyri in the parietal lobe. In effect, they "expanded" Wernicke's area. In addition, they identified a third language area known as the **supplementary motor cortex**, which lies in the superior region of the frontal lobe anterior to the primary motor cortex. These areas are illustrated in Figure 11–4. Moreover, they ranked these areas according to the degree of language dysfunction that damage to each area could be expected to cause. In descending order of importance, they are Wernicke's area, Broca's area, and the supplementary motor cortex.

Before leaving this section on the history of neurolinguistics, let us emphasize that we have touched on only a few major figures from the last 150 years. These scientists, however, have made some of the most significant contributions to the study of language and the brain.

## *Hemispherical Specialization*

One of the most interesting findings to come out of the study of language and brain is that the left and right hemispheres of the brain are specialized to carry out separate but complementary functions, a property apparently unique to humans. A central

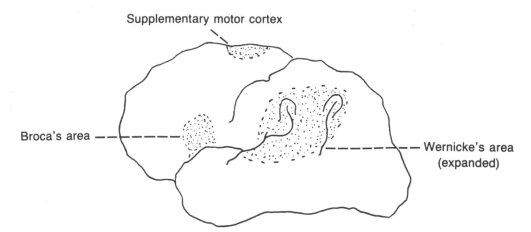

Supplementary motor cortex

Broca's area

Wernicke's area
(expanded)

**FIGURE 11–4.    Three major language areas of the cortex according to Penfield and Roberts.**

concept necessary to understanding the specific functions of each hemisphere is what is known as **dominance**.

## Left-Hemisphere Dominance for Language

Penfield and Roberts estimated that 98 percent of the population have their language centers in the left hemisphere. Thus, we might say that approximately 98 percent of the population is **left dominant** and approximately 2 percent is **right dominant**. (This is an oversimplification since a very small number of people have **bilateral dominance**, where the language function seems to be shared more or less equally by both hemispheres.) The term *dominance* as used here refers solely to the location of the primary language centers. The evidence for left-hemisphere dominance among humans comes from several sources.

**Aphasia.**  It has been estimated that damage to the left hemisphere causes some form of aphasia in approximately 70 percent of all adults; damage to the right hemisphere causes an aphasic disturbance in only about 1 percent of the adult population.

**Hemispherectomies.**  Adults undergoing a left hemisensphere (surgical removal of the left hemisphere) generally suffer a permanent loss of their ability to process language; right hemispherectomies among adults are less likely to cause complete or permanent loss of the language function.

**Planum Temporal.**  The planum temporal is a white fiber tract underneath both the left and right temporal lobes. Brain researchers have found that this structure is larger in the left hemisphere in approximately 65 percent of adults. Moreover, researchers have found that the planum temporal in fetuses is larger in the left hemi-sphere. Such findings may indicate that left-hemisphere dominance in humans is biologically determined; that is, that the genetic program actually builds more neu-ronal structure into the left hemisphere to "enable" it to acquire language.

**Subcortical System.**   The thalamus, part of the higher brain stem, is the low-est structure in the central nervous system to have a left and right hemisphere. Dam-age to the left side of the thalamus causes such linguistic dysfunctions as involuntary repetitions and naming difficulties; damage to the right side of the thalamus, how-ever, generally does not.

**Wada Test.**   In 1949 Juhn Wada reported on a new procedure for determining the brain dominance of an individual. In this procedure, the patient lies on his or her back in a comfortable position and is instructed to count and move the fingers of both hands rapidly. At this point, sodium amytal, a sedative, is injected into either the left or right internal carotid artery in the neck. If the sodium amytal is injected into the left internal carotid, it will depress activity in the left hemisphere, and vice versa. This has the effect of temporarily paralyzing the opposite side of the body. If the affected hemisphere is non-dominant, then the counting stops and starts again within 30 seconds. The patient is able to speak, name, and read correctly, and re-members the paralysis. However, if the affected hemisphere is dominant, then the patient stops counting for one minute or longer, has difficulty in speaking, naming, and reading, and does not recall the paralysis. The results of this test indicate that the vast majority of humans are left dominant.

**Dichotic Listening.**   In the 1960's, Doreen Kimura developed a technique called dichotic listening which also supports the claim that most humans are left dominant. In this procedure, a normal subject is fed two auditory signals simulta-neously through headphones. Even though each ear has neural connections to both hemispheres, the most direct pathway is to the contralateral hemisphere. Thus, for all practical purposes, a signal fed to the right ear will be sent to the left hemisphere for processing, and vice versa. When the two stimuli are linguistic (i.e., words), the subject reports hearing the word that was presented to the right ear. Thus, for ex-ample, a subject presented with *boy* to the right ear and *girl* to the left ear would report having heard *boy* but not *girl*. The vast majority of subjects have this **right ear advantage** for linguistic stimuli, a fact which supports the claim that most hu-mans are left dominant.

Subsequent dichotic listening experiments have shown that most subjects have a right ear (i.e., left hemisphere) advantage for all types of linguistic stimuli: speech, nonsense syllables (e.g., /kɛb/, /lʌb/), synthetic speech, speech played backwards, CV syllables, and even Morse code. On the other hand, these same subjects have a **left ear advantage** (i.e., right hemisphere) for environmental sounds: nonspeech sounds, clicks, tones, buzzes, laughter, coughing, and so forth. In short, it seems that most humans process any auditory signal that is perceived as language or language-like in the left hemisphere; any other sort of auditory signal will be processed by the right hemisphere. Once again, this evidence suggests that the left hemisphere in most humans is specialized for language processing.

**Split Brains.** In the 1960's, another major breakthrough in the theory of left hemispherical dominance was made by Roger Sperry and his colleagues, most notably Michael Gazzaniga. Earlier work had shown that severe cases of epilepsy could be treated by surgically severing the corpus callosum, the white fiber tract connecting the two cerebral hemispheres. The epileptic seizures originating in one hemisphere would travel to the other via the corpus callosum and increase the magnitude of the seizure. By severing the corpus callosum, the abnormal electrical discharges were confined to one hemisphere and, in fact, seizures dramatically decreased in both hemispheres. The effect of this operation is illustrated in Figure 11–5. Thus, the normal brain can send information back and forth between hemispheres, but the split brain cannot.

The effects of severing the corpus callosum might seem devastating; remarkably, however, they are not. In fact, the overt behavior of a split-brain patient does not differ significantly from that of a normal subject. This is because under ordinary circumstances, both hemispheres receive sensory information simultaneously. For example, when you look at an object, each eye sends information to both hemispheres simultaneously.

What is relevant to our purposes, however, is that Sperry and his colleagues discovered a way of sending visual information selectively to only one hemisphere. Unlike a normal brain, a split brain cannot transmit this information to the other hemisphere because the corpus callosum has been severed. The effect, then, is to "trap" information in one hemisphere or the other. By covering one of the patient's eyes completely and blocking out the left or right visual field of the remaining eye,

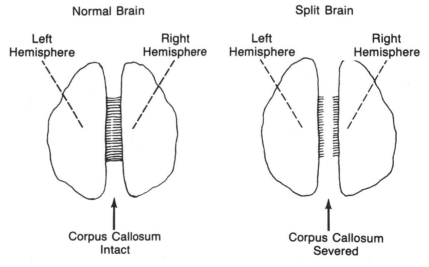

**FIGURE 11–5. Normal brain and split brain.**

Sperry could control which hemisphere received the information. This method depends on the fact that each eye has both a left and a right visual field; information from each visual field is transmitted to the contralateral hemisphere. Thus, if the left visual field were blocked, information (e.g., a written word) could be presented to the right visual field and thereby sent only to the left hemisphere. On the other hand, if the right visual field were blocked, information could be presented to the left visual field and thereby sent only to the right hemisphere. This procedure is diagrammed in Figure 11–6.

Now that we have some idea of how split-brain patients allow us to examine the processing capacity of each hemisphere independently of the other, let's take a look at some of the experiments that Sperry and his colleagues conducted. (In the following discussion, when we say that a stimulus was presented to either the left or right hemisphere, keep in mind that the stimulus was presented visually to one field of vision, as just described.) One experimental paradigm that Sperry used was to seat the patient at a desk, facing a screen. Hidden from view beneath the desk was a tray containing small objects. Sperry would flash a word onto the screen to one of the hemispheres. The patient would then be instructed to reach into the tray with the opposite hand (remember: contralateral control) and retrieve the appropriate object.

When Sperry presented a word such as key to the left hemisphere, the patient would retrieve a key from the hidden tray with his or her right hand; then, when asked to name the object, the patient would say *key*. However, when Sperry presented a word to the right hemisphere, the patient would be able to retrieve the object with the left hand, but *would not be able to name the object*. In fact, the patient had no conscious knowledge of what the left hand was doing. This suggests

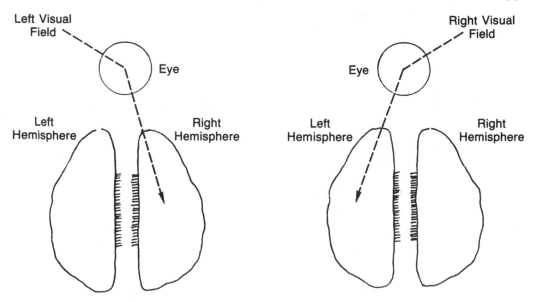

**FIGURE 11–6. Presentation of visual stimulus selectively to right and left hemispheres.**

that the dominant hemisphere (the left, in all of Sperry's subjects) can process language both actively and passively; that is, it can both comprehend and produce linguistic stimuli. On the other hand, the non-dominant (i.e., right) hemisphere can process language passively but not actively. It can "recognize" a word such as *key* but cannot "produce" the word. In other words, in order for a human to be conscious of a linguistic stimulus, the dominant hemisphere must have access to information regarding that stimulus.

In another experiment, Sperry presented verbs such as *nod, wink,* and *smile* to one hemisphere of split-brain patients. In each case, the subject was instructed to carry out the command presented on the screen. (Note that this would require a nonlinguistic response, just as the object-finding task in the first experiment did.) However, when the verb was presented to the right hemisphere, the patient not only failed to carry out the command, but also behaved as if he or she had seen nothing. Earlier we saw that the non-dominant hemisphere is able to process nouns at least passively (e.g., pick an object from a tray hidden from view). The results of this experiment, however, suggest that the non-dominant hemisphere cannot process verbs at all, either actively or passively.

In another experiment, Sperry presented incomplete sentences (e.g., *Mother loves* _____ ) to one hemisphere of his patients. In each case, the patient was instructed to complete the sentence by pointing with the left hand to one of four words (e.g., *nail, baby, broom, stone*), which were fed to the same hemisphere. However, when the stimuli were fed to the right hemisphere, the patients only randomly pointed to *baby.* Even though this experiment requires the patient to choose a noun, the patient must integrate the noun into a sentence in order to make an appropriate choice. This task requires processing syntactic information, namely that the correct noun can serve as the direct object of the structure *Mother loves* _____. The results of this experiment suggest that the non-dominant hemisphere cannot process syntactic information.

In sum, these and other experiments performed by Sperry and his colleagues provide rather dramatic evidence that the left hemisphere is specialized for language in most humans. In particular, this research provides at least tentative evidence that the dominant hemisphere alone can process language actively. On the other hand, the non-dominant hemisphere appears to have some capacity for processing noun-like stimuli passively.

## Left Brain vs. Right Brain

So far we have looked at evidence that most human beings are left dominant; that is, the left hemisphere houses the language centers in the brain and exercises primary control for the processing of language. In fact, each hemisphere is specialized for carrying out certain specific yet complementary types of tasks, which are summarized below.

**Left Hemisphere.** As we have seen, the left hemisphere is specialized for language. This includes not only speaking and listening, but also reading and wri ing. In addition, the left hemisphere is specialized for temporal order perception, the processing of any stimuli that arrive at different points in time. Suppose, for example, you were presented with a sequence of two tones, a buzz, and three more tones. If you were asked to determine where the buzz occurred in the series (i.e., third), your answer would require left-hemisphere processing. Similarly, the left hemisphere seems to be specialized for arithmetical calculations, such as determining that $1 + 2 + 3 = 6$. Related to this is logical reasoning; for example, determining that if A is greater than B and B is greater than C, then A is greater than C.

Note that all of these functions involve step-by-step processing. In order to process the sentence *Denny eats ketchup on fried chicken*, you need to know that *Denny* precedes *eats* and *eats* precedes *ketchup*. In order to determine when a buzz occurred amid a series of tones, you need to keep track of the tones. In order to determine that $1 + 2 + 3 = 6$, you need to know that $1 + 2 = 3$ and that $3 + 3 = 6$. In order to determine that A is greater than C, you need to know that A is greater than B and B is greater than C. All of these tasks require at least two sequential steps.

**Right Hemisphere.**    In contrast to the left hemisphere, the right hemisphere is specialized for nonlinguistic auditory stimuli. This includes environmental sounds such as horns, whistles, laughter, the squeal of tires, waves breaking on the beach, musical instruments, melodies, and so on. In short, any sound that is perceived as nonlinguistic is apparently processed by the right hemisphere. Likewise, the right hemisphere is specialized for visuospatial processing. This would include depth perception; orientation in space; the perception of pictures, paintings, photographs, and patterns; recognition of faces; and even the ability to dress oneself. Similarly, the right hemisphere seems to be specialized for tactile recognition tasks such as stereognosis (i.e., the ability to perceive the form and weight of an object by handling it or lifting it).

All of these right hemisphere functions involve holistic processing. That is, in order to process the sound of a horn or even a laugh, you do not need to divide it into meaningful parts. In order to recognize a familiar face, you presumably do not do it piece by piece but rather as an integrated unit. In order to tell that a box of feathers is lighter than a box of lead, you do not go through a series of mental calculations to determine their respective densities. Rather, all of these tasks require simultaneous integration of information.

By way of summary, we can make the following generalization: the left hemisphere is specialized for analysis, or breaking a whole into its parts, while the right hemisphere is specialized for synthesis, or combining the parts to form a whole. Because the study of hemispherical specialization is a relatively new field of inquiry, much of what is now being hypothesized is still subject to debate and further investigation. However, what we have covered here is summarized in the following table.

| *Left Hemisphere* | *Right Hemisphere* |
|---|---|
| Language | Nonlinguistic auditory processing |
| Temporal order perception | Visuospatial processing |
| Calculation | Stereognosis |
| Analysis | Synthesis |

Although the left hemisphere is dominant for language in most humans, the right hemisphere does subserve some language processing functions. One of these is the ability to produce and comprehend intonational patterns—for example, modulations of tone that express emotion. Right-hemisphere damage may also lead to difficulties in interpreting discourse. For example, consider the sentences *Linda bought a puppy for her daughter Susan. It barks when you wind it up.* A correct inference is 'Susan has a new toy'; an incorrect inference is 'Susan has a new pet.' Patients with right-hemisphere damage can recognize a correct inference; however, they are also more likely to accept an incorrect inference. Right-hemisphere damage can also lead to deficits in understanding humor, metaphor, and indirect speech acts. For example, a patient may give a literal interpretation to an expression like *He lost his shirt* to describe an unlucky gambler.

## Handedness

Before leaving this section on hemispherical specialization, we want to say something about the relationship between dominance and handedness. This topic is important because Broca introduced a misconception regarding this relationship, which unfortunately seems widespread even today. Broca inferred from one of his patients that left-handed people are right dominant, just as most right-handed people are left dominant.

As discussed earlier, Penfield and Roberts estimated that roughly 98 percent of the population is left dominant, while the remaining 2 percent is right dominant. However, about 95 percent of the population is right-handed and about 5 percent is left-handed. Since the match between these figures is not perfect, this raises the question of how handedness relates to dominance. In general, there is a high correlation between right-handedness and left dominance. However, most evidence indicates that left-handers are divided: about 40 percent (2 percent of the population) are left dominant, and 60 percent (3 percent of the population) are right dominant.

Two additional factors seem to affect the relationship between handedness and dominance. One is familial left-handedness: the more left-handed people in a family, the greater the likelihood of their right dominance. (Familial left-handedness also increases the likelihood of bilateral dominance in right-handers.) The second factor is strength of handedness (i.e., the number of tasks one does with the same hand). For example, someone who throws and bats with the left hand is more likely to be right dominant than someone who throws with the right hand but bats with the left.

The relation between these handedness factors and dominance can be illustrated graphically as follows.

*Left Dominance*        *Bilateral Dominance*            *Right Dominance*

Strong right-handedness
    Weak right-handedness
        Weak right-handedness and familial left-handedness
           Weak left-handedness
                Weak left-handedness and familial left-handedness
                Strong left-handedness
                    Strong left-handedness and familial left-handedness

In short, the farther to the right that a particular individual falls on this chart, the more likely that person is to have bilateral or right hemisphere dominance.

# Disorders

In this section, we will discuss four general types of brain disorders that can affect language: aphasia, agnosia, and apraxia. Let's begin by drawing some general distinctions among these four types of disorders. **Aphasia** is an acquired disorder of language due to cortical damage. It is important to note that aphasia is acquired; that is, only a person who has already developed a linguistic system can be stricken with aphasia. For example, a person with brain damage present at birth (or sustained immediately afterward) which prevents the acquisition of language would not properly be said to have aphasia. Moreover, aphasia is specifically a language disorder. Although brain damage may result in several different types of syndromes, only one that involves a language dysfunction is properly called an aphasia. Finally, aphasia is due to cortical damage, or to damage to the white fiber tracts immediately underlying language centers in the cortex. Thus, for example, a person sustaining damage to the brain stem which results in inarticulate speech would not properly be said to have aphasia.

    **Agnosia** is a loss of comprehension of sensation due to cortical damage. It is important to note that with this disorder, the sensory system is intact, yet the individual cannot comprehend or recognize what has been sensed. Thus, for example, a person with visual agnosia can see perfectly well but cannot recognize what is seen; a person with auditory agnosia can hear perfectly well but cannot recognize what is heard. In order to get a feel for this difference between sensing something but not recognizing it, imagine that you are listening to someone speak a language you do not understand, say, Greek. You can hear this person perfectly well, yet you cannot understand what you hear. This situation, of course, would not constitute an agnosia, since there has been no cortical damage or loss of your ability to understand Greek.

If, however, you had a stroke and could hear English but no longer understand it, this would be a form of agnosia.

As this example illustrates, aphasia and agnosia are not mutually exclusive. Thus, an acquired disorder of language due to cortical damage, which affects comprehension without disrupting the ability to sense, would be both an aphasia and an agnosia. In fact, such a syndrome describes an agnosia in general and a type of sensory aphasia in particular.

**Apraxia** is the loss of the ability to perform voluntary actions due to cortical damage, without the loss of motor power. It may be useful to think of apraxia as the mirror image of agnosia. Whereas agnosia affects comprehension, apraxia affects action. In both cases, however, the sensory-motor system for receiving stimuli and producing movement is intact. For example, a person who cannot smile on command, but later does so spontaneously, has a form of apraxia: the person is unable to perform a voluntary action, despite having the motor power to do so. As was the case with agnosia, aphasia and apraxia are not mutually exclusive. Thus, an acquired disorder of language due to cortical damage, which affects action without disrupting the motor power to act, would be both an aphasia and an apraxia. In fact, such a syndrome describes an apraxia in general and a type of expressive aphasia in particular.

Having distinguished among these various brain disorders, let's consider some specific types of aphasia, agnosia, and apraxia.

## Aphasia

Numerous types of aphasia have been proposed and discussed in the literature on the subject. Here, we look at three of the most common types (Broca's, Wernicke's, and conduction), as well as three other types found in the literature (anomia, semantic aphasia, and word deafness).

**Broca's Aphasia.** This type of disorder, also known as motor or expressive aphasia, typically involves a lesion in the third frontal convolution of the dominant hemisphere. Note that this lesion is close to the motor cortex controlling the speech musculature. Symptoms usually include the following. First, motor function is normal; that is, the articulators are fully functioning. However, there is typically some paralysis on the side opposite the dominant hemisphere. Second, the patient's speech output is non-fluent; that is, it is hesitant, halting, labored, and lacks normal intonation. Third, the output is "telegraphic" in that it generally lacks grammatical morphemes, such as articles, prepositions, plural and possessive markers, tense markers on verbs, and so on. Thus, the more highly inflected the patient's language (e.g., German), the more severe the disturbance appears. Fourth, reading and writing usually exhibit the same deficiencies as speech. On the other hand, the patient's comprehension is typically fairly good. And the patient is usually self-monitoring, that is, aware of his or her mistakes and difficulties in speaking.

Let's now look at some examples of actual speech produced by patients with Broca's aphasia. In an unpublished article entitled "Classification of Language Disorders from the Psycholinguistic Point of View," Myrna Schwartz cites examples of such patients trying to describe a picture of a girl giving flowers to her teacher. Here is a sample of responses.

(a)   *Girl is handing flowers to teacher.* Note the sporadic omission of grammatical morphemes. (Cf. *The girl is handing the flowers to her teacher.*)

(b)   *The young . . . the girl . . . the little girl is . . . the flower.* Note the hesitant style. At each pause the patient seems to be giving up and starting over.

(c)   *The girl is . . . is roses. The girl is rosing. The woman and the little girl was rosed.* Note here the use of *rose* as a verb.

**Wernicke's Aphasia.**   This type of disorder, also known as sensory or receptive aphasia, typically involves a lesion in the first temporal convolution of the dominant hemisphere. Note that this lesion is close to the primary auditory cortex (Heschl's gyrus). Symptoms usually include the following. First, hearing is normal. Second, the patient's speech output is typically fluent, rather than hesitant or halting, and has a normal intonation contour. Third, it generally consists of anywhere from 30 to 80 percent neologistic jargon. This term refers to "new words"—utterances that conform to the phonological structure of the patient's language, but are meaningless—for example, *bliven, glover,* and *devable.* Consequently, Wernicke's aphasia is sometimes called **neologistic jargon aphasia** (or simply jargon aphasia). In addition, the output is riddled with **phonemic paraphasia**, which includes repetition and reversal of phonemes. For example, *bowling shirt* might come out *bowling birt* or *showling birt.* (Phonemic paraphasia is sometimes called **literal paraphasia**, due to confusion in the older neurological literature between phonemes and letters of the alphabet. Patients were said to confuse "letters"; thus, "literal" paraphasia.) Fourth, the patient's comprehension is generally quite poor. Fifth, the patient is not self-monitoring; that is, the patient seems unaware that much of his or her output is error-ridden and incomprehensible.

On the other hand, the patient's syntax is relatively normal in the sense that, within a sentence, nouns appear where we would expect nouns, adjectives appear where we would expect adjectives, and so forth. For example, Brown cites a patient who responded to the question *What does 'swell-headed' mean?* with *She is selfice on purpiten* (1972: 65). Note that the syntactic structure of this sentence is perfectly normal: a subject (*she*) is followed by a verb (*is*) and a complement (*selfice on purpiten*). The problem is that in the complement, we get jargon where we would expect a lexical morpheme.

Let's consider some more actual examples of the speech output produced by patients with Wernicke's aphasia. In response to the question *What is your speech problem?*, Brown's patient answered *Because no one gotta scotta gowan thwa, thirst, gell, gerst, derund, gystrol, that's all.* Note the phonemic repetition: *gotta, scotta;*

*thwa, thirst; gell, gerst;* and *gystrol, that's all.* Schwartz, in the article cited earlier, gives examples of aphasic patients describing a picture of a boy taking a cookie out of a cookie jar; the boy's mother and sister are standing in the picture. One patient's response is as follows.

> You mean like this boy? I mean noy, and this, uh, meoy. This is a kaynit, kahken. I don't say it. I'm not getting anything from it. . . . These were ex-preshez, agrashenz and with the type of mechanic is standing like this . . . . And this is deli, this one is the one and this one and this one and . . . I don't know.

Note that the output is fluent; it is not labored and there are few hesitations. Like-wise, the syntax is relatively normal (*You mean like this boy?* ; *I'm not getting any-thing from it*; *I don't know*, etc.). On the other hand, the output is so jargon-ridden that it is unintelligible.

Before leaving this section, let us try to clear up one point of potential confusion. We have drawn a distinction between Broca's aphasia, which is primarily a deficit in linguistic expression, and Wernicke's aphasia, which is primarily a deficit in linguistic comprehension. It is clear, however, that a major symptom of Wernicke's aphasia is the production of neologistic jargon, which appears to be a problem in expression. This is not a contradiction. The expression problem in Wernicke's aphasia is thought to be primarily a *result* of the fundamental deficit in comprehension.

**Conduction Aphasia.** This type of disorder typically involves the **arcuate fasciculus**, the association fibers connecting Broca's area and Wernicke's area and the adjacent cortex. The primary symptom is the inability to repeat utterances. This makes sense anatomically, since linguistic input can be received (in Wernicke's area), but the information cannot be transmitted to the linguistic ex-pression center (in Broca's area). Likewise, reading aloud is difficult for someone with conduction aphasia. On the other hand, output is generally fluent, in con-trast to Broca's aphasia; but comprehension is typically normal or only mildly disturbed, in contrast to Wernicke's aphasia. Also, patients are generally self-monitoring. For example, Brown cites a patient who repeatedly interjected such comments as *Your baby could do better than I can* and *I can't do anything; what's wrong with me* (1972: 87).

Another of Brown's patients, when asked *Have you any headaches?*, responded *Had one three to four week . . . days, Monday, Tuesday, Wednesday, Thursday, and Thursday it started to go away* (1972: 87–88). Apparently, this patient was trying to access the word *Thursday* but could not do so directly. Thus, she started at the beginning of the week, went through the days of the week, and was able to continue when she got to *Thursday.* Note that this pathological behavior is an exaggeration of normal behavior. For example, if you were asked which letter of the alphabet precedes *L*, you might access *K* indirectly by reciting the alphabet up through Brown asked the same patient, *Can you give me the date (February 6)?* She replie

*It's the fu . . . 1–2–3–4–5, oh I don't know, there seems to me there must be something I could do but I don't know what it is* (1972: 88).

The major symptoms of Broca's, Wernicke's, and conduction aphasia are summarized in the following table.

|  | *Broca's* | *Wernicke's* | *Conduction* |
|---|---|---|---|
| *Lesion Site* | Third frontal convolution | First temporal convolution | Arcuate fasciculus |
| *Language Output* | Non-fluent | Fluent | Fluent |
| *Comprehension* | Unimpaired | Severely impaired | Unimpaired |
| *Self-monitoring* | Yes | No | Yes |
| *Paralysis* | Yes (contralateral) | No | Contralateral weakness |
| *Main characteristic* | Labored "tele-graphic" output | Neologistic jargon | Severely impaired repetition |

**Anomia.**  This disorder has been associated with a lesion of the angular gyrus in the dominant hemisphere, along with diffuse lesions in the temporal lobe. The primary symptom involves the inability to name objects and general problems in accessing specific words. Consequently, the speech output appears empty, vague, and ridden with clichés. Patients tend to use an abundance of indefinite nouns, such as *gismo, thingamabob, whatchamacallit,* and *thing.* Their speech contains numerous circumlocutions, for example *what you drink out of* for *cup.* On the other hand, the output is fluent (unlike that in Broca's aphasia), comprehension is normal (unlike that in Wernicke's aphasia), and repetition is normal (unlike that in conduction aphasia).

**Semantic Aphasia.**  This disorder has been associated with lesions in the temporal lobe of the dominant hemisphere. In fact, some specialists consider this disorder to be a mild form of Wernicke's aphasia. The primary symptom, **semantic paraphasia**, refers to the inappropriate use of words. For example, one of Brown's patients said *My son is just home from Ireland. He is a flying man* (1972: 32). Note the use of *flying man* for what appears to be *pilot.* Brown cites another example, this one written: *There are certain incidence which unfolded from my last living time in England Therefore I would rather not inform people of the last month of my Last England Life* (1972: 45). Once again, note *my last living time in England* and *my last England life* for something like *the last time I lived in England.*

**Word Deafness.**  This disorder has been associated with the border of Heschl's gyrus and Wernicke's area in the temporal lobe of the dominant hemisphere. Patients with this disorder have normal hearing but cannot understand speech. Obviously, they have a severe comprehension problem and their ability to repeat is profoundly disrupted. On the other hand, their self-generated speech output is fluent and correct. Patients' comments on their disorder are especially revealing.

Brown cites one patient who said *I can hear quite well but I don't understand; I can hear a fly flying past me* (1972: 127). Brown reports another patient as saying *Voice comes but no words. I can hear, sound comes, but words don't separate* (1972: 129).

## *Agnosia*

Several different types of agnosia (disorders involving comprehension) have been noted and discussed in the literature. Here, however, we will briefly discuss only three: apperceptive visual agnosia, prosopagnosia, and autotopagnosia. Although these disorders do not affect language, they are of interest because, first, they exhibit certain parallels with linguistic disorders and, second, they provide additional evidence for the localization of various cognitive functions.

**Apperceptive Visual Agnosia.**  This disorder typically involves bilateral lesions in the occipital lobe, which houses the visual centers in the cortex. The primary symptom of this disorder is the inability to recognize objects, even though vision itself is intact. (This disorder is similar to what is sometimes known as **cortical blindness**.) According to Brown, a patient with apperceptive visual agnosia can sometimes identify an object "upon touching it or perceiving it through another modality [e.g., smell]. . . . In recognition tasks, the patient will peer at or around an object. . . . or he will search for an object directly before him [as if nearsighted], at times identifying it when it falls in his peripheral field" (1972: 204–205). Once again, the point to note is that the patient has no vision problem, but simply cannot recognize objects. It would be as if you were presented with a typewriter and you could see it, yet were unable to recognize it. However, upon receiving stimuli through some other modality (e.g., touching the keys or listening to someone type), you then were able to identify it.

**Prosopagnosia.**  This disorder, which describes the inability to recognize faces, has been associated with lesions in the occipital lobe of the non-dominant hemisphere (usually the right). As with apperceptive visual agnosia, the patient's vision is perfectly normal, but in this case the symptoms are more specific—the primary disfunction lies in the inability to recognize faces. Of one patient, Brown states:

> he was unable to recognize members of his family, the hospital staff or his own face in the mirror. . . . Lincoln's face was excellently described from memory as "tall, angular with a small beard, large nose and tasseled [sic] hair," but he was uncertain about a standard portrait fitting this description quite perfectly. (1972: 226)

Note the correlation between the site of the lesion and the patient's symptoms: the right hemisphere controls visuospatial processing.

**Autotopagnosia.** This disorder, which describes the inability to recognize parts of the body, has been associated with lesions in the parietal lobes of both hemispheres. As with prosopagnosia, the disruption of comprehension is quite specific. Even though the peripheral sensory system is intact, the patient cannot identify body parts. Brown has this to say about autotopagnosia:

> one case, asked to show his elbow, said "My elbow, an elbow would be over there (pointing to the door)." A moment later, however, he was able to match the body part (elbow) to the correct name. . . . Patients may indicate through their response that they understand the command, as in De Renzi's case who, in connection with the word "wrist," said, "there is the wristwatch," or to "ankle" spoke of his children breaking their ankles, though still unable to point correctly. (1972: 246)

It is worth emphasizing that autotopagnosia is almost certainly not a special case of sensory aphasia. Note that the last-mentioned patient apparently had no trouble in comprehending the *words* for wrist and ankle (he was able to use them appropriately, as in *wristwatch*); instead, his problem was recognizing the *objects* themselves.

## *Apraxia*

Numerous types of apraxia (disorders of expression) have been discussed in the neurological literature. Here we will look briefly at three: facial, ideational, and dressing apraxia.

**Facial Apraxia.** This disorder, which describes the inability to perform voluntary actions with the face, lips, and tongue, is generally due to lesions near Broca's area. (Recall that Broca's area is very close to that part of the primary motor cortex which controls the facial musculature.) For example, a patient with facial apraxia may be unable to stick out his tongue on command, yet be able to do so spontaneously when licking his lips. Not surprisingly, some form of facial apraxia has been found in 90 percent of patients with Broca's aphasia and 33 percent of patients with conduction aphasia. However, this disorder has also been noted in left-brain-damaged patients without aphasia. Thus, it is a separate disorder from Broca's aphasia.

**Ideational Apraxia.** This disorder, which describes the inability to use objects appropriately, has been associated with lesions in the left hemisphere where the parietal and occipital lobes meet. Brown describes a patient with ideational apraxia as follows:

> when told to demonstrate how to brush his teeth, he did so promptly, but when given a toothbrush and asked to demonstrate its use, he first brushed his nails, then his pants, and only with much prompting did he finally use the toothbrush correctly. . . .
> [Another] patient is asked to call the operator on the telephone. He picks

up the receiver and holds it properly to his ear, then with his right hand presses down on the tone button, saying, "I don't know how to do it." Encouraged, he continues to push on the button, then runs his fingers over the dial, stumbles into the second hole, and dials #2 repeatedly. (1972: 166)

The important point to note here is that it is the use of objects that causes the greatest problems for the patient. The first patient can use his finger to show how he brushes his teeth; he just can't use a toothbrush. Similarly, the second patient recognizes the phone (he puts the receiver to his ear), but has difficulty in carrying out the voluntary action of dialing it.

**Dressing Apraxia.**    This disorder, which describes an inability to perform the voluntary actions involved in getting dressed, has been associated with lesions in the non-dominant hemisphere. Brown describes a patient, apparently the first case on record, "who did not know which was the inside or outside of his coat, put his clothes on upside down and his legs into the coat sleeves" (1972: 190). There is some sentiment that this disorder may actually be a type of agnosia, since some patients do not seem to comprehend the function of clothing. (A true apraxia would involve recognizing the clothes, yet being unable to perform the voluntary action of putting on.) In either case, note the correlation between damage to the non-dominant (usually right) hemisphere and the deficit in visuospatial processing.

Before leaving this section on disorders, let us reiterate a few points. First, although we have presented each disorder as a discrete, self-contained syndrome, it is important to understand that such isolated, well-defined cases are relatively rare. Rather, cortical damage, even when very localized, may cause symptoms of two or more disorders to appear. We noted, for example, that facial apraxia occurs with 90 percent of the cases of Broca's aphasia. Likewise, anomia may occur in conjunction with other aphasic syndromes. Moreover, keep in mind that the best we can do at present is to make correlational and statistical statements. That is, damage to a certain cortical area causes certain symptoms in some percent of the cases observed. Likewise, it is worth remembering that each syndrome (e.g., Broca's aphasia) is a cover term for a set of symptoms that typically coincide with damage to a certain cortical area (e.g., non-fluency, near-normal comprehension, right-sided paralysis, and so on).

Second, all the disorders we have discussed (with the exception of dysarthria) are higher level, in the sense that they involve damage to specific areas of the cerebral cortex or the white fiber tracts underlying them. That is, these disorders involve either the interpretation of sensations (on the comprehension side) or conscious voluntary action (on the expression side).

Third, even though they are not specific to language, various agnosias and apraxias are relevant to the neurology of language for two reasons. For one, language disorders involving comprehension and expression (Wernicke's and Broca's aphasia, respectively) parallel more general disorders involving comprehension and expression (agnosia and apraxia, respectively). For another, different types of agnosia and apraxia support the theories of both hemispherical specialization and localization of function, just as different types of aphasia do.

## *Summary*

Let's go over what we have covered in this chapter. We began with four observations about the neurology of language. However, we had no immediate explanation for these phenomena. Thus, we constructed a (partial) theory of neurolinguistics to account for our four original observations. This theory is based in part on the anatomy of the central nervous system—in particular, the left and the right hemispheres and the frontal, temporal, occipital, and parietal lobes. In addition, this theory makes use of such concepts as localization of function, hemispherical dominance, hemispherical specialization, and handedness. We have also seen that cortical damage can cause aphasia, an acquired disorder of language. Within this general category, different damage sites typically coincide with different syndromes, most notably Broca's aphasia, Wernicke's aphasia, and conduction aphasia. Finally, we have seen that damage to the cortex outside of the language centers can cause deficits in comprehension (agnosia) and expression (apraxia).

As usual, we want to emphasize that there is a great deal more to the study of neurolinguistics than what we have been able to cover in this one short chapter. However, you have now been exposed to some of the basic ideas in the field; if you want to learn more, the supplementary readings will introduce you to additional information about the neurology of language. Following the readings is a short set of practice problems with the answers, which you can use to check your understanding of the material in this chapter. After that is a set of 50 exercises for you to work on your own.

## *Supplementary Readings*

Brown, J. (1972). *Aphasia, apraxia, and agnosia.* Springfield, IL: Charles Thomas.

Davis, G. A. (1983). *A survey of adult aphasia.* Englewood Cliffs, NJ: Prentice-Hall.

Luria, A. R. (1973). *The working brain.* New York: Basic Books.

Penfield, W., and Roberts, L. (1959). *Speech and* *brain mechanisms.* Princeton, NJ: Princeton University Press.

Springer, S. P., and Deutsch, G. (1985). *Left brain, right brain.* Rev. ed. New York: W. H. Freeman and Company.

Young, R. (1970). *Mind, brain and adaptation in the nineteenth century.* Oxford: Clarendon Press.

You are now prepared to read the relevant sections of all these works. Luria provides a basic introduction to the brain sciences and it should be read first. Young is a rich source of information concerning advances in cerebral localization during the nineteenth century. Penfield and Roberts is a complete report of ten years of research on cerebral dominance and aphasia, using electrical stimulation of the cortex. Brown provides a detailed source of clinical information on aphasia, agnosia, and apraxia. Davis, a comprehensive introductory text for speech-language pathologists, covers basic research on aphasia and information about its diagnosis and treatment. Springer and Deutsch is an interesting and readable discussion of hemispherical asymmetry in normal and brain-damaged subjects, including chapters on split-brain research, handedness, and sex and age differences in brain asymmetry.

# Practice

1. True - False
   a. The cerebrum is essentially made up of the two hemispheres of the brain.
   b. Approximately 89 percent of all humans are left dominant.
   c. Ataxia is a type of aphasia characterized by the inability to name objects.
   d. Broca's aphasia is characterized by the absence of lexical morphemes.
   e. Dysarthria is the loss of motor power to speak distinctly; it typically involves damage to the lower brain stem.
   f. Right-handed people with a family history of left-handedness are more likely to be bilaterally dominant than other right-handed people.
   g. A patient with cortical blindness would be expected to have lesions in the parietal lobes.

2. When you go to sleep, you become unconscious, which suggests a decrease in cortical activity. However, you continue to breathe and your heart continues to beat. Does this mean that these functions are not controlled by the central nervous system? Explain.

3. Most patients cited in the neurolinguistics literature have incurred brain damage from strokes rather than from tumors or trauma. Why would stroke patients provide the most interesting evidence for the localization of linguistic function in the brain?

4. A normal subject is presented with two auditory stimuli simultaneously, *see* in the left ear and *saw* in the right ear. The subject reports hearing *saw* but not *see*. Is this person left dominant, right dominant, bilaterally dominant, or non-dominant?

5. Assume you are left-handed and have a history of left-handedness in your family. A team of neurologists performs the Wada test on your left and right hemispheres. In neither case do you have much trouble in speaking, reading, or naming. What is your cerebral dominance likely to be?

6. Assume that a normal subject has the input to the right visual field blocked. A written command (e.g., *smile*) is presented to the left visual field. The subject smiles when presented with the stimulus. Explain how the subject is able to do this.

7. Assume you are left-hemisphere dominant, you are not a musician, and you are listening to a musical composition by Bach. Which hemisphere is most likely to process this stimulus?

8. Dr. Drool claims that word deafness is a form of apraxia. Is he right or wrong? Explain.

9. An adult, right-handed stroke patient exhibits the following symptoms: normal (or near-normal) comprehension, fluent output, and the inability to repeat words and sentences.
   a. What type of aphasia is this most likely to be?
   b. Where is the lesion most likely to be?

**10.** What type of aphasia is illustrated by the following utterance, from a patient cited by Brown (1972: 64–65)?

Why my fytisset for, whattim tim saying got dok arne gimmen my suit, suit to Friday . . . . I ayre here what takes zwei the cuppen seffer effer sepped . . . .

# Answers

The following answers are, in some cases, not the only possible ones. Discussion of other possibilities is part of the practice.

**1.** a. T
   b. F (98 percent)
   c. F (anomia)
   d. F (grammatical morphemes)
   e. T
   f. T
   g. F (occipital)

**2.** No. Breathing and heart rate are controlled by the central nervous system, but they're controlled by the brain stem, not the cortex—the part of the brain that governs conscious mental activity.

**3.** The damage from a stroke is more likely to be localized.

**4.** Left dominant

**5.** Bilateral

**6.** The subject transfers the information from the right hemisphere through the corpus callosum to the left hemisphere, where the command can be interpreted.

**7.** The right (i.e., the non-dominant) hemisphere. (Now imagine the same situation, but this time assume that you *are* a musician. Speculate on which hemisphere might process the music, and why.)

**8.** Wrong. Word deafness is a deficit in comprehension; therefore, it would be more accurately classified as a type of agnosia.

**9.** a. Conduction aphasia
   b. Arcuate fasciculus of the left hemisphere

**10.** Wernicke's aphasia

# Exercises

**1.** Nonlinguistic dysfunctions such as dysmetria ("overshoot" and "undershoot") and ataxia (lack of muscular coordination) may result from damage to the _____, which lies posterior to the brain stem.

**2.** Heschl's gyrus is the part of the brain that _____.

    a. controls vision

    b. holds together the left and right hemispheres

    c. separates linguistic and nonlinguistic auditory stimuli

    d. controls the voluntary motor movements of the tongue and lips

**3.** True - False

    a. The cerebrum controls equilibrium.

    b. Neurons are composed of a cell body, an axon, and synapses.

    c. Wernicke was the first researcher to correlate expressive aphasia with a specific area of the brain.

**4.** True - False

    a. A right ear advantage for nonlinguistic sounds during a dichotic listening test would indicate left-hemisphere dominance for language.

    b. A left ear advantage for linguistic stimuli during a dichotic listening test would indicate right-hemisphere dominance for language.

    c. The left hemisphere of most split-brain patients can process nouns both actively and passively.

**5.** Stereognosis refers to _____.

    a. visual recognition of patterns

    b. temporal order processing

    c. recognition of form and weight through touch

    d. the ability to hear sounds through both ears

**6.** Consider a left dominant patient with a severe disturbance in spatial awareness, in musical ability, and in the recognition of other people, but with no paralysis or weakness. This patient's damage is most likely to be _____.

    a. in the anterior region of the left hemisphere

    b. in the posterior region of the left hemisphere

    c. in the anterior region of the right hemisphere

    d. in the posterior region of the right hemisphere

    e. in the anterior region of both hemispheres

**7.** Ability to report when a buzz occurs in a sequence of tone-buzz-tone-tone is typically a (right, left) hemisphere function.

**8.** Recognition of environmental noises such as horns, whistles, and screeching tires is typically a (right, left) hemisphere function.

**9.** Ability to orient oneself in space is typically a (right, left) hemisphere function.

**10.** Ability to determine that $1 + 2 + 3 = 6$ is typically a (right, left) hemisphere function.

**11.** True - False.

    a. Someone who is "strongly" left-handed is more likely to be left dominant than someone who is "weakly" left-handed.

    b. Someone who is "weakly" left-handed is more likely to be bilaterally dominant than someone who is "strongly" right-handed.

    c. The more left-handed people in a family, the greater the likelihood of right dominance in those left-handers.

**12.** According to Heny (1985: 179) "left-handed speakers are eight times more likely than right-handers to suffer from aphasia after damage to the right hemisphere only. For right-handers, the incidence of such aphasia is 3 percent, compared to 25 percent in their left-handed counterparts." Based on these observations, what generalizations might one make about cerebral dominance in left- and right-handers?

**13.** Heny (1985: 171) reports research on the linguistic ability of a 10-year-old child whose left hemisphere had been removed shortly after birth. The child had difficulty distinguishing (A) and (B) below and in recognizing the ambiguity of (C):

    A.  The boy kissed the girl.
    B.  The boy was kissed by the girl.
    C.  He gave her dog biscuits.

    a.  What area of the grammar do these tasks reveal a deficit in?
    b.  What is the specific relation between (A) and (B)?
    c.  What type of ambiguity does (C) exhibit?

**14.** Ornstein (1973: 92) states that scientists have concluded that in humans "the left hemisphere is organized in a focal manner and the right hemisphere is organized in a more diffuse manner." Which of the following facts can be used as evidence for this conclusion?

    a.  The human brain exhibits contralateral control.
    b.  Damage to the left hemisphere is more likely to cause an aphasic disturbance than damage to the right hemisphere.
    c.  Injuries in specific areas of the left hemisphere interfere with specific tasks, but no such specific disruptions are found following right-hemisphere lesions.
    d.  Split-brain patients are able to process more information at once than normal people can.

**15.** Ornstein (1973: 92) notes that "increased alpha [rhythm] production is a sign of decreased information processing." Assume you are left dominant and you are listening to a music composition by Bach. What happens to the alpha rhythm in your left hemisphere?

**16.** A stroke patient is asked to name the President of the United States. The patient responds, *I can't say his name. I know the man, but I just can't come out and say it.* This response is typical of _____.

    a.  Broca's aphasia             d.  anomia
    b.  Wernicke's aphasia         e.  semantic aphasia
    c.  conduction aphasia

**17.** Broca's aphasia is more likely than Wernicke's aphasia to be accompanied by paralysis. Why? (Hint: consider the areas surrounding the lesion site.)

**18.** Facial apraxia is often found in Broca's aphasics. Why? (Hint: what is the common denominator in the two disorders?)

**19.** Agnosias often involve a lesion in the _____ lobe of the non-dominant hemisphere. What is the connection between agnosia and this lobe?

**20.** An examiner shows a patient a clock and asks, *What do you call this?* The patient responds, *That's a timing machine.* This response is typical of _____.

    a. Broca's aphasia          d. anomia

    b. Wernicke's aphasia       e. semantic aphasia

    c. conduction aphasia

**21.** An examiner asks a patient to describe a picture of a boy taking a cookie. The patient responds, *Boy . . . cook . . . cookie . . . take . . . cookie.* This response is typical of _____.

    a. Broca's aphasia          d. anomia

    b. Wernicke's aphasia       e. semantic aphasia

    c. conduction aphasia

**22.** An examiner shows a patient a picture of a gun and asks, *What do you call this?* The patient responds, *That's a* [pínərəs pǽkrəs] . . . *a* [rǽkə]. *I'm sure it's* [nʌməri rébu]. This response is typical of _____.

    a. Broca's aphasia          d. anomia

    b. Wernicke's aphasia       e. semantic aphasia

    c. conduction aphasia

**23.** An examiner asks a patient to say the word *rifle*. The patient responds, [rífəl] . . . [rífdəl] . . . *Oh, I mean gun.* This response is typical of _____.

    a. Broca's aphasia          d. anomia

    b. Wernicke's aphasia       e. semantic aphasia

    c. conduction aphasia

**24.** Which of the following is not typically associated with Broca's aphasia?

    a. halting, telegraphic speech      d. absence of inflections

    b. damage to the left frontal lobe      e. generally good  comprehension

    c. neologistic jargon

**25.** Which of the following is not typically associated with Wernicke's aphasia?

    a. fluent speech           d. neologistic jargon

    b. relatively good comprehension      e. retention of inflections

    c. damage to the left temporal lobe

**26.** Consider the following patient's language (reported in Davis [1983: 14]):

I should have then convolve to the particular asculation . . . which would give me particulars to tendon.

This output is typical of _____ aphasia.

**27.** Which of the following illustrates phonemic paraphasia?

    a. *bowling birt* for *bowling shirt*

    b. *He is a flying man* for *He is a pilot*

    c. *Girl is handing flowers to teacher* for *The girl is handing the flowers to the teacher*

    d. *She is selfice on purpiten* for *She is swell-headed*

    e. use of indefinite nouns like *gismo, thingamabob,* and *whachamacallit*

**28.** Which of the following illustrates semantic paraphasia?

    a. *bowling birt* for *bowling shirt*

    b. *He is a flying man* for *He is a pilot*

    c. *Girl is handing flowers to teacher* for *The girl is handing the flowers to the teacher*
    d. *She is selfice on purpiten* for *She is swell-headed*
    e. use of indefinite nouns like *gismo, thingamabob,* and *whachamacallit*

**29.** Match each disorder (a–f) with its description.

    a. apperceptive visual agnosia      d. facial apraxia
    b. prosopagnosia      e. ideational apraxia
    c. autotopagnosia      f. dressing apraxia

    \_\_\_ inability to use objects appropriately
    \_\_\_ inability to recognize faces
    \_\_\_ inability to recognize objects
    \_\_\_ inability to perform voluntary actions with the face, lips, and tongue
    \_\_\_ inability to perform voluntary actions associated with getting dressed
    \_\_\_ inability to recognize parts of the body

**30.** Consider the following patient's language (reported in Davis [1983: 21]). The patient was asked to explain how to drive a car:

> When you get into the car, close your door. Put your feet on those two things on the floor. . . . You just put your thing which I know of which I cannot say right now but I can make a picture of it . . . you put it in . . . on your . . . inside the thing that turns the car on. You put your foot on the thing that makes the, uh, stuff come on. It's called the, uh . . .

This output is symptomatic of _____.

**31.** Gardner (1985: 185) reports the following exchange with an aphasic patient:

GARDNER:      What kind of work have you done, Mr. Johnson?
MR. JOHNSON:      We, the kids, all of us, and I, we were working for a long time in the . . . you know . . . it's the kind of space, I mean place rear to the spedwan . . .
GARDNER:      Excuse me, but I wanted to know what work you have been doing.
MR. JOHNSON:      If you had said that, we had said that, poomer, near the fortunate, forpunate, tamppoo, all around the fourth of martz. Oh, I get all confused.

What disorder does Mr. Johnson's speech appear to reflect?

**32.** Gardner (1985: 186) reports the following exchange with an aphasic patient:

GARDNER:      [Asks patient what kind of work he's been doing]
MR. COOPER:      Me . . . build—ing . . . chairs, no, no cab—in—nets. (This reply takes about 40 seconds.)
GARDNER:      Can you tell me how you would go about building a cabinet?
MR. COOPER:      One, saw . . . then, cutting wood . . . working . . . Jesus Christ, oh boy.

What disorder is Mr. Cooper's response typical of?

**33.** Head (1926, vol. 2: 141–42) describes a patient who was asked to read the following newspaper passage aloud:

SHIPBUILDING STOPPAGE. SUSPENSION OF LOCK-OUT NOTICES
Steps towards the settlement of two big labour disputes were taken yesterday. Lock-out notices to the forty-seven engineering units which have broken away, have been

suspended pending negotiations, which will open on Monday afternoon. The notices which would have expired today affected 600,000 men.

The patient read as follows:

Ship . . . buildin . . . stoppages . . . See . . . pep . . . I don't know the word . . . of lock-out notice . . . Steps . . . to-fore . . . to-ward . . . settle . . . of two big . . . Labour . . . de-speds . . . are taken yesterday . . . Lock-out notice to the . . . forty-seven . . . inde . . . inder . . . unions which will have broke away . . . have been . . . sus-pes-ed . . . I don't know that . . . which will . . . open on Monday afternoon . . . The notice which will have . . . expied . . . to-day . . . affect . . . six unded thousand men.

What disorder does this patient's response typify?

**34.** Head (1926, vol 2: 93) reports on a patient with a wound to the left parietal region around the left angular gyrus. The patient was asked to repeat the names of the months of the year as Head said each one aloud. This task produced the following results:

JANUARY:  Jan-jer-ley, Jan, Jan.
FEBRUARY:  Fenchurch, Jan-jey, Jan-jey.
MARCH:  Mart, Mar, Mar, Marts.
APRIL:  What was it? Aper, Aperl.
MAY:  Mage, Made, Mage.
JUNE:  Ju, June.
JULY:  June, June, June-eye.
AUGUST:  Orgeons, Or-just.
SEPTEMBER:  Eps-ten, Ex-pent, Ex-penst.
OCTOBER:  Ex, Ox, Ox, Ox-toe, Ox-tove.
NOVEMBER:  No-vendl, New-vender.
DECEMBER:  Ex. What was it? Ex-pend. Ex-cembr.

a.  What disorder does this patient's response typify?
b.  What type of behavior occurs in some of the responses (e.g., the naming of February and July)?

**35.** Head (1926, vol. 2: 8) describes a patient as follows: "He had recovered sufficient words to tell the time; but he was not only extremely slow in utterance, but confused 'past' and 'to' and stumbled over two of the numbers correcting himself each time." What disorder does this patient's behavior typify?

**36.** Head (1926, vol. 1: 98) reports the following concerning a patient:

The mechanical kinesis of the limb and the conception of the movements to be performed are intact, but the primary or initiating idea is at fault. . . . the patient cannot execute spontaneously some complex series of adjusted actions, although he is capable of making the necessary movements under other conditions. This is a general disturbance of function affecting the body as a whole and becomes evident if the task to be performed demands the orderly manipulation of a series of objects. Thus, when one of Liepmann's patients was given a cigar and a match-box, he opened it, inserted the tip of the cigar and shut the box as though to cut off the end. Then, taking out the cigar, he rubbed it on the box as if it were a match. All the movements required to execute the complex task were present, but they were not performed in the correct sequence; the general conception was imperfect. In the same way, if a patient is given a tooth-brush, he uses it to brush his hair or clothes and puts a match into his mouth instead of cigarette.

What disorder does this patient's behavior typify?

**37.** Head (1926, vol. 1: 232) reports a patient who called a pencil *blacking* or *black lead*. What disorder does this response typify?

**38.** Eisenson (1984: 21) reports the following interchange:

EXAMINER:  On what do you sleep?
PATIENT:    Alarm clock, wake up.
EXAMINER:  What's ink for?
PATIENT:    To do with a pen.

What disorder do these responses typify?

**39.** Eisenson (1984: 95) reports a patient who was asked to name the following objects: a key, a button, a spoon, and a fork. The patient called them *key, cutty, skoon,* and *sfork.* What phonological phenomenon is illustrated by these responses?

**40.** Head (1926, vol. 1: 52) cites a patient who referred to a kitten as a *little fur-child*. What disorder does this typify?

**41.** Head (1926, vol. 1: 97) describes the following behavior:

Given an object, such as a brush or a match-box, [the patient] fails to carry out the natural actions of brushing his hair or lighting a match. . . . He may be able to name a pair of scissors placed in his hand, although he cannot use them; or he explains that an envelope and a sheet of paper are "to send though the post," and yet fails to put them together and fasten the flap correctly. Shown a pencil he says it is "to make marks with"; but told to use it, he replies holding it aimlessly in his hand, "That's what I can't manage."

What disorder does this patient's behavior typify?

**42.** A stroke patient is asked to name several common objects. The patient gives the following responses:

PAD OF PAPER:  the stuff you write on
FORK:          it's the thing you use to eat with
SCREWDRIVER:   that's one of those gismos . . . you know . . . I have one in my garage

a. What type of language disorder does this patient appear to have?
b. What area of the brain is associated with this disorder?

**43.** A patient refers to her eyeglasses as her *lights*.

a. What disorder is this type of output characteristic of?
b. Explain.

**44.** A stroke patient utters the following: *I've* [tʌŋd] *it a little, but* [wítən dəvédən]. *I would say that* [mɪkdésəs nósɪs] *are* [spíktərz].

a. What disorder is this type of output characteristic of?
b. What area of the brain is associated with this disorder?
c. What is normal about the patient's output?

**45.** Oliver Sacks has written a book called *The Man Who Mistook His Wife for a Hat*.

a. Given only this information, what general type of disorder might the patient have?
b. Which lobe is likely to be the lesion site?

**46.** Heny (1985) notes that polyglots (i.e., speakers of more than one language) are five times more likely to exhibit aphasic symptoms from right-hemisphere damage than are monolinguals. What does this observation suggest about cerebral dominance in monolingual and polyglot speakers?

**47.** Research by Caramazza et al. (1976) compared the ability of normal subjects and subjects with right-hemisphere damage to solve problems of the following types:

TYPE 1: John is taller than Bill; who is taller?
TYPE 2: John is taller than Bill; who is shorter?

Normal and right-hemisphere-damaged subjects performed equally well on Type 1 problems. However, the right-hemisphere-damaged patients performed much more poorly on the Type 2 problems. Based on these results, what semantic relation appears to require an unimpaired right hemisphere?

**48.** Winner & Gardner (1977) conducted research on aphasic patients and on patients with right-hemisphere damage. The patients were shown different pictures for the same expression and asked to choose the most appropriate picture. For example, for the expression *He has a heavy heart*, the pictures included one of a crying person and another of a man carrying a huge heart-shaped object. Aphasic patients (i.e., those with left-hemisphere damage) were more likely to choose the first picture and to laugh at the second picture, rejecting it as inappropriate. In contrast, patients with right-hemisphere damage were equally likely to choose either picture and found nothing humorous about the second one. Given these responses, what capacity appears to be lost by patients with right-hemisphere damage?

**49.** Consider the following news account of an accident victim. What type of aphasia does the accident victim appear to have? List five symptoms mentioned in the passage that would support your answer.

BOSTON (AP)—A man whose brain was impaled by a 7-foot crowbar is home from the hospital, asking about neighborhood events and rousting slugabed teen-aged sons, his wife said Tuesday. . . .

Thompson's head was pierced by the metal crowbar when the station wagon he was driving struck a tree and the crowbar hurled forward from the back seat.

When rescuers reached Thompson after the May 1 accident, the crowbar was extended three feet from his forehead and three feet from the back of his head.

The ends of the 40-pound tool had to be sawed off before he could be removed from the car, but the rest of the crowbar remained in his head until he got to the hospital. The injury was on the left side of the brain, which controls speech.

Doctors say Thompson's vision and hearing were not impaired in the accident and he can understand everything that is said to him. . . . "His speech is still halted and requires a good deal of effort, but we are very encouraged that he keeps doing better."

Thompson is able to work, though his right leg is weak. His right arm is paralyzed, but he is gradually learning to move it.

**50.** Consider the following passage from "The Last Words of Joseph Chaikin" (*Hippocrates*, Jan./Feb. 1989).

When Chaikin woke up after the surgery, words like "piddle-poodle" popped out of his mouth. "His speech was all blather," says van Itallie, who was one of the first people to see him. Chaikin couldn't understand what was being said to him, and didn't know that others didn't understand him. If he could have spoken, he would have told his doctors that he felt . . . "very pain my right."

The operation had left his heart stronger than ever. But it had also sent a blood clot shooting into . . . his brain . . . . He couldn't read music, do mathematical functions, use sign language or speak.

Use evidence from the passage itself to answer the following questions.

a.  What is the evidence that Chaikin was non-self-monitoring?
b.  What is the evidence that Chaikin had a sensory type of aphasia?
c.  What hemisphere was the blood clot in?
d.  What is the evidence for your answer to (c)?
e.  What type of aphasia did Chaikin most likely have?

# Chapter *12*

# *Conclusion*

In Chapter 1, we discussed some examples of linguistic phenomena that specialists in allied fields might encounter and also outlined the general methodology that underlies theory construction in linguistics. In subsequent chapters, we continued this dual emphasis on data and theory. Each chapter began with some observations (data) that an adequate theory of linguistics should be able to explain and proceeded to construct a partial theory to account for these observations. In short, this book has continually emphasized the interdependence of data and theory that is at the heart of linguistics (as well as any other empirical field of inquiry). In this chapter we would like to elaborate a little on two contributions that linguistic theory can make to related disciplines. The more obvious one is that linguistic theory provides a way of explaining a vast array of phenomena that professionals in allied fields encounter on a daily basis. Somewhat less obvious is the fact that linguistic theory provides a model for explanation which professionals in neighboring fields may be able to transfer to their own disciplines. In short, linguistic theory can benefit allied fields on two levels: a practical level, by providing explanations for particular observations, and a theoretical level, by providing a model for analyzing data. We will take these up one at a time.

First, let's consider the practical contribution: explanation of data. By way of illustration, let us return briefly to the phenomena mentioned at the beginning of Chapter 1 and consider how the discussion in Chapters 2 through 11 might enable us to explain these phenomena. We started with the hypothetical case of a researcher in business communication who is trying to characterize how different management styles are reflected in the way that managers give directions to their employees. The researcher notes that one group of managers tends to give instructions like *Type this memo*, while another group gives instructions like *Could you type this memo?* Principles from pragmatics, in particular the distinction between direct and indirect speech acts, can be used to characterize these two different styles of giving directions. In this case, the researcher might note that the first group of managers tends toward direct speech acts, those in which the syntactic form (an imperative) matches the illocutionary force (a directive). In contrast, the second group tend toward indirect speech acts, those in which the syntactic form (a *yes-no* interrogative) does not match the illocutionary force (a directive).

We also looked at phenomena that might be encountered in the fields of education and composition. We saw that a kindergarten teacher might observe that students tend to give more correct responses to questions like *Which of these girls is taller?* than to questions like *Which of these girls is shorter?* The teacher might draw upon semantic theory and principles of language acquisition in order to explain this phenomenon, noting that children tend to acquire the positive member of a pair of antonyms (*tall*) earlier than the negative member (*short*). Note that *tall* carries fewer presuppositions than *short*. The question *How tall was the girl?* presupposes nothing about the girl's height—she might be 7 feet tall or only 4 feet tall. On the other hand, the question *How short was the girl?* presupposes that the girl is relatively short.

Principles from linguistic theory would also enable a composition instructor to understand the source of a syntactic structure like *I wanted to know what could I do* when encountered in a student's writing. The difference between this form and the standard form *I wanted to know what I could do* has a straightforward syntactic explanation. In standard English, *wh*-interrogatives in subordinate clauses do not undergo the rule of I-Movement (i.e., move the tensed auxiliary to the left of the subject). Some speakers, however, do apply this rule in indirect *wh*-interrogatives, leading to forms such as *I wanted to know what could I do.* (Note that the tensed auxiliary verb, *could*, has been moved to the left of the subject NP, *I*.) Furthermore, the instructor would note that such forms, because they are somewhat socially marked, may reflect negatively on the writer.

The last two phenomena mentioned in Chapter 1 were drawn from ESL and speech-language pathology. We pointed out that an ESL teacher might encounter a student who writes *I will taking physics next semester.* In trying to offer the student an explicit principle for constructing sentences of this type, the teacher can draw upon morphological and syntactic principles governing the relation between auxiliary verbs and the affix on the following verb form. The relevant rules here are (a) within a single clause the verb form following a modal (e.g., *will*) is always uninflected (e.g., *take*) and (b) the verb form preceding a present participle (e.g., *taking*) is always a form of *be*. The first principle alone would yield *I will take*; the second alone would yield *I am taking*; and the two together would yield *I will be taking*. Thus, any combination of principles that the student tries will result in an acceptable form.

Turning to speech-language pathology, we saw that a specialist in this field might encounter a child who says *tay* for *stay* but never *say* for *stay*. In order to evaluate and explain this form, the speech-language pathologist can draw upon principles from phonology and language acquisition. Here, for example, the omission of the /s/ in the /st/ cluster reflects the principle that single consonants are generally acquired before clusters. In fact, CV syllables are apparently universal, whereas CCV syllables are not. Moreover, the omission of the /s/ rather than the /t/ is explained by the tendency for stops (/t/) to be acquired before fricatives (/s/).

In short, language-related phenomena similar to those just described are encountered every day by researchers and teachers in the fields that neighbor linguistics. Linguistic theory, in turn, provides a system of categories and rules which can be used to analyze and explain such phenomena.

Now let's turn to the theoretical contribution that linguistic theory can make to specialists in allied fields: it may provide them with a model for analyzing the nonlinguistic (or quasilinguistic) phenomena within their fields. This, however, is not just speculation about a future state of affairs. During the last 30 years, a number of fields in the humanities and social sciences have looked to linguistic theory as a model for analyzing phenomena within their respective domains. Among these fields are those as diverse as folklore and anthropology, literary criticism, and rhetoric and composition.

Representative examples of this interest in linguistics among those outside the field are not hard to find. For instance, Robert Georges, a folklorist, states that "the theory and work of generative-transformational grammarians has direct implications for the study of traditional narrative [i.e., folktales]" (1970: 14). Similarly, Roger Fowler, a literary critic, states that "description *per se* is not the only way in which linguistics has been . . . employed in literary studies. . . . linguistic concepts have often been used . . . metaphorically to provide *models* of textual structure rather than *accounts* of the specific structures of sentences and texts" (1981: 19). Likewise, Ross Winterowd, a rhetorician, states that since the publication of Chomsky's *Syntactic Structures* in 1957, "composition teachers have been dazzled by the elegance of the notational system of the new grammar . . . , have been intrigued by the complexity and ingenuity of grammatical arguments; and . . . have allowed themselves to hope that from the new field would emerge *the* panacea for the ills of teaching composition" (1976: 197). The attraction that linguistic theory has had for specialists in other disciplines is summed up by the folklorist Lauri Honko, who states that "the only success-story in the humanities in the recent past [is] modern linguistic theor[y]" (1979–1980: 6). Even though some of these high expectations have met with disappointment (see Newmeyer, 1983, Chapter 5, for discussion), there has nonetheless been a sustained interest in linguistic theory from practitioners in neighboring fields. Let's now take a look at some of the properties which the theory presented in this book has (or at least should have) and which may be applicable to other fields in the humanities and social sciences.

First, the theory should be **testable**; and therefore, it must necessarily be **explicit**. This criterion is necessary in order to make empirical (testable) claims about the structure of the phenomenon of interest; vague, inexplicit claims are impossible to test. Consider, for example, the following hypothetical statements.

(1)   We are living in the most corrupt era this country has ever seen.
(2)   More elected officials were indicted for felonies during the 1980's than during the entire first half of the twentieth century.

The claim in statement (1) is simply too inexplicit to test. What indices is the writer using to define "corruption"? What length of time constitutes an "era"? The claim can be supported or denied only if these terms are made explicit. The claim in statement (2), on the other hand, is explicit enough to be tested. The subjects are well defined (elected officials), the criterion is well defined (felonies), and the time frames are well defined (1980 through 1989 and 1900 through 1949).

Consider how this principle applies to linguistic theory. You may recall from Chapter 1 that we tried to develop a theory of the distribution of antecedents for personal and reflexive pronouns: a personal pronoun cannot have an antecedent within its clause, and a reflexive pronoun must have an antecedent within its clause. Note that the statement of these two rules depends crucially on the concept of **clause**. Without a precise definition of this term, it is not possible to test our rules to see if they work (indeed, it would be impossible to hypothesize such rules in the first place). Even though we didn't define clause in Chapter 1, we could start with the following working definition: a clause is a syntactic structure consisting of one and only one main verb and its optional NP arguments (subject, object, indirect object, and so forth). Regardless of whether this definition is completely accurate, the point is that a precise definition of clause is absolutely essential for us to be able to test our theory.

The main point of this discussion is that demands of testability force linguists into stating their theories in precise, explicit terms. This, in turn, accounts for the widespread use of formal notation in linguistic theory. Even though nothing can be put into formal notation that cannot be put into words, the notation encourages the analyst to be precise and explicit.

Second, the theory should be **revealing**: that is, it should capture significant generalizations. This criterion is necessary because revelation is the primary reason for constructing a model in the first place; any analysis that is opaque or unrevealing is by definition useless. Failure to meet this criterion is similar to the freshman classification theme that sorts the seasons of the year into four and proceeds to point out that one follows the other in the order spring, summer, fall, and winter. Even though it is impossible to give a precise definition of what constitutes a revealing analysis, it is worth noting that we have relied on this concept, at least implicitly, throughout this book in choosing one analysis over another.

For example, in Chapter 4 we discussed the syntax of the following sentences.

(3)   Tiny Abner concealed the document.
(4)   Did Tiny Abner conceal the document?
(5)   What did Tiny Abner conceal?

Based on such sentences (among others), we constructed two theories concerning whether or not *conceal* takes an object. In our first theory, we proposed that if *conceal* appears in a declarative sentence (3) or a *yes-no* interrogative (4), it must have a direct object; however, if *conceal* appears in a *wh*-interrogative (5), it cannot have a direct object. This theory accounts for the data in (3–5), as well as all of the related data we discussed in Chapter 4. This theory, however, is not revealing. That is, it does not provide us with a clue as to why *conceal* sometimes is required to have an object and other times is prohibited from having one. Moreover, under this theory, it is completely unclear why one type of interrogative (*yes-no*) is required to have an object, while another type of interrogative (*wh*) may not have one.

On the other hand, our second theory proposed that in sentence (5), *what* originated in direct object position and was moved into clause-initial position by a transformation. This theory, in contrast to our first, is revealing. That is, it does explain why *conceal* appears to have an object in some cases but not in others. In particular, this theory provides the following explanation: *conceal* has a direct object in all cases. If the object is not a *wh*-item (e.g., *the document*), it remains in object position. If, however, the object is a *wh*-item (e.g., *what*), it moves to clause-initial position. Even though this theory does not explain why a language would have a rule of *wh*-Movement in the first place, it is nonetheless revealing in that it provides a straightforward and intuitively satisfying account of some rather perplexing data.

Third, the theory should be restricted to a characterization of **systematic** phenomena. This criterion is necessary because a theory is a model of a system that can't be observed directly, and only predictable, rule-governed phenomena can be modelled. Failure to meet this criterion results in a description in which the analyst "can't see the forest for the trees." In other words, the systematic properties of the phenomenon at hand are camouflaged by attention to unassociated detail. It would be like a theory of the game of baseball which, in addition to modelling systematic properties of the game such as the number of players, the number of innings, and the number of outs per inning, tried to account for idiosyncratic properties of the game such as depth of the outfield, the playing surface (grass versus astroturf), or the color of the players' uniforms or eyes.

It is just as difficult to give a precise definition of systematic phenomena as it was to define a revealing analysis earlier. One reason is that what may be systematic within one field may not be systematic within another. For example, the color of baseball players' eyes may be perfectly systematic within a theory of genetics, but it isn't systematic within a theory of baseball. Another difficulty is that the notion of systematic phenomena is somewhat dependent upon the point of view of the researcher. No researcher is going to study a phenomenon that he or she believes is not governed by principles which can be inferred through examination. The problem, of course, is that analysts sometimes disagree over what seems to be rule governed and principled versus what seems to be random and idiosyncratic.

Aside from such problems in defining the term, it is worth pointing out that we have relied on the concept of systematic phenomena throughout this book. For example, in our discussion of phonology in Chapter 6, we hypothesized that English has two systematic vowel lengths: relatively long and relatively short. This we characterized by means of the feature [±long]; and, through examining some relevant data, we postulated that a vowel is [+long] before a voiced consonant and [−long] before a voiceless consonant. At the same time, it is a well-documented fact that two speakers of English will pronounce the same vowel in the same phonological environment with different absolute lengths. Moreover, even the same speaker pronouncing the same word over and over will vary the vowel length. How then can we say that English has two degrees of vowel length? The answer is simple. We can do this by stipulating that the two degrees of vowel length are *systematic*. By using this term, we are essentially claiming that within the system of any speaker, there will be two types of vowels: relatively long and relatively short. Moreover, the relative length of the vowel is determined by the voicing characteristics of the following segment. The reason we don't try to model vowel lengths for individual speakers is that we assume that variation from speaker to speaker is idiosyncratic and for the most part unprincipled, at least within a theory of language. In short, by trying to account for all facets of some range of phenomena, the analyst risks confusing the systematic with the unsystematic and the relevant with the irrelevant.

At this point, it is appropriate to discuss how linguistic theory attempts to distill the abstract system from the raw data. The theory articulated by Chomsky is what is termed a **competence** model. That is, it is a theory of the psychological system of unconscious knowledge that underlies our ability to produce and interpret utterances in a language. (You will recall that this is how we defined language in the first chapter.) In contrast to a competence model is a **performance** model; that is, a theory of the actual physical and psychological processes that a speaker might go through in producing and interpreting an utterance. Over 25 years ago, Chomsky made this distinction in a landmark book entitled *Aspects of the Theory of Syntax*:

> We thus make a fundamental distinction between *competence* (the speaker-hearer's knowledge of his language) and *performance* (the actual use of language in concrete situations). . . . linguistic theory is mentalistic, since it is concerned with discovering a mental reality [i.e., competence] underlying actual behavior [i.e., performance]. (1965: 4)

This is not to say that linguists have no interest in performance; certainly, performance data provides a way of studying competence. Instead, the point is that the central goal of linguistic theory, at least according to Chomsky, is to model the psychological system of unconscious knowledge that underlies behavior (competence) rather than the behavior itself (performance).

A good example of this distinction is provided by comparing two different interpretations of our rule of *wh*-Movement (move a *wh*-item to sentence-initial position). One interpretation of this rule would be to take it as a statement about performance. That is, when speakers of English produce an utterance such as *What did Tiny Abner conceal?*, they actually go through the following steps. First, they formulate a mental structure in which *what* is the direct object of *conceal* (did-Tiny Abner-conceal-what). Then they move *what* to sentence-initial position, thus creating another mental structure (what-did-Tiny Abner-conceal). Finally, they utter the sentence.

This, however, is not the way that *wh*-Movement is understood within linguistic theory. Instead, this rule is interpreted as part of competence. In postulating such a rule, the linguist is actually making a statement of the following sort: in order to make the judgments that speakers of English do in fact make about *wh*-interrogatives, they need to know that certain verbs (e.g., *conceal*) require a direct object. Moreover, they need to know that if the direct object is a non-*wh*-item (e.g., *document*), it is uttered in direct object position; however, if it is a *wh*-item (e.g., *what*), it is uttered in clause-initial position. The linguist will try to explain this state of affairs by using the metaphor of movement; that is, the *wh*-item is "moved" from direct object position to clause-initial position. In a competence model, the linguist is not claiming that speakers of English actually move *wh*-items from one position to another when they utter *wh*-interrogatives. Instead, "movement" is a convenient metaphor for describing the psychological system of unconscious knowledge which speakers possess, at least with respect to the distribution of *wh*-items and non-*wh*-items in English.

At this point it is appropriate to bring up a final concept closely associated with the study of competence, namely **generative grammar**. Simply put, a generative grammar is a theory of competence: a model of the psychological system of unconscious knowledge that underlies a speaker's ability to produce and interpret utterances in a language. Chomsky defines a generative grammar as follows:

> a generative grammar is not a model for a speaker or a hearer. It attempts to characterize in the most neutral possible terms the knowledge of the language [i.e., competence] that provides the basis for actual use of language by a speaker-hearer. . . . When we say that a sentence has a certain derivation with respect to a particular generative grammar, we say nothing about how the speaker or hearer might proceed . . . to construct such a derivation. These questions belong to . . . the theory of performance. No doubt, a reasonable model of language use will incorporate, as a basic component, the generative grammar that expresses the speaker-hearer's knowledge of the language; but this generative grammar does not, in itself, prescribe the character or functioning of a perceptual model or a model of speech production. (1965: 9)

A good way of trying to understand Chomsky's point is to think of a generative grammar as essentially a *definition* of competence: a set of criteria that linguistic structures must meet to be judged acceptable.

An analogy might make the point clearer. In *Transformational Grammar*, Andrew Radford compares a generative grammar to a municipal housing code, where the housing code is essentially a definition of house: that is, a set of criteria that housing structures must meet to be judged acceptable. Radford states:

> To interpret generative rules as well-formedness . . . conditions [i.e., as a definition of competence] . . . is to disclaim any implications about the processes and mechanisms by which sentence-structures might be formed. . . . Municipal regulations specify certain conditions that houses must meet: viz. they must be built out of certain materials, not others; they must contain so many windows of such-and-such a size, and so many doors; they must have a roof which conforms to certain standards . . . and so on and so forth. Such regulations are in effect well-formedness conditions on houses. What they do not do is tell you HOW to go about building a house; for that you need a completely different set of instructions, such as might be found e.g. in *Teach Yourself Housebuilding*. (1981: 90–91)

The analogy between a generative grammar and a municipal housing code is summarized in Figure 12–1. In short, to produce an acceptable sentence, a speaker needs

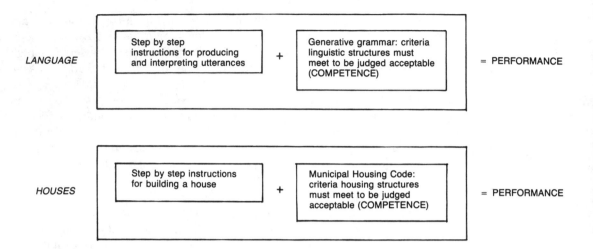

**FIGURE 12–1.  Relationship between competence and performance.**

*both* the step-by-step instructions specifying how to proceed *and* a generative grammar identifying the criteria linguistic structures must meet. Likewise, to construct an acceptable house, a building needs *both* the step-by-step instructions specifying how to proceed *and* a municipal housing code identifying the criteria that housing structures must meet.

Let's review what we have covered in this chapter. We discussed two levels on which linguistic theory might benefit specialists in related fields. First, it is of practical use in that it provides explanations for phenomena that crop up every day in language-related disciplines. Second, it is of theoretical use in that it provides a model which professionals in allied fields may find helpful in analyzing nonlinguistic or quasilinguistic phenomena. In particular, linguistic theory attempts to be testable, revealing, and restricted to systematic phenomena. Specifically, it attempts to model linguistic competence (the psychological system of unconscious knowledge that underlies our ability to produce and interpret utterances in a language) by constructing a generative grammar (a set of criteria that linguistic structures must meet to be judged acceptable).

# References

Adams, V. (1973). *An introduction to modern English word formation*. London: Longman.

Adjémian, C. (1983). The transferability of lexical properties. In Gass and Selinker, pp. 250–268.

Aitchison, J. (1985). Predestinate grooves: Is there a preordained language "program"? In Clark et al., pp. 90–110.

Akmajian, A., and Heny, F. W. (1975). *An introduction to the principles of transformational syntax*. Cambridge, MA: MIT Press.

Allen, H. B. (1973). *The linguistic atlas of the Upper Midwest*, 3 vols. Minneapolis: University of Minnesota Press. Copyright 1982, Gale Research Inc., Detroit.

Allwood, J., Andersson, L.-G., and Dahl, Ö. (1977). *Logic in linguistics*. Cambridge, England: Cambridge University Press.

Anderson, R. (1983). Transfer to somewhere. In Gass and Selinker, pp. 177–201.

Anderson, S. R. (1985). *Phonology in the twentieth century*. Chicago: University of Chicago Press.

Aronoff, M. (1976). *Word formation in generative grammar*. Cambridge, MA: MIT Press.

Atwood, E. B. (1953). *A survey of verb forms in the eastern United States*. Ann Arbor: University of Michigan Press.

Austin, J. L. (1962). *How to do things with words*. Oxford: Clarendon Press.

Bach, K., and Harnish, R. M. (1979). *Linguistic communication and speech acts*. Cambridge, MA: MIT Press.

Bates, E. (1976). *Language and context: The acquisition of pragmatics*. New York: Academic Press.

Bauer, L. (1983) *English word-formation*. Cambridge, England: Cambridge University Press.

Beebe, L. (Ed.) (1988). *Issues in second language acquisition*. New York: Newbury House.

Broselow, E. (1987). Non-obvious transfer: On predicting epenthesis errors. In Ioup and Weinberger, pp. 292–304.

Brown, J. (1972). *Aphasia, apraxia, and agnosia*. Springfield, IL: Charles Thomas.

Brown, R. (1973). *A first language: The early stages*. Cambridge, MA: Harvard University Press.

Campbell, K. S. (1990). Explanations in negative messages: More insights from speech act theory. *Journal of Business Communication, 20,* 357–375.

Campbell, K. S., Riley, K., and Parker, F. (1990). *You*-perspective: Insights from speech act theory. *Journal of Technical Writing and Communication, 20,* 189–199.

Caramazza, A., Gordon, J., Zurif, E. B., and DeLuca, D. (1976). Right-hemispheric damage and verbal problem solving behavior. *Brain and Language, 3,* 41–46.

Carver, C. M. (1987). *American regional dialects: A word geography*. Ann Arbor: University of Michigan.

Cassidy, F. (1981). DARE. *National Forum* (Summer), 36–37.

Cassidy, F. (1985, 1992). *Dictionary of American regional English*, 2 vols. Cambridge, MA: Harvard University Press.

Chierchia, G., and McConnell-Ginet, S. (1991). *Meaning and grammar: An introduction to semantics*. Cambridge, MA: MIT Press.

Chomsky, C. (1969). *The acquisition of syntax in children from 5 to 10*. Cambridge, MA: MIT Press.

Chomsky, N. (1959). A review of B. F. Skinner's *Verbal behavior. Language, 35,* 26–58.

Chomsky, N. (1965). *Aspects of the theory of syntax*. Cambridge, MA: MIT Press.

Chomsky, N. (1980). *Rules and representations*. New York: Columbia University Press.

Chomsky, N. (1983). Interview. *Omni* (November), 113–118, 171–174.

Chomsky, N., and Halle, M. (1968). *The sound pattern of English*. New York: Harper and Row.

Clark, E. V. (1975). Knowledge, context, and strategy in the acquisition of meaning. In Dato, pp. 77–98.

Clark, H. H., and Clark, E. V. (1977). *Psychology and language: An introduction to psycholinguistics*. New York: Harcourt Brace Jovanovich.

Clark, V. P., Escholz, P. A., and Rosa, F. (Eds.) (1985). *Language: Introductory readings* (4th ed.). New York: St. Martins Press.

Cole, P., and Morgan, J. L. (Eds.) (1975). *Syntax*

*and semantics 3: Speech acts.* New York: Academic Press.

Coulthard, M. (1977). *Discourse analysis.* London: Longman.

Cowper, E. (1992). *A concise introduction to syntactic theory: The government-binding approach.* Chicago: University of Chicago Press.

Cruse, D. A. (1986). *Lexical semantics.* Cambridge, England: Cambridge University Press.

Curtiss, S. (1977). *Genie: A psycholinguistic study of a modern-day "wild child."* New York: Academic Press.

Dato, D. P. (Ed.) (1975). *Georgetown University round table on languages and linguistics 1975.* Washington, DC: Georgetown University Press.

Davis, G. A. (1983). *A survey of adult aphasia.* Englewood Cliffs, NJ: Prentice-Hall.

Dillard, J. (1972). *Black English: Its history and usage in the United States.* New York: Random House.

Dulay, H., and Burt, M. (1983). Goofing: An indicator of children's second language learning and strategies. In Gass and Selinker, pp. 54–68.

Eckman, F. (1987). Markedness and the contrastive analysis hypothesis. In Ioup and Weinberger, pp. 55–69.

Einstein, A., and Infeld, L. (1938). *The evolution of physics.* New York: Simon and Schuster.

Eisenson, J. (1984). *Adult aphasia* (2nd ed.). Englewood Cliffs, NJ: Prentice-Hall.

Fasold, R. (1981). The relation between black and white speech in the south. *American Speech, 56,* 163–189.

Fasold, R. (1984). *The sociolinguistics of society.* New York: Blackwell.

Fasold, R. (1990). *The sociolinguistics of language.* Cambridge, MA: Blackwell.

Ferguson, C. A., and Heath, S. B. (1981). *Language in the USA.* Cambridge, England: Cambridge University Press.

Ferguson, K. S., and Parker, F. (1990). Grammar and technical writing. *Journal of Technical Writing and Communication, 20,* 357–367.

Fishman, J. (1972). *The Sociology of Language.* Rowley, MA: Newbury House.

Flanagan, O. J. (1984). *The science of the mind.* Cambridge, MA: MIT Press.

Fowler, R. (1981). *Literature as social discourse.* Bloomington, IN: Indiana University Press.

Francis, W. N. (Ed.) (1958). *The structure of American English.* New York: Ronald Press.

Fromkin, V. A. (1971). The non-anomalous nature of anomalous utterances. *Language, 47,* 27–52.

Gardner, H. (1985). The loss of language. In Clark et al., pp. 184–194.

Gass, S., and Schachter, J. (1989). *Linguistic perspectives on second language acquisition.* Cambridge, England: Cambridge University Press.

Gass, S., and Selinker, L. (1983). *Language transfer in language learning.* Rowley, MA: Newbury House.

Gelb, I. J. (1963). *A study of writing.* Chicago: University of Chicago Press.

Georges, R. (1970). Structure in folktales: A generative-transformational approach. *The Conch, II,* #2 (September), 4–17.

Graddol, D., and J. Swann. (1989). *Gender voices.* Oxford: Blackwell.

Grice, H. P. (1975). Logic and conversation. In Cole and Morgan, pp. 41–58.

Haegeman, L. (1991). *Introduction to government and binding theory.* Cambridge, MA: Blackwell.

Halle, M. (1985). The rules of language. In Clark et al., pp. 236–248.

Hatch, E. (1983). *Psycholinguistics: A second language perspective.* Rowley, MA: Newbury House.

Head, H. (1926). *Aphasia and kindred disorders of speech,* 2 vols. Cambridge, England: Cambridge University Press.

Heny, J. (1985). Brain and language. In Clark et al., pp. 159–182.

Hogg, R., and McCully, C. B. (1987). *Metrical phonology: A coursebook.* Cambridge, England: Cambridge University Press.

Honko, L. (1979–1980). Methods in folk-narrative research. *Ethnologica Europaea, 11,* 6–27.

How genes shape personality. (1987). *US News and World Report* (April 13), 58–62.

Hurford, J. R., and Heasley, B. (1983). *Semantics: A coursebook.* New York: Cambridge University Press.

Hyman, L. M. (1975). *Phonology: Theory and analysis.* New York: Holt, Rinehart and Winston.

Ingram, D. (1988). *First language acquisition:*

*Method, description, and explanation*. Cambridge, England: Cambridge University Press.

Ioup, G., and Weinberger, S. (1987). *Interlanguage phonology: The acquisition of a second language sound system*. Cambridge, MA: Newbury House.

Jakobson, R., Fant, G., and Halle, M. (1963). *Preliminaries to speech analysis*. Cambridge, MA: MIT Press.

Katz, J., and Fodor, J. (Eds.) (1964). *The structure of language*. Englewood Cliffs, NJ: Prentice-Hall.

Katzner, K. (1975). *The languages of the world*. New York: Funk & Wagnalls.

Kempson, R. (1977). *Semantic theory*. Cambridge, England: Cambridge University Press.

Kurath, H. (1939–43). *Linguistic atlas of New England*, 3 vols. Providence: Brown University Press.

Kurath, H. (1949). *A word geography of the eastern United States*. Ann Arbor: University of Michigan Press.

Kurath, H., and McDavid, R. I. (1961). *The pronunciation of English in the Atlantic states*. Ann Arbor: University of Michigan Press.

Labov, W. (1972). Academic ignorance and black intelligence. *The Atlantic* (June), 59–67.

Lakoff, R. (1975). *Language and women's place*. New York: Harper and Row.

Laufer, B. (1990). Why are some words more difficult than others? Some intralexical factors that affect the learning of words. *IRAL, 28*, 293–307.

Leiber, J. (1975). *Noam Chomsky: A philosophic overview*. New York: St. Martin's Press.

Lenneberg, E. (1964). The capacity for language acquisition. In Katz and Fodor, pp. 579–603.

Levinson, S. (1983). *Pragmatics*. Cambridge, England: Cambridge University Press.

Lightfoot, D. (1982). *The language lottery*. Cambridge, MA: MIT Press.

Limber, J. (1973). The genesis of complex sentences. In Moore, pp. 169–185.

Luria, A. R. (1973). *The working brain*. New York: Basic Books.

Lyons, J. (1977). *Noam Chomsky*. New York: Penguin.

Lyons, J. (1977). *Semantics*, 2 vols. New York: Cambridge University Press.

Major, R. (1987). A model for interlanguage phonology. In Ioup and Weinberger, pp. 101–124.

Marchand, H. (1969). *The categories and types of present-day English word-formation* (2nd ed.). Munich: Beck.

Matthews, P. H. (1974). *Morphology: An introduction to the theory of word-structure*. Cambridge, England: Cambridge University Press.

McDavid, R. I. (1958). The dialects of American English. In Francis, pp. 480–543.

McLaughlin, B. (1987). *Theories of second language learning*. London: Edward Arnold.

Moore, T.E. (Ed.) (1973). *Cognitive development and the acquisition of language*. New York: Academic Press.

Moskowitz, B. A. (1979). The acquisition of language. *Scientific American* (November), 82–96.

Newmeyer, F. J. (1983). *Grammatical theory*. Chicago: University of Chicago Press.

Newmeyer, F. J. (1986). *Linguistic theory in America* (2nd ed.). Orlando: Academic Press.

O'Barr, W. M. (1981). The language of the law. In Ferguson and Heath, pp. 386–406.

Ornstein, R. (1973). Right and left thinking. *Psychology Today* (May), 87–92.

Palmer, F. R. (1976). *Semantics: A new outline*. New York: Cambridge University Press.

Parker, F., and Campbell, K. S. (forthcoming). Linguistics and writing: A reassessment. *College Composition and Communication*.

Penfield, W., and Roberts, L. (1959). *Speech and brain mechanisms*. Princeton, NJ: Princeton University Press.

Radford, A. (1981). *Transformational syntax*. Cambridge, England: Cambridge University Press.

Riley, K. (1988). Speech act theory and degrees of directness in professional writing. *The Technical Writing Teacher, 15*, 1–29.

Riley, K. (1993). Telling more than the truth: Implicature, speech acts, and ethics in professional communication. *Journal of Business Ethics 12*, 179–96.

Riley, K., and Parker, F. (1988). Tone as a function of presupposition in technical and business writing. *Journal of Technical Writing and Communication, 18*, 325–343.

Salmon, W. C. (1973). *Logic* (2nd ed.). Englewood Cliffs, NJ: Prentice-Hall.

Sampson, G. (1985). *Writing systems*. London: Hutchinson.

Say rabbit, not wabbit. (1971). *Newsweek* (March 22), 98.

Schane, S. (1973). *Generative phonology*. Englewood Cliffs, NJ: Prentice-Hall.

Schane, S., and Bendixen, B. (1978). *Workbook in generative phonology*. Englewood Cliffs, NJ: Prentice-Hall.

Searle, J. R. (1969). *Speech acts*. Cambridge, England: Cambridge University Press.

Searle, J. R. (1975). Indirect speech acts. In Cole and Morgan, pp. 59–82.

Searle, J. R. (1976). The classification of illocutionary acts. *Language in Society, 5*, 1–24.

Selkirk, E. O. (1982). *The syntax of words*. Cambridge, MA: MIT Press.

Shaughnessy, M. P. (1977). *Errors and expectations*. New York: Oxford University Press.

Skinner, B. F. (1957). *Verbal behavior*. New York: Appleton-Century-Crofts.

Smith, N., and Wilson, D. (1985). What is a language? In Clark et al., pp. 325–339.

Sperber, D., and Wilson, D. (1986). *Relevance*. Cambridge, MA: Harvard University Press.

Springer, S. P., and Deutsch, G. (1985). *Left brain, right brain* (rev. ed.). New York: W. H. Freeman and Company.

Tannen, D. (1990). *You just don't understand: Women and men in conversation*. New York: William Morrow and Company.

Tate, G. (Ed.) (1976). *Teaching composition*. Fort Worth: Texas Christian University Press.

Traugott, E. C., and Pratt, M. L. (1980). *Linguistics for students of literature*. San Diego: Harcourt Brace Jovanovich.

Vande Kopple, W. J. (1982). Functional sentence perspective, composition, and reading. *College Composition and Communication, 33*, 50–63.

Warden, D. A. (1976). The influence of context on children's use of identifying expressions and references. *British Journal of Psychology, 67*, 101–112.

White, L. (1989). *Universal grammar and second language acquisition*. Amsterdam: John Benjamins.

Winner, E., and Gardner, H. (1977). The comprehension of metaphor in brain-damaged persons. *Brain, 100*, 719–727.

Winterowd, R. (1976). Linguistics and composition. In Tate, pp. 197–221.

Wolfram, W. (1982). Language knowledge and other dialects. *American Speech, 57*, 3–18.

Wolfram, W. (1991). *Dialects and American English*. Englewood Cliffs, NJ: Prentice-Hall.

Wolfram, W., and Christian, D. (1989). *Dialects and education: Issues and answers*. Englewood Cliffs, NJ: Prentice-Hall.

Wolfram, W., and Fasold, R. (1974). *The study of social dialects in American English*. Englewood Cliffs, NJ: Prentice-Hall.

Wolfram, W., and Johnson, R. (1982). *Phonological analysis: Focus on American English*. Washington, DC: Center for Applied Linguistics.

Young, R. (1970). *Mind, brain and adaptation in the nineteenth century*. Oxford: Clarendon Press.

Zughoul, M. (1991). Lexical choice: Towards writing problematic word lists. *IRAL, 29*, 45–60.

# *Glossary*

**active sentence.** One which does *not* contain a form of *be* followed by a past participle (cf. **passive**).

**affix.** The category of **bound, grammatical morphemes**, including both prefixes and suffixes.

**affricate.** A **segment** associated with complete closure in the vocal tract (i.e., a stop) followed by restricted airflow (i.e., a fricative) (e.g., /č/).

**agent.** An NP representing an entity capable of acting under its own volition (e.g., *John* but not *lightning*).

**agnosia.** The loss of the ability to *interpret* incoming stimuli, due to cortical damage.

**allophone.** A **segment** which is a systematic variant of a **phoneme** (e.g., [tʰ] is an allophone of /t/ in English because any time /t/ is syllable-initial before a stressed vowel, it is aspirated).

**alphabetic.** Describing a writing system in which each symbol represents a phonological **segment** (e.g., *c-a-t*).

**analytic sentence.** One that is necessarily true as a result of the words in it (e.g., *A triangle has three sides*).

**anaphora.** Describing a linguistic expression (the anaphor) which must have another expression to refer to (the **antecedent**) (e.g., all **reflexive pronouns** are anaphors).

**anomia.** A type of **aphasia** characterized by the inability to name objects and difficulty in accessing nouns.

**antecedent.** A linguistic expression that another expression refers to (e.g., *They* is the antecedent of *each other* in *They ran into each other*).

**anticipation.** Accessing an item that occurs *later* in a series (e.g., *tig and tall* for *big and tall*).

**antonymy.** Two words whose senses differ only in the value of a single semantic feature (e.g., *man* and *boy* differ only in [±adult]).

**aphasia.** An acquired language dysfunction caused by cortical damage.

**apraxia.**  The loss of the ability to *perform* voluntary actions, due to cortical damage.

**assimilation.**  Any phonological process by which one **segment** becomes more like a neighboring segment (e.g., Vowel Nasalization).

**auxiliary verb.**  Any verb preceding the right-most verb in a simple sentence; auxiliaries in English are the **modals** and forms of *be, have,* and *do.*

**bare infinitive.**  An infinitive verb form (e.g., *to go*) with no overt subject (e.g., *John told you where to go*).

**basic-level terms.**  Words of intermediate generality, typically acquired first (e.g., *car* acquired before *vehicle* [general] or *four-by-four* [specific]).

**beneficiary.**  An NP representing an entity which benefits from an action (e.g., *Mary* in *John baked a cake for Mary*).

**binary antonyms.**  Antonyms that describe all possibilities along a single dimension (e.g., *sane* and *insane*).

**blending.**  A phonological process combining features of two adjacent **segments** into one (e.g., [m̥ok] for *smoke*).

**bound morpheme.**  One which cannot stand alone as a word (e.g., *un-*).

**Broca's aphasia.**  A type of **aphasia** characterized by labored "telegraphic" output; caused by damage to **Broca's area**. Also known as motor or expressive aphasia.

**Broca's area.**  The area in the frontal lobe of the **dominant hemisphere**, near the primary motor cortex (which controls movement).

**category.**  A class of words that share a characteristic (e.g., nouns can be made plural, verbs can be inflected for tense, etc.).

**circumlocution.**  A descriptive phrase substituted for a single word the speaker either has not yet learned or is unable to retrieve (e.g., *thing you write with* for *pencil*).

**coda.**  One or more consonants ending a syllable.

**code-switching.**  A bilingual speaker changing from one language to another during the course of a conversation; often triggered by a change in topic or attitude.

**commissive.**  An utterance used to commit the speaker to do something (e.g., a promise).

**competence.**  The psychological system of unconscious knowledge that underlies a speaker's ability to produce and interpret utterances in a language (cf. **performance**)

**complementary distribution.**  The relation between two items that never occur in the same environment (e.g., in English [tʰ] always occurs before a stressed vowel, but [ɾ] never does).

**conduction aphasia.**  A type of **aphasia** characterized by the inability to repeat words; caused by damage to the arcuate fasciculus.

**connotation.**  The associations attached to a word, apart from its core sense (e.g., *train* and *choo-choo* have different connotations) (cf. **denotation**).

**constituent.**  Two or more words dominated entirely and exclusively by a single **node** (i.e., the node dominates those words and no others).

**contradictory sentence.**  One that is necessarily false as a result of the words in it (e.g., *A triangle has four sides*).

**contrast.** Two **segments** contrast if substituting one for the other causes a change in meaning. The **phonemes** of a language are all and only those segments that contrast with each other.

**contralateral control.** The property of the brain (not peculiar to humans) such that each hemisphere controls activity on the opposite side of the body.

**contrastive analysis.** A point-by-point comparison of the grammars of two languages.

**conversational maxims.** Four principles (Quality, Quantity, Relation, and Manner) in terms of which speakers interpret utterances.

**converse antonyms.** Antonyms that describe the relationship between two entities from opposite perspectives (e.g., *employer* and *employee*).

**coreference.** The condition of two expressions having the same **referent** (e.g., *President of the U.S.* and *Commander-in-Chief*).

**count noun.** One that has a plural form (e.g., *boy/boys*). Any other noun is noncount (e.g., *water*).

**creole.** A **pidgin** which has become the native language of a group of speakers.

**declaration.** An utterance used to change the status of some entity (e.g., a resignation).

**deixis.** The ability of one expression to refer systematically to two or more distinct entities in the same context (e.g., *you* and *I*)

**denotation.** The core sense of a word (e.g., *train* and *choo-choo* have the same denotation) (cf. **connotation**).

**derivation.** A step-by-step "history" of a linguistic form, from its **underlying structure** through all the rules that apply to it, resulting in its **surface structure**.

**derivational morpheme.** All prefixes and all non-inflectional suffixes (in English); derivational suffixes typically change the **category** of the root (e.g., *-ize*: *critic* is a noun, but *criticize* is a verb).

**determiner.** A syntactic **category** including articles, demonstratives (e.g., *this*, *that*, etc.), possessive pronouns, and perhaps quantifiers (e.g., *some, many*, etc.).

**developmental process.** A process in second-language acquisition that is similar to one in first-language acquisition (e.g., **simplification** of consonant clusters).

**dialect.** A systematic variety of a language specific to a particular region or social group (e.g., Australian English, Black English).

**direct illocutionary act.** One performed by an utterance whose syntactic form matches its illocutionary force (e.g., an imperative used to issue a directive). Any other illocutionary act is indirect.

**directive.** An utterance used to try to get the hearer to do something (e.g., a request).

**distinctive features.** Two-valued dimensions which serve as basic building blocks of **segments** (e.g., /m/ and /n/ are both [+nasal] and [+voice]).

**dominant hemisphere.** The one that is primarily responsible for processing language (i.e., the left in most people).

**empiricism.** The view that we are born with relatively *little* of the unconscious knowledge we will have as adults; also known as behaviorism (cf. **nativism**).

**entailment.** A proposition (expressed in a sentence) that follows *necessarily* from another sentence (e.g., *John murdered Bill* entails *Bill died*).

**epenthesis.** The insertion of a **segment** into a series. Vowel epenthesis inserts a vowel between two consonants, and consonant epenthesis inserts a consonant between two vowels.

**error analysis.** A procedure for identifying regularities in **interlanguage** forms; the learner's productions are compared to the grammar of the second language.

**explicit performative.** An utterance containing a performative verb used in its performative sense (e.g., *I apologize for . . .* ). Any other utterance is a non-explicit performative.

**expressed locutionary act.** One actually expressing the propositional content condition for the illocutionary act involved (e.g., a promise must predicate a future act of the speaker, so *I promise I'll help you with your homework* is expressed). Any other locutionary act is implied (e.g., *I promise you won't have to do your homework alone*).

**expressive.** An utterance used to express the emotional state of the speaker (e.g., an apology).

**extension.** The set of all potential **referents** (if any) for a linguistic expression.

**extraposition.** A transformation which moves a relative clause or prepositional phrase away from the NP it modifies to clause-final position (e.g., *A rumor about you just surfaced* ---> *A rumor just surfaced about you*).

**factive verb.** A main clause verb that presupposes the truth of the proposition in the subordinate clause (e.g., *I realize that you are a coward* presupposes 'You are a coward').

**felicity conditions.** Conditions that must be met for the valid performance of an **illocutionary act** (i.e., participants and circumstances must be appropriate, participants must have appropriate intentions, etc.).

**field dependence.** A style of learning where the individual attempts to analyze all data at once.

**field independence.** A style of learning where the individual is able to foreground specific data and analyze them.

**final consonant reduction.** A phonological process deleting a post-vocalic, word-final **obstruent** (e.g., [dɔ] for *dog*).

**final devoicing.** A phonological process devoicing a word-final **obstruent** (e.g., [hɛt] for *head*).

**free morpheme.** One which can stand alone as a word (e.g., *not*) (cf. **bound morpheme**).

**free variation.** Two items that can occur in the same environment without causing a change in meaning (e.g., [ǰ] and [ž] are in free variation in *garage*).

**fricative.** A **segment** associated with restricted but uninterrupted airflow, creating turbulence (e.g., /s/).

**gender.** A morphological category, usually indicated by affixation (e.g., *actor/actress*); also, the social and psychological roles, attitudes, and traits associated with biological sex.

**general cognitive capacities.** Innate knowledge that relates to all domains of human cognition (e.g., the ability to serialize items).

**generative grammar.** A theory of the psychological system of unconscious knowledge that underlies a speaker's ability to produce and interpret utterances in a language.

**given information.** That which the speaker assumes is already known to the hearer; normally expressed as the subject of a sentence (cf. **new information**).

**glide.** A **segment** associated with restricted air flow, but not enough to create turbulence (e.g., /y/).

**gliding.** A phonological process changing a **liquid** into a **glide** (e.g., [kéwi] for *Kelly*.

**gradable antonyms.** Antonyms that describe opposite poles of a single dimension (e.g., *tall* and *short*).

**grammatical morpheme.** One whose function is to modify the sense of a **lexical morpheme**; prepositions, articles, conjunctions, and **affixes** are grammatical.

**hemispherical specialization.** The control of separate cognitive functions by the left and right hemispheres.

**holophrastic.** Describing a stage of language acquisition characterized by one-word utterances.

**hyponymy.** The sense of one word (the superordinate) being entirely contained in the sense of another word (the hyponym) (e.g., the sense of *talk* is entirely contained within the sense of *mumble*).

**iconic.** See **writing**.

**ideograph.** A drawing of an object used to represent that object and related concepts (e.g., a bumper sticker depicting a heart, representing love).

**idiolect.** The specific linguistic system of a particular speaker, with all its attendant idiosyncrasies.

**idiom.** An expression whose meaning cannot be derived from its component words (e.g., *bought the farm* 'died').

**illocutionary act.** The act of *doing* something by saying something (e.g., making a request).

**illocutionary force.** The illocutionary act performed by a given utterance.

**implicative verb.** A main clause verb that presupposes a particular attitude on the part of the speaker toward the proposition in the subordinate clause (e.g., *I managed to find your keys* presupposes 'finding your keys was difficult,' vs. *I happened to find your keys* presupposes 'finding your keys was accidental').

**implicature.** A proposition *implied* by an utterance but not part of that utterance or a necessary consequence of that utterance.

**implied locutionary act.** See **expressed locutionary act**.

**inflectional morpheme.** One of eight suffixes (in English) that do not change the category of the root (e.g., {PLU}: *chair* is a noun and plural *chairs* is a noun) (cf. **derivational morpheme**).

**instrument.** An NP representing an entity used to perform an action (e.g., *a knife* in *John cut the cake with a knife*).

**instrumental motivation.**  The desire to learn a second language for some practical purpose (e.g., conducting business).

**integrative motivation.**  The desire to learn a second language in order to make oneself part of the community or culture.

**interference.**  See **language transfer**.

**interlanguage.**  In second-language acquisition, a grammar different from both the speaker's native language and the second language.

**intonation.**  A pitch change over an entire sentence; pitch falls in declaratives and *wh*-interrogatives, but rises in *yes-no* interrogatives.

**isogloss.**  A line demarcating the area in which some linguistic feature can be found. Numerous isoglosses that coincide indicate the presence of a **dialect** boundary.

**jargon.**  Technical vocabulary of a particular occupational or social group.

**jargon aphasia.**  See **Wernicke's aphasia**.

**language-specific capacities.**  Innate knowledge that relates only to the acquisition of language and to no other domain of cognition (e.g., the subjacency constraint).

**language transfer.**  Properties of a first language that are carried over into a second language. Positive transfer enhances second-language acquisition, and negative transfer (or **interference**) impedes it.

**language universals.**  Properties that all human languages have in common. Chomsky attributes some of these to the initial state of the human mind to account for the rapidity and uniformity of language acquisition; he calls them universal grammar.

**left ear advantage.**  See **right ear advantage**.

**level of representation.**  A particular point of view from which language can be described (e.g., *John kissed Mary* and *Mary was kissed by John* are the same on the semantic level of representation [they express the same proposition], but different on the syntactic level of representation [one is active and the other is passive]).

**lexical ambiguity.**  The condition of a word having more than one sense (e.g., *star* means both 'heavenly body' and 'celebrity').

**lexical decomposition.**  The representation of the sense of a word in terms of **semantic features**.

**lexical morpheme.**  One having an independent sense; most nouns, verbs, and adjectives are lexical (e.g., *man, run, tall*) (cf. **grammatical morpheme**).

**liquid.**  Any /l/- or /r/-like **segment**.

**literal locutionary act.**  An utterance in which the words mean exactly what they say (i.e., one that is not sarcastic or exaggerated). An other locutionary act is nonliteral.

**localization of function.**  The control of different cognitive functions by different parts of each hemisphere (e.g., the front part of the **dominant hemisphere** controls speaking, and the rear part controls comprehension).

**locutionary act.**  The act of simply *saying* something.

**main verb.** The right-most verb in a simple sentence (e.g., *did* is the main verb in *John did his work* but not in *John did not finish his work*).

**markedness.** Properties consistent with language universals are unmarked; those inconsistent with language universals are marked.

**markedness differential hypothesis.** Eckman's theory of second-language acquisition which states that, of those structures *not* shared by the first and second language, difficulty increases with markedness.

**metathesis.** Reversing two items in a series (e.g., *tig and ball* for *big and tall*).

**minimum distance principle.** A general rule for interpreting **bare infinitives**: the subject of a bare infinitive is assumed to be the closest NP to its left (e.g., *John told you where to go* = 'You go').

**modal verb.** One lacking the present tense *-s* suffix with a third-person singular subject (e.g., *She can go/\*She cans go*); modals in English are forms of *can, will, shall, may,* and *must*).

**morpheme.** A minimal element of meaning associated with a particular form (e.g., *-pel* means 'push' as in *repel, compel,* etc.).

**morphographic.** Describing a writing system in which each symbol represents a morpheme (e.g., 2 x 2 = 4).

**morphophoneme.** A phonological segment representing a morpheme; typically written in capital letters within double slashes (e.g., {PLU} = //Z//).

**nasal.** A **segment** associated with a lowered velum, allowing air to escape through the nose (e.g., /n/).

**nativism.** The view that we are born with relatively *much* of the unconscious knowledge we will have as adults; also known as mentalism (cf. **empiricism**).

**neologistic jargon.** Nonsense words characteristic of **Wernicke's aphasia**; also known as neologisms.

**neutralization.** Any phonological process which wipes out the contrast between two **segments** (e.g., Flapping).

**new information.** That which the speaker assumes is not already known to the hearer; normally expressed as the predicate of a sentence (i.e., after the subject) (cf. **given information**).

**node.** A point in a tree structure which can branch.

**nonstandard English.** Any variety of English which contains **socially marked** forms.

**np-movement.** A **transformation** which moves an NP to any other empty NP position (e.g., ____-*was-found-the key* ---> *the key-was-found-*____).

**nucleus.** The vowel in a syllable.

**obstruent.** Any member of the class of **stops**, **fricatives**, and **affricates**.

**onset.** One or more consonants beginning a syllable.

**operational definition.** Defining an entity by stipulating a procedure for producing it (e.g., the direct object of a sentence is the NP that moves to subject position when the sentence is made passive).

**order of mention.** A general principle for interpreting the sequence of events reported in two adjacent clauses: the event in the first clause is assumed to have occurred before the event in the second clause.

**overgeneralization.** A semantic process of using a word to refer to more things than it normally does (e.g., *car* 'any vehicle').

**overlap.** The condition of two words having the same value for some (but not all) **semantic features** (e.g., *nun* and *niece* share [– male]).

**passive sentence.** One which contains a form of *be* followed by a **past participle** (e.g., *The vehicle could have <u>been driven</u> by John*) (cf. **active**).

**past participle.** The verb form following auxiliary *have* (e.g., *driven* as in *You should have driven*).

**patient.** An NP representing an entity being acted upon (e.g., *beans* in *John ate beans*).

**performance.** The actual physical and psychological processes that a speaker might go through in producing or interpreting an utterance (cf. **competence**).

**performative verb.** A verb that actually names the **illocutionary act** it is used to perform (e.g., *state, order, question*, etc.).

**perseveration.** Accessing an item that occurred earlier in a series (e.g., *big and ball* for *big and tall*).

**phoneme.** The type of **segment** we *think* we hear when we interpret speech.

**phonemic paraphasia. Anticipation, perseveration,** and **metathesis** of phonological **segments**, as a consequence of **aphasia**. Also known as literal paraphasia.

**phonotactics.** Restrictions on the permissible sequences of **segments** in a language (e.g., if three consonants begin a word in English, the first one must be /s/ and the third one must be a liquid or a glide).

**phrase structure rules.** Rules which specify the hierarchical arrangement and left-to-right ordering of categories (e.g., S ---> NP - VP).

**pictograph.** A drawing of an object used to represent that object (e.g., a highway sign depicting a deer).

**pidgin.** A mixture of two existing languages brought into contact by trade or colonization.

**post-vocalic liquid deletion.** A phonological process deleting an /l/ or /r/ following a vowel (e.g., [hɛp] for *help*).

**present participle.** The verb form following auxiliary *be* in an active sentence (e.g., *driving* as in *You should not be driving*).

**presupposition.** A proposition (expressed in a sentence) that is assumed to be true in order to judge the truth of another sentence (e.g., *Hart passed the bar exam* presupposes *Hart took the bar exam*).

**projection problem.** The hypothesis that language learners acquire linguistic principles that cannot be inferred solely from the data they are exposed to.

**prototype.** A typical member of the **extension** of a linguistic expression (e.g., Lassie is a prototype of *dog*).

**question.** An utterance used to try to get the hearer to provide information.

**reduplication.** A process by which a morpheme or a syllable is repeated (e.g., *dada*).

**reference.** The relation between linguistic expressions (e.g., words and sentences) and objects in the real (or imagined) world.

**referent.** The entity (if any) identified by the use of a linguistic expression (e.g., the referent of *The White House* is the building at 1600 Pennsylvania Avenue in Washington, D.C.).

**reflexive pronoun.** A pronoun formed by adding *-self/selves* to a personal pronoun.

**register.** One of many styles of language, ranging from formal to informal.

**representative.** An utterance used to describe some state of affairs (e.g., a statement).

**right ear advantage.** The ability to process auditory stimuli presented to the right ear to the exclusion of stimuli presented simultaneously to the left ear. Most humans, being left dominant, have a right ear advantage for linguistic stimuli and a **left ear advantage** for nonlinguistic stimuli.

**segment.** A psychological unit of phonology corresponding roughly to "speech sound"; **allophones**, **phonemes**, and **morphophonemes** are all segments. We interpret the physical speech signal in terms of segments.

**selectional restrictions.** Semantic constraints on the NPs that a particular lexical item can take (e.g., *regret* requires a human subject).

**semantic feature.** A dimension of sense typically having two values (e.g., [±human]).

**semantic paraphasia.** The use of inappropriate but closely related words, as a consequence of **aphasia** (e.g., *phone* for *radio*).

**sense.** The literal meaning of an expression, independent of situational context.

**simplification.** A phonological process reducing the number of consonants in a cluster (e.g., [pínəč] for *spinach*).

**socially marked.** Any linguistic form that can cause a listener to form a negative social judgement of the speaker (e.g., *ain't*).

**sonorant.** Any member of the class of **nasals**, **liquids**, and **glides**.

**speech act.** A **locutionary act** (i.e., the act of saying something) plus an **illocutionary act** (i.e., the act of doing something).

**standard English.** Any variety of English which contains no **socially marked** forms.

**stereotype.** A list of characteristics describing a **prototype** of a linguistic expression (e.g., barks, wags tail, has fur, etc. is a stereotype of *dog*).

**stop.** A **segment** associated with complete closure in the vocal tract (e.g., /t/).

**stopping.** The phonological process of a **fricative** becoming a **stop** (e.g., [dɪs] for *this*).

**structural ambiguity.** The condition whereby an expression can be assigned more than one syntactic structure (e.g., *old men and women* = old [men and women] or [old men] and women).

**structural hypercorrection.** The use of a form in a context where it is not normally used; usually occurs among speakers trying to affect a more formal style (e.g., *between you and I* for *between you and me*).

**subcategorization restrictions.** Syntactic constraints on the types of complements that a particular lexical item can take (e.g., the verb *sleep* cannot have a direct object).

**superordinate.** See **hyponymy**.

**surface structure.** A syntactic configuration after all applicable **transformations** have applied.

**syllabic.** Describing a writing system in which each symbol represents a syllable (e.g., *LO* = 'hello').

**synonymy.** Two words having the same **sense** (e.g., *student* and *pupil*).

**synthetic sentence.** One that can be judged true or false only by evaluating the state of affairs it describes (e.g., *Al Gore is President of the U.S. Senate*).

**telegraphic.** Describing a stage of language acquisition characterized by utterances that are open-ended in length but lack most **grammatical morphemes**.

**tense.** In English, one of two verb inflections (present or past) which occurs on the first verb form in a simple sentence (e.g., *John may/might have been eating*).

**thematic progression.** The arrangement of given and new information in a discourse. Linear progression (AB:BC) makes new information in one sentence the given information in the next. Hierarchical progression (AB:AC) retains the same given information in successive sentences.

**theory.** A hypothesis about the workings of a mechanism (physical or psychological) that cannot be observed directly; designed to explain observations that otherwise would remain unexplained.

**transformation.** An operation that alters syntactic structure (e.g., the I-Movement transformation changes *He-has-gone* into *Has-he-gone*).

**truth conditions.** The conditions under which a sentence can be judged as true, false, or having no truth value.

**umlaut.** A phonological process in Germanic languages whereby the vowel in a suffix has an effect on the vowel in the root of a word (e.g., historically, the vowel in *mice* [< *mouse*] is the result of umlaut).

**underlying structure.** A syntactic configuration before any **transformations** have applied.

**uninflected verb form.** The form following infinitival *to* (e.g., *give* as in *to give*).

**universal grammar.** See **language universals**.

**Wernicke's aphasia.** A type of **aphasia** characterized by **neologisms**; caused by damage to **Wernicke's area**. Also known as sensory, receptive, or jargon aphasia.

**Wernicke's area.** The area in the temporal lobe of the **dominant hemisphere**, near the primary auditory cortex (which processes sounds).

*wh*-**movement.** A **transformation** which moves a *wh*-item into clause-initial position (e.g., *has-John-gone-where* ---> *where-has-John-gone*).

**writing.** A representational system in which the symbols no longer depict the objects they represent (i.e., one which is not **iconic**).

# Author Index

# Subject Index